FISCHER BLACK

and the

REVOLUTIONARY IDEA
of
FINANCE

FISCHER BLACK

and the

REVOLUTIONARY IDEA

of

FINANCE

PERRY MEHRLING

WILEY

John Wiley & Sons, Inc.

Published by John Wiley & Sons, Inc., Hoboken, New Jersey.
Published simultaneously in Canada.

Fischer Black's published and unpublished work is quoted with permission of the
estate of Fischer Black. Courtesy Alethea Black.

For general information on our other products and services or for technical
support, please contact our Customer Care Department within the United States at
(800) 762-2974, outside the United States at (317) 572-3993 or fax (317) 572-4002.

Wiley also publishes its books in a variety of electronic formats. Some content that
appears in print may not be available in electronic books. For more information about
Wiley products, visit our web site at www.wiley.com.

Library of Congress Cataloging-in-Publication Data:
Merhling, Perry.
    Fischer Black and the revolutionary idea of finance / by Perry Mehrling.
        p. cm.
    ISBN-13 978-0-471-45732-9 (cloth)
    ISBN-10 0-471-45732-9 (cloth)
    1. Black, Fischer, 1938–   2. Finance—United States—History—20th century.   3.
Economists—United States—Biography.   4. Finance—Mathematical models.   5.
Investments—Mathematical models.   I. Title.
    HG172.F53M44   2005
    332'.092—dc22
                                                                    2005007460

Printed in the United States of America.

10   9   8   7   6   5   4   3   2   1

To
Judy

The true search for knowledge is not like the voyage of Columbus but like that of Ulysses. Man is born abroad, living means seeking your home, and thinking means living. . . .

A cowardly fear of thinking curbs us all; the censorship of public opinion is more oppressive than that of governments. Most writers are no better than they are because they have ideas but no character. . . .

To be original you must listen to the voice of your heart rather than the clamor of the world—and have the courage to teach publicly what you have learned. The source of all genius is sincerity; men would be wiser if they were more moral.

Ludwig Borne (1823), quoted in
Rudolf Flesch, *How to Make Sense* (1954)

Contents

Acknowledgments

This book has been seven years in the making. Along the way I have received help from very many people, in very many forms. My largest debt is to Fischer's family, especially to Cathy Tawes Black, who provided access to Fischer's extensive professional files at MIT as well as student records at Harvard, and to Fischer's parents (now deceased), who welcomed me to their Tampa home and opened the family archives to me. Fischer's siblings Blakeney and Lee, his daughters (especially Alethea), his ex-wives Cynthia Linton and Miriam Black, and his cousin Stanley Black and aunt Corinne Black all provided invaluable help in understanding issues of character. I am also indebted to Fischer's high school buddies, college and graduate school roommates, friends and housemates, for their insights.

The most important intellectual influences on Fischer were Jack Treynor and Merton Miller, whose help and support were therefore especially valuable and appreciated, especially that of Merton Miller, who took the time to meet with me despite his own failing health. Thanks also to Franco Modigliani, whose passionate advocacy of neo-Keynesian orthodoxy gave Fischer something to respond to, and to Serena Modigliani for access to her husband's papers, which allowed me to trace the origin of Fischer's interest in macroeconomics and monetary theory. Special thanks also to Robert Merton and Myron Scholes, whose lives were from the beginning inextricably intertwined with Fischer's on account of the options formula.

My interest in writing about Fischer Black stemmed originally from an interest in understanding the evolution of twentieth-century American monetary thought, and initially I conceived of the book as providing a window on certain ideas and institutional developments in finance that have transformed both the way banking is done and the way we think about it. The book was supposed to carry into the present the story I had begun to tell in my previous book *The Money Interest and the Public Interest, American Monetary Thought, 1920–1970*. Fischer Black was clearly the best subject on whom to hang such a story since he, more than anyone else of his generation of financial economists, maintained a lifelong engagement with the problems of macroeconomics and monetary theory. In my original conception, the research for the project was to be almost entirely archival. I owe thanks especially to Nora Murphy and Jeffrey Mifflin for their help during a summer spent at the MIT Institute Archives and Special Collections.

My original project survives as Chapters 6 through 8 in the present volume, but the initial research revealed that there was an even larger story that needed to be told, namely the story of the rise of modern finance itself. For this story also, the career of Fischer Black seemed to provide an almost perfect narrative frame, since he spent his life straddling the world of academia and the world of practical business. As I was expanding my sense of the project, Pamela van Giessen at John Wiley & Sons approached me with the suggestion to expand my horizons even more. She urged me to write a book that would not only straddle the worlds in which Fischer lived, both academia and business, but also the personal life that supported the intellectual venture of this unusual mind. I was intrigued by the challenge, but also more than a little intimidated. I thank my agent Susan Rabiner for helping me to discover how concretely to proceed.

In the end, I interviewed more than a hundred people, some several times. It soon became clear to me that Fischer had the habit—I would go so far as to call it an intellectual strategy—of gravitating to people he thought he could learn from. The key to understanding the evolution of his ideas was therefore to find the people he was interacting with at each stage in his life. In each setting—Arthur D. Little (ADL), Wells Fargo Bank, the University of Chicago, the Massachusetts Institute of Technology, and Goldman Sachs—there was a different group, but in every case I found that group more than willing to share with me their remembrances of interactions with Fischer. The overall intellectual arc of the book would have been largely the same without these interviews, but it would have lacked the texture and detail that make the story of ideas into a human drama. I owe a great debt to all who made time to talk with me, in person or by phone, over the years.

For their help in understanding the ADL years, thanks to Barry Anson, Keith Butters, Robert J. Fahey, Robert Glauber, Michael Jensen, Eleanor Lintner, Alan L. Loss, Franco Modigliani, Stewart Myers, Paul Samuelson, William Sharpe, and Jeremy Siegel. For the Wells Fargo years, thanks to Hossein Askari, Larry Cuneo, James Farrell, William Fouse, John Andrew McQuown, James Stone, Oldrich Vasicek, and Wayne Wagner. For the Chicago years, thanks to Truman Clark, David DeRosa, Eugene Fama, Sally Fama, Milton Friedman, Dan Galai, Jack Gould, Robert Hetzel, Roger Ibbotson, Arthur Laffer, James Lorie, Gershon Mandelker, Bill Margrabe, Ron Masulis, Rachel McCulloch, Richard Posner, Bill Spangler, Charles Upton, Joseph T. Williams, Richard Zecher, and Arnold Zellner. For the MIT years, thanks to Sudipto Bhattacharya, Thierry Bollier, John Cox, Moray Dewhurst, Susan Dudley, Marc Freed, Peter Glasser, Richard Homonoff, John Lacey, Mark Latham, Saman Majd, Terry A. Marsh, Charles Plosser, Ed Prescott, Stephen Ross, Robert Solow, and Steve Zeldes.

At Goldman Sachs, special thanks are due to Richard Witten, and to Robert Rubin and Jon Corzine, whose support of this project opened doors that might otherwise have remained closed to me. Beverly Bell, Fischer's editor, provided invaluable guidance to the range of Fischer's contacts at the firm and access to his unpublished papers. I thank Armen Avanessians, John Coates, Emanuel Derman, Stanley Diller, Michael Dubno, Jacob Goldfield, Erol Hakanoglu, Rob Jones, Iraj Kani, Piotr Karasinski, Robert Litterman, Bob Litzenberger, Scott Pinkus, Richard Roll, Ramine Rouhani, Mark Rubinstein, Alan Shuch, Jeff Wecker, Larry Weiss, Mark Winkelman, and Mark Zurack. During Fischer's later years at Goldman, he began once again to reengage with academics, including Ed Glaeser, Larry Glosten, Boyan Jovanovic, Larry Kotlikoff, Albert Pete Kyle, Robert Lucas, Hersh Shefrin, and Meir Statman.

I have benefited along the way from scholarly feedback in a number of settings, beginning with the invitation by David Colander to lecture on Fischer Black at Middlebury College in April 1999, continuing in a series of presentations to the annual meeting of the History of Economics Society (1999 at the University of North Carolina at Greensboro, 2001 at Wake Forest University, 2003 at Duke University, and 2004 at Victoria College in Toronto), and continuing also in a series of presentations to my Columbia University colleagues at the regular Tuesday Macroeconomics Lunch Group and Thursday Finance Lunch Group. Thanks to Robert Dimand, Franck Jovanovic, Philip Mirowski, Goulven Rubin, and Neil Skaggs, and to Larry Glosten, Gur Huberman, Rick Mishkin, and Steve Zeldes. Thank you to my colleagues at Barnard College, especially Andre Burgstaller, Duncan Foley, and Carl Wennerlind, who read early drafts, to my graduate students Goetz von Peter and Paul Sengmuller, and to Brian Bedner for superior research assistance.

I would also like to thank Warren Samuels for the opportunity to write about Irving Fisher when I needed it as background for the book. Thanks also to the Austrian Economics Colloquium at New York University, to Zvi Bodie for an invitation to talk at the Boston University School of Business, and to Craufurd Goodwin for an invitation to present the 2002 Johnson Distinguished Economist Lecture at Duke University. For valuable opportunities to pull together the broad themes of the book, thanks to Luca Fiorito for arranging a lecture to the Italian Association for the History of Economic Thought (AISPE) in Palermo, Italy, in October 2004; to Michel DeVroey for an invitation to address the History of Macroeconomics conference in Louvain, Belgium, in January 2005; and to Wade Hands for an invitation to address the History of Economics Society in Tacoma, Washington, in June 2005.

In the final stages of the book, I took further advantage of some of my interview contacts to provide comments on draft chapters. I do not claim to have met satisfactorily all of the criticisms I have received, but I do know that I have repeatedly been impelled to deepen and broaden the argument because of them. I thank especially Michael Adler, Peter Bernstein, Emanuel Derman, Benjamin Friedman, Kevin Hoover, Thomas Humphrey, David Laidler, Robert Litterman, James Lorie, John McQuown, Robert Merton, Myron Scholes, William Sharpe, Robert Solow, Jack Treynor, and Richard Zecher.

Finally, I thank my employer, Barnard College, for allowing me a semester Senior Faculty Research Leave in Spring 2002 to get the book started. Thanks to Franco Modigliani for arranging for me to spend that semester at the Sloan School in Cambridge, Massachusetts, and to John

Cox and Stewart Myers for making me more than welcome. In the end, I needed a further year and a half leave in order to produce the final manuscript, and I thank Barnard for that as well. But as anyone who has ever written a book knows, free time is only a necessary, not a sufficient, condition. It is my family who have provided the sufficient conditions.

What a writer needs is stability and constancy during the inevitable ups and downs of the writing process, even as the book swells to absorb more and more space, both physical and emotional. A book is like a guest who arrives one day and settles in, increasingly demanding and ill-tempered, with no sign of imminent departure. It takes a very gracious host to find room for such a guest, even while gently moving him day by day closer to the exit. My wife Judy has been that gracious host. It is because of her that I was able to take on a project that I knew would stretch me more anything I have previously done. And it is because of her that I have now been able to bring that project to conclusion. The dedication is only a token of the debt I owe.

PERRY MEHRLING

FISCHER
BLACK

and the

REVOLUTIONARY IDEA

of

FINANCE

THE PRICE OF RISK

Preferring a search for objective reality over revelation is another way of satisfying religious hunger. . . . It aims to save the spirit, not by surrender but by liberation of the human mind. Its central tenet, as Einstein knew, is the unification of knowledge. When we have unified enough certain knowledge, we will understand who we are and why we are here.
                                   Edward O. Wilson, *Consilience* (1998, p. 7)

On Wednesday, September 24, 1997, Jack Treynor flew into Boston on the red-eye from California, where he ran his own small money management business. The weather was sunny but only in the 50s, and a gusty northwest wind made it feel colder. Treynor's destination that morning was the annual conference of the International Association of Financial Engineers (IAFE), already under way downtown at the Park Plaza Hotel, just a block from the Boston Common. He was flying in for the day to give a talk at lunch about his old friend Fischer Black, who had died two years before (only 57 years old) shortly after receiving the association's highest honor, Financial Engineer of the Year.

Unbeknownst to Treynor, Paul Samuelson, the Nobel Prize-winning economist from the Massachusetts Institute of Technology (MIT) across the river in Cambridge, had been the featured speaker at the Monday dinner that opened the conference. In anticipation of the October announcement of that year's Nobel Prize, Samuelson had offered his own "Hall of Fame of Theoretical Finance," in which he suggested that the time was overdue for recognition of the work of Fischer Black, Myron

Scholes, and especially his own student Robert Merton. He planned to conclude with the words: "If the modern corpus of financial engineering came into existence in any one instant, by my vote that instant was when Merton constructed the boundary-value solutions to the partial-differential equations of continuously diffusing Bachelier probabilities."[1] The reference was to Merton's 1973 paper "Theory of Rational Option Pricing," published in the same year as "The Pricing of Options and Corporate Liabilities" by Black and Scholes. Both papers contained the option pricing formula that everyone in the industry had come to know colloquially as "Black-Scholes."

But Samuelson got only halfway through his speech before there was an interruption from the floor. He had been listing names on a flip chart, starting with Louis Bachelier, an obscure turn-of-the-century French mathematician who had anticipated the line that Merton would later follow, but including along the way other greats whose contributions had followed different lines. The talk was going fine until he reached 1964 and wrote "John Lintner and William Sharpe: independent innovators." The innovation in question was the capital asset pricing model (CAPM), for which Sharpe had been awarded the Nobel Prize in 1990. Samuelson's next entry would have been for Black, Scholes, and Merton, but there was a voice from the audience. "What about Treynor? You forgot Treynor!"

It was Franco Modigliani, Samuelson's Nobel-winning colleague at MIT, rising unsteadily to his feet to spoil the punch line, and he was rising from Samuelson's own chair! He had come in after Samuelson was already under way and sat in the only empty place he could find. Hard of hearing as he was, and having forgotten his hearing aid, he could well have mistaken what Samuelson was saying. But there could be no mistake about what Samuelson had written on the flip chart, and Modigliani had good reason to be sensitive about it. He knew that Treynor had developed his own version of the capital asset pricing model, and even before Sharpe or Lintner, because Treynor had shown it to him. At the time, Modigliani had not recognized its importance because it seemed to him too simple. But in retrospect Treynor had been right, and forever after Modigliani felt badly that he had not encouraged Treynor more strongly.

Suddenly the after-dinner entertainment got very interesting. Here were two Nobelists, both well past normal retirement age, going at it like men half their age. At the podium Samuelson was dapper as always in blue blazer and bow tie. On the floor Modigliani was comfortably unkempt in his favorite ivory silk jacket (tailor-made with cloth bought wholesale from Italy through his brother). Friends and colleagues at MIT for almost 40 years, both men knew all the moves of the other. Modigliani, in particular, was famous for taking over seminars being offered by other people. "Don't give Franco the chalk," visiting scholars would be warned, "or you'll never get it back." So Samuelson was not about to let his friend begin adding names to his list.

And anyway, Treynor hardly qualified for the Hall of Fame of *Theoretical* Finance since he was a practitioner, not an academic. Samuelson's famous line in his presidential address to the American Economic Association—"In the long run, the economic scholar works for the only coin worth having—our own applause"—implicitly defined Treynor out of the running.[2] No doubt Samuelson had heard the whispers that John Lintner might have gotten the idea for the CAPM from Treynor, who had been his student at the Harvard Business School. But they were only whispers, not proofs.[3] The important point was that the two bona fide academics, Sharpe and Lintner, had both clearly developed the result independently of one another. It was simply an accident of fate that only Sharpe got the Nobel for it, because Lintner died before the Nobel committee finally judged the field of finance worthy of recognition. (The Nobel is never given posthumously.)

So Samuelson held both the chalk and his ground until Modigliani sat down and let him finish. By then the damage was done, so no one remembered his plug for Merton, but it was only a matter of weeks before Samuelson's pick would be endorsed where it really mattered. On October 14, the Nobel Prize Committee would issue a press release announcing the prize for 1997: "Robert C. Merton and Myron S. Scholes have, in collaboration with the late Fischer Black, developed a pioneering formula for the valuation of stock options. Their methodology has paved the way for economic valuations in many areas. It has also generated new types of financial instruments and facilitated more efficient risk management in society."

The Committee's unusual posthumous nod to Fischer Black would mean, however, that Merton shared the accolade not only with fellow academic Scholes, but also with a man who had spent the majority of his career in nonacademic positions. At the time Black and Scholes came up with the formula, Scholes was at MIT but Black was at the business consulting firm Arthur D. Little, Inc. (ADL). Subsequently, Black did enjoy an appointment as professor at the University of Chicago, and also at MIT. But he gave up academic tenure to join the investment bank Goldman, Sachs & Co., where he spent the last 10 years of his life. Academic or practitioner, fish or fowl? In fact, and most transgressive of all, Fischer Black had always been both. His very existence stood as a challenge to any neat division between theory and practice.

Jack Treynor was the natural choice for a talk to the IAFE about Fischer Black. He was the one who first stimulated Black's interest in finance way back in 1965 when they met as junior analysts at ADL. He had shown Black his capital asset pricing model and the two had gone on to co-author a piece of work that proved to be seminal for the young profession of financial engineering, "How to Use Security Analysis to Improve Portfolio Selection."[4] By showing how to blend traditional security analysis techniques with the new CAPM, Treynor and Black had provided a framework for managing the transition from traditional craft practice to the modern scientific methods that would transform investment management over the ensuing 30 years.

It was that very transformation that gave rise to the community of financial engineers who were sitting in Treynor's audience that day. Originally a somewhat motley bunch of ex-physicists, mathematicians, and computer scientists, joined by a very few finance academics, they had been drawn to Wall Street by the demand for quantitative skills to support the increasing technical sophistication of investment practice at the leading investment houses. There they had retooled, learning on the job what they needed to know, and the result was a new profession that eventually came together in the International Association of Financial Engineers, founded in 1992.[5] Most of the members had listened respectfully to Samuelson the previous evening, but he was not really one of them. Treynor was, and so was Fischer Black.

Treynor was the natural choice to talk about Black but no one knew what he would say, despite the fact that his advertised title "Remembering Fischer Black" duplicated the title of a brief memoir by him that had already been published.[6] Treynor had a reputation as one of the oddest ducks in the pond, brilliant but unbalanced, with a grip on reality a bit too loose to be reliable. Over the years, many people had the experience of talking with him at some length without ever getting a clear idea what he was trying to tell them. He would say that's what made him such a good money manager, since his somewhat inchoate ideas were unlikely to be already reflected in existing security prices. "It's one thing to have a clear vision of the investment future; it's another to be right." He would also say that's what made him such a small money manager, since most people are more comfortable following the crowd.[7] What would such a man say about Fischer Black, a man with his own reputation for oddness to rival that of Treynor? The room was packed with people who wanted to hear for themselves.

Mark Kritzman, organizer of the conference, had an idea about how to introduce Treynor. Back in 1981, when Treynor was stepping down as editor of the *Financial Analysts Journal* in order to try his hand at money management, Black had written an appreciation of Treynor as a letter to the editor. Kritzman dug up the letter and read it aloud as his introduction.

> Your own research has been very important. You developed the capital asset pricing model before anyone else. But perhaps your greatest contribution has been through the work of others as editor of the *Financial Analysts Journal*. Balancing academic interest, readability and practical interest in a unique way, you guided issue after brilliant issue toward publication. I hope the profession will be able to repay you in some way.[8]

Hearing these words, Treynor was visibly moved. It was, he would later say, the first time he heard them since Fischer had conspired with the assistant editor to publish the letter without Treynor's knowledge.

Stepping up to the podium, Treynor, dressed conventionally if a bit unseasonably in a beige poplin suit and patterned tie, stood about average height and build, with a slight stoop born of natural diffidence as much as age. With his handsome, angular face framed by a full head of well-groomed hair just starting to go silver at the temples, in appearance he could have been any other son of the WASP ascendancy. He spoke quietly and hesitantly even from his prepared text, as though wondering afresh whether the written words adequately express what he now wanted to say. For those in the front row, who could see his eyes, the impression was even stronger of a man who was thinking, not performing, and feeling strong emotion as he remembered his time with Fischer.

Risk and time, he said, are the problems that define the modern field of finance, and Fischer Black's proposed solutions to specific problems in the field should all be understood as bits of a larger proposed solution to those deeper problems. Fischer's special genius was for developing models, "insightful, elegant models that changed the way we look at the world." The most famous of these was the Black-Scholes formula that made possible the subsequent derivatives revolution on Wall Street, but there were others as well.

> In a field full of accomplished learners, Fischer Black was an accomplished thinker.
>
> In a field now full of talented mathematicians, Fischer was a mathematically talented physicist.
>
> In a field where so many profit from confusion, Fischer made a career out of analytical precision.[9]

Fischer never took a course in either economics or finance, so he never learned the way you were supposed to do things. But that lack of training proved to be an advantage, Treynor suggested, since the traditional methods in those fields were better at producing academic careers than new knowledge. Fischer's intellectual formation was instead in physics and mathematics, and his success in finance came from applying the methods of astrophysics. Lacking the ability to run controlled experiments on the stars, the astrophysicist relies on careful observation and then imagination to find the simplicity underlying apparent complexity. In Fischer's hands, the same habits of research turned out to be effective for producing new knowledge in finance.

Indeed, the quest for new knowledge was the motivation behind almost everything that Fischer ever did. Said Treynor, "Fischer's surrender to intellectual curiosity was as complete as his surrender to conscience." Surrender to conscience meant telling the truth at all times, even when it is uncomfortable, indeed especially when it is uncomfortable. Having become convinced of the truth of modern finance, Fischer never wavered no matter what form resistance and opposition might take.

"Never uncomfortable being a minority of one," he refused to tailor his views to the audience. "He was a beacon to harried finance teachers, who loved him for his courage."

Fischer got away with his persistent nonconformity mainly because he was so clearly sincere. He wasn't chasing status, or money, or personal power, only ideas. That meant "letting go of the old, in order to grasp the new," whether it was the old ideas of traditional finance and economics or the old ideas he himself had espoused not long before. Because he was sincere, you could not embarrass him by pointing to a flaw in his thinking. "He never said, 'That's a deeply troubling idea. Maybe someday, when I have more time, I'll think about it.'"[10] Instead he would tell people, "I don't like errors, and I'd appreciate help in finding them."[11]

In Treynor's remembrance, a picture of Fischer Black began to emerge as a kind of alter ego to Treynor himself. Fischer Black was the man who managed to do what Treynor had long ago recognized needed doing, but had himself been unable to do. Looking back now over his own life, with Fischer's public appreciation reverberating in his head, Treynor was overwhelmed by emotion. He broke down at the podium, unable to complete his intended remarks.

"One of the things I like about doing science," Fischer once said, "the thing that is the most fun, is coming up with something that seems ridiculous when you first hear it, but finally seems obvious when you're finished."[12] Fischer not only didn't mind being a minority of one, he actually found it fun, and along multiple dimensions.

Most important, he simply enjoyed the process of using his mind to solve problems. One telltale symptom: At Goldman Sachs he had to leave his Game Boy at home lest he be tempted to play his favorite video game, Super Mario Brothers, when he should be working. Problems in finance were much like video games for him. He would try one way, and then another, and then another, playing around with the problem until he understood it. And then he would come up with an approach that no one had ever before considered, a way of thinking about the problem that was new. His goal was not merely to find his way through all the levels of the Mushroom Kingdom in order to free Princess Toadstool from the evil Koopa turtle king, but even more to find a way to best the top score that had yet been achieved. His competition was not so much against other players, as it was against the game itself, and the game was play, not work.

Satisfying as it was to achieve new solutions, most of the fun actually came from all the other things one inevitably learned along the way. Fischer was never one to learn passively what others told him he ought to know. He preferred to learn whatever he needed in order to solve whatever problem he was working on at the time. "Research should have a goal," he would say. Luckily there were lots of problems that interested him, enough so that moving from one to the next kept him learning new things for his entire life. Fischer was like a toddler in a room full of toys, picking up each one in turn and exhausting its fascination before moving on to the next.

The best problems, like the best toys, are hard to exhaust. You can approach them from a variety of different angles, each new angle making the problem fresh again, and bringing the opportunity to discover something new. Any idea, no matter how crazy seeming, might work and can be worth exploring. Indeed, the harder the problem, the more degrees of freedom one can allow in tackling it. Fischer relished hard problems because he relished that freedom, but in practice he did not try just anything. In his view, if a problem does not yield to known methods, that doesn't mean we need more sophisticated methods, indeed probably just the opposite. Usually problems are hard not because our technique is deficient but because our understanding is deficient.

Fischer's instinct was therefore to limit himself to elementary and direct approaches in an effort to find his way in to the very heart of the problem. Emanuel Derman, Fischer's colleague at Goldman Sachs, remembers: "His approach seemed to me to consist of unafraid hard thinking, intuition, and no great reliance on advanced mathematics. He attacked problems directly, with whatever skills he had at his command, and often they worked."[13] Hard problems offer the possibility of fundamental discovery—that's what makes them so exciting to work on—but only if we approach them in a fundamental way.

An openness to fundamental discovery involves implicit challenge to conventional wisdom, and that dimension of the scientific enterprise especially appealed to Fischer. Behind the protective coloration of his habitual three-piece suit, he was a rebel whose instinctive iconoclasm posed a threat to any institution in which he found himself. But his attacks on established orthodoxy were never only negative (though those under attack sometimes felt otherwise). They were always about replacing the old with something new and better. Fischer was happy being a minority of one, not for its own sake, but only for so long as it took his radical innovations to be accepted as the new orthodoxy, or to be surpassed by something even better.

For Fischer, the ultimate test of any innovation was its practical usefulness. In finance, he had one spectacular success, when the Black-Scholes formula moved almost immediately from the pages of an academic journal to concrete practice at the Chicago Board Options Exchange. Others of his innovative ideas took longer, and none achieved the same widespread and pervasive influence. His proposal for what we now know as portfolio insurance was premature by almost two decades, and his proposals for a radical shift in pension fund investment practice and a radical overhaul of accounting practice remain controversial, even today. But even without the Black-Scholes formula, Fischer would still have been famous for his work on pricing commodity futures, his work on bond swaps and interest rate futures (the famous Black-Derman-Toy model), and the famous Black-Litterman model of global asset allocation, all of which have become standards in the industry.

Fischer's work in finance would have been enough for a brilliant career and a permanent place in the pantheon of greats, but in fact it was only half of what Fischer did in his brief career, and the less important half as well, by Fischer's own reckoning. From the very beginning, and through to the end of his career, Fischer thought of macroeconomics, not finance, as the area where intellectual advance could do the most practical good. What causes unemployment, inflation, and the fluctuations in business that seem such basic features of economic experience? And what, if anything, should the government be doing about them? Fischer entered academia in 1971 in large part because he was attracted by the debates then raging between the Keynesian and monetarist schools of macroeconomics, and while there he mounted a sustained intellectual project to develop an alternative theory of business fluctuations. Unlike in finance, however, he had little success getting economists to take his views seriously.

In economics, he couldn't get his most important papers published in the main journals, so after he left academia he published them as a book, *Business Cycles and Equilibrium* (1987). And once having established himself at Goldman Sachs, he tried again, producing a second book: *Exploring General Equilibrium* (1995), which he considered his magnum opus, was published only months before he died. Here we find the end result of almost 30 years of sustained thinking about some of the deepest problems in economics, all from the fresh angle of finance. Not surprisingly, it made hardly a ripple among economists when it was published. Most had long before made up their minds about this trespasser on their turf.

Today, as the integration and globalization of financial markets has become the most salient feature of our times, the perspective of finance seems more natural than it did when Fischer was starting out. And traditional macroeconomics, a body of thought that emerged to provide guidance for individual nation states in a world fragmented by Depression and World War, seems increasingly out of touch. Was Fischer wrong, or just premature?

The revolutionary idea of finance is about risk, about when and how to avoid it but also about when and how to embrace it. For individuals, it tells how to get the most out of whatever risk tolerance you may have, by distinguishing risks that have a commensurate expected payoff from those that do not. The capital asset pricing model tells how you can improve the expected return on your portfolio of risky stocks without increasing your exposure to risk, simply by holding a widely diversified market portfolio and then using leverage, rather than stock selection, to adjust your overall risk exposure. This works because the risk in the market portfolio comes with a commensurate expected payoff, whereas the risk in an individual stock may not.

The reason is market equilibrium. In a world where people get to choose whether to take a risk or to play it safe, they will take the risk only if there is a prospect of sufficient expected return. The return associated with a given risk is the price of that risk, the price that needs to be paid in order to induce people to take it. It doesn't make sense to take risks unless you get paid for doing so. But it also doesn't make sense to avoid risks that do pay, since risk is the cost of reward.

Although the CAPM seems to be about stocks and the stock market, its argument is more widely applicable, and that wider application is what caught the imagination of the young Fischer Black. Most compelling, the capital asset pricing model could be read as a scientific version of the guiding beliefs that swept over a new generation in the 1960s, in opposition to the Depression-era conservatism of their parents. Growing up in the prosperous postwar years, the new generation saw no reason to play it safe, and insisted on the freedom to take risks of their own choosing. Born in 1938, Fischer Black was on the leading edge of that new generation, instinctively attracted to risky behavior but lacking a rational basis for choosing among alternative risks.

Before he found CAPM, Fischer already embraced risk as the cost of education. Convinced that the best way to learn was by experience, he deliberately chose to embrace all kinds of new experience, and brooked no obstacles to his freedom to do so. The bohemian lifestyle endorsed an experimental approach to life, so Fischer called himself a bohemian while he explored the pleasures of casual sex and mind-expanding drugs. He was willing to pay the cost, and would not be held back by the costs that others around him might also have to pay. He learned from experience just how high both costs could be. The wreck of a first marriage and the wasting death of his much-loved second fiancée left him wondering if maybe his parents had been right. The CAPM gave him a new lease on the risk-taking life, a rational reason for turning away from the known past in favor of an unknown future, and a scientific basis for his intuitive life philosophy.

After CAPM, Fischer chose more carefully what specific risks to bear. He continued to seek out new experience so long as the potential benefit outweighed the cost, which for him it often did since mere embarrassment was not a cost that he weighed very heavily. The biggest change was in his greater attention to factors affecting his own personal health and safety. He became a careful driver of cars that were highly rated for safety, and he always wore a seat belt. He always drank a lot of water, ever since a bout with kidney stones in graduate school. Now he cut out alcohol almost completely. All this was about avoiding risks that do not pay.

As time went on his health regime became more and more elaborate. Because there was early-onset cancer on both sides of his family, his Uncle Stanley on his father's side and Grandfather Zemp on his mother's, he took care to avoid adding environmental risk factors to the genetic risk factor he was surely born with. Concerned about exposure to electromagnetic radiation from computer screens, he bought a radiation meter to test the places where he spent most of his time, and bought an extra-long cord for his computer keyboard so he could sit away from the screen. Concerned about the association of dietary fat with cancer, he would eat frozen vegetables with applesauce for breakfast, and plain broiled fish with a baked potato for lunch, no butter or aluminum foil on the potato.

What about risks that do pay? After learning CAPM, Fischer switched from individual stock holding to mutual funds, and he never switched back. As a young man he thought he had high tolerance for financial risk, so he borrowed in order to increase his risk exposure, but experience with market fluctuations taught him about his true preferences. Later on, as a partner at Goldman Sachs, he would say, "I have little tolerance for risk."[14] Except for the money he had in the firm, he kept the rest in money market funds and other short-term securities. For him, intellectual risk in the life of the mind was a better bet than financial risk in the stock market. The downside was much less, and the potential upside quite as large.

The apparent paradox that Fischer presented to the outside world, a freethinker in conservative clothes, is thus no paradox at all. Nor is there any contradiction between the man who lived on the Wild West frontier of new knowledge and the man who lived his life by the dictates of rational choice theory. It was fun to think up the theory, but it was also fun to try it out. For Fischer, living by CAPM was a discipline, but it was also an experiment in an alternative lifestyle, and that made it great fun. It gave him a kick not only to view the world through different glasses from other people, but actually to live and be different from them.

Variation is what makes life interesting, and it is also what makes for progress since it gives natural selection something to work on. Fischer purposely chose to make himself into the first CAPM man, an outlier in the range of human possibility. Other people who were looking for a rational approach to the risk of modern life were free to imitate him, or not, just as they pleased. It would be interesting, which is to say that it would be fun, to see how it all worked out. In the end, we're all playing the same game, and we can't know what strategy works best until the screen flashes "Game Over."

In all investment decisions, the biggest source of risk is time. The world in which we live is always changing, and it is impossible to know what the future holds. Modern finance tells us how to reduce risk by diversifying over time, if only we know the expected return and so can confine our attention to fluctuations around that return. In that case we simply adjust our risk exposure so that we hold constant the fraction of our wealth invested in risky assets. There is, unfortunately, no particular reason to suppose that expected return is constant over time, and there is also no particular way to know how it changes. Said Fischer, "Our estimates of how expected return changes are so poor they are almost laughable."[15] So we need a different approach to the problem.

For most people, future wage income is the largest part of their wealth, so anything that reduces the riskiness of wage income can play a large role in reducing risk over time. Unfortunately, high income tends to require specialized skill, and specialization tends to increase risk because the demand for any particular specialty can change dramatically over even a few years. One solution is diversification by means of multiple specializations, and we see Fischer adopting that strategy in his straddle between academia and business. Another solution is flexibility, meaning the ability and willingness to change direction during the course of a career as the fog of the future lifts. A career based, as Fischer's was, on general-purpose skills, such as logical thinking and clear writing, is thus less risky than one based on highly specific technical skills such as sophisticated mathematics or statistics.

Another way to achieve personal stability in an unstable world is to enter into long-term contracts with other people. Traditional marriage, with its rather well-defined sex roles, is perhaps the epitome of such a contract, but there are others as well, such as academic tenure and the partnership structure at Goldman Sachs. Long-term contracts, Fischer would insist, are often safer than short-term contracts because, even though you lose flexibility, you gain by reducing your exposure to instantaneous jumps.

In all these ways, the science of modern finance operates as a force for stability in an inherently unstable world by inducing regular behavior in all those who use it for guidance. In a world where nothing is constant, and where multiple futures are entirely possible, people need something to hold on to. By providing a rational account of the working of an ideal world in which stocks are like dice, the CAPM offers people something they can understand and use to organize their thinking about the more difficult real world. The Black-Scholes option pricing model does the same for options and other derivatives by providing a rational account of a world in which volatility is constant.

Both CAPM and Black-Scholes are thus much simpler than the world they seek to illuminate, but according to Fischer that's a good thing, not a bad thing. In a world where nothing is constant, complex models are inherently fragile, and are prone to break down when you lean on them too hard. Simple models are potentially more robust, and easier to adapt as the world changes. Fischer embraced simple models as his anchor in the flux because he thought they were more likely to survive Darwinian selection as the system changes.

Fischer's image of the development of finance was thus as a kind of cultural ecology, in which models and behavior co-evolve with the environment. For him, finance is fundamentally unlike physics with its immutable laws of nature, and more like a social science such as anthropology or psychology. Evolution of financial institutions and markets is only the most visible face of a much larger social process of co-evolution. One reason evolution proceeds so fast in the narrow finance field is that the discipline of the profit motive in free markets works much faster than Darwinian selection in the natural world. Another reason is that the creative powers of human beings are always anticipating the future by offering up new ideas. As a consequence, there is a much wider range of variation for the selection process to work on in the social world than there is in the natural world.

In finance, Fischer's models changed the world by changing the way people look at it, but he himself would have been to first to insist that it was the ideas, not himself, that made the change. He saw himself not as an actor on a world stage, but only as a conduit channeling forces already at work within the system. The CAPM showed a different way to think about risk and time, and everything that followed after was merely playing out the consequences of that fundamental shift in thinking. It was inevitable that such a fundamental shift would have extremely widespread repercussions. Fischer's entire career was built on his ability to surf the wave of repercussions in the field of finance, but he always understood that wave as only part of an even larger story.

More important than the transformation of financial institutions was the way that a changed understanding of risk and time would allow people to live different lives, by freeing them from the superstition that guides action wherever science has yet to penetrate. And even more important was the way that a changed understanding of risk and time would allow people to live different collective lives, by understanding better the larger society of which they are a part, and their place in it. Fischer chose to be a pioneer in both respects, organizing both his personal life and his conception of the society in which he lived along lines suggested by the theory of modern finance. He was like a man from the CAPM future sent back in time to plant the seeds that would produce that future.

One reason for Fischer's success in surfing the revolution in financial markets was his sense of the broader project of which it was a part; he could see the future better than others because he was already living it. But he also worked, and very hard, to figure out the actual world in which he found himself, and to communicate with the actual people with whom he came into contact. His strategies of research and communication must be regarded as equally crucial for explaining the success he enjoyed, as well as the limits of that success.

Although a deeply introverted and shy man by nature, Fischer found that he needed interaction with other people as a stimulus to the high-variance thinking he wanted to do, and also as a regulator of that thinking. All his life, he gravitated to people he could learn from, even as he usually drifted away from them after having learned what they had to teach. Almost all of these interactions were one-on-one, face-to-face with immediate colleagues and then increasingly by phone and e-mail as his intellectual range (and communication technology) expanded. There was never any chitchat, and each interaction focused on the specific problem that he was working on at the moment. As a result, although he interacted with literally hundreds of people, none saw any more of Fischer than the sliver where his interests overlapped with their own, and maybe not even that because he typically would not explain the larger issue behind his specific questions.

His use of other people to regulate his thinking was also largely one-on-one, but with a much smaller set of trusted longtime colleagues.

Here is where his craziest ideas got left behind. But if his colleagues could not convince him to drop an idea, sooner or later he would try it out on a wider group, typically an academic seminar and later maybe a class he was teaching. Unlike standard practice in academia, there was very little back-and-forth in one of Fischer's seminars, since he was not really trying to persuade his audience, but only to catalog their responses for later reflection. He would lay some outrageous notion on the table and then sit quietly while people reacted to it.

Whether asking questions directly or provoking responses in a larger forum, Fischer got people to talk, and then took notes on what they said. He always carried with him a package of note cards, and would pull them out to make a note the very moment the thought occurred, while you were talking, or even in the middle of his classroom lecture. You always wondered what it was that he was writing, but you just had to wonder, and wait until he was done. It made for a strangely syncopated style of interaction, which some people tolerated better than others. But if you couldn't tolerate it, too bad, because Fischer wasn't about to change.

What happened to all the notes? They all got taken back to his office where he would review them and decide what to save and what to throw out. Everything that got saved then got placed into an elaborate filing system where Fischer could put his hand on it within seconds should he ever need it again. Each note had its own sturdy manila file folder, with straight-cut tabs across the top to provide room for a detailed label, usually indicating the problem that the note addressed. As computer technology improved, Fischer augmented this paper filing system with an equally elaborate electronic filing system. People who worked closely with Fischer at Goldman Sachs joked that Fischer was becoming such an appendage to his filing system that one day they expected to arrive at work to find that the bodily Fischer had completely disappeared!

In effect, Fischer surrendered himself to the problem he was working on, and allowed it to take control of his interactions with other people. When possessed by a problem, Fischer tended to treat the people around him as little more than data banks for his central processing unit (CPU) to query. It was as though he shut down that part of the brain that looks after the give-and-take of human intercourse in order to provide maximal resources to the problem-solving module. Somewhere deep inside, he was having fun, but from the outside it could be hard to tell. For the most part, only people who shared Fischer's cultural origin as a science geek were able to see, much less engage, the laughter inside.

Not for nothing did Franco Modigliani characterize Fischer as a "computer with blood in its veins." Another MIT colleague, the Nobel economist Robert Solow, reaching for a metaphor that would encompass as well Fischer's unusual physical appearance, came up with "extraterrestrial," an image that aptly conveys the impression of Fischer's outsized head perched on an unusually skinny neck, like Steven Spielberg's E.T. A third colleague, John Cox, said it best: "Fischer is the only real genius I've ever met in finance. Other people, like Robert Merton or Stephen Ross, are just very smart and quick, but they think like me. Fischer came from someplace else entirely."

And yet, appearances to the contrary notwithstanding, Fischer never viewed his mind as a "meat machine." In early encounters with the artificial intelligence community during his graduate student years, he concluded that computers would one day completely outclass human beings in some dimensions, certainly in terms of memory and speed of calculation. But they would never be able to create; that was the special genius left to human beings. Fischer took the lesson that it was futile to spend energy training his memory or improving his proficiency in calculation. Computers would one day do all that, so all such effort would be wasted. Far better to devote energy to improving one's creative powers, relying on the rapidly improving computer as a memory and calculation prosthesis. Only human beings can think, so that's what they should do, and anyway thinking is great fun.

If ever anyone remarked on Fischer's habit of taking notes during conversations, he would tell them he did it because he had such a bad memory. The more complete answer is that *all* human beings have bad memories. What made Fischer different was that he decided not to fight that natural weakness but instead to compensate with an elaborate filing system. If his natural memory was weaker than others, it was because he relied so much on his artificial external memory that his natural capacity atrophied. What probably started out as just a personal experiment, motivated perhaps by some philosophical debates in the artificial intelligence community, turned into a way of life for Fischer because it worked.

Because of his filing system, Fischer was able to work simultaneously on an unusually large number of different projects, and also to sustain significant projects over an unusually long period of time until they achieved results. The risk reduction that came from such intellectual diversification provided much-needed balance for the high-variance intellectual strategy that Fischer followed in each individual project. Because of his filing system, Fischer could do more work but also he could do better work. The constant cross-fertilization among all the different projects he kept open at one time provided further stimulus to the creativity that was the whole point of the enterprise.

Thinking is one thing that humans do better than machines, and communication with human beings is another. Some people are naturally good at communicating with other people, but Fischer was not one of them. He was too much in his own head to ever become very good at reading others, and consequently he was a terrible judge of character. The devious complexity of office politics, whether in academia or business, simply defeated him, and he learned to keep himself out of it as much as he could. With the exception of fellow science geeks, the people with whom he connected most successfully were, generally speaking, people who could connect to almost anybody. All his life, Fischer relied on select gifted communicators around him to help him interface with the outside world on a day-to-day basis. But he was too independent of spirit and mind to allow others to speak for him when it came to the hard-won product of his own creative thought.

The solution he found was to rely on communication at a distance through his pen. Here again, instead of devoting precious energy to overcoming a natural deficit, Fischer found a way to compensate. Relying initially on the manuals of Rudolf Flesch, he taught himself to write in a simple, declarative style that turned out to be almost perfectly suited to the fundamental character of the questions he wanted to treat. Like the pianist Glenn Gould, he found a way to achieve tremendous impact with a direct, apparently artless style. There were no grammatical flourishes, and almost no adjectives, but somehow he was able to plug directly into a reader's mind, bypassing the editor that translates external input into the internal language of the mind. Fischer wrote in a kind of universal code that could run on any brain. "Let us imagine a world in which money does not exist," he invites us in his first published article, and we find ourselves disarmed, already entering into his world and engaging his thought processes.[16]

Fischer's favorite source of news about the outside world was the British news magazine the *Economist*, not least because of its distinctive house writing style. So when the Christmas 1990 issue announced a competition to translate St. Matthew, Chapter 5, into "Economese," Fischer rose to the challenge. The challenge was "to squeeze out unnecessary metaphors, adjectives, and other argument-obscuring figures of speech so that the same point is got across clearly and economically." Fischer's entry did not win, even though it was shorter than the one that did win. He had gone too far, translating not into Economese but into Fischerese.

The Sermon on the Mount
January 2, 1991

Then Jesus went to a mountain with his disciples and preached to them:

Blessed are the weak and the needy; peacemakers; and the righteous, especially when they are persecuted for their beliefs. The earth is for the meek, and heaven for the oppressed.

Light the world with your faith. Let everyone see God's hand in your good deeds.

God forbids murder. I say it's as bad to feel anger without cause, or even to ridicule someone, as to kill.

God forbids adultery. I say it's adultery when you marry an unjustly divorced woman, or even when you look at a woman with lust in your heart.

If you should do or think evil, confess and take your punishment. Better to suffer now than to end up in hell.

Withdraw from conflict. If someone slaps one cheek, turn the other cheek. If he sues you for $1,000, offer him $2,000.

An eye for an eye, and a tooth for a tooth? No. Submit willingly to your enemies, and hold nothing against them. Indeed, *love* your enemies.

In this way you can create heaven on earth.[17]

Here we get a rare glimpse of Fischer's distinctive form separate from his distinctive content, two sides of the man that are fused into an integrated whole in everything else he ever wrote.

Imagine Fischer at work, alone in his office with the door closed, surrounded by file cabinets, with his phone and computer keyboard both within easy reach. This is Fischer in interactive mode, connected to his internal memory bank and his external network of informants, playing with a problem. You can almost hear the cables humming as the CPU sends out a request for new data, places the response in short-term memory, combines it with other responses to distill a new nugget of information, and then finally adds the new information to the permanent database. Fischer is at work, exploring the Mushroom Kingdom, and he is happy, lost in the problem at hand.

Now imagine Fischer at home, with no files, no computer, and the phone unplugged. Maybe it's a long weekend, or the Christmas vacation lull. He sits at a different desk now, with only a white lined pad and his favorite mechanical pencil. This is Fischer in creation mode, alone with his mind, composing. He writes from the top down, beginning with an outline, which is really only a list, with two or three words holding the place that will become a paragraph, or a page, or an entire section. He is calm and relaxed, weighing each word as though he has all the time in the world.

Now his attention is entirely on communication, on converting thoughts into sentences that his readers can convert back into thoughts again. The object is not to enter our world but rather to provide an entry point for us to join him in his. He has figured out the game by now, and is writing tips and clues for those who are stuck back on level three, to help us find our way to where he is. He remembers being stuck himself many times, so he sympathizes, but still he doesn't tell everything he knows since that would spoil the fun (ours and his). He points us in the right direction and then leaves us to work the rest out for ourselves, knowing that we will learn only by doing.

Fischer spent as much of his life as he could in one or the other of these two modes. There is a lot of aloneness in such a life; that is the price of independence in the life of the mind. It was a price that Fischer was willing to pay, and he had the personal reserves to afford it. But at the end of the day, he often found himself spent, and yearned for the simple comfort of the family life he had known growing up. Not passion, such as his parents had in their marriage, just the comfort and security that he had felt as their much-loved son. He lived for the work he loved, and so had no need for fulfillment in his private life to substitute for disappointment elsewhere. But after a day of mountaineering up where the air is thin, he needed a base camp to which he could return for restoration.

Unfortunately, it took two divorces before he knew himself well enough to choose wisely what he needed. Meanwhile, he learned to find comfort outside the marriage. An elegant and always meticulously groomed man, he loved women and often they loved him back, and it wasn't at all always about sex. He made friends with the wives of colleagues and used them as confidantes, much as he would his sister Blakeney or his aunt Corinne.

And now and then there was even a male acquaintance who would become a personal friend, usually someone junior or one of his older students. One such friend, the accounting professor John Lacey, recalls the pleasure he shared with Fischer in the California comedy clubs while they were both going through difficult divorces. Fischer's favorite comedian was Gallagher, the redhead famous for punctuating his one-liners by smashing watermelons with a giant sledgehammer.

But Fischer's greatest comfort, and deepest emotional connection, came from his interaction with his four daughters by his second wife. He loved being a dad, reading to the kids before tucking them into bed at night, and singing them his favorite Broadway show tunes to get them up in the morning. No doubt these moments reminded him of his own childhood. As in his relations with adults, his emotional range remained rather limited. He was sensitive, nurturing, and kind, but not really empathetic, and certainly never much of a disciplinarian. Although quite open to the world of simple emotions, he was easily defeated by emotional complexity. For children, it could be enough.

There was always a lot of child in Fischer. In Treynor's talk remembering Fischer, he drew attention to the picture that the *New York Times* had used in their obituary notice, a picture that had been taken when Fischer joined the MIT faculty in 1975. "What is jarring about Fischer's picture is that his expression shows the kind of joy, curiosity, anticipation, and love of life that we normally see only in babies."[18]

Here, finally, we come to the secret of Fischer Black's extraordinary creativity as a thinker. He approached the world with the naive innocence of a child, without prejudging what he would find there. More often than not he found something new that more sophisticated approaches had missed.

But it wasn't enough just to think like a child. The conditions of creativity mattered, too. Without his strategies for research and communication, he would have had nothing to create with and no one to create for, and could very well have remained locked within his own mind as a kind of autistic savant. And even given those strategies, without CAPM to provide an overriding focus and purpose, he could very well have become nothing more than a dilettante. By the time he found CAPM, he was already almost 30 years old, the dreaded age when creativity begins to decline in fields such as theoretical physics, pure mathematics, and lyrical poetry.[19] But he did find CAPM, and the result was an absolute torrent of creativity for the next 30 years. The CAPM was, for Fischer, the final jump he needed to solve the problem of what to do with his life. From then on he knew what he had to do, and so he did it.

■ Chapter One ■

THOU LIVING RAY OF INTELLECTUAL FIRE

The machine is useful, the system in terms of which the machines gain their use is efficient, but what is man?

 The artist, the writer, and to a new degree the scientist seek an answer in the nature of their acts. They create or they seek to create, and this in itself endows the process with dignity. There is "creative" writing and "pure" science, each justifying the work of its producer in its own right. It is implied, I think, that the act of a man creating is the act of a whole man, that it is this rather than the product that makes it good and worthy.

Jerome S. Bruner, On Knowing (1962, p. 17)

When his parents drove him up to visit Harvard College in the fall of 1954, young Fischer Black refused even to get out of the car. But once they were back home in Bronxville, New York, it was the only college to which he applied. There was never any question that Fischer would get in. He was a math and science geek, and the "number 1 candidate" from the elite Bronxville High School, according to the school's report. But he always liked to tell people that he chose Harvard because of the Freshman Glee Club.

It is true that he liked to sing. But what he wrote on his college application was that choral singing groups "provide social contacts." It was only one of many strategies that Fischer used to compensate for his awkwardness in social situations. At 17 years old, he already stood 6 feet

2 inches but weighed only 150 pounds, his outsized head perched atop an underdeveloped body. The high school's report put the best spin on it: "For one of his ability he is unusually well-balanced, although at times a little shy."

Growing up in Bronxville, young Fischer could not help but be acutely aware of his social deficits. One square mile in area and just north of New York City, Bronxville was populated mostly by people from somewhere else on their way up the corporate ladder. Parents kept busy with sports (golf and tennis) and cocktail parties, and children were expected to do their bit for the family cause, starting with the passing of hors d'oeuvres and drinks. Girls were expected to "come out" in elaborate debutante balls, and boys were assumed to be college bound, on their way to careers in business or one of the more remunerative professions. It goes without saying that the town was lily-white; thanks to an infamous so-called gentlemen's agreement, no Jews or blacks were allowed to own property.[1] Casual racism and anti-Semitism were shared ground for a community whose principle anxiety was about class status.

Given his intellectual gifts, Fischer's parents thought he might become a doctor, and so were pleased when he won acceptance to the prestigious Precollegiate Research Training Program at the Jackson Memorial Laboratory in Bar Harbor, Maine, during the summer before his senior year in high school. But nine weeks of cutting open mice left him unsure whether a career in science was for him. A better clue to his future direction was the discussion group he organized with his high school friends "to try to work out effective methods of true discussion," as he would write on his college application.

He called the group the American Society of Creators, Apostles, and Prophets, and it had four members.[2] George Amis was the Father. He went to Amherst College and became a professor of literature. Robert Helmreich was the Son. He went to Yale and became a professor of psychology. Fischer himself was the Holy Ghost, and Helmreich's girlfriend Eva Augenblick was Virgin Mary pro tempore. She went to Radcliffe and became a research medical doctor. Fischer's high school friends were not math and science geeks, but rather the intellectual leaders of the school, the backbone of the school's theatrical productions, and reliable producers of juvenile poetry for the student newspaper.

It was Amis, then in full flight from his stockbroker father's ambitions for him, who was the closest to being Fischer's best friend at the time.

They built rockets together and blew them up in Fischer's backyard, and they traveled into New York to see the theater. In their junior year they were both in the school production of *Lost Horizons*, Amis as the second male lead and Fischer as the mysterious High Lama. According to the class yearbook, Fischer was "the personification of Oriental mystery." In the student newspaper, alongside a poem by Amis, is one by Fischer titled "Life or Death," which concludes with the stanza: "Death./All dies./Nothing is left./To be good?/No use./Death, death, death. . . ."[3]

Fischer signed Amis' yearbook with a passage from Samuel Taylor Coleridge's *Rime of the Ancient Mariner*: "With my crossbow I shot the albatross." For his own yearbook quotation, he chose a passage from William Falconer's famous poem "The Shipwreck": "Thou living ray of intellectual fire,/Whose voluntary gleams my verse inspire."[4] The poet is invoking his muse, and asking how it can be that heroic sailors venture forth on such a shallow motive as material gain. The passage continues: "Can sons of Neptune, generous, brave and bold,/In pain and hazard toil for sordid gold?/They can. . . ." The poet is preparing the reader to understand the eventual shipwreck as cosmic punishment for human greed. Fischer is signaling his own imminent rebellion against the values of Bronxville, and his determination to find another way.

Τhe Black family came originally from Illinois farming stock. In 1898, however, the farm was sold to pay off mounting debts, and the center of the family shifted to Bryson City in North Carolina, where Amy Black moved after marrying Thad Bryson, son of the town's founder. Amy's older brother Stanley soon joined her and, in partnership with Thad, he built a thriving law practice around the land transfers involved in the growing timber and hydroelectric industries. Stanley Black married Marianna Fischer, a college classmate of Amy's from back in Illinois, and they raised four children in the big house up on Black Hill. There were two girls and two boys, and the youngest of them all was Fischer Sheffey Black, Fischer's father, born January 26, 1911.

Notwithstanding its name, Bryson City was at that time a town of fewer than 500 people, buried deep in the Great Smoky Mountains in the far western part of North Carolina. It was an island of sorts in the sea of southern Appalachian hill culture, a sea populated by rugged but impoverished backwoodsmen, isolated, inbred, and suspicious of "furriners."[5] Marianna was determined not to drown in that sea, and she set the standard for the rest of the family. Energetic, strong-willed, and optimistic, Marianna's advice to her children was always "Be good and you will be happy." But she also took concrete steps to ensure her children's education as the road to a better life, by founding the local library and teaching in the local school. Following her lead, Stanley became trustee of the Bryson City School District, and served as chairman of the county board of education.

The two girls followed the example that Marianna set, continuing their education at Converse College in South Carolina. The eldest, Ellen Engleman Black, went on for her PhD in Sociology at the University of Chicago, became Commissioner of Public Welfare for North Carolina in 1944, and subsequently served as the first U.S. Commissioner of Welfare in the Department of Health, Education, and Welfare from 1963 to 1969.[6] The second daughter, Louise Bryson Black, known as the pioneer of the family, sought her fortune in New York City in the middle of the Depression, where she became a model, a dance partner of Fred Astaire, and chief buyer for a major department store. There she met and married Oscar Cox, an up-and-coming lawyer working for Mayor Fiorello LaGuardia. He would subsequently go on to the Treasury Department in Washington where, working under Henry Morgenthau Jr. during the war, he wrote the lend-lease agreement with Russia.

The two boys took more after their father. In addition to his law practice, Stanley was also involved in real estate dealings on his own account, and was a founder of the local Bryson City Bank, of which he became president in the singularly inauspicious year of 1929. (The bank survived the Depression thanks to an infusion of capital from Marianna's brother, Louis E. Fischer, an engineer and businessman in Chicago, and thanks to the stratagem of paying off depositors with preferred stock.) The eldest son, Stanley Warren Black Jr., carried on the Black banking tradition, rising in the ranks of the American Trust Company to become executive vice president of the successor North Carolina National Bank, which would become NationsBank in 1991, only to merge with Bank of America in 1998.

The youngest son, Fischer Sheffey Black, inherited his father's sense of the main chance, moving from one thing to another as the opportunity arose. An electrical engineer by training, Fischer got his start at the Potomac Electric Power Company, in Washington, D.C., through family connections (Uncle Louis again). But soon he migrated to the business side of the company, while acquiring a law degree on the side. After the war, when the opportunity arose to try his hand as editor of the trade journal *Electrical World* in New York City, he jumped at the chance and subsequently became publisher as well. When that position began to seem shaky,[7] he moved back onto the business side as executive vice president of Tampa Electric in Florida, while acquiring a broker's license and starting a brokerage business on the side. The constant through all these career changes, he would say, is that he was "never out of top management." Like his father before him, Fischer Sheffey attributed much of his business success to his fortunate choice of a mate, Elizabeth Zemp, called Libby. She made all the big decisions, and that was fine with him.

On the Zemp side, the family home was in Camden, the oldest inland town in South Carolina.[8] Libby's mother, Albertus "Bertie" Moore Lenoir Zemp, traced her ancestry to pre–Revolutionary War days, and even earlier to the minister who officiated at the marriage of Pocahontas to John Rolfe. Libby's father's family were more recent arrivals, but nonetheless Libby remembers her father, James Blakeney Zemp, as the "most loved man in Camden." Bertie ran a local private school, while James was a jack-of-all-trades, operating a trucking business and a small vegetable farm, but also dabbling in real estate and serving as partner in the local bank. In the latter capacity, he was obliged to put up money of his own to save the bank during the Depression. The parental models in the Zemp family were thus quite similar to those in the Black family.

An only child, Libby led a charmed childhood full of afternoon horse rides with myriad cousins, Saturday tennis and picnics, parties, and even occasional circuses put on for self-amusement. It was a childhood without much money, but always there was enough for a cook and a maid. Great grandmother Elizabeth Peay Clark kept alive memories of pre–Civil War days when the family had owned a plantation, illustrating her stories about General William Tecumseh Sherman's march with a silver pitcher that had been punctured by a Union sword probing the ground where it was buried. As Libby put it, there were no famous people in her family, but they were people of strong character and self-discipline, with a reputation for honesty and loyalty, and that was plenty of which to be proud. She grew up identifying with Mary Chesnut, author of the famous *Diary from Dixie* about her life at Mulberry Plantation in Camden during the Civil War. Libby graduated as valedictorian from the local public school and went on to Converse College on scholarship with a major in mathematics and a minor in English. "Math is like a puzzle to me," she would say.

During the Depression, both Fischer and Libby came to Washington to find more economic opportunity, as well as a wider selection of potential mates. In September 1935, Libby was working for the Works Progress Administration (WPA) and the Federal Housing Administration (FHA), and Fischer was working for Potomac Electric, when they met at a party; they fell in love, and married in June 1936. Fischer recognized in Libby the qualities he had known and admired in his mother and his accomplished older sisters. And Libby recognized in Fischer the qualities she admired in her father, but also the opportunity to live out something of the life Mary Chesnut had led when she moved to Washington after her husband was elected to the Senate. Thanks to the social connections of Fischer's sister Louise, Fischer and Libby traveled in a "semifast set" on the edges of the Washington social scene. As newlyweds, they lived in Georgetown at 2530 Q Street.

The marriage was bound to succeed, Libby reflects, because she and Fischer had so much in common. "We were both Presbyterians, both bridge players, and both Southern." In fact, she was more genuinely Southern than he, and more genuinely Presbyterian as well since he was never very religious. But both were genuinely bridge players, and more generally both took pleasure in a rich social life filled with parties and dances, cocktails before dinner and sometimes after as well. Like her mother, Libby would always have a maid to take care of the house and the cooking. But she would also insist on putting aside at least $50 a week, which was half of their joint income at the time they married. As a consequence, there was always plenty of money in reserve. As children of the Depression, they always thought of themselves as savers even as they lived a country club life.

Fischer Sheffey Black Jr. was born January 11, 1938, the first of three children, "a love child if ever there was one" according to Libby—albeit a legitimate one. They called him Fish for short. Soon thereafter the family moved from the apartment in Georgetown to a small house on four acres of land on Old Dominion Drive in rural Falls Church outside the city. The first 10 years of young Fischer's life were thus spent in a kind of rural idyll, playing with his younger sister Janice Blakeney Black and brother Louis Engleman Black, tending the victory garden with his father, catching crawfish in the stream behind the house with his cousins Peter and Warren Cox, shooting squirrels while visiting his maternal grandmother in Camden, and fishing the mountain streams while visiting his paternal grandparents in Bryson City. The junior Fischer's early childhood was not so different from that of his parents.

The consequence was an abiding sense of security and acceptance that never left him. The simple country life built around loving family relations was a very good life, and always available in case other plans didn't work out. Later on, when sister Blakeney married a Jewish mathematician with two children of his own and moved to Quebec to raise goats, Fischer said he wanted to join her. He drove everyone up to see the farm and announced, "I think I'd like that." Probably he would not have lasted a week—he didn't even like exercise, much less actual physical labor—but that's not the important thing. His childhood life in the country was always a place he could go in his mind to find peace and calm.

From the beginning, it was clear that Fischer was special. His father taught him to read when he was only four years old, and his kindergarten teacher said he was the smartest student she ever had. He took obvious pleasure in learning new things, and also in teaching what he knew to his sister and brother. The move to Bronxville, when Fischer was 10 and already entering sixth grade—he had skipped a year—placed Fischer in one of the top public school systems in the country and confirmed his bookish nature. Schoolmates would come to the house at 46 Elm Rock Road and call for him to come out, but he wouldn't go despite his mother's encouragement. "They just want to hack around, and I don't like to hack around." He was always most comfortable at home, surrounded by his family, and his books and magazines.

As he got exposed to new ideas and ways of thinking at school, he would bring them home and try them out on his family. Knowing his father's conventionally conservative political preferences, he would make the case for Russian communism. Knowing his mother's strong views on proper etiquette, he would dismiss manners as mere convention, and defend the bohemian lifestyle that was then growing up in nearby Greenwich Village. More generally, he rejected the status-conscious corporate climber culture of Bronxville, as well as the casual prejudice against outsiders. His sister and brother remember rip-roaring arguments at the dinner table. But there was never any danger of a lasting rift. Fischer's parents understood that Fischer was playing around with ideas, just as he always liked to play around with words.

As Fischer gained experience with this kind of robust intellectual interchange on ground that was fundamentally safe for him, he began to try it out in other more risky locations. A favorite target at school was the physics teacher, Joseph "Cappy" Ricketts. "You're wrong, Mr. Ricketts," Fischer would interject calmly. "According to the laws of physics bumble bees can't fly." Here began a lifelong habit of questioning authority that could easily be mistaken for personal attack. Probably Fischer had no sense of how his comments made other people feel. Certainly he never felt the need to develop such a sense since he never had the slightest interest in fitting in. He was different from other people, and he knew it.

The American Society of Creators, Apostles, and Prophets was Fischer's attempt to expand his experiments with intellectual interchange to a select circle of his peers. They read *Scientific American* and discussed all the latest developments, such as Norbert Wiener's cybernetic theory of the human nervous system. They read Aldous Huxley on altered states of consciousness and tried their hand at hypnosis. But even with his closest friends, Fischer always came across as a very closed and private person, cerebral and isolated, detached and aloof. Everyone knew he was the brightest person in the class, but no one knew who he was.

The first person outside his family with whom Fischer made a significant emotional connection was his very first girlfriend, Cynthia "Tinna" Carpenter, from neighboring Scarsdale, whom he met on a school trip to France and Switzerland during the summer between high school and college. They connected right away, and the tour leaders spent the rest of the trip trying to keep them apart. By the time they got back, it was all arranged that she would be his steady girlfriend when he went off to Harvard. Throughout his college years, he and Tinna would write to one another almost daily, and visit regularly. The first year she was still finishing high school, and after that she was at Smith College in western Massachusetts.

Tinna was a quiet girl, serious, shy, studious, and, until she met Fischer, obedient to her parents' wishes. Her father, Ralph Emerson

Carpenter Jr., from a very old New England family, had made plenty of money in the pensions and investments business, and used it to support his passion for antique collection and the preservation of historic homes.[9] In the latter field, he made his reputation by constructing his own Georgian-style home on Morris Lane in Scarsdale, called Mowbra Hall, as a bow to Mowbra Castle, from which three rooms of the home had been salvaged. In 1956, Tinna would make her debut at the Westchester Cotillion and the Holly Ball. Suffice it to say that the Carpenters were a step up on the social ladder from the Blacks, and as such more than suitable for an eventual family merger.

The only problem was that Tinna's parents didn't much like young Fischer and his challenging ways. Tinna called him a nonconformist, and was attracted by his willingness to question God, materialism, and social conventions more generally. Under Fischer's influence, she fancied herself as something of a bohemian as well. No doubt her parents hoped that this infatuation would pass, but no such luck. In fact, Fischer was already talking to his own parents about getting married, and they only insisted that he wait until after graduation. In his first semester at Harvard, Fischer wrote to his grandmother: "Ya know, it looks like you'll be a great grandmother before yer very old—in 6–8 years. Congratulations (6th anniversary before yer 1st grandchild). Ya know, ya might even have some great great grandchildren. How odd."[10] Fischer was always a great one for making plans.

Instead of waiting four years, Fischer and Tinna married after three in July 1958, when Fischer still had one more year to go at Harvard—and soon thereafter they produced the first grandchild. Ultimately the marriage did not work out, but throughout Fischer's early college years the idea of marriage and children was always in the back of his mind as a source of personal security, as he threw himself into the intellectual ferment that was Harvard in the late 1950s.

To the chagrin of his parents, Fischer would put no constraints on the choice of his college roommates, except that they have different interests from his own. When asked to characterize his interests, he would only say "the human being." When asked about a potential major, he would only say "education." There were four of them assigned to the suite in Wigglesworth D-31. Fischer shared a room with Steven Jervis, a New Yorker who would go on to become a professor of English literature. The next year he and Jervis would continue together in Adams House B-42 joined by Elliot Elson, a native of St. Louis whom Fischer had met during his summer at the Jackson Memorial Laboratory. Elson would go on to become a professor of biochemistry. Jervis and Elson were both friends of Fischer, but again not really intimates.

Unlike his roommates, Fischer never focused on conventional academic success. He would write papers on his own topic, not the assignment, and was more interested in finding new and unconventional approaches to problems than in learning the standard stuff. Even then his way was to make an intuitive leap, and leave the details for later. In daily life, he was unwilling to accept normal conventions, such as waiting until others have read the newspaper before tearing out an article than interests you. He was always challenging and provoking arguments about even the smallest thing, and would not brook obstacles to his own independence, including other people's feelings and opinions. When he and Jervis were called on the carpet for snickering and exchanging glances during the weekly section meeting of Social Science 2, the famous introduction to "Western Thought and Institutions" taught by Professor Samuel Beer, Fischer simply switched to a section leader he liked better.

Behind the outward show of childishness and immaturity, Fischer led a simple, almost monastic life with large areas kept completely private. Tinna was one of those areas, and also his own family, but the most significant was Fischer's own internal life. He kept detailed records of his emotional state over time, writing down numbers on a little pad he kept with him. Probably he was looking for patterns, or causal connections with outside stimuli, but he never talked about it. Scientific findings about himself were more about himself than they were about science. And anyway, he always knew he was different from other people, so his findings were unlikely to have any general application.

Fischer's course selection seems to have been similarly directed by a scientific interest, now directed outward at other people. In his first semester, he took an introduction to anthropology "all about how early man and institutions developed" and decided to major in Social Relations, which he described as a "conglomeration of sociology, anthropology, psychology, psychiatry, etc."[11] As a sophomore, he jumped immediately into advanced classes that could also be taken by graduate students in the field. By his own account, the most important of these was "Psychological Foundations of Social Behavior," taught by Jerome Bruner.[12]

Bruner was at that time in the forefront of the new cognitive approach to psychology that was rising up to challenge the old behaviorist approach championed by fellow Harvard professor B. F. Skinner. Instead of viewing behavior as a conditioned response to stimuli, the cognitive psychologists were focusing on the internal thought processes that mediated any such response. Bruner's specific focus was on education, and he had a message that Fischer liked. "Intuitive thinking, the training of hunches, is a much-neglected and essential feature of productive thinking not only in formal academic disciplines but also in everyday life. . . . Usually intuitive thinking rests on familiarity with the domain of knowledge involved and with its structure, which makes it possible for the thinker to leap about, skipping steps and employing shortcuts in a manner that requires a later rechecking of conclusions by more analytical means, whether deductive or inductive."[13] In effect, Bruner gave Fischer permission to proceed with his own education in the way he was already inclined. Even more, Bruner's ruminations about "The Conditions of Creativity"—detachment and commitment, passion and decorum, freedom to be dominated by the object, deferral and immediacy, and the internal drama—provided Fischer with a kind of road map showing how to get where he wanted to go.[14]

A second course, "The Socialization Process in Variable Family Structures," taught by Clyde Kluckhohn, gave Fischer greater appreciation for the parenting he had received, and he told his parents so.[15] "Cultural Ecology," taught by Clifford Geertz, offered an account of broader human culture as the product of co-evolution along with the natural environment. Fischer was so captivated by the latter course that, in summer 1957, he and Tinna typed up the lecture notes Geertz had prepared, and distributed them to interested graduate students. Geertz concluded the course with an ecological critique of modern culture: "Production per se has thus become a central value in our society; our utopian image is the ever-expanding economy. Such an image, though it is held by some of the most prudent, realistic, and practical men in our society, is truly utopian for it rests on the false premise that the potentialities of the environment in which we live are infinite, that 'science' will always find a way to make any damage we do to nature unimportant and will enable us to go on forever milking the cow without feeding her."[16]

As a sophomore, Fischer spent much of his spare time with the graduate students he was meeting in his classes. His closest connection was with the graduate student Karl Reisman, his sophomore tutor in the fall semester, the section leader in Beer's course to whose section Fischer transferred, and a classmate in the Geertz course. Hanging around with Reisman's crowd, Fischer tried once to interest them in his experimentation with hallucinogenic drugs, apparently some kind of mushroom. As usual, he approached the experience like a scientist, taking notes every half hour on what he was feeling. At about this same time, Tinna recalls that Fischer was also experimenting with changing his sleep patterns, alternating four hours of sleep with four hours awake, to see how it affected his mental state. He took lab notes on that experiment as well. Neither experiment was sufficiently successful to cause him to change his ways permanently. In fact, by the end of the sophomore year he seems to have exhausted his interest in pursuing his study of social relations any further, and he was going on to other things.

All the while he was pursuing his intensive study of social relations, he had also been taking courses in mathematics and physics. He seems to have had the idea that he could always return to physics for graduate school if nothing else worked out. In May 1957 he wrote to his parents that physics was not interesting to him but would lead to the kind of job he wanted, namely in research. "In social relations the subject matter would be more interesting and everything would be great if I could get the right kind of job, but I doubt if such jobs even exist. I'm now considering other fields, even economics."[17] Given the timing, it seems reasonable to infer that he was thinking about jobs because he was thinking about marriage. He had to have something to say when Tinna's father asked the inevitable question.

Fischer spent the fall of 1957 trying out biology and chemistry as possible alternatives to physics before he accepted the inevitable. (He also took the philosopher Van Quine's course "Deductive Logic" for his own interest, and was sufficiently engaged to urge Tinna to take a logic course as well.) In May 1958 he switched his major to physics, and on July 12 he and Tinna were married and set up housekeeping at 2 Ware Street right next to campus. Tinna transferred from Smith College to

Boston University, while Fischer continued on to complete his degree, making up for lost time by taking a full load of physics courses, several of them intended only for graduate students.

In October of his senior year he applied to graduate school in physics, once again only to Harvard. He seems to have had the idea that if he showed he could do the work, Harvard would have to accept him, but he made sure of acceptance by scoring 870 (out of 900) on the Graduate Record Exam in Physics. It probably also helped that, after the shock of Sputnik in October 1957, graduate schools were flooded with government money. Fischer won a National Science Foundation fellowship to study theoretical physics, and Harvard took him in, just as he had planned.

He wrote to his parents: "I'm interested only in fundamental theory and physics. Fundamental work is done both at the universities and in industry, but primarily at universities. So it will probably be best for me to be at a university. I don't particularly care what I'm doing to 'earn my salary'—in industry I would spend part of my time on company projects, and at a university I would spend part of my time teaching. This is more or less irrelevant to me, though I think I might like teaching best. I am not interested in creating 'better things for better living,' but rather in making better sense out of the physical world. It is a great challenge to me."[18]

But once he got to graduate school, he took only one physics course—Julian Schwinger's famous course on "Quantum Mechanics"—and barely passed it, no doubt because he paid it little attention. Instead he was focusing his attention on Howard Aiken's course on the theory of switching and Van Quine's advanced course on "Mathematical Logic." Apparently he had gotten interested in computers. In November he petitioned to switch officially from theoretical physics to applied mathematics in the Division of Engineering and Applied Sciences, and in spring 1960 he enrolled in Marvin Minsky's course down the road at MIT, "Automata and Artificial Intelligence." Back at Harvard, one of his mathematics professors set the students a challenge problem, with the prize being a fellowship for the next year. Fischer was by no means getting the best grade in the class, but he focused his energies and within two weeks solved the problem and won the Gordon McKay Fellowship.

Possibly it was this accomplishment that gave Fischer and Tinna the confidence to accelerate their plan to have a child. At any rate, soon thereafter Tinna realized that she was pregnant. Working at the Harvard Computation Lab in the summer of 1960, Fischer wrote to his parents: "One of the things I am most interested in is building computers which can think like human beings. I think it will be possible within 20 years. We don't really care if the baby is a boy or a girl." Fischer's interest in computers had thus morphed into an interest in artificial intelligence, and got connected in his mind with the prospect of raising a child. "I am working on a general plan for a machine which will be able to do 'anything' you or I can do—learn languages, make decisions, solve problems, etc. . . . The general idea is that it starts out like a child, with some basic learning principle but no knowledge, and it slowly is taught all it needs to know."[19]

To help him think about the problem of raising a computer/child, in fall 1960 he took a course on the "Psychology of Learning" that explored the behaviorist approach of B. F. Skinner, but fatefully managed to fail it. More interesting to him was the cognitive approach that he had been exposed to as an undergraduate, and was now exploring in a graduate seminar with Jerome Bruner on "The Cognitive Functions of Personality," and in a reading course with the experimental psychologist George Miller.[20] As an alternative to the stimulus-response framework of the behaviorist, Miller taught, the cognitive theorists propose an Image-Plan framework. An individual formulates an Image of the goal, and a Plan to get there, and then uses that Image-Plan to evaluate all received stimuli and potential actions. The computer, Miller suggested, is a material metaphor for this process.[21]

It is probably from Miller that Fischer got the idea to use the computer to simulate the higher-order cognitive functions. And it is probably through Miller's connections with the RAND Corporation in California that Fischer got offered a job there to pursue the idea over the summer of 1961. The plan was for him to collaborate with the leaders in the field, two professors from Carnegie-Mellon University, Henry Simon and Alan Newell. All the stars seemed to be lining up in his favor.

But in the midst of this exciting intellectual voyage, relations in Fischer's marriage had begun to seriously deteriorate. Conflict had begun to build soon after Tinna got pregnant, and only worsened after the baby, Fischer Sheffey Black III, was born on December 10, 1960. When Fischer went to California, Tinna stayed in Cambridge with the baby. And when Fischer returned, he found a place of his own. He and Tinna got a legal separation in November 1961 and then a Mexican divorce over the Christmas holidays, and Fischer gave up all rights to the child. After a few years, Tinna found someone else, remarried, renamed the child, and moved away. It was the first big reversal of Fischer's life.

And marital trouble was only the tip of the iceberg. Fischer's willful failure in the "Psychology of Learning" had drawn the attention of department authorities, initially only because it threatened his satisfactory progress through the program. More troublesome was Fischer's unwillingness to be tied down to a specific program of work. December 14, 1960, only four days after the birth of his son, in his formal application for admission to the thesis-writing stage of the PhD, Fischer listed his proposed subject as "artificial intelligence or foundations of mathematics." Well, which was it to be? In February 1961, his adviser, Anthony Oettinger, wrote a note to the Committee on Higher Degrees: "I have reason to be concerned about his intellectual discipline so that, while recognizing his ability and his desire for independence, I am concerned lest he lapse into dilettantism."

On April 21, the same Oettinger would chair the oral qualifying examination that Fischer had to pass in order to be allowed to continue on to write a thesis.[22] Fischer did pass, but with the explicit requirement that he produce by the next January 1962 "a coherent, lucid thesis outline reflecting a thorough survey of the relevant literature." More immediately, he had also to pass on May 5 yet another oral examination, this one in the field of psychology to make up for the course he had failed, and once again Oettinger would sit in judgment. Fischer's state of mind can be judged by what happened in the interim.

The spring of 1961 was, in the larger world, a time when the currents that would produce the upheavals of the 1960s were just beginning to come to the surface. President John F. Kennedy was newly in the White House, and change was in the air. On April 15, the daily *Harvard Crimson* editorialized for relaxation of the parietal rules regulating dormitory visits by members of the opposite sex, and on April 28 the weekly *Crimson Review* carried an article on "Oral Contraceptives and the College Community." The Pill had come to Harvard, and not just the contraceptive variety. Over on Divinity Avenue, at the Harvard Center for Personality Research, Timothy Leary and Richard Alpert were completing their first year of experiments with the hallucinogen psilocybin, using Harvard graduate students as their experimental subjects. By the spring of 1961, they had given hallucinogenic drugs to more than 200 experimental subjects.[23]

Meanwhile, in the politics of the day, the 1950s-era activity of the House Un-American Activities Committee still loomed large, as the folk singer Pete Seeger was sentenced to a year in prison for his refusal to cooperate back in 1955. Other headlines spoke of new concerns. "Kennedy warns Soviets against armed support of war in Laos." "Malcolm X demands states for Negroes." "Anti-Castro invasion of Cuba collapses." On Thursday, April 27 the *Crimson* landed on Fischer's doorstep with the banner headline, "2000 Riot After Protest on Widener Steps." On Friday, the headline was even bigger: "Police Use Tear Gas Smoke Bombs to Dispel 4000 Students in Second Riot." Having read these headlines, Fischer found himself in Harvard Square being told by a nervous Cambridge policeman to move on. He refused, and was promptly arrested and thrown in jail.

The irony of the story is that the April 1961 riots were not about Vietnam, or civil rights, or even the Bay of Pigs. The riots were about the decision of Harvard president Nathan Pusey to print diplomas in English, rather than Latin, in a radical departure from 325 years of tradition. Thus did the 1960s begin at Harvard. Eight years later, in April 1969, several hundred students would occupy University Hall with a list of demands, provoking the same President Pusey to order their forcible removal at dawn by more than 400 Cambridge police, an action that prompted a student strike that shut down the entire university. But in 1961, nothing like this was remotely imaginable.

A Harvard dean who was called to the jail to talk to Fischer found him quite unrepentant, indeed "surly" and "insolent." "Black remarked that he hated authority, and seemed to want for a while to stay in jail, but then decided to accept the chance to get out."[24] Of course the authority that Fischer hated was not the police, but Oettinger, and even that target was misplaced. In truth, there was nothing very unusual about Oettinger's actions. Probably he was trying to help Fischer to focus his energies, but Fischer was in no condition to see that. Oettinger was throwing up obstacles to what he wanted to do, and Fischer had only one way of dealing with obstacles, namely stubborn refusal to recognize their legitimacy.

In any event, Fischer managed to pull himself together sufficiently to pass the May 5 psychology exam, but that was the end of it. By spring 1962, his lack of progress toward a viable thesis was evident to everyone, and Oettinger graded his work unsatisfactory. In June he was officially informed that he would not be allowed to register in the fall. Fischer had always said that he wanted independence, and now he had it. There was anger, and disappointment, but also relief. "For the first time in 19 years I am out of school for more than a summer."[25]

Long before the official end finally came, Fischer had begun to take steps to build a new life for himself, beginning with the summer of 1961 in Santa Monica, when he was ostensibly working on a computer simulation project at RAND. On his own, away from both Harvard and Tinna, he tried the California lifestyle and found that he liked it: beaches and mountain climbing, folk dancing and recorder lessons, and the easy company of women not his wife. One girlfriend that summer was Jewish, a fact Fischer was pleased to point out to his parents. "Friendships are one thing and marriage is another. A friendship can be terminated at any time if it stops being enjoyable or meaningful. Therefore there is no reason whatever to be cautious in one's choice of friends. It is good to be close friends with a variety of people."[26] To his grandmother he wrote: "I like the west coast a great deal. It's like a frontier. I think I would like to come out here to work when I finish school."[27]

Back in Cambridge in the fall of 1961, Fischer shared an apartment at 1560 Cambridge Street with three physicists and a historian, Bart Bernstein, whom Fischer would view as his closest friend during this period. Fischer described his life with his roommates: "Hard to get much work done from all the talking, but fun. I have been doing many more things than I ever did before—lots of reading, parties, political work, etc. . . . We helped elect some reasonable politicians in Cambridge." The reference is to the Cambridge Civic Association, a liberal reform movement in town politics. In national politics, Fischer was a supporter of Kennedy.

Separated from Tinna, Fischer was also doing a great deal of dating, including an affair with the wife of a neighbor. Fischer himself understood this period in his life as "a rapid, if delayed, adolescence."[28] It was like a return to his first college days, only without the tie to Tinna. He was supposed to be writing his thesis, but no one was watching over him, so he was in fact free to do whatever he wanted, and he did. After a year of this, the consequence was that he got kicked out of graduate school, but after the initial annoyance that turned out not to be such a big consequence. In May 1962, shortly before the official end, Fischer was making plans to stay in Cambridge for the summer and take a course on the modern American short story. "I like Hemingway, Ring Lardner, Fitzgerald, Farrell, and Salinger the best."

Like so many who drift away from graduate study at Harvard or MIT, he found a job at the local consulting firm Bolt Beranek and Newman (BBN). In July, only a month after his expulsion from graduate school, he described his life: "I am studying modern art in summer school, taking guitar lessons, taking a speed reading course, working on my thesis, working at Bolt Beranek and Newman, participating in psychological experiments on hypnotism. Therefore I am very busy. You don't seem to approve of my social life, so I won't tell you about it."[29]

Needless to say, there was a lot for a parent to disapprove of. Hardest to take, the break with Tinna meant the loss of their first grandchild, who was supposed to carry the Fischer Sheffey Black name into the next generation. (At Libby's suggestion, Tinna changed the child's name to Terry, short for Tertius, as a lasting reference to the missing III.) And yet, no matter how much they disapproved of what their son was doing, Fischer's parents never ceased to support him, both financially and emotionally. In March 1962, after the divorce from Tinna but before the divorce from Harvard, Fischer wrote to his father: "I was just thinking about how much of a difference the money you gave me is making and will make in my life, and I thought I would thank you again."[30] A year later, after he had started to get his life back in some order, he reflected: "My current theory of wisdom is that he is wise who speaks not about the empires he will build until he is emperor. Too many people talk endlessly about their plans and accomplish nothing."[31]

Fischer's roommate Bernstein remembers Fischer during this period as "the most disengaged person I've ever known," quite friendly and generous, gentle and easygoing, but completely incapable of emotional intimacy. He was curious about other people, but always as an outsider and from a distance. "It was as though everyone spoke a different language from him. He could learn it, but he was not a native speaker." Most people conceal their deficits, but Fischer revealed and even emphasized them, because he learned that his differences held some benefit. The Fischer that his college roommates remember, the one who challenged everything and everyone, was apparently gone only to be replaced by a wide-eyed Candide, willing to try everything but unwilling to commit to anything in particular.

One of the benefits of this style was a certain attractiveness to women, who tended to appreciate Fischer's softness and honesty. Soon after Fischer settled down to his job at BBN, he settled down with a steady girlfriend as well. Shirley Noakes was studying humanities and comparative literature, while supporting herself with part-time secretarial work in the physics department. Fischer spent Thanksgiving and Christmas of 1962 with Shirley and her sister Tina, who lived in New York. Shirley remembers Fischer playfully interacting with Tina's two small children. Thus did Fischer discover the kind of family involvement that most suited him.

He could help Shirley and her sister with money and kindness—Shirley remembers Fischer as both "rescuer" and "nurturer"—without being bound by any more complicated emotional bond. In turn Shirley could provide a comfortable home where Fischer was always welcome, but never obligated. He was focused on his work and she was focused on hers, so both needed someone regular, but neither one was thinking about marriage. He taught her to play Space Wars on the PDP-1 computer at BBN, and she took him to her music theory class. They were lovers for the year, and friends afterward.

BBN hired Fischer initially to work on automatic simplification of computer programs, and toward the end of his time there he worked on a syntax-directed compiler,[32] but mostly he worked on computer-based information retrieval systems for a study about "Libraries of the Future," sponsored by the Council on Library Resources and directed by J. C. R. Licklider. Vice president of BBN, Licklider was just leaving for a position in the Defense Department in Washington where he would control the funds that would finance the next step of the computer revolution, what we now know as the Internet.[33]

The library study grew out of Licklider's famous 1960 article on "Man-Computer Symbiosis," which promoted the idea that the main use of the new digital computer, at least in the short to medium run, would not be to replace humans entirely but rather to extend and enhance human capabilities. "The hope is that, in not too many years, human brains and computing machines will be coupled together very tightly, and that the resulting partnership will think as no human brain has ever thought and process data in a way not approached by the information-handling machines we know today. . . . Those years should be intellectually the most creative and exciting in the history of mankind."[34]

Licklider's focus was on designing what he called a "procognitive system," a system for knowledge that would not only do what humans don't do well, such as calculate and retrieve information, but would also aid humans in doing better what they already do well, such as formulate new questions. "It is both our hypothesis and our conviction that people can handle the major part of their interaction with the fund of knowledge better by controlling and monitoring the processing of information than by handling all the detail themselves." The point was not division of labor between man and machines, but interlocking dependency in a dynamically "adaptive, self-organizing process."[35]

In September 1962, Fischer's boss, Tom Marill, suggested that he try his hand at writing a computer program that would be able to deduce answers to questions from a set of given statements, using as a framework the predicate logic that Fischer had learned from Quine. (John McCarthy had suggested something like this as early as 1958 in his proposal for an "Advice Taker," but apparently Fischer didn't know that, and anyway by 1962 McCarthy was no longer in Cambridge, having left MIT for Stanford University.)[36] The goal was to produce a few concrete demonstrations in order to stimulate further investigation. Over the next year, Fischer built a system that was able to understand simple questions—"What is the largest planet?"—and work out the answer from information it had stored in its database. Limitations of computer memory and calculation speed kept the system from being very useful, but that would presumably be overcome eventually. In his final report, Licklider chose to highlight Fischer's "Question Answering System," calling it "a signal advance in automated question answering."[37]

As part of that project, in spring 1963 Fischer sat in on courses at MIT in the grammar of English and in semantics.[38] He was trying to learn about how natural language works in the hope that it might help him with the tricky problem of programming a computer to understand questions posed in natural language. He never made much progress on the problem, but along the way he did gain a lasting respect for the power and flexibility of natural language. For the rest of his life, he would consciously choose to express himself whenever possible in English rather than the formal language of mathematics. And the kind of English he would choose was the "Fairly Easy" English recommended by Rudolf Flesch, whose books Fischer first encountered at this crucial moment in his life.[39] It was Flesch who finally gave Fischer the effective method of true discussion he had been looking for since high school days, and a workable technology for communicating ideas from one mind to another.

Flesch wrote how-to guides—*The Art of Plain Talk* (1946), *The Art of Readable Writing* (1949), and *How to Make Sense* (1954). Here is the origin of Fischer's distinctive mature writing style, a style that is at once plain, direct, simple, informal, and yet strangely compelling. Twenty years later, at Goldman Sachs, when Fischer hired an editor into the Quantitative Strategies Group in order to improve the readability of the departmental memos he was reading, he wanted someone familiar with the Flesch approach.[40]

It would take much practice before he mastered the style, but already in July 1963 Fischer was consciously using the Flesch method to present a talk on his year's work at BBN. A second talk on "Styles of Programming," given at a conference at Stanford University, not only adopted the Flesch method, but also adapted the Flesch content. The point of programming style, Fischer argued, is not so much to communicate effectively with the computer, since the compiler takes care of that, but to communicate with oneself and with other human programmers in later revisions of the program. "Make your style simple, not complicated, even though the complicated style may seem to have some abstract virtues."[41]

When Fischer's work at BBN came to the attention of Marvin Minsky at MIT, it opened the possibility for a return to school. Minsky agreed to take responsibility for him, and at Harvard a new junior professor, Patrick Fischer, agreed to sign off on the formalities. Over the next year, Fischer wrote a dissertation that was accepted for the PhD in applied mathematics in June 1964. The title of the dissertation was "A Deductive Question Answering System." He dedicated it to his parents and singled out for special thanks "S. Noakes for help and encouragement."[42]

The original idea behind the question-answering system was to use the logical structure of the question itself to guide the search for an answer. We start by thinking of the question as a logical statement that follows at the end of some chain of deductive reasoning, and then we work backwards to construct possible earlier links in the chain. Eventually we arrive at a link that matches a statement we already know is true, and that tells us one answer to the question. When we have examined all possible logical chains, we know we have all the possible answers, and we are done.

The main conceptual problem with implementing such a system is how to avoid endless deduction. Fischer's idea for how to handle that problem was to work forward from the corpus of known statements by making all possible deductions once and for all. (He notes the alternative to classify statements hierarchically, but does not pursue it.) Essentially we ask the computer to figure out all the logical consequences of what we already know, and then we use it also to keep a record of those consequences until we have a question to ask.

Given the extremely limited capacity of computers at the time, there was no hope of actually implementing Fischer's question-answering system, but the same could be said of almost everything then being developed in the infant field of artificial intelligence. Had Fischer wanted to continue working in this area, it seems highly probable that funds would have been forthcoming, not least from Licklider at the Defense Department. More generally, Fischer was in contact with essentially all of the key players in artificial intelligence during the years that one historian has called the "Dawn of the Golden Years" (1956–1963).[43] There are any number of ways he could have parlayed his contacts and skills into a career, but he didn't. After finishing his thesis he essentially turned his back on the field.

Even as he was writing the thesis, he wrote to his parents: "I'm trying to decide what I want to do after I get my degree. The field is wide open. I don't really like any of these labels: scientist, engineer, researcher. I'm not at all sure I want to stay in the computer field. . . . I'm not sure

I like computer people very much. I suppose they're no different from anyone else, but they strike me as being overenthusiastic about their ideas—like the people in the electric utility business who are putting in expensive nuclear plants."[44]

Unlike most computer people, Fischer was interested not so much in the underlying technology of the computer but rather in how it could be used to enhance human capabilities, not least his own. From his studies in psychology, he knew well both the strengths and weaknesses of the human mind. No computer would ever have the creative and intuitive cognitive powers that Bruner emphasized as characteristically human. But also no human would ever have the memory and information retrieval powers that computers could offer, at least potentially. (Fischer's professor George Miller had a famous paper "The Magical Number Seven" pointing out that humans are typically unable to hold more than seven separate items in memory simultaneously.) But computers were as yet far too primitive to make Licklider's man-computer symbiosis practical. For the time being, and for some time to come, a well-organized paper filing system could do a lot better.

In this regard, the most important visible legacy of Fischer's exposure to artificial intelligence was the filing system that he used throughout his life as an ever-expanding corpus to keep track of every paper he read and every idea he had. At his death, 30 years later, there were more than 6,000 letter-sized manila folders. His editor at Goldman Sachs describes how he used them: "In going about his research, Fischer made the most of three ordinary tools: pencils, paper, and manila folders. As ideas played about in his head, he was quick to write everything down, and he kept copies of the material he needed or might need. Then, he filed it all where he could find it and use it. It was a simple, elegant approach that freed his mind to do the work he loved."[45] It was, one might say, a paper version of his "Deductive Question Answering System."

A deeper legacy of Fischer's encounter with the idea of man-computer symbiosis was finally to achieve an integration of the two sides of his character, the wildly creative and the ruthlessly logical. Thirty years later, a colleague would remember Fischer: "No one's mind is, or will ever be, as fertile as Fischer's was. No one is even close. He was crazy and logical at the same time. The force of his logic would push you into corners you didn't like, or it could open vistas you had not imagined.

The crazy streak freed him from conventional wisdom. He was intellectually fearless."[46]

Fischer's childhood ambition was to create something new, to think ideas that no one had ever thought before. But creativity unharnessed is close to madness, and anyway society will not tolerate it, as Fischer found out the hard way. In this regard, the most important thing that Fischer's version of man-computer symbiosis gave him was a way to discipline and channel his creative impulse. As "man" he could be as wildly creative as he wanted to be, knowing always that as "computer" he could rigorously check the logic behind any of the ideas he might come up with. And in the interval between ideas, instead of "man" restlessly switching fields in search of fresh stimulation, "computer" could be kept busy extending and organizing the corpus for future use, or answering routine questions posed by other people.

In retrospect, it is clear that the metaphor of man-computer symbiosis helped Fischer to stabilize himself, and so made it possible for him to work productively. But at the time, this was not clear at all, least of all to Fischer himself, mainly because he had not yet found any work that he wanted to do. Throughout his final year at Harvard, there is a sense that he was trying to pack in as much enjoyment of his freedom as he could before the door shut behind him. He moved into a new apartment at 334 Harvard Street, Apt. E-2, and led a very active social life, including some peripheral involvement in the civil rights movement of the day. He attended a concert to raise money for the March on Washington for Jobs and Freedom where Martin Luther King Jr. gave his famous "I Have a Dream" speech. And as the year came to a close, he began looking for a job.

His father, of course, pressed him to consider a career in business, preferably at a big company like IBM. Fischer responded: "I think maybe the best way for me to get things done is to write—papers for journals, articles for magazines, and books. Being an executive and writing are about equally good as ways of getting things done, and I think I would prefer writing. Besides technical articles, I might write books like [Rachel Carson's] *Silent Spring* or [Jessica Mitford's] *The American Way of Death*."[47] Other possibilities included a postdoctoral fellowship in Harvard's new University Program on Technology and Society, or a position with a start-up time-sharing technology company called Real Applications, Inc., and there were other possibilities as well.

In the end, none of the alternatives Fischer explored came through, so he wound up taking a position at Arthur D. Little, Inc. (ADL), a local consulting firm where he got an interview through his father's business contacts. Fischer told himself that the job at ADL was more or less a continuation of his job at BBN, but with industry rather than the government as the primary client. One good thing was that such work was more likely to be of practical use to someone. At BBN, the culture was that consultants decide what they want to work on and then find some argument why the government should fund it. Fischer always thought this put the cart before the horse, and he looked forward to a different culture at ADL. His job would be to help businesses make better use of their computers, and he would start work in January 1965.

■ Chapter Two ■

AN IDEA IN THE ROUGH

Practical experience is not merely the ultimate test of ideas; it is also the ultimate source. At their beginnings, most ideas are dimly perceived.

Ideas are most clearly viewed when presented as abstractions, hence the common assumption that academics—who are proficient at presenting and discussing abstractions—are the source of most ideas.

One of the dangers in our system of formal education, however, is that a student can go all the way through to an advanced degree in many fields without ever having seen an idea in the rough. An academic with this kind of background may even have trouble recognizing a new idea when he has one.

Jack Treynor, "Editor's Comment," *Financial Analysts Journal* (March/April 1973, p. 6)

Founded in 1886, Arthur D. Little, Inc. (ADL) claims to be the oldest management consulting firm in the world, but this is only partly true.[1] Arthur Little himself was a chemical engineer, and for the first 50 years of the firm's life industrial research was its bread and butter. Indeed, Little's "Research Palace," built in 1917 at 30 Charles River Road right next to the Massachusetts Institute of Technology, was in 1977 designated a national historic site as the birthplace of industrial research. The shift toward management consulting happened after World War II, and grew out of the firm's wartime expertise in operations research. As in the other divisions, the goal of the new Management Services division was to use technology to solve business problems.

The new division grew up largely in North Cambridge at the new Acorn Park site, 40 acres of woodland next to a main arterial route, where the firm moved in 1956. To a modern visitor, the place feels like an early incarnation of the modern industrial park, an architectural form designed to mimic the university campuses on which so many of its prospective occupants spend their formative years. In 1965, the boxy facade of the main building, with its upper floors a kind of plaid of pink, gray, and purple granite, would have signaled confident modernity. Fischer was hired into the Operations Research section of Management Services, a section conceived as providing technical support to the Business Research unit. He was supposed to be an analyst, supporting the consultants who talked directly with business clients.

Fischer's office was room 427 in Building 35, a drab three-story brick-faced structure that sprawls to one side of the main building. (In a bow to its MIT roots, ADL adopted the MIT custom of numbering rather than naming its buildings.) By contrast to the main structure, the outbuildings were entirely functional, the private sector's equivalent of wartime barracks, thrown up rapidly and cheaply to meet an immediate need. Inside, the offices were cinderblock cells opening off an endless hallway that echoed whenever the public address system paged someone to take a phone call. The individual offices were spartanly furnished with functional steel desks and file cabinets. It was a place for working, not lounging. Visiting clients would see that their fees went into the work, not the overhead.

Visiting clients were entertained in the Reservation Dining Room in the main building, but everyone else ate in the cafeteria, and that's where a new employee like Fischer would most easily meet people from other sections of the firm. The way the firm worked, every consulting job (or "case") was carried out by a team assembled from around the firm, with each member of the team billing hours to the job. The immediate way to get work was to have an expertise that case managers could use. And the way to get ahead was to become a case manager, bringing in business from your own clients and running a portfolio of cases. For both purposes, you needed to know who else was in the firm and what they were doing. That happened at lunch.

One day, shortly after he arrived, Fischer was eating lunch alone at one of the 12-person tables over by the windows, when Alan Loss set down his tray and struck up the conversation that led to Fischer's first commercial case. Like Fischer, Loss was in the Operations Research section. His undergraduate degree in applied math and computer science at MIT provided the initial opening for a connection with Fischer. But his 1963 MBA from MIT's Sloan School qualified him for more direct contact with clients. Fischer talked about how much he had hated the government projects at Bolt Beranek and Newman, and how much he was looking forward to working with commercial clients instead. Loss talked about his case for the insurance company MetLife.

MetLife had a Honeywell 1800 computer, but they were nevertheless feeling themselves computer constrained, and they had hired ADL to figure out whether they needed a second one. Loss and Fischer investigated and discovered that the actual computer was idle as much as 50 percent of the time. The computing constraint came not from the central processing unit but rather from the availability of tape drives. MetLife already had 30 drives, but it turned out that the routine for sorting data used eight of them. What the company needed was more tape drives and an optimization routine for assigning them. Loss called in Ed Silver, a PhD mathematician, to solve the optimization problem, and the job was done. The client saved the expense of a second computer, and the team of Silver, Loss, and Black published "A Quantitative Rule for the Use of Resources in a Multiprogrammed Computer System" in the Canadian Operational Research Society's Journal, *INFOR*. (The initiative to publish came from Silver, who had his eye on a possible teaching career in Toronto.)

ADL also ran a training operation for MetLife's operations research people in New York, and Loss involved Fischer in that as well. One week, Loss had not had the time to prepare a homework assignment, so he told Fischer his plan to let the class run late, knowing that the senior manager needed to catch a train and so could be depended upon to call the class over before homework was assigned. Everything went according to plan, and the class was breaking up, when Fischer piped up from the back of the room, "You forgot the homework assignment!" It was a chilly cab ride back to LaGuardia Airport, as Fischer stubbornly insisted, "I refuse to lie." Late that night, back in Boston, Loss got a phone call. It was Fischer, calling to apologize. He had been reviewing the incident with his girlfriend and she had helped him to understand it in a new light. No one had been asking him to lie.

The girlfriend was Frances Marshall Watkins, a graduate of Boston University and a third-grade teacher in Quincy, a suburb of Boston. They had met soon after Fischer started at ADL and fallen in love. She was, by all accounts, a wonderful person, both sweet and intelligent, well-adjusted and a joy to be around, tall and slender, with blond hair worn long and straight. Soon Fischer and Loss were double-dating, most often to go bowling. By June Fischer and Fran were engaged to be married, on August 28, 1965, at her great-uncle and aunt's home on Martha's Vineyard.

During this period of Fischer's life, probably as a consequence of lingering parental disapproval, his primary family connection was his great-uncle Floyd Black who had retired to the Cambridge area with his vivacious Bulgarian wife Zarafinca Kirova. They were known as the intellectuals of the family. Floyd had begun his career teaching at Robert College (now Bosphorus University) in Istanbul, Turkey, and gone on to serve as president of the American College in Sofia, Bulgaria. Their son, Cyril Edwin Black, a contemporary of Fischer's father, had built a brilliant career as a professor of history at Princeton University (including service as a consultant for the Central Intelligence Agency during the 1960s).

Fischer's first interaction with the Floyd Blacks had come during his engagement to Tinna. She stayed with them during her visits from Smith College. But Fischer and Floyd hit it off, and so the connection continued on after the marriage and divorce. The model for Fischer's first marriage had pretty clearly been his own parents, and with Tinna he had made the kind of match that they could heartily endorse. Now, as Fischer was once again considering marriage, Floyd and Zarafinca offered a different model, not just for marriage but also for life. Fran was Fischer's Zarafinca, and probably he would have had a wonderful life with her, but it was not to be.

Only weeks before the wedding date, Fran was diagnosed with amyotrophic lateral sclerosis (ALS), commonly known as Lou Gehrig's disease. They canceled the wedding, but she moved in with Fischer and they continued to socialize with friends and family as her health declined. In April 1966, she was still able to walk with help when she caught cold and died in a matter of days as her lungs filled with fluid.[2] The funeral was the first time Fischer's brother had ever seen him cry.

One Friday, in spring of 1966, Fischer was working late at ADL when his friend Alan Loss poked his head in the door to ask if Fischer wanted to go bowling. Loss had a date with a senior at Simmons College and she wanted to include her roommate. That's how Fischer first met Miriam "Mimi" Allen, a 1964 graduate of Simmons College in psychology and a fourth-grade teacher in Arlington. Fischer impressed her as something of a lost soul who needed someone to take care of him.

A native of Arlington, a working-class town north of Cambridge, Mimi had been raised as a Catholic. Her father worked for New England Telephone, but the dominant force in the family was her mother, who ran a successful real estate brokerage business. More important than all this for Fischer, however, Mimi was a stunning beauty. She wore her shoulder-length blond hair styled in a classic flip, accentuating her high cheekbones and long neck.

After their initial introduction, Mimi and Fischer met again on Memorial Day at a party at the house of a mutual friend, and he drove her home. During the summer they both continued to see other people—Fischer was taking advantage of the new technology of computer dating—but by the fall they began dating each other more seriously. Friends at ADL whose advice Fischer sought did not think it was such a good match, but Fischer would not be dissuaded. Later he would explain that he thought she would make a fine mother for the children he very much wanted to have.

In November, Fischer took Mimi to New York to meet his brother and sister, and then over Christmas to meet his parents. The visit did not go well. In his parents' mind, she was no match for Tinna, and they could not imagine wanting to socialize with her parents. For her part, she was appalled by the daytime drinking, not to mention the overt social prejudice. Once back in Cambridge, Fischer and Mimi broke up for a while, but then in February he proposed; in March they bought a house at 209 Jason Street in Arlington; and on July 15, 1967, they were married. (Tinna agreed to have the first marriage annulled so that the second could be recognized by the Catholic authorities.) Fischer's ADL colleagues, Alan Loss and Ed Silver, served as his ushers, along with Mimi's brothers Carl and Ted. Fischer's brother Lee was his best man.

Once he began to date Mimi exclusively, Fischer took the opportunity to reengage with his job at ADL, which had taken a backseat after Fran's death. Fischer's friend Jack Treynor had left for a new job at Merrill Lynch in New York, but not before training Fischer to be his replacement. Now Fischer made the connection with Bob Fahey, who had been the case leader for Treynor's finance cases.

Unlike Treynor or Fischer, Fahey was an accomplished people person whom the principals at ADL trusted to deal directly with clients. He had joined ADL 10 years before and built a thriving practice consulting to large U.S. corporations on issues around long-term planning and organizational structure. Treynor's last case with Fahey had been an evaluation of "Investment Fund Management" for Yale University, completed in July 1966. Fischer's first case with Fahey was for the Continental Bank in Chicago.

The case was about whether the bank should release the second tranche of a large loan to Management Assistance Inc., a company that was trying to challenge IBM in the computer leasing business. Fischer did a day's work and decided that the company couldn't possibly pay back the first tranche, which was $100 million. But when he and Fahey presented the analysis, the client rejected it. As lead lender, the bank was not happy to hear bad news that it would be obligated to pass along to other members of the loan syndicate. Fischer thought that was funny, and giggled about it on the plane home.

Fischer's analysis for the Continental case would have come directly from Treynor who, 10 years before, had begun his own intellectual journey by thinking about the economics of leasing.[3] Here at the very start, Fischer was following in Treynor's footsteps. Years later, Fischer would write an open letter to honor Treynor:

> You started me out in finance and showed me the beauty of the way markets balance bulls and bears, speculators and investors. You taught me to look for buried treasure rather than surface nuggets in the unexplored wilds of research. You listened patiently to my random thoughts, and helped to make them less random. I cannot repay my debt to you.[4]

These are not just nice words. An understanding of how Fischer Black viewed the world of finance and economics begins with Jack Treynor, Black's first and most significant teacher.

A mathematics major at Haverford College, Jack Treynor received his MBA from Harvard Business School in 1955, and stayed on for a year to work with Professor Robert Anthony. One of his tasks that year was to write up a case on machine tool leasing. From an analytical standpoint, the leasing problem is just a specific form of the capital budgeting problem that asks whether it makes sense to purchase a particular capital good. Treynor's teachers had taught him to attack such problems by discounting future benefits back to the present and comparing the sum with initial cost. But they had nothing much to say about what the discount rate should be, and that was troubling since in most practical applications the discount rate turned out to be the critical input. It seemed clear that the rate should be higher than the rate on risk-free government bonds in order to take into account the riskiness of the capital spending project, but how much higher?[5] Treynor resolved to try to understand the relation between risk and the discount rate. This was the problem in the back of his mind as he joined the Operations Research section of ADL in 1956.

His initial breakthrough in thinking about the problem dates from an intensive work period during a three-week vacation in Colorado in summer 1958, during which he produced 44 pages of mathematical notes. Subsequently, he spent weekends at his ADL office putting together a manuscript. At some point, he showed an early draft of the paper to John Lintner at Harvard Business School, "the only economist I knew even slightly," but Lintner offered no encouragement. The end result was a 45-page paper titled "Market Value, Time, and Risk," dated August 8, 1961. An ADL colleague sent the paper to Merton Miller at the University of Chicago, who forwarded it on to Franco Modigliani at MIT, who invited Treynor to spend a year (1962–1963) at MIT further developing the ideas under his supervision. Treynor accepted the invitation, and ADL agreed to support him for the year.

In the 1961 paper, Treynor's analysis built primarily on the foundations laid by a famous 1958 paper of Modigliani and Miller, "The Cost of Capital, Corporation Finance, and the Theory of Investment," in which they introduced economists to a new kind of arbitrage argument. Treynor begins by considering the relative price of assets that are perfectly correlated (single risk factor), expands the analysis to incorporate multiple risk factors, and then expands further to consider diversifiable risk. Throughout the argument, the problem of portfolio choice enters the argument only very briefly, and then more or less as a kind of example to show how we might think about the multiple risk premiums being determined in market equilibrium. In Treynor's setup the problem of portfolio choice is trivial because, given borrowing and lending at the riskless interest rate, one portfolio dominates all others in the sense that it will be chosen by everyone regardless of their attitude toward risk.

This idea of a dominant portfolio would have been familiar to Franco Modigliani from a 1958 paper of Yale professor James Tobin, "Liquidity Preference as Behavior toward Risk." (Tobin would receive the Nobel Prize in 1981 "for his analysis of financial markets and their relations to expenditure decisions, employment, production, and prices.") However, Tobin did not take the crucial step of associating the portfolio proportions in the dominant portfolio with the available supply of assets, and so did not derive market-clearing risk premiums. Under Modigliani's supervision, and building on his own 1961 paper, that is exactly what Treynor would do.

At one level, Treynor's capital asset pricing model (CAPM) was nothing more than the application of some standard ideas from statistics to the question of determining stock prices. The CAPM treats stocks as if they were dice, so the return to owning a stock is like the random number generated by the roll of a die. An ordinary die has six sides and each side has an equal chance of turning up, so the average dice roll is 3.5 = (1 + 2 + 3 + 4 + 5 + 6)/6. In any one roll, an extreme roll of 1 or 6 is just as likely as a near-average roll of 3 or 4, but over a sequence of many rolls we expect that the average will be near 3.5. Furthermore, and this is the key point, if we have many dice and roll them all at the same time, we expect the average of all the rolls to be near 3.5. Average rolls of 1 or 6 are of course possible, but they are not very probable since they can be achieved only if every single die turns up the same extreme roll. If you have enough dice, it's a very good bet that the average roll will be very near to 3.5.

The CAPM applies this dice reasoning to stocks, pointing out first of all that it is less risky to hold a portfolio of many stocks that it is to hold a single stock. An extreme return on a portfolio of many stocks is much less likely than an extreme return on an individual stock. However, unlike the dice analogy, a portfolio of stocks remains a risky investment even after diversification because the average return on a portfolio of stocks is not a fixed number like 3.5 but rather is itself subject to random fluctuation. Unlike dice, stocks tend to move together so their individual fluctuation does not all average out.

It's as if the roll of each die were influenced by fluctuations in temperature, magnetic field, humidity, and such. Even if each die is affected differently by these fluctuating systematic forces, the systematic character of the fluctuation means that the average over many dice will itself fluctuate. In fact, the fluctuation of the dice average is just the sum of all the covariances of each die with every other die. That average fluctuation is systematic risk. Applying this idea to stocks, CAPM says that the price of an individual stock depends only on its systematic risk, which is measured by its covariance with the portfolio of all stocks. In technical terms, Treynor wrote:

> In our idealized equity market, therefore, the risk premium per share for the *i*th investment is proportional to the covariance of the investment with the total value of all the investments in the market.[6]

Treynor had this essential insight of CAPM in 1962, but didn't realize its importance because he was not primarily trying to solve the problem of pricing stocks. He still had his mind on valuing a risky stream of future earnings, and he was trying to grapple with that problem by attributing the risk in earnings to the risk in a set of underlying economic variables. His idea had been first to calculate the market-clearing risk premium on each of the underlying economic variables at a moment in time, and then second to trace the evolution of these variables and their associated risk premiums through the life of the earning asset in question. The CAPM was the first step, but the second step continued to defeat him. He had, however, developed a model of the determination of stock prices, though not one he thought was very applicable to real-world stock pricing on account of its highly idealized nature. Back at ADL and facing pressure from his boss to justify his year away, Treynor turned his attention to possible practical implications of his idealized model.

The model says that returns on a diversified portfolio of stocks can be expected to fluctuate with returns on the market as a whole, more or less widely depending on the risk exposure of the stocks within the portfolio. Further, it says that a portfolio of risky stocks should have higher average returns but greater volatility than a portfolio of less risky stocks. Finally and crucially, since this pattern of returns should arise quite independent of anything the person picking the stocks might be doing, the model suggests an approach to assessing the performance of that person. Using the model, we can factor out the return attributable merely to risk exposure, and what we're left with must be a measure of performance. This is the idea behind Treynor's famous 1965 *Harvard Business Review* paper "How to Rate Management of Investment Funds" and his 1966 follow-up (with Kay Mazuy) "Can Mutual Funds Outguess the Market?" Treynor called this residual the "appraisal premium."

What had begun for Treynor as research into the problem of identifying *ex ante* superior capital investments thus found its first practical application to the problem of identifying *ex post* superior portfolio managers, but in one sense it was really the same problem. If the risk-adjusted present value of a capital investment project looking into the future is greater than its cost, then we know we have a superior project. If the appraisal premium for a manager looking back into his demonstrated record is consistently positive, then we know we have a superior portfolio manager. (Consistency is important to rule out luck.)

Treynor thought that some managers were able to add value, and he therefore constructed a measure that would indicate who had been able to add the most. That meant correcting gross returns for market risk, but then also scaling the resulting risk-adjusted returns to correct for different management styles (low risk or high risk). Treynor's resulting rank list would never have survived a formal test of statistical significance, but it never occurred to him to offer one.[7] His objective was to create a practical benchmark against which managers could be measured. Even if it turned out that the average manager added no value, that would only be evidence of the primitive state of management skill. The important thing was to set up a dynamic of promoting those managers who added value, and eliminating those managers who didn't, and in so doing to improve the performance of the industry as a whole.

Treynor apparently felt sure that any moderately skillful manager would do well under a risk-adjusted assessment, if only because the measure was really fairly crude. Indeed, he seems to have thought that the best managers would welcome the new assessment measure, both as a means of demonstrating the superiority of their product, and as a benchmark for improving it. He was wrong about that, of course. The real impetus for change came not from the managers, but rather from the large institutional investors who adopted Treynor's measure, or one like it, as a way of comparing managers. That is what really caused the change in investment practice, but that was all yet in the future. Treynor's last case at ADL, for Yale University, pointed the way toward that future.

The purpose of the Yale case was to develop methods for evaluating the performance of Yale's new hotshot portfolio managers who were taking a much more active and aggressive approach to their job in an effort to generate more out of the endowment in order to support the ambitious growth plans of Yale's new president Kingman Brewster. The ADL report was supposed to reassure trustees of the prudence, and hence the fiduciary responsibility, of such risk taking. If you can measure it, then you can control it. After reviewing the "three dimensions of investment management"—aggressive versus defensive investment policy, innovation-oriented versus traditional stocks, and active versus passive management—the report concluded that the reason most funds do not perform well is that they are managed by committee. "It seems to us that the key to active portfolio management lies in giving the fund manager the freedom to determine his own style of investment management and to act independently and quickly."[8]

Unfortunately, the top management at ADL did not recognize the potential value of Treynor's methods. (It would be a long time, and a long battle, before the financial industry would adopt them.) Bob Fahey tried to get more money for Treynor but without success. So Treynor made plans to take himself to Merrill Lynch in New York, and in fall 1966, Fischer began to work with Fahey, all the while remaining in touch with Treynor by phone. What Fischer subsequently learned about finance and economics he learned on the job, with Treynor at a distance serving as his guide.

The most significant development in financial markets in the two decades after World War II was the increasing importance of the so-called institutional investor, meaning mainly mutual funds and pension funds.

When the Investment Company Act of 1940 was passed, in the wake of all the other Depression-era financial reforms, mutual funds were a relatively unimportant part of the investment scene, with only 300,000 shareholders and $450 million in assets under management. By 1967, there were 3.5 million shareholders and $40 billion in assets under management. The Securities and Exchange Commission (SEC), the government agency charged with regulatory responsibility, tracked this development with growing concern in a number of studies until finally it felt ready to act. Its proposal was the Investment Company Amendments Act of 1967.[9]

One recurring theme in the studies leading up to the proposed legislation was the failure of mutual funds to provide consumers with investment performance sufficient to justify their high sales commissions and management fee charges. In a sense, it was a hard claim to make stick since there was no agreed way to assess portfolio performance in the presence of risk, but for that same reason it was also a hard claim to refute. Even very crude comparisons of gross returns with the Dow Jones Industrial Average were enough to raise suspicions. The 1967 Act proposed, therefore, to bring mutual fund sales charges and management fees under regulatory control. The mutual fund industry naturally opposed the change, and hired ADL to provide intellectual backup for their position.

The idea was to use Treynor's new method of assessing portfolio performance, a method clearly superior to the crude comparisons on which the SEC was relying, to demonstrate how well mutual funds had performed. But at the eventual SEC hearings, Bob Fahey offered only two rather bland arguments in defense of the industry position. First, mutual fund ownership is the lowest-cost method of owning securities available to most people. Second, the mutual fund industry is competitive and regulated by market forces. It was hardly the ringing endorsement that the Investment Company Institute (ICI) had expected.

What happened was that Fahey's assistant, Fischer Black, heard about a young fellow at the University of Chicago named Michael Jensen who was writing his PhD dissertation on exactly the question that the ICI wanted answered, and using a method very similar to Treynor's to answer it. What Jensen had found was that, over the period 1955–1964, none of the 115 mutual funds for which data was available had a statistically significant record of consistent excess returns once you corrected for their exposure to market risk.[10]

All of Jensen's tests compared the performance of a mutual fund (adjusted for its exposure to market risk) with the performance of a simple market index. He asked whether the measured excess returns, which he called α (or alpha), are sufficiently positive that we can conclude that a fund beats the market. If not, as Jensen found, then we are unable to reject the null hypothesis that professional portfolio managers perform no better than a strategy of mindlessly buying the entire market portfolio and holding on, since the α for that strategy is identically zero. Fischer arranged to hire Jensen as a consultant for a day, and they met in a hotel at O'Hare International Airport in Chicago, sometime in late March 1967.

Fischer also flew in William Sharpe from Seattle, where he was a professor at the University of Washington. Sharpe had in 1966 published his own paper on "Mutual Fund Performance" that proposed yet a third measure of performance, excess return divided by total variability, which came to be called the Sharpe ratio (though not by Sharpe). Sharpe's measure built on his own version of the CAPM, which, unlike Treynor's version, he had developed as an extension of the portfolio choice problem studied by James Tobin and by Sharpe's mentor Harry Markowitz. (See the next chapter for the full story.) Sharpe's measure of portfolio performance was recognizably inspired by the consumer's portfolio choice problem, since it is total variability that presumably enters the consumer's utility function.

Thus, on that one day in that one small hotel room, the three leading methods of mutual fund performance evaluation were represented, each having emerged from a different way of thinking about the problem. It was exactly the kind of setup that excited Fischer, who always loved attacking a problem from multiple angles simultaneously. For both Jensen and Sharpe, it was their first time meeting Fischer, and both came away impressed. For Fischer, especially in his meeting with Jensen, it was his first face-to-face encounter with the Chicago efficient markets interpretation of CAPM, and he also came away deeply impressed. From this day forward, it would fascinate him to reason about the world as if both CAPM and the efficient markets hypothesis were true.

The efficient markets hypothesis (EMH) is about information, not equilibrium. In analytical terms, it says that a firm's stock price fully reflects all available information about the prospects of the firm. If prices change only because of new information, and if new information arises randomly, then prices will fluctuate randomly.[11] If that is what the world is like, then it will be impossible for anyone to pick a group of stocks that can be expected to outperform another group of stocks. Active portfolio management will not be able to improve expected performance and, to the extent that active management uses real resources, it can be expected instead to degrade performance.

The efficient markets hypothesis originated as an attempt to explain a startling empirical fact. If you draw a chart showing how the price of a stock (or stock index) has moved over some period of time, it will typically bear a striking resemblance to similar charts showing the movement of variables that we know to be random, such as coin flips. If you keep track of a series of coin flips, counting heads as +1 and tails as −1, the cumulative sum will go up and down in a way that is hard to distinguish from the movement of a stock price. Harry Roberts, a statistician at the Graduate School of Business at the University of Chicago, convinced himself of this random walk theory by showing charts of stock prices and cumulative coin flips to stock market analysts, who could not tell the difference. Over the next few years Roberts' students, most notably Eugene Fama, applying more sophisticated statistical techniques to the data, came to more sophisticated versions of more or less the same conclusion.[12]

Those students took as their model of sophisticated statistical work the careful 1953 study of British stock prices by the famous British statistician M. G. Kendall, who had found that: "In series of prices which are observed at fairly close intervals the random changes from one term to the next are so large as to swamp any systematic effect which may be present. The data behave almost like wandering series . . . almost as if once a week the Demon of Chance drew a random number from a symmetrical population of fixed dispersion and added it to the current price to determine the next week's price."[13] This way of thinking about the data focused attention on two questions: the independence of successive price changes over time, and the shape of the probability distribution of price changes at a point in time.

For economists, the independence question seemed naturally the more important of the two, since statistical independence would imply zero expected speculative profit, which economists recognized as a characterization of equilibrium in competitive markets. Thus the so-called random walk theory, which was initially only a statistical characterization of the data, came to be endowed with implicit economic content, and began to be called the efficient markets theory instead. At Chicago in 1967, the efficient markets hypothesis was the null hypothesis that empirical tests were expected not to reject. Jensen's results on mutual fund performance were more or less exactly what his academic mentors (specifically Eugene Fama) expected him to find.

Jensen's results were not, however, what the mutual funds wanted to hear at all. Fischer wrote to his parents: "We had a meeting in New York today at which we told some men from the mutual fund industry that our data shows that no mutual funds consistently outperform the market averages. They were surprised. Indeed, one might say they didn't believe us." Undeterred by the negative reaction, he summarized his findings in a memo "Summary of Research Results" dated April 20, 1967.[14] He made two points. First, mutual funds are a better value than brokerage accounts. Second, data from 115 mutual funds for the period 1955–1964 show that none of them beat the market.[15]

The Investment Company Institute wanted the Jensen findings expunged from the ADL report, but Fahey and Fischer refused. What happened instead was a compromise. The ADL report, titled "Economic Studies of the Mutual Fund Industry, June 1967," was included in the committee files, but *not* published as part of the official hearings. And in his testimony to the committee, Fahey presented a statement that made no reference to the Jensen findings, or indeed to any other findings on mutual fund performance. Fischer attended the hearings, but did not testify.

Testimony about the record of mutual fund performance came only on the day after Fahey testified when Paul Samuelson, Institute Professor at MIT, spoke in support of the proposed regulation. His main argument was that the mutual fund industry was a classic case of monopolistic competition, in which prices tend to be kept inefficiently high. As a side remark, he mentioned a PhD thesis written by a student at Yale who found that the distribution of mutual fund performance records is indistinguishable from the distribution of a random selection of any 20 publicly traded stocks.[16] The senators perked up and took interest. In written testimony submitted later, Samuelson expanded his remarks to include a reference to his own version of the efficient markets hypothesis and concluded: "To say that mutual fund portfolios do not do better than sample portfolios selected purely at random is equivalent to saying that they do not do better than the market as a whole."[17]

For Fischer, his work preparing the ICI case was completely exhilarating, so much so that, after getting married on July 15, he called off his planned honeymoon (a trip to London and Paris) and returned instead to work. One imagines that his mind was on the upcoming hearings in Washington on August 1. And then, immediately after the hearings, he threw himself into work again, producing the first of what would be a series of working papers developing his own ideas about finance, independent of any specific case.

In August 1967, he wrote a paper titled simply "Financial Risk" and labeled it Financial Note No. 1. In September he followed up with a second, Financial Note No. 2, titled "Corporate Investment Decisions." How could he produce such papers, and so fast? The answer is that they were not really original work, but rather versions of the two papers Treynor had written during his 1962–1963 sojourn at MIT. The first one was Fischer's account of CAPM (notably including multiple sources of systematic risk), and the second his account of Treynor's capital budgeting problem.[18] Fischer was learning how to write papers in finance, using Treynor's papers as a starting place and Treynor himself as a co-author. And he was preparing for his next big case, which would be for the Ford Foundation.

McGeorge Bundy, newly president of the Ford Foundation, wanted to shift the energy and funds (to the tune of $500 million annually) of the foundation away from support of colleges and universities and into new areas. His idea was to wean them away gradually, by helping them to learn how to make more money from their own endowments. Meanwhile, at the Center for Research in Security Prices (CRSP) at the University of Chicago, Lawrence Fisher and James Lorie had just completed a massive study documenting the superior returns of common stock over the long run. Additionally, the Bank Administration Institute had just completed its report on investment performance of pension funds, a project chaired by the director of CRSP James Lorie. Bundy formed an Advisory Committee on Endowment Management, and tapped Lorie to be the economist on the committee.

The first thing the committee did was to commission a study of the legal framework controlling endowment management, which concluded that there was no legal obstacle in the way of investing in stocks, and nothing to prevent spending realized capital gains as well as interest and dividends.[19] The way thus cleared, the committee produced in 1969 its conclusions in a report *Managing Educational Endowments* that would serve as the industry template for decades to come.

The first paragraph of the summary chapter catches the tone of the whole:

> The record of endowment management by most colleges and universities in the United States has not been good. We believe the fundamental reason is that primary emphasis has been given to avoiding losses and sustaining income. In our opinion, the most important present responsibility of the trustees of these institutions with respect to endowment is to shift their objective to maximizing long-term total return. We believe the total return can be increased sufficiently to permit both a larger annual contribution to operations and greater long-term growth.

Writing under his own name, Lorie added the caveat that it was important to focus also on the increased risk that comes with increased return. Performance can only be evaluated in relation to a definite risk objective. "Inasmuch as there are ways to describe that objective by measuring the riskiness of the portfolio, I hope that the measurement of investment results of endowment funds eventually will include a measure of risk."

Though the published report makes no mention of it, the data on which the report was based had all been gathered and evaluated under a contract arranged by Lorie with Arthur D. Little, meaning Bob Fahey and Fischer Black. Lorie had first met Fischer in January or February 1967 when he stopped off at ADL to talk about the ICI case. (Lorie had just lost his wife and was on his way to a Caribbean vacation to recuperate.) It was probably at that meeting that Fischer learned about Jensen's results on mutual fund performance. Lorie came away very impressed by Fischer's intellectual power and personal integrity. Here perhaps was planted the idea of some day getting Fischer to the University of Chicago. Lorie was, after all, a member of the appointments committee and so always on the lookout for new talent. Obviously Fischer was not ready for anything like that yet, and his degree was anyway in the wrong field, but meanwhile Lorie was happy to recommend Fischer for anything else. When the Ford case came up, Fischer was a natural choice.

The case began in September 1967 and ran throughout the next year. The main task was to gather information on investment practice and performance from university treasurers around the country. The groundwork for this part of the project had already been laid by Treynor, who had done a more limited study as part of the Yale case. The larger study found that no two institutions did it the same way, and on average university endowments achieved investment results even worse than mutual funds. Clearly there was a case for increased professionalism in investment management.

The secondary task was to develop appropriate methods of portfolio performance evaluation in order to support the proposed shift into riskier assets. For Fischer this naturally meant synthesizing the work of Treynor, Jensen, and Sharpe that he had encountered during the ICI case. His Financial Note No. 3, "Measuring Portfolio Performance," completed November 15, 1967, in collaboration with Treynor and Jensen, did just that, but also went beyond the task assigned to consider the question of how to use measures of portfolio performance to guide asset allocation.[20]

At the invitation of James Lorie, Fischer and Treynor used this paper as the basis for a talk to the biannual seminar of CRSP at the University of Chicago in November 1967. The seminar was already a famous meeting ground where practitioners (whose firms sponsored the Center) gathered to hear the latest academic research before it became public. The title of the Treynor-Black talk was "How to Use Security Analysis to Improve Portfolio Selection."

The whole point of security analysis is to identify securities that will perform better than the market. If markets are efficient, as academics tend to believe, then security analysis should be futile. But if markets are not efficient, as practitioners tend to believe, then some forms of security analysis should improve portfolio performance. What Treynor and Black proposed was a way to allocate funds between two portfolios, a "passive" portfolio that is invested broadly in the market and so can be expected to yield the market risk premium, and an "active" portfolio that attempts to earn an additional appraisal premium by exploiting market inefficiencies through picking stocks, timing the market, or whatever. Basically the first fund reflects the advice of academicians, and the second the ambition of practitioners.

In effect, Treynor and Black proposed not to take a position on whether academicians or practitioners are right about market efficiency, but instead to allow experience to decide the case. In their proposal, a statistical algorithm shifts money between the two different funds, based on a comparison of analysts' projections with subsequent experience. "If the analysts are very accurate, the active portfolio will dominate the total portfolio, and it will have a high turnover rate. If the analysts are not very accurate, the market portfolio will dominate the total portfolio, and it will have a low turnover rate."[21]

Even so, the proposal involves a presumption that markets are not completely efficient—else why make room for any active management at all—and that got them into trouble. Said Treynor and Black: "We make the assumption that security analysis, properly used, can improve portfolio performance."[22] At Chicago these were fighting words. The whole point of the CRSP seminar was to proselytize for the efficient markets side of the great religious war then being waged between the new academic thinking on the one side and traditional practice on the other. In that setting, the Treynor-Black paper came across as giving too much ground to the enemy. Treynor remembers that the talk did not go well.

In fact, as both men realized, the Treynor-Black proposal to let experience decide doesn't really solve the problem, since it is almost impossible to distinguish good analysis from good luck purely on the basis of performance. Even the best analysis can easily be swamped by a run of bad luck, so it takes a long run of experience to distinguish good analysis from good luck. In the short run, how one interprets performance will depend on one's prior beliefs. Although Fischer had started out with Treynor believing that a more scientific and systematic approach to portfolio management could improve on current performance, increasingly he found himself fascinated by the opposite efficient markets point of view. His response to criticism of the Treynor-Black talk was a Solomon-like act—he split the paper into two, one for the academics and one for the practitioners.

In Fischer's next talk to the CRSP seminar, "Risk and Evaluation of Portfolio Performance" in March 1968, he presented the academic half, and that's the part that made it into the final report to Lorie and the Ford Foundation. Meanwhile, he produced a separate paper in February 1968, Financial Note No. 4A, "How to Use Security Analysis to Improve Portfolio Selection," as part of another case he was doing for the Massachusetts Investors Trust, a large mutual fund company that had hired ADL to propose ways of using computers to improve their investment management practice.[23] This fourth note would eventually be published in 1973, and would become a seminal document in the "quant" revolution that would eventually sweep Wall Street.

On the one hand, like any good consultant, Fischer was playing both sides of the street. But on the other hand, this kind of dualistic approach was quite characteristic of the way he always liked to work, by attacking the same problem from two points of view simultaneously. If markets are efficient, you do one thing, and if they are inefficient you do another. The fact that almost no one seemed able to beat the market did not mean that no one ever would. If anyone ever did, it would be because they had some advantage over other investors, such as a better theory of asset prices or a better implementation of that theory. That is what Treynor was trying to do at Merrill Lynch. But suppose that markets are efficient and CAPM is true. What else would be true? With the Ford Foundation case winding down, Fischer began to explore this other side of the question in greater depth.

As Treynor had done before him, he began setting aside time, in the evenings and on weekends, to work on his own theories. In July 1968 he produced Financial Note No. 6, "The Time Diversification of Investments," about lifetime portfolio selection in a CAPM world, his first really independent piece of financial thinking without Treynor. And in September 1968 he produced Financial Note No. 7, "Banking, Money, and Interest Rates," about the role of money in a CAPM world, his first foray into macroeconomics. In the waning months of 1968, Fischer was engaged and happy to be at ADL, where he felt he could balance the pull of research with work on real-world problems.

Meanwhile, Treynor was coming to the end of the road at Merrill Lynch. He had been hired by Donald Regan to organize the first quant operation, but was having difficulty persuading the company to implement his ideas. Having failed to convince Fischer to join forces with him, he was beginning to look at other opportunities when suddenly Nicholas Molodovsky, the longtime editor of the *Financial Analysts Journal (FAJ)*, died of a heart attack on March 7, 1969. Treynor got the job, and was introduced to subscribers in the September/October issue.

The profession of financial analyst grew up with the postwar growth of the stock market, but it wasn't until 1959 that a professional organization arose to serve the industry. And it was not until 1963 that the Institute of Chartered Financial Analysts gave its first examination and awarded its first charter.[24] Nowadays chartered financial analysts (CFAs) are everywhere, but back then it was a new designation, struggling to be recognized as a mark of professional distinction.

The purpose of the first exam was mainly to grandfather the leading older members of the Financial Analysts Federation, but farsighted observers could see the future. Nicholas Molodovsky had used his position as editor of the *FAJ* to urge his readers to open themselves to new methods of financial analysis or risk becoming irrelevant. The new portfolio choice theories of Harry Markowitz and James Tobin were here to stay, he would say, and advances in computer technology were every day making it more possible to implement them. Even more, the rising importance of institutional investors was bringing a demand for increased professionalism in investment management, a demand that financial analysts could not meet without retooling.[25]

An article Treynor (et al.) had written for the *Financial Analysts Journal* in 1968, "Using Portfolio Composition to Estimate Risk," based on his work at Merrill Lynch, was a shining example of the new methods in action, a fact recognized by award of the Graham and Dodd Scroll for best article of the year. (Benjamin Graham and David L. Dodd's *Security Analysis*, originally published in 1934, represented the state of the quantitative art now being surpassed by people like Treynor.) Treynor was also well known to the New York Society of Financial Analysts as chair of their Computer Applications Committee. On both counts, he seemed a natural choice to take Molodovsky's place as editor, and to carry the torch for increased professionalism.

Treynor's first "Editorial Viewpoint," published in the March/April 1971 issue, threw down the gauntlet. Until recently, he wrote, it was impossible to tell whether a portfolio manager was any good. The background fluctuation in asset prices is simply so large that it obscures the contribution of the manager. But now, for the first time, new financial theories provide a way of separating out that background fluctuation. And new, more sophisticated professional clients, the institutional investors, are taking an interest. The consequence, Treynor foresaw, would be a new technological dynamism in the field of investment management. "The impact on the rate at which the quality of investment thinking improves can scarcely be overestimated."[26]

In part, Treynor was simply amplifying his predecessor's vision that the future of the profession would involve the replacement of craft by science. The old-breed financial analysts were like blacksmiths who had specialized in forging horseshoes and were now facing mass production of the Model T automobile. "Hammers flashing, anvils ringing, the blacksmiths passed into folklore."[27] Where the craftsman focuses on the uniqueness of each security, the engineer sees each as a member of a class whose essential properties can be summarized and compared using statistical methods. What standardization and mass production opened up for Henry Ford, the computer opened up for the new methods of investment analysis.

What was new was Treynor's insistence that the goal of achieving professional status for financial analysts would require a reorientation of their attention (and employment) away from the securities industry and toward the "ultimate customer," who was increasingly an institutional investor such as a mutual fund or pension fund. Instead of serving the interests of brokers and dealers by generating trades, the financial analyst should serve the interests of the ultimate owner of securities even if that meant decreased commissions for brokers and dealers. "The test of an investment idea has been whether it would sell, rather than its intrinsic value." Treynor's admonitions seem quaint today but at the time many viewed them as heresy.

Countering Treynor's Parable of the Blacksmiths, one of the old guard proposed his own Parable of the Horses: "Once upon a time there lived in the rolling fields of Kentucky a wealthy man who dealt in horses. He bred them, groomed them, and trained them; sometimes sold them, sometimes showed them, and sometimes raced them. From the total of these activities he made a profit. . . . In addition, however, he derived another kind of satisfaction because he loved horses, enjoyed the wide open spaces, and felt he was creating beauty and helping to maintain the quality of life."[28] Into this happy scene enter the new breed of men, interested only in wagering on horse races, and not at all in horses themselves. The predictable outcome of the new approach will be decline in the quality of horses, not to mention the quality of life.

The subtext of this fraternal debate among financial analysts was subsequently brought out into the open by the academic William Sharpe, who offered a parable of his own. Once upon a time, money managers passed the time making bets with one another, enjoying themselves, and enriching the casino owner at the expense of their investing clients. Then one day "a group of professors at Indicia U." came into town raising uncomfortable questions about this cozy arrangement, and the clients responded by moving their funds to new managers who agreed to shun the casino in favor of simply holding the market portfolio. "And everyone but the casino owner lived happily ever after."[29] Sharpe saw the professors of "Indicia U." as the prime movers, while Treynor emphasized the institutional investors, but both agreed that the era of the gentleman farmer-adviser was over.

Treynor's job was to preside over the transition to something new while retaining the support of the old guard. To help him, Treynor added Fischer (by then an academic himself) to the board of *FAJ*. It is thus no accident that Fischer's first article for the journal, "Implications of the Random Walk Hypothesis for Portfolio Management," was published in the same 1971 issue that carried Treynor's manifesto. In return Treynor would publish work of Fischer's that was too much for Fischer's own academic old guard throughout the 1970s and 1980s: "Fact and Fantasy in the Use of Options," "The Ins and Outs of Foreign Investment," "The ABCs of Business Cycles," and "The Trouble with Econometric Models." But there was more to the continuing Treynor-Black relationship than mutual back-scratching.

As editor of *FAJ*, Treynor lived in the world of practical experience, and he transformed that experience into a series of "ideas in the rough" that Fischer would pick up, rework, and feed back. Just so, in 1971, Treynor, writing under the pseudonym Walter Bagehot, thinks about the economics of the dealer function in his "The Only Game in Town," and Black responds with his visionary "Toward a Fully Automated Stock Exchange." And then in 1972 Treynor, still as Bagehot, thinks about different options for pension fund reform, and Black responds with his "The Investment Policy Spectrum."[30] Also in 1972, now under

his own name, Treynor critiques certain long-standing accounting practices in "The Trouble with Earnings," and Black responds with "Yes, Virginia, There Is Hope: Tests of the Value Line Ranking System" and "The
Magic in Earnings."

And this was just the beginning of Treynor and Black's lifelong partnership. In each of these three areas, both men would continue to make
contributions, and almost always in the pages of the *FAJ*. The implicit
dialogue would continue even after Treynor left the *FAJ*, in 1981, to try
his hand at investment management, and after Black left academia, in
1984, to join Goldman Sachs. Among the last articles Black published
before he died were three—"Equilibrium Exchanges," "The Plan Sponsor's Goal," and "Choosing Accounting Rules"—that stated his last position on the three debates he had opened with Treynor more than 20
years before.

At the root of this lifelong dialogue lies CAPM, a root to which both
men held fast throughout their lives even as those around them chased
the next new thing. As late as the May/June 1993 issue of *FAJ* Treynor
writes "In Defense of CAPM," and in the September/October issue
Black responds with "Estimating Expected Return."[31] On the surface
both were defending a particular model and analytical approach. Below
the surface, they were defending the worldview that model had crystallized for them many years before.

■ Chapter Three ■

SOME KIND OF AN EDUCATION

Ideas have great value: both commercial value and intangible value. People love to create ideas, just as actors love to perform.

We don't have to pay actors. They spend their own money taking lessons, auditioning, and even performing. For each one who makes a living at it, perhaps thousands pay money from other sources to stay involved.

We don't have to pay researchers either. Some will earn a living by doing research with commercial value, but many others will support their research with their own funds. They may even earn money in fields entirely unrelated to their research.

Fischer Black, "Doctoral Education, the Business School, and the University" (1992, p. 2)

Fischer Black learned the capital asset pricing model (CAPM) from Jack Treynor, but no one else did. Fischer and Jack talked the same language, but everyone else talked economics. That's why no one got the point when Treynor's CAPM got passed around to the economists. CAPM would have to be invented again twice, and by economists this time, before the new idea could take root and grow. Only after the fact, indeed after the 1990 Nobel award shared by Harry Markowitz, William Sharpe, and Merton Miller, would economists be able to look back and recognize Treynor's paper as an independent discovery of CAPM.[1]

The first bona fide economist to bring the idea of CAPM into print was recent UCLA Economics PhD William Sharpe in 1964, followed

73

closely in 1965 by the established professor John Lintner at Harvard. But even though Sharpe and Lintner spoke the right language, it still took a while for people to get the point. Even Sharpe and Lintner themselves failed to recognize that they were saying essentially the same thing. Lintner claimed that his version of CAPM was more general than Sharpe's, a claim that Sharpe accepted in print in 1966, before Eugene Fama in 1968 showed how the two papers might, under one interpretation, be seen to be saying the same thing.[2] And so, for several years, the two economist versions of CAPM developed independently, Sharpe's version mainly at Chicago and Lintner's version mainly at Harvard.

Sharpe approached the problem from the perspective of the individual investor buying shares of stock. He got to his version of CAPM by extending the portfolio choice theory that had been developed by Harry Markowitz in his 1959 book *Portfolio Selection: Efficient Diversification of Investments*. Markowitz' book was an extension of his 1952 paper "Portfolio Selection," which applied the mathematical technique of quadratic programming to the problem of selecting an optimal portfolio. Markowitz was always more a mathematics and computer person than he was an economist, so much so that Milton Friedman famously came near to rejecting his 1955 dissertation on the grounds that it wasn't economics.[3]

Lintner, by contrast, approached the problem from the perspective of a corporation issuing shares of stock. He got to his version of CAPM by extending the famous 1958 paper of Modigliani and Miller, the very same paper that got Treynor started. But Treynor wanted to build on Modigliani-Miller, while Lintner wanted to refute them. Here is the likely root of Lintner's failure to encourage Treynor. Lintner, like Modigliani, thought Treynor was certainly overly simple, but also probably outright wrong, at least insofar as the theory he was developing was supposed to say something about the real world.

The accident of geography meant that Fischer's exposure to the economists' alternative CAPMs began with the Harvard version, and John Lintner. He spent almost three years shuttling back and forth between Arthur D. Little and the Harvard Business School. Lintner would tell him his view of the way it is in economics, and then Fischer would take that back to Treynor, who would tell him, "No, that can't possibly be true." And then Fischer would return to Lintner and tell him that

Treynor didn't agree, at which point Lintner would effectively tell him, "Treynor's all wet." Treynor remembers: "That strange dialogue went on for a long time, and in the process Fischer got some kind of an education in economics."[4]

The Harvard Business School lies just across the Charles River from the main Harvard campus, only a five-minute walk from Harvard Square across the Lars Anderson bridge, but a world apart. The neo-Georgian red brick architecture tells you you're still at Harvard, but everything else is different. At the Business School they follow the case method of instruction and research, and reject as unrealistic the abstract academic economics as practiced at the Faculty of Arts and Sciences. Teaching and research always begin with the specific instance, in all its detail and complexity, not with the general principles of economic theory. It was not a very likely place to find a PhD economist. And yet there he was, John Lintner, the George Gund Professor of Business and Economics, firmly ensconced in his corner office on the back side of Baker Library overlooking the parking lot and the soccer field.

John Virgil Lintner Jr. arrived at Harvard for graduate study in 1940 from the University of Kansas, where he had earned his BA the previous year. At 24, he was older than the typical graduate student because he had spent two years in a sanatorium recovering from tuberculosis between high school and college. Those two years of forced rest produced a disciplined young man of regular habits, mature beyond his years, and a scholar's scholar very much at home in the world of books and ideas. His undergraduate mentor, John Ise, had recognized his special talents, and provided the encouragement and recommendation that got Lintner from Kansas to Harvard. Once there, his scholarly virtues quickly impressed the faculty, and in 1942 they elected him to the Society of Fellows, a three-year paid fellowship with no duties except study and research in an area of one's own choosing.

Recurrence of tuberculosis in late 1942 forced another break in Lintner's studies and another spell of forced rest in a sanatorium. The threat to his life was serious, but the threat to his studies was not, because most of the professors and students were away on war duty, and the ivory tower had been transformed into a rather hectic training operation for departing troops. By 1944 he had recovered and was back in town, more determined than ever to restrict his activity in order to avoid another relapse. His friend Keith Butters, a 1941 PhD in economics who had taken a position at the Business School, recruited his part-time help on a monograph studying the effect of taxes on growing enterprises.[5] A portion of that project became Lintner's 1945 PhD thesis "Tax Restrictions on Financing Business Expansion" and the origin of Lintner's later research focus in the area of corporate finance.

Lintner's official employment at the Business School began in 1946 when he was tapped to teach Financial Accounting to the burgeoning enrollment of returning soldiers. Two further monographs, both safely empirical, secured for him a permanent position against the opposition of senior faculty who objected to the appointment of any more economists.[6] In 1952, a five-year grant from the Rockefeller Foundation, renewed in 1956 for another five years, finally bought him the time and freedom to pursue his own interests in the way he thought best. The grant was for an open-ended project somewhat vaguely titled "Profits and the Functioning of the American Economy."

Coincidently, two PhD students at Harvard, John R. Meyer and Edwin Kuh, were then both working on dissertations on the economics of business investment decisions. In summer 1952 a chance encounter at the Coke machine in the basement of Baker Library brought Meyer and Kuh together with Lintner. Thus began a decade of collaboration, the product of which came to be called the Charles River Theory of the Firm.[7] Lintner's primary contribution was on financial policy, comprising managerial decisions about dividend payout and debt leverage.

From that point on, Lintner would always have one foot on each side of the river, involving a succession of economics students in his research projects, and himself in theirs. In 1964, the Gund Chair institutionalized this bridging operation with a joint appointment in both the Economics Department and the Business School, and established Lintner as director of a new PhD program in economics and business. Shortly thereafter, in February 1965, he published his version of CAPM in Harvard's *Review of Economics and Statistics*.

He had announced the paper as forthcoming two years earlier, but had run into problems that were still not fully resolved. He warned his readers: "The results are not being presented as directly applicable to practical decisions at this stage. Too many factors that matter very significantly have been left out (or assumed away)." It would be 1969, another four years, before he managed to work out the more realistic general model that came closer to capturing his intuitive understanding of how financial markets work.[8]

The years between his first and last CAPM papers were exactly the years when Fischer was visiting Lintner. He would climb the stairs to Baker 333, shyly enter the room, and look around for somewhere to sit. The room would be hot to Lintner's liking, and thick with pipe smoke that had over the years blackened the green walls. Lintner sat at his desk, facing the door, and drank bottle after bottle of warm Coke as he talked, placing each empty in the stack of wooden cases behind the desk as he plucked a full one to take its place. Lintner would have welcomed Fischer, as he had welcomed Meyer and Kuh, as a potential collaborator. (There were also grounds for personal sympathy between the men, since Lintner had lost his wife to a cerebral hemorrhage in January 1961, and remarried in June 1963.)

Lintner always started from the idea that investment spending is constrained by the availability of internal funds, meaning profits after taxes and dividends. This was especially the case, he thought, for the smaller, more innovative, faster-growing firms on which the dynamism of the economy depends.[9] Not only are the internal funds from realized profits lower in these firms, but for that very reason their ability to raise funds from external sources such as bank loans and capital markets is also more limited. Banks and security markets tend to think of smaller firms as too risky, and prefer to channel their funds to a limited number of large blue-chip firms. The result, at least potentially, is a misallocation of investment spending.

How to fix the problem? One way is to influence the distribution of internal funds. In order to do that, we need to understand the determinants of corporate profits, and of taxes and dividends, which are the major deductions from corporate profits. This was the focus of Lintner's early work, leading up to his famous 1956 paper on dividend policy. Another way is to influence the distribution of external funds. In order to do that, we need to understand how the major stock- and bondholders, mainly financial intermediaries such as insurance companies and pension funds, assess the value of the securities that firms might offer. This is the focus of the work leading up to Lintner's famous 1965 paper on CAPM.[10]

In both lines of work, Lintner's approach was, characteristically for him, initially empirical. He pored over the balance sheet data that publicly traded companies are required to file, looking for patterns. Dividends, for example, are related to measures of earnings and past dividends. Unusually for an economist, he went beyond the published data, conducting field interviews to find out what the patterns mean, or at any rate what managers think they mean. Only when that work was done did he turn to economic theory and attempt to characterize his findings as some kind of rational maximizing behavior. For Lintner, empirical work always preceded theory.

The overarching theoretical question for the Charles River Theory of the Firm was always the optimum level of investment spending. The part of that question that interested Lintner was how the supply of finance capital, from both internal and external sources, affects investment. The usual economist's rule says that you should increase investment spending so long as the prospective return on marginal investment is greater than the cost of capital. The problem with the economist's rule is that it doesn't tell how to account for the uncertainty involved in the return on a risky investment. What exactly is the cost of capital appropriate for risky investment projects? Lintner's question was essentially the same as Treynor's.

Before CAPM, the usual practice was simply to add an arbitrary risk premium to the risk-free rate of interest. For example, in a consulting project in 1956 conducted for Pittsburg Plate Glass (now PPG Industries), Lintner and his Harvard colleague James Duesenberry proposed classifying projects into four risk classes, each with a successively higher risk premium.[11] Neither they nor anyone else had a theory of how big the premium should be, but it didn't seem to matter so much, at least at first. So long as there was a backlog of investment opportunities, the primary constraint on investment was the availability of internal funds, not their price. But as the 1950s wore on and the backlog got used up, the question of the appropriate risk premium became more pressing.

In fact, there began to be concern that managers of the largest firms were investing too much, not too little, and pursuing growth for its own sake (and for their own sake). At the very same time, financial intermediaries such as insurance companies and pension funds were rising in importance as suppliers of external funds to the large corporations. These intermediaries were in a position to serve as countervailing power to the excesses of entrenched corporate managers, but to do so they needed a theory of the cost of capital. This is the context and motivation behind Lintner's turn away from empiricism and toward theory.[12]

Like Treynor, Lintner started his analysis with the famous 1958 paper of Franco Modigliani and Merton Miller in which they argue that, whatever might be the cost of capital, the value of the firm is independent of its financial policy. In the ideal world that they analyze, neither dividend policy nor leverage has any effect on the value of the firm. So much the worse for their ideal world, Lintner thought, since he knew from his empirical researches that both managers and shareholders pay a lot of attention to financial policy. Well before M&M (as the famous paper came to be called), Lintner had already concluded that managers systematically pay out less in dividends than shareholders would like.[13] His problem was to identify exactly where Modigliani and Miller went wrong.

Uncertainty, Lintner came to think, was the most important feature of the real world that was absent from the ideal world of Modigliani and Miller. His intuition told him that if you take into account the effect of financial policy on the riskiness of the firm, then their results collapse. His first attempt to express that intuition in proper economic language was in a long paper titled "A New Model of the Cost of Capital: Dividends, Earnings, Leverage, Expectations and Stock Prices," which he delivered at the annual meeting of the Econometric Society on December 29, 1960.[14] In the very same session, Modigliani and Miller offered a follow-up paper of their own, "Leverage, Dividend Policy and the Cost of Capital: The Theory and Some Evidence." Thus was launched the line of work that led Lintner to the CAPM.

In a nutshell, Lintner's idea was that financial policy affects the firm by affecting the riskiness of future profit flows. Since managers and shareholders are both risk averse, they will accept additional risk only if it comes with additional expected profit. In principle there is no reason to expect managers and shareholders to have identical attitudes toward risk, so conflict of interest is possible. But if the firm is publicly traded, then financial policy can be directed toward the unambiguous goal of maximizing share price. Presumably additional risk tends to lower the share price, so we can sketch the outlines of a theory of optimal dividends and optimal capital structure even without completely solving the problem of how risk affects the stock price. But to go beyond that sketch, and to mount a really effective critique of Modigliani and Miller, we need a theory of the "Valuation of Risk Assets."[15] We need CAPM.

Like everyone else, Lintner knew quite well how to value any stream of future earnings, provided that they are known with certainty. It's all in Irving Fisher's book *The Theory of Interest* (1930). You just discount each flow back to the present using the risk-free rate of interest—$10 today is the same as $10(1 + r)$ a year from now, so $10 a year from now is the same as $10/(1 + r)$ today. But suppose the quantity to be received in a year is a gamble, say either $0 or $20 with equal probability. The expected future value is $10, but what is the present value of that expected future value? Lintner's approach to the problem replaces troublesome expected values with "certainty equivalents" and then proceeds just the same as if the quantities were known with certainty.

A "certainty equivalent" is the quantity of money that, if received for certain, would be equivalent to the risky gamble. For example, suppose someone is willing to pay $8 for a gamble that will pay either $0 or $20 with equal probability. We say that $8 is the certainty equivalent for that person. The difference between expected profit and the certainty equivalent is a premium for risk, in this case $10 − $8 = $2, and the present value of our gamble is then $($10 − $2)/(1 + r)$. According to this argument, the size of the risk premium will be larger or smaller depending on the variance of profits, and depending on the risk aversion of the person evaluating that variance.

But suppose, more realistically, that this gamble is only one of many possible gambles. The portfolio theory of Harry Markowitz made clear that certainty equivalents depend not just on the variance of the individual gamble, but also on its covariance with other gambles that have already been chosen. For example, a gamble that pays $20 when other gambles pay $0, and vice versa, actually reduces overall risk. In this case, someone might be willing to pay more than the expected value in order to participate, and the risk premium would be negative. The general point is that certainty equivalents, and also risk premiums, depend not just on variance but also on covariance.

Empirically, Lintner knew that positive covariance is the general rule both for stocks and for investment projects, and the reason for this seems to be the business cycle.[16] In a boom, the returns on capital projects of all kinds rise, and in recessions they fall. In this sense covariances are caused by whatever causes business cycles, *not* by anything that individual firms can influence by their own financial policy. In the heyday of Keynesianism, some extremists thought that stabilization policy might be able to eliminate business cycles entirely, but Lintner was always more skeptical. For him, the business cycle was a fact of life—like the weather—which meant that risk premiums were larger than they would otherwise be. The important point is that, in thinking about asset pricing, Lintner found it natural to abstract from the general level of stock prices and to focus instead on the price of one stock relative to another, or relative to some market index. His stated reason for doing so was to abstract from the noise introduced by speculation.[17] But the effect was to abstract also from other more fundamental sources of price co-movement, such as business cycle fluctuation.

For example, suppose that the yield of security i is related to attributes specific to the firm and to some index of market performance I according to the following equation:

$$R_i = a_i + b_i I + u_i$$

Here a_i and b_i are constant parameters, and u_i is residual independent risk. Then the expected yield is $E(R_i) = a_i + b_i E(I)$, and the variance around that expected yield is $\sigma_r^2 = b_i^2 \sigma_I^2 + \sigma_u^2$. Lintner's focus on financial policy led him to look for a theory of how the variance of a firm's profit stream affects the level of its stock price. The equation shows how part of that variance is *covariance* common to all firms (σ_I), and part is unique to the individual firm (σ_u). Crucially, Lintner chose to abstract from the former and focus on the latter because that's where he thought a firm's unique financial policy must have its effect.

Lintner's mental model of asset pricing thus focused on the independent risk that is unique to the individual firm. For him, the key insight is that the larger the number of independent risks over which you diversify a given investment, the lower is the risk of the investment. It follows that, in a world of independent risk, the best thing a stockholder can do is to hold a widely diversified portfolio, including both high- and low-variance stocks. Financial intermediaries that are concerned about risk should not favor safe blue-chip stocks over the risky stocks of smaller, more innovative firms, but should instead choose a diversified portfolio of stocks that offer the best risk-reward trade-off. And managers who seek to maximize their stock value should set financial policy to ensure that the firm's own risk/return trade-off is equal to the market's risk/return trade-off. Some firms will have high variance, but also high expected excess returns. Other firms will have low variance, and so also low expected excess returns. For Lintner, these were the most important lessons of his CAPM.

But there was a problem. In Lintner's mental model, variance was the essential thing and covariance a complication arising from waves of speculation or business cycles. But when you work out the mathematics, what it says is that expected returns depend on covariance, and *only* covariance. Ironically, the reason is exactly the diversification that Lintner advocated. (A key assumption behind this result is that all business is done without risk of bankruptcy, an assumption that Lintner shared with Modigliani and Miller, but would not recognize as crucial until much later.)

Lintner seems to have discovered this problem only at a late stage in his research. As late as May 1963 he announced his asset pricing paper as forthcoming in November, but come November it didn't appear. In February 1964 he again announced it as forthcoming, this time without a specific date. But another year went by before it finally appeared in February 1965, and even then in a form that is not fully digested. The uncharacteristically turbid prose, the proliferation of footnotes (77 in all), and the sprawling Appendix Notes (five in all), are all symptoms of a work rushed into print.

Around May 6, 1963, Lintner realized that he had a problem when he presented a draft of his asset pricing paper to his colleagues Howard Raiffa and Robert Schlaifer in their Seminar on Decisions under Uncertainty.[18] Raiffa and Schlaifer were using the seminar as a forum to help them work out the fundamental problems in statistical decision theory. Their ultimate goal was a workable set of tools they could teach to the MBAs, and they were hard at work on class notes that would become their 1965 textbook (with John Pratt) *Introduction to Statistical Decision Theory*. The portfolio choice problem was a natural application, and they had already directed some students toward the problem.[19] In short, they were ready for Lintner.

There is no record of what exactly Lintner said at that seminar, nor does the draft paper survive. But by June 20, 1963, Robert Schlaifer produced a 16-page typed memo, titled "Some Results on Portfolio Analysis Due to Lintner."[20] The purpose of the memo seems to be to translate the argument of Lintner's talk into the framework, and mathematical notation, of Pratt-Raiffa-Schlaifer decision theory. A comparison of the 1963 Schlaifer memo with Lintner's 1965 CAPM paper reveals that Lintner leaned heavily on it in his exposition of the mathematical core of his argument.

The focus of Schlaifer's memo was on the portfolio problem, and especially the "separation theorem" that allows us to treat separately the problem of optimal portfolio size and the problem of optimal portfolio weights. In 1963, Schlaifer thought there was nothing in the memo that went beyond what Tobin had already done, but in fact there was. Schlaifer's Section 7 (pp. 12–14) extends the portfolio analysis to market equilibrium in the case where all investors have the same information and the same risk preferences. And he concludes that: "When the i'th stock is correlated with some of the other stocks, . . . the [risk premium] deduction D_i increases with . . . the 'total covariance' of the i'th stock with all other stocks." This, and the associated equation, is recognizably the essential insight of CAPM.

It was not, however, the insight that Lintner wanted to transmit. The whole point of his theoretical research had been to refute Modigliani–Miller by showing why shareholders care about variance, and hence why managers should care about the firm's financial policy. But now the math was saying that shareholders care only about covariance which, in Lintner's mind, had nothing to do with financial policy. He had intended to refute Modigliani-Miller, but wound up confirming them. And yet his intuition remained unshaken, based as it was on deep knowledge of how the world actually works. Schlaifer's memo meant that he hadn't yet identified exactly where Modigliani-Miller went wrong.

Uncertainty was still the most likely suspect, but apparently the uncertainty in CAPM was yet too idealized to capture the essential characteristics of the real world. Lintner's 1969 CAPM paper would treat the more general case where individual investors have different information and different preferences, where short selling is limited, and where there is no riskless asset to combine with the risky portfolio of stocks. And later still, the application of Black-Scholes option pricing to stock prices would provide a rigorous model in which total variance, not covariance, is what matters.[21] But in 1965, given the publication of Sharpe's CAPM, Lintner didn't have the time to work all this out, so he went with what he had. He was an old-timer playing catch-up with younger and quicker minds.

In 1965, all he had was a model in which stock price depends on covariance. But the covariance of a risky asset with the portfolio in which it is held must always include a term for the covariance of the asset with itself, which is to say the asset's own variance. So variance is still in the picture. Indeed, in the very special case where *all* other covariance terms are zero, *only* variance matters. It was a slim reed, but it allowed Lintner to cling to his original intuition, and to assert that asset prices depend on both variance and covariance.

He couldn't be sure that his CAPM was the answer, but he apparently felt sure that Sharpe's CAPM wasn't. The juices that had first stimulated him to refute Modigliani-Miller now urged him on against Sharpe. First he convinced himself, and then Sharpe, too, that his own CAPM, with its supposed role for variance, superseded Sharpe's. And then he worked to assemble empirical evidence that covariance alone was not enough to explain the patterns we observe in real-world stock prices, and that variance also comes in as at least as important. Total risk, he would argue, is the sum of business risk, financial risk, and market risk. Sharpe's focus on market risk is much too narrow since market risk accounts for at most 2 percent of the excess return on stocks.[22]

What was at stake? At root, Lintner was trying to find a way to correct what he saw as a bias in the flow of external funds in favor of large and safe companies at the expense of small and risky companies. The energy he devoted to refuting Sharpe came from his reading of Sharpe as a defense of traditional fund management practice, a practice that urged concentration of stock holdings in a select list of approved stocks, and so starved the most dynamic firms of the funds they needed.

William Sharpe's CAPM grew out of his June 1961 dissertation at UCLA titled "Portfolio Analysis Based on a Simplified Model of the Relationships among Securities." It was his second attempt at a dissertation after his adviser poured cold water on the first idea, so he was in a hurry. Working mainly with Harry Markowitz at the RAND Corporation, where Sharpe had been employed throughout his graduate study, he wrote the thesis in only a year, just in time to start a job as an assistant professor at the University of Washington in Seattle.

Sharpe's basic idea was to connect up the portfolio choice framework of Markowitz with the operational mind-set of an actual stock analyst. Introduced to a bona fide analyst by one of his professors, Sharpe soon discovered that analysts know quite well that stock prices tend to move together, and so habitually think of the risk in an individual stock as composed of both risk that is specific to that stock and risk that comes from the stock's sensitivity to the market as a whole. What Sharpe did was to show how to go from estimates of these two kinds of risk to the portfolio weights that optimize the risk/return trade-off for the portfolio as a whole.

He started with the 1959 one-factor market model of Markowitz that relates yield to attributes specific to the firm and an index of market performance according to the following equation:[23]

$$R_i = a_i + b_i I + u_i$$

Sharpe's idea was to use the analyst's estimates of "market sensitivity" and "specific risk" as measures of b_i and σ_u. The key point is that, because diversification tends to mute the portfolio impact of independent risk, optimal portfolio weights depend mainly on market sensitivities. The larger the number of securities held, the more this is the case, but a portfolio of as few as 20 stocks provides almost all the diversification you can get. Here is the origin of Lintner's impression that Sharpe was merely bolstering the traditional analyst's predilection.[24]

But Sharpe was doing more than that. In Section V of his thesis he asks what asset prices would be if *everyone* followed his procedure for selecting portfolio weights, and he offers the answer as "A Positive Theory of Security Market Behavior." This chapter is the origin of Sharpe's CAPM. In the thesis, it reads almost as an afterthought, added perhaps with one specific reader on his thesis committee in mind. "I knew Armen Alchian would like the equilibrium stuff," Sharpe remembers. But he knew he had something important, and he devoted his energies to developing the idea further as his first post-thesis research project.

The intuition behind Sharpe's CAPM is simple. Suppose everyone used the Sharpe-Markowitz procedure to choose portfolio weights. Then if any stock offered a lower expected return than required by its market sensitivity, people would shift their portfolio weights away from the stock, its price would fall, and its expected return would rise. Similarly, if any stock offered a higher expected return than required by its market sensitivity, people would shift their portfolio weights in favor of the stock, its price would rise, and its expected return would fall. It follows that, in equilibrium, all stocks must offer the same trade-off between expected return and exposure to market risk.

This is recognizably CAPM, but only for the very special case where asset returns are generated by a one-factor model. In this special case, the efficient frontier is linear and there are many efficient equilibrium portfolios. As Sharpe explains, "When the market has reached equilibrium, no quadratic program is required to distinguish between inefficient and efficient portfolios; the set of efficient portfolios is merely the set of diversified portfolios."[25]

Once there are two factors driving market returns, or even more, then it's much harder to see intuitively how the equilibration process would work, and in general the efficient frontier will no longer be linear. That's probably why, in the 1964 published CAPM paper, Sharpe shifted away from his equilibrium argument and instead derived his asset pricing formula from the relationship between the yield on an individual security and the yield on any efficient portfolio containing that security.[26] Because it's a portfolio choice argument, the formula will hold for any set of asset prices, not just equilibrium prices that clear markets. That's also probably why, in the published paper, Sharpe's characterization of equilibrium continues to rely on the single-factor intuition in his dissertation, so that his diagrams show a linear efficient frontier and the consequent multiplicity of efficient equilibrium portfolios.

All this led to a certain amount of confusion when Sharpe's article came out, some bad and some good. On the bad side, it left the door open for Lintner to claim that his own version of CAPM was more general than Sharpe's. On the good side, it left the door open for Fama and others at Chicago to see Sharpe's CAPM as merely a theoretical justification, by way of Markowitz, of the empirical market model suggested by the work of Chicago graduate student Benjamin King. In fact, the market model is actually inconsistent with equilibrium and hence also with CAPM, but it would take a while before that fact was widely appreciated.[27] Even so, the temporary confusion was on balance a good thing because it meant that Chicago promoted Sharpe's CAPM as a way of promoting their own empiricist research program.

At Chicago, Benjamin King had been working from the efficient markets idea that stock prices change because of new information. Some information affects the entire market, while other information affects only certain industries, and yet other information is specific to an individual firm. We do not observe any of the information directly, only its effect on stock prices. But if we have enough data, we might be able to construct factors (f_{1t}, f_{2t}, f_{3t}) and decompose individual price movements (γ_{jt}) into changes in those factors and an individual stock's sensitivity $(\lambda_{j1}, \lambda_{j2}, \lambda_{j3})$ to each of the different factors. King explained stock price changes as:

$$\gamma_{jt} = \lambda_{j1} f_{1t} + \lambda_{j2} f_{2t} + \lambda_{j3} f_{3t} + \ldots +$$

It is important to emphasize that King was doing statistics, not economics. He was simply trying to find a low-dimension statistical characterization of the interdependence of stock returns (technically speaking, the covariance matrix). What he found was that as much as half of stock price fluctuation could be accounted for by a common factor that he called the market factor (because it was quite highly correlated with the Standard & Poor's 500 index), and another 10 percent by industry-specific factors. In effect, King's results suggested that the one-factor market model was a pretty good statistical characterization of the data.

Eventually King would write all this up in his 1964 dissertation, "The Latent Statistical Structure of Security Price Changes,"[28] but preliminary results were already in the air in January 1962 when Sharpe came to the Quadrangle Club at the University of Chicago to present his dissertation results. Merton Miller and James Lorie, both supervisors of King's research, and Eugene Fama, then still a graduate student like King, all attended Sharpe's talk and came away very excited. What Sharpe was saying seemed to offer a way to link up Chicago's program of empirical research with proper economic theory. The business school offered Sharpe a job, but he decided to stay in Seattle. They didn't get Sharpe, but they did get his CAPM, and the rest is history.

In 1962, the finance program at the Graduate School of Business was just getting off the ground. In 1961, Merton Miller had come from Carnegie-Mellon so they had one of the best theorists available. The lack of a proper theory of asset prices, however, left a vacuum that at Chicago got filled with pure empiricism. The core of the empirical research effort was the Center for Research in Security Prices (CRSP), founded and directed by James Lorie starting in March 1960. Lawrence Fisher, associate professor of finance and associate director of CRSP, took operational charge of the center. The New York investment firm Merrill Lynch provided the initial funding of $50,000, a commitment that was renewed annually until the Center got off the ground. Wall Street had long been touting stocks as a superior investment for the long term. Now, for the first time, the actual fact of the matter would be calculated.

The first CRSP project was to construct a comprehensive database of historical asset prices, covering monthly closing prices of all common stocks traded on the New York Stock Exchange from 1926 to 1960. The second project was to construct a more detailed daily record—including daily high, low, and closing prices for each stock—starting July 1, 1960, and going forward. It was a massive undertaking, occupying a staff of approximately 40 full-time and part-time clerks for six months just to complete the initial coding of 400,000 punch cards.

The project would have been unthinkable before electronic computing, and even then it stretched the capability of the computers available at the time. The project got started on the UNIVAC I machine at the University of Chicago. The first file of prices took 33 reels of magnetic tape and, when printed, occupied 22,000 pages of 11-by-15-inch paper. Partway through the project, the University installed a new IBM 7090 (later upgraded to the 7094), requiring transfer of the data to a new set of tapes with new formatting. It took almost four years of cleaning and cross-checking before the data could be pronounced "99 44/100% pure" and ready for use. Now, what to do with it?

In the first publication to use the new database, in 1964 Fisher and Lorie simply calculated the return on an equal-weighted portfolio of all stocks in the database over the period January 1926 to December 1960. The idea was to see what an investor might have earned simply by choosing a random portfolio, with equal probability of investing in every stock. "In one pass of the data, [the computer] can compute results for six starting dates, twelve ending dates, and three sets of tax rates (one of which is zero) in about 22 minutes."[29] The average return over the entire period was 9 percent, much in excess of the yields available on alternative investments, such as bonds.

During the long wait for the CRSP data, eager graduate students jumped on the empirical program bandwagon using whatever data they could get their hands on. Benjamin King, for example, used a subset of the CRSP data that he cleaned himself. And Eugene Fama used several years of daily price data that he had brought with him when he enrolled in the School of Business in 1960, only 21 years old at the time. He had collected it for Martin Ernst, one of his professors during his undergraduate years at Tufts University, and had already combed through it looking for profitable trading strategies that Ernst could tout to readers of his market newsletter. To his surprise, none of the strategies that would have made money on past data proved successful going forward. The patterns were illusory, just as Harry Roberts had suggested. Fama was thus an easy convert to the random walk theory. In his 1963 dissertation, he hardly bothered to test independence but focused instead on the secondary question of the shape of the probability distribution of returns.[30]

The immediate stimulus for Fama's work was the observation by mathematician Benoit Mandelbrot that certain asset prices fluctuate more widely than is consistent with the standard Gaussian or normal distribution. In Mandelbrot's view, this evidence called for "a radically new approach to the problem of price variation."[31] What came to be known as the problem of "fat tails"—too many outliers—had been pointed out long before.[32] What Mandelbrot added was the proposal to treat these distributions as members of a class of probability distributions called the stable Paretian. When Mandelbrot visited Chicago for one quarter, Fama learned about all this from the man himself. What

Fama did in his dissertation was to show that the price distribution for his 30 U.S. stocks conformed to the Mandelbrot hypothesis.

At first glance, the Mandelbrot hypothesis doesn't sound like such a radical idea, just a generalization of the familiar Gaussian random walk. Paul Cootner, a professor at MIT, sounded the alarm at a meeting of the Econometric Society, December 29, 1962: "Mandelbrot, like Prime Minister Churchill before him, promises us not utopia but blood, sweat, toil, and tears. If he is right, almost all of our statistical tools are obsolete—least squares, spectral analysis, workable maximum likelihood solutions, all our established sample theory, closed distribution functions. Almost without exception, past econometric work is meaningless. Surely, before consigning centuries of work to the ash pile, we should like to have some assurance that all our work is truly useless."[33] We see here the instinct of the established professor to defend his intellectual capital accumulation, but the instinct of the young student Fama was just the opposite. His only intellectual investment was in efficient markets and, so far as he could see, the Mandelbrot hypothesis did *not* require giving up efficient markets. Quite the contrary, efficient markets (in the sense of serial independence) plus the Mandelbrot hypothesis (in the sense of fat tails) together seemed like a pretty good empirical characterization of the data.

Mandelbrot himself, however, had a different view. For him, the arbitrage trading that works to eliminate serial dependence is also responsible for the price jumps that cause fat tails, as prices move to discount the entire future consequences of any new piece of information. But if there is a limit to how far prices can jump, then there is also a limit to how much serial dependence can be eliminated by arbitrage.[34] Serial dependence is therefore likely to be just as permanent a feature of the data as fat tails. For Mandelbrot, inefficient markets and Paretian distributions go together as a package, as a matter of theoretical logic, just as efficient markets and Gaussian distributions do.[35]

In 1964, Fama joined the business school faculty at Chicago. Given the underdeveloped state of theory, his empiricism won the day and his package of efficient markets and fat tails became the defining feature of the Chicago finance program. Fama's first assignment was to design and teach the very first efficient markets finance course, a course that would eventually be incorporated into the standard Chicago textbook *The Theory of Finance*, written with Merton Miller and published in 1972.

Soon after Fama started his course, Paul Samuelson and Benoit Mandelbrot both came out with formal treatments of the statistical implications of efficient markets.[36] Both men couched their results in language that made clear they viewed efficiency as an idealization unlikely to hold reliably in the real world, hence not an attractive null hypothesis and certainly not a useful maintained hypothesis. By contrast, Fama's 1970 survey article "Efficient Capital Markets: A Review of Theory and Empirical Work" was the work of a true believer, and it became the classic professional reference. His characterization of three levels of efficiency—weak, semistrong, and strong, depending on the information set captured by prices—shifted the debate from the qualitative (efficient or inefficient?) to the quantitative (how efficient?).

But Fama's package of efficient markets plus Paretian price distributions was still not much of a theory. It characterized the fluctuation of prices but not their level, the fluctuation of returns but not the average around which they fluctuate. Sharpe's CAPM arrived just in time to fill the gap, or rather Sharpe's CAPM extended to the case of Paretian return distributions.[37] But Fama's allegiance was always more to efficient markets than to any particular theory of expected return. In time, he would give up CAPM to save efficient markets even as his erstwhile colleague Fischer Black would do the opposite.[38] But that is getting ahead of the story.

When Sharpe first met Fischer in the O'Hare International Airport in March 1967, he came away with the impression that Fischer had learned more finance, from a standing start, than many of his colleagues who had the benefit of background and training. He put it down to native ability: "Fischer was one really smart guy." But Fischer also had his own head start, from Treynor, and that helped a lot. Unlike most people around Harvard, he never had to fight his way through the thicket of Lintner's writing to access the insights of CAPM. Even more of an advantage, unlike most people around Chicago, he had no prior commitment to the nonequilibrium market model that would need to be overcome.

Treynor's emphasis on CAPM as a model of multiple risk factors provided a further advantage. In this respect, Treynor's CAPM looks less like the Sharpe-Lintner CAPM and more like an early version of the

1976 "Arbitrage Theory of Capital Asset Pricing" of Stephen Ross. Like arbitrage pricing theory (APT), Treynor's theory treats the risk premium appropriate for a share (or any other "investment with general uncertainty") as the weighted sum of multiple basic risk premiums, with the weights depending on the investment's exposure to the various forms of underlying systematic risk.[39] In this respect, his understanding of CAPM would differ from that of most academics. As Ross has observed, for most people the single-factor "diagonal" model, the model of Sharpe's thesis, is "the intuitive grey eminence behind the CAPM," a grey eminence that moreover made the multifactor "generalization" of APT necessary. The important point is that Treynor, and Black also, never had any such grey eminence to overcome. In this regard Treynor, and Black also, started out well ahead of everyone else.[40]

As a consequence, while everyone else was sorting out the differences between Sharpe and Lintner, and the relationship of the theoretical CAPM to the empirical market model, Fischer was already extending the CAPM he had learned from Treynor into a theory of the economy as a whole. Whereas Sharpe started from the problem faced by the individual investor, and Lintner started from the problem faced by the individual firm, Fischer consistently took the perspective of the economy as a whole. Everyone else used the idea of equilibrium only to help solve the problem. Only Fischer adopted the idea of equilibrium as the very essence of the problem. As he himself would say: "I can't help trying to look at the big picture."

Twenty years later, speaking as a partner at Goldman Sachs to a sellout audience in Japan, he would reflect on how he got started:

> I liked the beauty and symmetry in Mr. Treynor's equilibrium models so much that I started designing them myself. I worked on models in several areas:
>
> > Monetary theory
> > Business cycles
> > Options and warrants
>
> For 20 years I have been struggling to show people the beauty in these models to pass on the knowledge I received from Mr. Treynor.

In monetary theory—the theory of how money is related to economic activity—I am still struggling. In business cycle theory—the theory of fluctuations in the economy—I am still struggling. In options and warrants, though, people see the beauty.[41]

The work on monetary theory to which he refers began with Financial Note No. 7, which became Black's first published paper in economics. The business cycle theory began with Financial Note No. 8, "Equilibrium in the Creation of Investment Goods under Uncertainty," first presented in August 1969 at the first Wells Fargo conference organized by Jensen at the University of Rochester. The options and warrants work took a little longer, but Fischer remembers having derived the correct differential equation by June 1969.

June 7, 1969, coincidentally, was also the birth date of Fischer's first-born daughter, named Alethea, which is Greek for truth, and Winston for Fischer's accomplished aunt Ellen. Everyone else would remember the summer of 1969 as the summer of the great Woodstock music festival, as well as the very peak of the Vietnam War that would, come the fall, spark the largest antiwar protests in U.S. history. Not Fischer. He was busy spinning a countercultural vision of his own, starting from Treynor and the idea of equilibrium. The ideal CAPM world that Fischer imagined was not perhaps the "brotherhood of man" famously imagined by John Lennon. Indeed, it was the opposite of a world with "no possessions." But it was arguably just as utopian.

The CAPM world that Fischer imagined back in 1969 is a world much simpler than the one we live in. It is a world of only two financial instruments, risky equity and riskless debt, in which households hold a diversified market portfolio of the equity issued by firms, and borrow and lend among themselves in order to achieve their desired risk exposure. It is a world of index mutual funds and uncontrolled banking. It is a world in which risk is the price of reward, and economic fluctuation the price of economic growth and expansion. It is a libertarian world in which individuals interact freely in market exchange, without any role for government intervention, indeed without even a central bank monetary authority.

Fischer's first step toward imagining such a world was to extend the CAPM idea of equilibrium in the market for risky stocks to include also equilibrium in the market for riskless borrowing and lending. Both Sharpe and Lintner treated the riskless interest rate as an exogenous parameter controlled by the monetary authorities. Not Fischer. Only one interest rate, he would insist, is consistent with equilibrium in the market for riskless borrowing and lending, and CAPM is therefore just as much a theory of the determination of that interest rate as it is a theory of the price of risk. Here is how the first extension of CAPM works.

In the world of CAPM, everyone holds exactly the same mix of stocks, namely the market portfolio. Therefore, in this world there is a natural role for an index mutual fund that holds all the equity shares issued by firms, and issues shares in that portfolio for individual investors to hold. Over time, as the market fluctuates, some individuals may want to redeem their shares but there is always someone else to buy them, so there is little need for trading in the underlying stock shares. The world of CAPM is a world of mutual funds with very little trading in individual stocks.

In the world of CAPM, people with low tolerance for risk hold only a fraction of their wealth in the stock portfolio and the rest in safe assets, so that the return on their overall portfolio won't vary much. For example, a person with low tolerance might have $100 split between $50 in stocks and $50 in bank deposits. Then, when the stock market moves 10 percent up or down, the overall portfolio moves only 5 percent up or down. People with high tolerance for risk, by contrast, borrow in order to increase their risk exposure, and this borrowing leverage means that the return on their overall portfolio will vary a lot. Such a person might have $100, borrow an additional $50, and invest the entire $150 in stocks. Then, when the stock market moves 10 percent up or down, the overall portfolio moves 15 percent up or down.

The aggregation of individual portfolio allocation decisions is what determines equilibrium prices in the market as a whole. Equilibrium refers to a situation in which demand equals supply; so, for example, the quantity of money borrowed from banks by high-tolerance people equals the quantity held as bank deposits by low-tolerance people. Just so, in this example, the high-tolerance person in effect borrows $50 from the low-tolerance person through the intermediation of the bank.

This equality between borrowing and lending is brought about by changes in the interest rate charged on bank loans and paid on bank deposits. Similarly, equality between the supply and demand for risky stocks is brought about by changes in the "price of risk," which means the expected extra return from holding the portfolio of risky stocks. Day by day and minute by minute, the rate of interest and the price of risk fluctuate in order to ensure that borrowing equals lending, and that risky assets are all willingly held.

As the value of the market portfolio fluctuates over time, households rebalance their exposure by changing their borrowing and lending. If timid people want only half of their wealth in the market portfolio, then a rise in the market induces them to sell equity and extend their riskless lending position. Aggressive people do just the opposite, extending their riskless borrowing in order to finance purchases of additional market exposure as the market rises. There is therefore a natural role for banks to facilitate riskless borrowing and lending among households, and to allow easy adjustment of net borrowing or lending as the market fluctuates. When the market rises, we expect expansion of both bank assets and bank liabilities. When the market falls, we expect the reverse.

In a CAPM world, Fischer concluded, the money supply (defined as the sum of all bank deposits) will fluctuate in order to accommodate optimal portfolio rebalancing. It follows that the traditional economist's story about the Federal Reserve controlling the money supply in order to stabilize the price level cannot be true, at least not in a CAPM world. A world in which the central bank controls the money supply is a world out of equilibrium, which means there are profit opportunities for the savvy investor to exploit. A world in equilibrium is a world with no role for monetary policy. This radical conclusion was the simple logical consequence of Fischer's first extension of CAPM.

Fischer's second extension of CAPM went even further by looking through the risky equity shares to the real productive capital assets underneath, and allowing both the quantity and risk of such capital assets to change over time as a response to changes in the price of risk. In this extension, CAPM expands from a model of the financial market to a model of the economy as a whole. Even so, the model inherits the essential feature of CAPM that the prices of all capital goods derive from just two fundamental prices of capital, the rate of interest and the price of risk. These two prices, and two prices only, are sufficient statistics that summarize production opportunities and investor preferences through the entire economy.

In a CAPM world, firms make real investments, each combining exposure to market risk and independent risk, guided by the risk tolerance of the community as reflected in the two prices of capital. The consequence is that communities with high risk tolerance get high expected excess returns, which means high average growth over time, but at the cost of tolerating greater aggregate fluctuation. Communities with low risk tolerance get low growth but greater stability.

For example, think of a simple world in which the only produced commodity is wheat, but there are many different ways of producing it, each with its own risk and expected return. Suppose that a community has a high tolerance for risk. The consequence is that firms in that community will choose methods of farming that have high expected yield but also high risk. The aggregate wheat crop might range between 100 and 150 bushels, with an average of 125. If we observe this community over time, we will observe fluctuations in the aggregate wheat crop, sometimes as low as 100, sometimes as high as 150 but on average about 125.

Another community, by contrast, might have a low tolerance for risk, so that its farmers choose varieties of wheat that have low expected yield but also low risk. If we observe the second community over time, we might observe different fluctuations in the aggregate wheat crop, sometimes as low as 110, sometimes as high as 130, but on average around 120. In both cases, we might call the fluctuation in the wheat crop a business cycle. What it actually is, however, is the fluctuating return on capital. A boom is just a period in which the market return is high. A recession is just a period in which the market return is low.

But if business fluctuation is really just the same thing as stock market fluctuation, and markets are efficient, there can be no role for government intervention to stabilize the economy. All the attention that economists pay to stabilizing business cycles must therefore be misplaced. The business cycle we get is the business cycle we choose, based on the community tolerance for risk. If we want an economy that produces a lot of wheat on average, then we simply have to learn to live with a rather wide range of fluctuation. If we can't learn to live with the fluctuation, then we will have to learn to live with an economy that produces less wheat on average. This radical conclusion was the simple logical consequence of Fischer's second extension of CAPM.

The real world is, of course, not this ideal CAPM world. It is not even the narrower world of CAPM applied only to the market for risky stocks. Why not? In time Fischer would come up with three good reasons: costly information, costly management, and costly selling, all frictions that cause the real world to deviate systematically from the ideal.[42] But mostly the reasons for deviation are historical accident, ill-considered regulation, and plain lack of knowledge of finance, which are not good reasons. The great contribution of CAPM is that it gives us the knowledge we need to reconstruct the world on rational grounds, starting with index mutual funds and uncontrolled banking.

Even more, the theory suggests a natural evolutionary mechanism for that reconstruction to arise naturally on account of the profit motive. The idea that the CAPM world is an *equilibrium* means that any deviation from it must offer an opportunity for profit somewhere. It might be hard to exploit, but as a matter of logic it must be there. Maybe all one needs to do is point in the right direction, and profit seekers will do the rest. As time goes on, CAPM should only become more and more true. The CAPM ideal is, Fischer decided, the future, and he would devote his life to helping realize that future.

The main obstacle in the way would be the entrenched interests that profit by harvesting rents from existing inefficiencies. Monopoly always hates competition and can be expected to do its best to thwart it. Treynor felt this adversarial nature of the enterprise more keenly than did Fischer. At the *Financial Analysts Journal* he was on the front lines and faced every day the brokers and dealers whose future role would likely be drastically curtailed. Fischer, by contrast, focused instead on the aggregate gains that should accrue to society as a whole as it moved toward the ideal, and he cast his lot instead with the new financial institutions that would help move society in the right direction.

In the end, Fischer decided to believe in CAPM and efficient markets, too, mainly because, as a student of Quine, he found the logic compelling. Neither CAPM nor efficient markets was a fully accurate description of the world as it is. But there were good reasons to believe they might be more accurate descriptions of the world as it was coming to be, and that's where Fischer fixed his eyes. Finally, after half a lifetime spent moving from one thing to another, he had found a project with enough breadth and depth to absorb the energy of his restless intelligence. He knew the road he was to travel, and he would not be distracted from it, no matter what.

Fischer had joined Arthur D. Little as a way out of the excessively abstract world of academia, but once he learned about Treynor's CAPM he found that solving practical problems was not enough. The big ideas kept distracting him. In 1968–1969 those big ideas were mainly about macroeconomics, meaning the theory of money and business cycles. Working at night and on the weekends, for the sheer love of the work, he managed to get the central intuitions down on paper, but not much more. The next few years would sweep Fischer up in a whirlwind of activity, mainly on other matters, but he never lost sight of what the big problems were, and he always retained his intellectual ambition to contribute to their solution. When the opportunity came to join academia, he would grasp it and use the opportunity to return to these big problems.

■ Chapter Four ■

LIVING UP TO THE MODEL

The totality of our so-called knowledge or beliefs, from the most casual matters of geography and history to the profoundest laws of atomic physics or even of pure mathematics and logic, is a man-made fabric which impinges on experience only along the edges. Or, to change the figure, total science is like a field of force whose boundary conditions are experience. A conflict with experience at the periphery occasions readjustments in the interior of the field. But the total field is so underdetermined by its boundary conditions, experience, that there is much latitude of choice as to what statements to reevaluate in the light of any single contrary experience.

W. V. O. Quine, "Two Dogmas of Empiricism" (1953, p. 42)

In September 1968, 27-year-old Myron Scholes arrived at MIT as assistant professor of finance at the Sloan School of Management, having just completed his PhD at the University of Chicago. A self-described computer nerd, he had supported himself through graduate school by helping members of the faculty with their computer programming problems, research assistance that in some cases evolved into research collaboration. One of his original faculty clients was Merton Miller. Scholes wrote his dissertation under Miller's supervision, and went on to co-author multiple papers.[1]

Upon arriving in Cambridge, one of the first things Scholes did, following up on the suggestion of fellow graduate student Michael Jensen, was to phone up Fischer Black at Arthur D. Little (ADL). They met for lunch in the ADL cafeteria. Fischer would have talked about the Ford

Foundation project he had just completed, and also about the work he was doing for the Massachusetts Investors Trust on how to use computers to streamline their traditional security analysis operation. He had been very happy the previous year with the combination of fundamental research and practical problems, but he was also looking into the future and wondering how long it could last. If he was eventually going to have to leave, as Treynor did after 10 years, better to leave now and get started with something that had more of a future.

Scholes would have talked about his dissertation work testing the efficient markets hypothesis,[2] and also his consulting work for Wells Fargo Bank in San Francisco, where John "Mac" McQuown was leading the charge to build a practical business around the new academic theories of finance. Like Fischer, Scholes had a strong interest in developing applications of the new financial theory. Both men were also just starting new families; their first children would both be born within days of each other in the next year. Most important of all, Fischer and Scholes had complementary intellectual styles and so could potentially help one another. Fischer was a theory guy, while Myron was a data guy. Fischer was questioning and reserved; Myron brash and outgoing.

A few months later, the opportunity arose for them to make use of that complementarity. In his consulting work for Wells Fargo, Scholes had been a persistent voice carrying the Chicago message of efficient markets. McQuown had tried hard to hire him full-time, but the lure of academia and MIT proved the stronger attraction. Now McQuown had approval from Dick Cooley, the CEO of the bank, to give the new ideas a try and he approached Scholes about a possible consulting arrangement. Unable to spare sufficient time from his professorial duties, Scholes suggested that Wells Fargo hire Fischer as well. McQuown had already seen Fischer in action at the Center for Research in Security Prices (CRSP), and he got a strong reference from Treynor, so he said yes.

His timing was perfect. At Mimi's urging, Fischer had finally screwed up the courage to ask for a substantial pay raise at ADL, but he didn't get it; so he quit effective March 31, 1969. With Mimi's help, he rented an office at 68 Leonard Street in Belmont, hired a part-time secretary, and started his own consulting practice, which he called Associates in Finance. Myron Scholes was the first associate, but he anticipated collaborating with others as well, such as Michael Jensen. Fischer took with him two or three of his existing ADL clients, but the big client was Wells Fargo Bank, which contracted for fully half of his time for an indefinite period. During intensive work periods, Scholes would leave MIT at three o'clock every day and stop by Fischer's office for a few hours before going home.

The project itself could hardly have been more exciting. It seemed like the folks at Wells Fargo seriously wanted to try something new and different, and were willing to spend substantial money for the purpose. Indeed, Fischer and Scholes were only two of a long list of consultants, a list that included essentially all of the leading finance academics: Sharpe and Lintner, of course, but mostly the Chicago gang comprising Merton Miller, James Lorie, Eugene Fama, plus Chicago students such as Michael Jensen and Richard Roll. Everyone was on the Wells Fargo gravy train. For Fischer it was a chance to start making the capital asset pricing model (CAPM) world a reality. If Wells Fargo could use CAPM to make money, everybody else would follow, and the world would change.

It was also a chance to visit California regularly, where Fischer had always wanted to return since his first visit in the summer of 1961. He would get to know Northern California this time, since Wells Fargo was in San Francisco, indeed smack in the middle of downtown at the corner of Market Street and Montgomery Street. About once a month for the next three years he would fly out for meetings, sometimes bringing Mimi and baby Alethea along. They were good years.

Fischer's role was more or less exactly to his taste. The staff at Wells Fargo did all the dirty work with data and computer simulation, and Fischer's job was simply to review what they had done periodically and make suggestions for next steps. His job was to use the theory to guide their empirical investigation. Most of the time he was 3,000 miles away in Boston, far away from the day-to-day activity. But once a month he spent a day at a conference table in San Francisco. The combination of detachment and engagement was exactly how Fischer liked to work.

The Fischer that the Wells Fargo people saw during his periodic visits was intensely engaged, able to spend hour after hour going carefully through their work without ever seeming to need a break, fueled only by endless glasses of super-sweetened iced tea. They would joke about Fischer's apparently limitless bladder capacity, but it was his capacity to digest a month's worth of their hard work in a single day that most impressed. Of all the academic consultants they hired over the years, Fischer and Scholes worked out the best. They were actually interested in helping Wells Fargo to produce a product that would make money.

Of course it wasn't so much about the money itself as it was about the intellectual challenge. The stimulation Fischer derived from his interactions at Wells Fargo shows up in the incredible outpouring of Financial Notes he produced during his years consulting for them, every one of the Notes an attempt to apply CAPM thinking to a different problem of practical investment management: "Expanding the Market for Short Term Securities," "Variable Options," "Investment with Leverage and without Taxes," "The Term Structure of Interest Rates," "Capital Market Equilibrium with No Riskless Borrowing or Lending," "The Effects of Dividends on Common Stock Prices: A New Methodology" (with Scholes), and "A Fully Computerized Stock Exchange." Ultimately it didn't last. When McQuown resigned in frustration, it would be over for Fischer as well. But it was lots of fun while it lasted.

Years later, when the opportunity arose to leave academia for Goldman Sachs, Fischer's memory of the excitement of the Wells Fargo years would tip the scale. Not only that, in thinking about the role he might be able to play at Goldman Sachs, Fischer no doubt had in mind as a model the Management Sciences department that McQuown had founded within Wells Fargo as the institutional means to bring new thinking into a traditional banking culture. His job at Goldman was not so different from McQuown's at Wells Fargo.

Wells Fargo was founded by Henry Wells and William Fargo in 1852 to capitalize on the California Gold Rush that had been triggered by the discovery of gold at Sutter's Mill on January 24, 1848. The miners needed a reliable way to convert gold dust into ready money, both gold coin and bank deposits, so Wells Fargo became a bank. They also needed a reliable way to obtain goods and mail, so Wells Fargo also operated an express service. Soon a network of Wells Fargo agents was shipping out gold and receiving packages of all kinds. The gold traveled in green treasure boxes stored under the stagecoach driver's seat. In a nod to that history, the stagecoach was designated as the corporate logo of Wells Fargo. The importance of the Black–Scholes contribution to Wells Fargo was signaled by the decision to market the strategy they proposed as the Stagecoach Fund.[3]

Inside Wells Fargo, McQuown was the most important advocate for the new finance of efficient markets, but he had not always been so. A mechanical engineer by training but a stock speculator by inclination, he had begun his finance career in New York working as a conventional investment banker during the week, while on weekends looking for quantitative patterns in stock price data using the IBM 7094 in the basement of the Time Life building. Back then, investment management was driven by the views of a few "water walkers" who were supposed to have the magic touch of picking stocks that would outperform. Whenever performance disappointed, the discredited seer would be replaced by a new one, but the system itself remained unchanged. McQuown wanted to replace the entire system with a more systematic and scientific approach based on quantitative analysis. He wanted to use science and technology to beat the market.

It was summer 1963 when McQuown first heard about the Fisher-Lorie results on common stock returns. A Chicago native himself, McQuown made arrangements through mutual connections to meet James Lorie in fall 1963, and Lorie introduced him to Fama and the rest of the Chicago gang. This was his initiation into the efficient markets worldview. The empirical finding of Benjamin King that half of the variance in stock market returns can be attributed to a common market factor struck him as confirmation that the water walkers were all wet.

Meanwhile, McQuown's intensive use of the computer had attracted the attention of IBM and he was asked to give a talk on his work at a forum in San Jose. In the audience was Ransom Cook, then CEO of Wells Fargo Bank, who invited him to talk further. In March 1964 McQuown joined Wells Fargo as the founder and head of the new Management Sciences department with the charge to develop quantitative technology for money management. The goal was to develop something that Wells Fargo could sell as a technology for beating the market, and to do it independently from the existing money management operation in the Financial Analysis department, where traditional water walking reigned supreme. From the beginning, McQuown was an outsider—a computer guy, not a finance guy, in the lowly computing department, not the prestigious finance department—but he had the ear of the top of the house and everybody knew it.

By the time he joined Wells Fargo, McQuown had already become suspicious that markets were sufficiently efficient that apparent patterns in stock price movements were largely illusory and could not easily be exploited for profit. But it still seemed possible that fundamental analysis might help. So he hired two young quants, Wayne Wagner for his background in statistics in 1964, and Larry Cuneo for his background in electrical engineering in 1965. He didn't want anyone with a background in finance. He could teach them whatever they needed to know.

He set them to work initially using balance sheet data on individual firms to forecast earnings and identify outperforming stocks. They bought the CRSP tapes and rented computer time from Standard Oil, which at that time owned the only IBM 7094 in San Francisco. As the project began to produce results, McQuown brought Myron Scholes in from Chicago to provide an outside academic perspective. Scholes gave it the thumbs-down, and McQuown agreed. From then on, he would focus his efforts on efficient market portfolio strategies. Once he got the go-ahead from the CEO, he started to spend big money.

The strategy was to bring in from academia the leading thinkers in modern portfolio theory, sometimes as consultants and sometimes as full-time employees, to help Wells Fargo develop marketable products. In return Wells Fargo would finance their research, including a series of academic conferences where the professors would present work in progress to each other, with Wells Fargo staff sitting in and trying to follow along.

The very first such conference was held in August 1969 at the University of Rochester in New York State on the banks of the Genessee River, which spills into Lake Ontario. That same month, down the road at the other end of the New York Thruway, the Woodstock Festival and Concert was held in the town of Bethel in the Catskill Mountains. Only the month before, the Apollo 11 astronauts had walked on the moon. It was a heady time.

The focus of the first Wells Fargo conference was on empirical tests of CAPM, since McQuown could hardly propose a product based on an untested theory. From this point of view the most significant output of the first conference was the paper of Fischer Black, Michael Jensen, and Myron Scholes (BJS), titled "The Capital Asset Pricing Model: Some Empirical Tests," eventually published in 1972. By the time of the conference, confusion about the various versions of CAPM had been resolved and everyone had begun using a common language. In a nutshell, CAPM said that the expected return on a particular stock j could be divided into two components, the risk-free rate of interest plus a term that multiplied the price of risk times the quantity of risk in the stock:

$$E(r_j) = r_F + [E(r_M) - r_F]\beta_j$$

In this formula β (or beta) represents the quantity of risk, measured as the covariance of the stock with the market portfolio.

One important consequence of the BJS tests was to confirm earlier suggestions that low-beta stocks tend to have higher returns and high-beta stocks tend to have lower returns than the theory predicts. This empirical fact, as it seemed to be at the time, would provide the focus for the Stagecoach Fund that Black and Scholes would propose.

In April 1969, McQuown had contracted with Fischer's Associates in Finance to develop a passive portfolio strategy. "By passive portfolio strategy, we mean the best we can do in managing a portfolio without using subjective estimates of the future performance of selected stocks, or the market as a whole."[4] The CAPM suggests that the best passive portfolio strategy is simply to hold a value-weighted market portfolio, but that's not what Black and Scholes proposed, nor would such a proposal have been welcome. At the time, the idea was still to develop an investment technology that would beat the market, because conventional wisdom said that was what would sell. Academic theory said that you could beat the market systematically only if there was an inefficiency somewhere and you could figure out how to exploit it. Everyone else was trying to exploit informational inefficiencies and, as a consequence, markets appeared to reflect pretty well the publicly available information. But any kind of inefficiency would do, and Scholes had reason to suspect where one might be.

Scholes came to the Wells Fargo project fresh from work with Merton Miller that suggested that low-beta stocks tend to be underpriced and high-beta stocks tend to be overpriced relative to CAPM predictions.[5] (This is the same regularity that Black-Jensen-Scholes would confirm in their more rigorous tests.) Miller and Scholes had been trying to counter work by George Douglas and John Lintner, who argued that empirical asset returns depend not just on covariance but also on variance. Douglas and Lintner interpreted their empirical results as a rejection of the CAPM theory, but the same results could alternatively be interpreted as a rejection of market efficiency—and that's where Black and Scholes started their analysis.

For Black and Scholes, the evidence on mispricing suggested the existence of an "alpha effect" that could potentially be exploited for profit. Their idea was that markets might be trying to set prices in accordance with CAPM, but something was getting in the way. All you needed to do was to figure out what the obstacle was, and find a way to overcome it, and untold profit would be yours. From the beginning, the pattern of deviation from CAPM pointed to borrowing constraints as a likely candidate. If low-beta stocks are underpriced, then a portfolio of low-beta stocks leveraged up with borrowing to have the same risk as the market should have a higher expected return than the market.

In other words, underpricing of low-beta stocks is not consistent with equilibrium unless borrowing constraints prevent leverage. But if investors can't use leverage to achieve their desired risk exposure, then maybe they try some other way. Maybe they try to buy more risky stocks, and that could explain the apparent overpricing of high-beta stocks. In short, borrowing constraints might possibly induce an alpha effect. The only way to find out for sure was to devise a portfolio strategy to exploit the anomaly for profit.

In their first report to Wells Fargo, submitted December 1, 1969, Black and Scholes proposed three different ways to exploit the alpha effect, and showed how these three strategies would have performed in the past relative to a strategy of simply holding high-beta stocks. The first portfolio they consider is simply the market portfolio, levered to have the same risk as the high-beta portfolio. The second is a portfolio of low-beta stocks, levered so that it, too, has the same risk as the high-beta portfolio. The third is a mixture of long positions in low-beta stocks, short positions in high-beta stocks, and more borrowing to match the risk of the high-beta portfolio. Today we recognize the first strategy as a kind of index fund, and the third as a kind of hedge fund. In 1969, none of these three ideas had yet been tried.

In their report to Wells Fargo, Black and Scholes show that, over the postwar period, all three strategies would have done substantially better than the high-beta strategy:[6]

Portfolio	Annual Excess Return
High-risk decile portfolio	13 percent
Leveraged market portfolio	20 percent
Leveraged low-risk decile portfolio	27 percent
Leveraged long/short portfolio	34 percent

To produce these calculations, they presume that it is possible to borrow without constraint at the interest rate paid by the government on Treasury bills, and that there is no constraint on short selling the high-beta stocks. They also ignore taxes and transactions costs, so their results certainly overestimate the potential returns. But the historical excess returns are so high that it seemed very likely that a more realistic model would confirm the opportunity. Stimulated by this report, the Wells Fargo staff took over the task of building a more realistic model, focusing their attention on the leveraged low-risk decile portfolio strategy.[7] This middle ground between an index fund and a hedge fund was the original Stagecoach Fund.

Inside Wells Fargo, the decisive objection to the Stagecoach Fund came from Bill Fouse. He had been hired into the more traditional Financial Analysis department in 1970 to give it the capability to mount its own activist program of quantitative portfolio management after McQuown decided that Management Sciences would henceforth focus its efforts exclusively on passive strategies. Fouse came to Wells Fargo from Mellon Bank in Pittsburgh, where he had developed a quantitative system for picking stocks based on the Dividend Discount Model. At Wells Fargo, he developed that model further, and built also an asset allocation model focused on selecting the optimal blend of stocks and bonds.

Fouse pointed out that a portfolio of low-risk stocks would be highly undiversified. It might not have much exposure to overall market risk, but it would likely have considerable exposure to industry-specific risk, since low-beta stocks tend to be found in only a few special sectors. At the decisive meeting, Fouse prevailed and Fischer Black stomped out, an event memorable as the nearly unique instance when Fischer lost his cool.[8] In subsequent lore, the meeting would be remembered as "The Day Alpha Died."

As a result, the Stagecoach Fund that came to market in January 1972 was not a leveraged low-risk portfolio, but only a leveraged market portfolio. It was the most conservative of the three portfolio strategies originally proposed by Black and Scholes, and the one that offered the smallest excess return. But it was still something new that no one else had. In fact, it was exactly the kind of thing CAPM said you should want if you were a risk-tolerant investor in an efficient market. On a risk-adjusted basis, the fund could not expect to beat the market. But the product could still be attractive to the extent that the bank could offer a lower cost of leverage than individuals could get on their own, and also much greater convenience by taking care of all the trading required to maintain the target leverage ratio. It seemed to be a good product, and the firm got behind it; but legal tangles delayed the launch, while regulatory restrictions blighted the marketing effort. On August 16, 1973, the decision was made to pull the plug, and that was the end of the Stagecoach Fund.

For Fischer, however, the Stagecoach Fund had actually died on the day alpha died. At the time, it seemed to him a completely irrational decision. If he had not been so personally involved, he would have simply laughed at the result, just as he did when Continental Bank rejected his analysis back in ADL days. Willful ignorance and political infighting were always equally amusing to him. But he *was* personally involved. He had, with Jensen and Scholes, been part of the team that confirmed the existence of the alpha effect. And also, more emotionally significant, he had produced an extension of CAPM to explain how the alpha effect might arise in equilibrium simply because of borrowing constraints. The relevant paper was Financial Note No. 15, the first version dated August 26, 1970, but by May 1971 already in its third and final revision. He had given them both data and theory; what more could they want?

He forgot about one thing, costly selling. In 1971, CAPM was still only an academic theory, indeed a theory only very recently stabilized among academics themselves. It was too much to expect rapid acceptance even among Wells Fargo staff from other departments, who had watched the Stagecoach idea hatch but remained uncomfortable with the underlying CAPM theory. And if you couldn't sell the idea to other Wells Fargo departments, how could you expect to sell it to clients out in the world who had never even heard of CAPM?

It only made matters worse that respectable academics, namely Richard Roll, questioned whether the alpha effect even existed. Because the collection of publicly traded stocks is only part of the larger universe of financial assets, Roll argued, the market factor measured from this subset of assets can be a biased estimate of the true market factor. From this point of view, the low-beta strategy was likely to involve inefficient portfolios with excess variability that is not compensated by commensurate excess return.[9] Roll's concern gave Fouse the ammunition he needed.

In retrospect, the problem was simply that they were trying to do too much too soon. As events proved, it was even too soon for a levered market portfolio. It was all the much more too soon for a levered low-beta portfolio.

Only months after the Stagecoach Fund was abandoned, the Financial Analysis department offered to institutional clients its own unlevered market index fund. If clients wanted leverage they would have to do it on their own. The goal of the fund was simply to track the S&P 500—not to beat the market but only to match it. In this respect its most immediate intellectual predecessor was not the Stagecoach Fund, but rather the unlevered portfolio that McQuown's Management Sciences had devised for the pension fund of the Samsonite Corporation and launched in July 1971. (The son of the president had been a student at Chicago, and so knew about the theoretical advantages of index funds.) The objective of that portfolio had been to track the performance of an equal-weighted index of the entire New York Stock Exchange. It wasn't exactly the market portfolio recommended by CAPM—for that matter neither was the S&P 500—but it came close. And anyway, it turned out to be something much easier to understand, and hence to sell. The Samsonite portfolio and the S&P 500 Fund became the first implementations of the index fund idea; the investment technology developed in Management Sciences showed the way forward for an entire industry to develop subsequently.

Since the Samsonite portfolio was not trying to beat the market but only to track an index, attention naturally focused on reducing costs, most importantly the cost of trading. An unlevered fund does not involve as much trading as a levered fund, since you don't have to be constantly buying and selling in order to maintain the desired leverage ratio as prices change. But you do incur trading costs when you initially set up the fund. Every time you buy a stock you pay an explicit broker's commission, plus an implicit commission in the spread between the bid and ask prices, plus an additional charge to the extent that purchasing pressure drives the stock price above its equilibrium level.

Fischer had an idea about how it might be possible to reduce these trading costs, maybe even to zero. He knew from Treynor that market makers tend to lose money to informed traders and make it back from uninformed liquidity traders.[10] Since an index fund is obviously not an informed trader, the problem of reducing trading costs was about reducing losses on trades with market makers. Fischer's idea was to take advantage of the fact that, although an index fund manager is a liquidity trader, he is generally indifferent about which particular stock he buys or sells. He may want a low-beta stock, but there are lots of low-beta stocks and any one will do.

Fischer's idea was to use that flexibility to get a better price by openly advertising an entire list of stocks and the prices at which one was prepared to trade.[11] In effect, the index fund manager should try to act like a one-sided dealer. He would still lose to informed traders, just as all dealers do, but he would not lose to (other) market makers. That was the theory, and it turned out to be true, at least in the Samsonite portfolio experiment. Not only was it possible to trade in this way, but also executed trades cost only 0.61 percent per trade, as compared with 1.45 percent for normal trades made on the same day.[12] This was good news for the Stagecoach Fund, but it was good news also for index funds of all kinds. This initial experiment showed the way forward for the index fund industry to develop by competing on cost rather than return.

Fischer had a further idea about how to reduce costs for a leveraged fund like the abortive Stagecoach Fund. If CAPM is true, then it should be possible to borrow at the risk-free rate in order to leverage up the portfolio. The problem was that a leveraged fund needs continuous access to borrowing since it can maintain desired leverage in the face of fluctuating securities prices only by borrowing to buy more stock when prices go up, and selling stock to repay loans when prices go down. Given the relatively underdeveloped character of short-term securities markets at the time, it seemed clear that the fund would need to rely on bank lending.[13] At that time, commercial lending was typically tied to the so-called prime rate, a short-term interest rate charged to the most creditworthy customers. But Fischer thought they could do better than prime.

Because CAPM applied most naturally to a very short time period, the appropriate interest rate for any application of the theory was as close as you could get to a spot money rate. In the market, the nearest to a spot money rate was the federal funds rate that banks charge one another when a bank with more deposits than loans lends to a bank with more loans than deposits. Fischer's idea was that banks might be willing to lend to the Stagecoach Fund at a spread over the fed funds rate. Because loans to the fund could be completely secured by its portfolio of stocks, the spread should be pretty low, perhaps 25 or 50 basis points.[14]

Whatever the spread turned out to be, the central innovation was the idea of borrowing at a rate that would change daily.[15] Fischer thought that banks would prefer such an arrangement to the standard prime rate loan because the spread guarantees a profitable loan even if interest rates rise. That was the theory, and it seemed to be true insofar as Wells Fargo was able to negotiate preliminary lending arrangements along these lines with other banks.[16] This was good news for the Stagecoach Fund, but it was also good news for the future of security trading operations of all kinds. The money market instrument that Wells Fargo was trying to develop can be seen as a clumsy precursor of today's ubiquitous repurchase agreement, a fully secured overnight loan legally organized as a separate sale and repurchase of the assets that secure the loan.

"Innovation is expensive and risky," Black and Scholes concluded in their 1974 postmortem. The Stagecoach Fund didn't ultimately work out, partly because of government restrictions and partly because of the difficulties involved in attracting customers to any really new product. "It is our view that in spite of the problems, the creation of market funds, levered market funds, unlevered market funds, and related products is inevitable. Sooner or later there will be a fund for individuals." And so it proved to be. The S&P 500 Fund that Wells Fargo launched for institutional investors in 1973 did not go unnoticed. It was followed in 1976 by Jack Bogle's Vanguard 500 Fund for retail investors, which would grow to become the largest mutual fund in the world with $90 billion under management.

Quite apart from the lesson about how difficult it could be to create a CAPM world, Fischer also learned from the Wells Fargo case a lesson about the limits of empiricism. It was a lesson he had learned in abstract form years before from his professor, the logician Van Quine. Now, in his collaboration with Jensen and Scholes, he would learn it again more concretely.

The style of empiricism that Fischer always preferred is well illustrated by the method he and Scholes used to quantify potential returns from their three hypothetical portfolio strategies. Essentially they show that, if you had adopted the leveraged low-beta strategy, you would have made money that CAPM says you shouldn't be able to make. In Fischer's view, this demonstration by itself should be quite enough to convince anyone that something is wrong with the theory; there is no need for anything fancier. Indeed, in a sense the portfolio test (as he called his method) is better than a more sophisticated statistical test because it tends to point to how we can improve our theory. After all, as Fischer would always insist, if we reject a theory we are not just going to throw it out. In practice we are going to tinker with it, enhance it in some way, so that it won't be rejected next time. The point of empirical work is not so much to test theories as it is to give us guidance on where to look for the next most promising theoretical enhancement.

In fact, Fischer's preferred portfolio method is really nothing more than the Treynor–Black proposal for portfolio management, but run on past data. Like Treynor–Black, the portfolio method runs a race between an active and a passive portfolio strategy. If the active strategy winds up with excess returns, that says that the active managers must be doing something right. Of course, if we only run the race on past data, we can never really be sure we have found new truth. We do it only as a preliminary to the real test, which will involve trying out the strategy in real time, going forward, and using real money. Fischer's disappointment at Wells Fargo's refusal to try out the leveraged low-beta fund was, at root, the disappointment of a scientist denied the chance to run the crucial experiment that would tell him where to look for the next most promising theoretical enhancement.

But even past data can give you a lot of information about how to improve your theory if you use it in the right way. The empirical work that Black and Scholes did for Wells Fargo shows the way. Using the CRSP monthly data for January 1926 to March 1966, they estimated the beta for each individual stock, separated the low-beta stocks and high-beta stocks into separate portfolios, and tracked the performance of each portfolio separately. In effect, what they did was to group the universe of stocks into 10 hypothetical mutual funds, one for each beta decile ranging from the lowest to the highest. Adjusting for risk, they found that the low-beta funds did a lot better than the high-beta funds. From this Black and Scholes concluded that the alpha effect was real. They could equally well have concluded that CAPM needed enhancement.

The problem, as always, is that there are numerous patterns in the data that prove to be illusory once you try to exploit them. How could they be sure that the alpha effect was not one of them? For academics, especially those trained within the efficient markets tradition to reject as illusory any seeming patterns in stock prices, it just didn't seem plausible that the market could be leaving such a large profit opportunity unexploited. Such skeptics found it easy to dismiss the original Black-Scholes report on scientific grounds, since their argument made no use at all of the standard academic apparatus of statistical hypothesis testing. To convince the skeptics, Black and Scholes recruited Michael Jensen to help them, and rewrote the paper in approved academic style. The resulting "BJS" paper became famous as the first methodologically satisfactory test of CAPM, but it was methodologically satisfactory only to the academics, not to Fischer.

In the academic version, the original clean intuition about hypothetical mutual funds is buried deep beneath the apparatus of proper statistical procedure. The use of a five-year rolling data window to estimate the individual betas is now justified as an instrumental variables procedure robust to possible nonstationarity. The decile grouping procedure is now supposed to be about increasing statistical efficiency. The entire paper is organized as a test of the null hypothesis that the alpha effect is zero, and the excess returns from hypothetical portfolio strategies have been replaced by excess returns on a hypothetical "beta factor" that, together with the CAPM market factor, is supposed to characterize the co-movement of stock prices. It's a lot of jargon, and a lot of work, for no more genuine insight than was already achieved by the simple portfolio method.

The "beta factor" is the only genuinely new idea added, and even it is only important from the standpoint of statistical modeling, not theory.

The model says that the expected return on stock j depends on the stock's beta β_j, the expected return on the market r_M, and the expected return on the beta factor r_Z:

$$E(r_j) = E(r_Z)(1 - \beta_j) + E(r_M)\beta_j$$

or

$$E(r_j) = E(r_Z) + [E(r_M) - E(r_Z)]\beta_j$$

The second form of their pricing equation makes clear that, notwithstanding the rejection of CAPM by their statistical tests, BJS came not to bury CAPM but to praise it. Compare the equation with the CAPM equation describing the expected return on an individual stock, where r_F is the risk-free rate of interest:

$$E(r_j) = r_F + [E(r_M) - r_F]\beta_j$$

Empirically, the problem with CAPM is that the predicted intercept r_F is too small and the predicted slope $[E(r_M) - r_F]$ is too large. The simplest way to make the equation fit the data is to replace r_F with something larger, since that would both raise the intercept and lower the slope. And that is exactly what BJS do when they replace r_F with $E(r_Z)$. In fact, they use the data to calculate the beta factor that gives the best fit! For those looking only for statistical representations of the data, BJS was a clear improvement on CAPM, but not for anyone else. The beta-factor statistical model was a statistical regularity in search of a theoretical explanation. Fischer had an idea about that.

In thinking about how best to exploit the alpha effect, he and Scholes had already come up with the idea of a zero-beta portfolio. If you hold long positions in low-beta stocks and short positions in high-beta stocks, you can exploit the underpricing effect and the overpricing effect simultaneously while at the same time creating a portfolio with very little systematic risk. In fact, you can create a portfolio with near zero beta.[17] You might think about adding leverage to this portfolio in order to increase risk exposure, but in fact you can do even better by first combining the zero-beta portfolio with the market portfolio in order to maximize the ratio of expected return to portfolio variance. The end result of this procedure is the long/short portfolio that Black and Scholes proposed as the third and most aggressive strategy in their first report to Wells Fargo.

This same idea of combining a zero-beta portfolio with the market portfolio in order to exploit the alpha effect became the centerpiece of the so-called zero-beta model that Black proposed both as a theoretical rationalization of the empirical alpha effect and as a theoretical under-pinning of the beta factor.[18] (The Z in the BJS notation $E(R_z)$ stands for zero-beta portfolio.) In ordinary CAPM, the set of efficient portfo-lios is generated by combining the market portfolio with the risk-free asset in different proportions. In Black's "weak form" CAPM, there is no riskless asset, and the set of efficient portfolios is generated by com-bining the market portfolio with the zero-beta portfolio in different proportions. Several authors had already pointed out that, in the absence of borrowing and lending, any portfolio on the efficient frontier could be characterized as a blend of two basic portfolios.[19] But not until Fischer Black did anyone think that one of those portfolios might be the mar-ket portfolio and the other a zero-beta portfolio. If the alpha effect is real then strong form CAPM is dead; long live weak form CAPM.

The original intuition about the source of the alpha effect had been borrowing constraints, and this intuition continues to inform Black's zero-beta model. (Government regulation gets most of the blame.) But at a deeper level, his model is about a world in which borrowing and lending are unconstrained but risky. The experience of the 1970s, when price level inflation eroded the value of purportedly riskless Treasury bills and bonds, would make Black's formulation seem more and more relevant, as time went by.

Of course Black's zero-beta theoretical model wasn't the only possi-ble rationalization of the BJS two-factor statistical model. From the be-ginning, the leading alternative explanation was Roll's idea about the statistical problem stemming from the use of an incomplete market portfolio to measure the return on the market.[20] If your measure of the market portfolio is not complete, then all your estimates of market co-variance will be biased. You'll find an alpha effect but it will be merely a statistical artifact, the consequence of mismeasurement. Strong form CAPM is not dead; it is just unobservable.

That's the way it always is in science. Lack of correspondence between the data and the theory is either the fault of the theory or the fault of the data, and one or the other must give way. Looking back on his Wells Fargo experience, Fischer reflected: "We don't know whether to believe the theory or the data. . . . In the light of the uncertainty about the reasons for the difference between the theory and the data, the safest course may be to assume that the theory is correct."[21] In context, he seems to be saying that Wells Fargo was right to go for the market index fund suggested by CAPM and efficient markets theory rather than the low-beta fund suggested by the data. But in fact his position is more complicated than that.

Although he was bound to accept the Wells Fargo decision to abandon the original Stagecoach Fund, Fischer himself never felt much uncertainty about the matter. Two things convinced him that the low-beta fund was worth trying. First, the results of the hypothetical mutual fund test had been completely unambiguous. No matter how you sliced the data, the excess returns were high. For Fischer, this test set a very high hurdle, and one that is typically not satisfied by other supposed effects that people seem perfectly willing to trade on. For example, the very same test says that we can't tell whether high-dividend stocks have higher or lower expected return than low-dividend stocks, but Wells Fargo had no qualms about bringing to market a dividend-tilted index fund.[22] Why, then, not try a low-beta fund?

But the empirical test was only ever half of the story. For Fischer you also needed a theory to explain what was causing the empirical result. For example, the stock rating service Value Line passed Fischer's portfolio test, but that empirical result provided insufficient reason to use the Value Line ratings to pick stocks. "According to the analysis that Value Line performed with my help, its ranking system appears to be one of the few exceptions to the rule that attempts to separate good stocks from bad stocks are futile."[23] But "the rankings are based almost completely on ten years of published information on the earnings and common stock prices of the companies followed." According to efficient markets theory, all this information should already be in the price. Fischer's subsequent work on the theory of accounting (see Chapter 9) can be understood as an attempt to work out a satisfactory theoretical explanation of the Value Line empirical result.[24] Once again, the great value of the portfolio test method was that it pointed to the direction for improving the theory. Only after achieving that improvement was Fischer prepared to recommend trading on the result.

The way that Fischer worked was to use "recalcitrant experience"— the expression is Quine's—to stimulate further refinement of his theory of how the world works. Indeed, he actively sought examples of recalcitrant experience for this purpose. For him, almost all recalcitrant experience would turn out, on closer examination, to be amenable to equilibrium analysis. "I see the world through equilibrium glasses; I don't think they fail me very often." For Fischer, the process of enhancing our conception of equilibrium to make room for recalcitrant experience was what learning about the world was all about.

This is the way Fischer always worked, and it is also the way that he tried to get others around him to work. With Myron Scholes, he made a connection and it worked extremely well. Scholes remembers his collaboration with Fischer as an "ideal research protocol" in which empirical anomalies stimulated theoretical work, which stimulated empirical work that uncovered new anomalies. It worked so well, in fact, that Scholes always counted it a loss to economics that Fischer let himself get distracted from valuable empirical work by his subsequent quixotic attempts to reform macroeconomics.

Other academics would have a harder time understanding Fischer, and the communication difficulty was mutual. The experience of rewriting the Wells Fargo report to satisfy the mores of a standard academic audience seems to have left Fischer with an abiding aversion to standard econometric technique, and he never tried it again. For his taste, econometrics meant too much statistics and not enough economics. He would say: "I define an econometric model as one whose structure is dictated primarily by the data, and only secondarily by theoretical considerations. Most often it is a model that uses linear regression methods. . . . I have read and heard a number of papers attempting to use econometrics in analyzing data, and I have almost always concluded that the attempt was a failure.

"The big problems arise when we specify a linear regression model, fit it to some data, and attempt to interpret the coefficients. The model is almost always seriously misspecified. A correctly specified model would almost always have identification problems, even if the independent variables could be observed without error. The independent variables are almost always observed with error, and they are almost always collinear. The errors of observation of the independent variables are rarely independent, either across variables or through time. As a result of all these problems the estimated coefficients of the model are virtually meaningless."[25]

All of Fischer's criticisms of econometric method were and are well known to practitioners, but they go ahead anyway, relying on various technical fixes to handle the situation as best they can. Not Fischer. He needed recalcitrant data points to stimulate his thinking, but would not waste his time on empirical results that could easily be spurious. Notwithstanding his criticisms of econometrics, he continued to believe in the power of his own portfolio test, even though most often the results of that kind of test were inconclusive, as in the case of dividends. Inconclusive was fine with him. Better to know the extent of your ignorance than to waste time building theories on insubstantial empirical foundations. More generally, he favored simply exploring the data quite directly, without very much in the way of elaborate statistical apparatus. He was not testing theories or estimating coefficients, but rather searching for new knowledge.

Having sorted out these methodological issues to his satisfaction, Fischer never saw any reason to change his mind. Twenty-five years later, at Goldman Sachs, he ruminated about how best to manage traders: "Observing a puzzle is not enough. A crooked yield curve or an unexplained stock price move is suggestive, but I generally want to know why these patterns exist before I trade. Stories can be wrong, but I'm uncomfortable trading without one. I want to know what kind of supply and demand imbalance is creating the trading opportunity."[26] Such is the long shadow cast by Fischer's early encounter with Quine.

Appendix 4.A   FINANCIAL NOTES CHRONOLOGY

Most of the Financial Notes went through multiple drafts, successive drafts being indicated by the letters A, B, and so forth. The chronology below lists the date and title of the first surviving draft, and the date of the published article in cases where the final draft was published.

No. 1: "Financial Risk" (August 21, 1967).

No. 2: "Corporate Investment Decisions" (September 12, 1967), published as Treynor and Black (1976).

No. 3: "Measuring Portfolio Performance" (November 15, 1967).

No. 4A: "How to Use Security Analysis to Improve Portfolio Selection" (February 1, 1968), published as Treynor-Black (1973).

No. 5: "Differences in Ability among Professional Portfolio Managers" (June 10, 1968).

No. 6: "The Time Diversification of Investments" (July 1, 1968), published as Black (1988c).

No. 7: "Banking, Money, and Interest Rates" (September 5, 1968), published as Black (1970).

No. 8B: "Equilibrium in the Creation of Investment Goods under Uncertainty" (October 23, 1969), published as Black (1972c).

No. 9: "How to Evaluate a Merger" (September 15, 1969).

No. 10: "Expanding the Market for Short Term Securities" (November 26, 1969).

No. 11: "Variable Options" (December 3, 1969).

No. 12: "Investment with Leverage and without Taxes" (December 9, 1969).

No. 13: "Implications of the Random Walk Hypothesis for Investment Management" (December 11, 1969), published as Black (1971a).

No. 14: "The Term Structure of Interest Rates" (February 6, 1970).

No. 15: "Capital Market Equilibrium with No Riskless Borrowing or Lending" (August 26, 1970), published as Black (1972b).

No. 16: (with Scholes) "A Theoretical Valuation Formula for Options, Warrants, and Other Securities" (August 1970), published as Black and Scholes (1973).

No. 17: "Dynamic Equilibrium and Monetary Policy" (December 1, 1970), published as Black (1972a).

No. 18: "Means of Payment with Uncontrolled Banking" (December 4, 1970).

No. 19: (with Scholes) "The Effects of Dividends on Common Stock Prices: A New Methodology" (January 26, 1971), published as Black and Scholes (1974a).

No. 20: "A Fully Computerized Stock Exchange" (February 15, 1971), published as Black (1971b).

No. 21: "Taxes and Capital Market Equilibrium" (April 23, 1971).

No. 22: "Capital Mobility and the Public Debt in a Neoclassical Model" (June 1971).

No. 23: "Barriers to Trade in a Neoclassical Model" (November 1971).

No. 24: "Capital Market Theory" (December 1971).

No. 25: "Trade Theory with Free Flow of Securities" (February 1972).

No. 26C: "Rational Economic Behavior and the Balance of Payments" (January 1973), published as Black (1987, Ch. 3).

No. 27B: "The Uniqueness of the Price Level in Monetary Growth Models with Rational Expectations" (November 1972), published as Black (1974c).

No. 28: "The Investment Policy Spectrum: Individuals, Endowment Funds, and Pension Funds" (July 1973), published as Black (1976d).

No. 29: "Optimality of Equilibrium" (July 1973).

No. 30: "Bank Funds Management in an Efficient Market" (July 1973), published as Black (1975a).

■ Chapter Five ■

TORTUOUS
ECONOMIC INTUITION

What we need are new iterated integrals $Q_1(Z), \ldots, Q_n(Z)$ *which reflect the compound probabilities for 2, $\ldots$, n periods ahead when the proper non-frozen portfolio changes have been made. Rather than derive these by tortuous economic intuition, let us give the mathematics its head and merely make successive substitutions.*

Paul A. Samuelson and Robert C. Merton, "A Complete Model of Warrant Pricing That Maximizes Utility" (1969)

In the summer of 1968, a 24-year-old graduate student, the applied mathematician–turned–economist Robert C. Merton (son of the famous Columbia University sociologist Robert K. Merton) was talking with his professor and mentor Paul Samuelson, who would soon become the first American to win the Nobel Prize in Economics. They sat in Samuelson's office at MIT, which looked out over Memorial Drive to the Charles River Basin, dotted with sailboats, and then on beyond to the big city on the opposite shore. But neither one noticed the view, Samuelson because it was familiar, and Merton because he was focused instead on Samuelson, who started off the conversation with the words that ambitious graduate students dream of hearing, "Why don't we write a paper together?"

The precipitating event for the suggestion seems to have been the publication in 1967 of Edward Thorp and Sheen Kassouf's *Beat the*

Market, which purported to offer a scientific system for making money in the stock market by buying stock and at the same time selling short something called a "warrant" on the same stock. A warrant is a kind of stock option issued by a corporation that gives the holder the right to buy shares in the company at a specified price at any time up to a specified date in the future. In 1968 there was no organized options exchange, but there were over one hundred traded warrants. Thorp and Kassouf claimed to have found a way to identify warrants that were overvalued, and to profit by setting up an arbitrage with the stock. In his review of their book, Samuelson had written: "Just as astronomers loathe astrology, scientists rightly resent vulgarization of their craft and false claims made on its behalf."[1]

Samuelson had been thinking about the problem of how to price warrants for more than a decade, and had published a first attempt at a solution in 1965, in the student-run MIT journal *Industrial Management Review*. In that paper he derived (with the help of MIT mathematics professor Henry McKean) a pricing equation based on the assumption that the expected return on a company's stock and its associated warrant were both known and constant through the life of the warrant. (Because he used α for the former and β for the latter, this paper came to be known as Samuelson's alpha-beta model.) If we project forward the assumed return on the stock, we can value the warrant at its termination date and then discount that value back to the present using the assumed return on the warrant. This procedure gives a formula for the value of the warrant at a point in time, and also a partial differential equation for how the value changes over time. The only problem is that we don't know the assumed expected returns, and anyway they are unlikely to be constant over time.

In 1968, Kassouf pointed out the limitations of Samuelson's 1965 model, and an effective response seemed to require a more sophisticated mathematical approach. For this purpose, Merton's extensive math training was just the resource Samuelson needed, and Merton already had considerable experience trading warrants for his own account, so the project interested him. Together Samuelson and Merton wrote their paper, "A Complete Model of Warrant Pricing That Maximizes Utility," and arranged to publish it also in the *Industrial Management Review*. In this paper, instead of positing α and β as exogenous parameters, they proposed an equilibrium model in which both quantities are deter-

mined, period by period, by supply and demand, given the risk preferences of investors.

That might have been the end of it, except that in October 1968
Samuelson was slated to give the inaugural lecture for the new
MIT–Harvard Joint Seminar in Mathematical Economics. It was to be a
big event, held in a special room in Holyoke Center at Harvard, and
Samuelson's name was the featured draw on all the publicity notices.
All the big Harvard names would be there—Kenneth Arrow, Wassily
Leontief, Zvi Griliches, Robert Dorfman, Hendrik Houthakker—and
important faculty would be visiting from other area universities as well.
As a further mark of the event's special status, no students would be al-
lowed to attend—no students, that is, except for Robert Merton, who
Samuelson arranged to give the talk in his place, but without telling any
of the organizers.

When the moment came, after the requisite ceremony and introduction, Samuelson stood up at one end of the long conference table and
spoke. "This is a joint paper, and my co-author will present it. I'd like
to introduce him as professor, but he is not a professor. I'd like to introduce him as Doctor, but he has no PhD. So I'll just introduce him as
Mr. Robert Merton." Thus did Merton come to the attention of the
mathematical economics elite, for a joint paper with Paul Samuelson on
the apparently esoteric topic of warrant pricing.

And then that was the end of it. For Merton, the warrant pricing
work led to a consulting assignment at a Southern California bank, but
no further. In the autobiography that Merton later wrote for the Nobel
Committee, he remembered that consulting work. "Ironically, had the
'equal yield for equal sigma risk' model I developed *ad hoc* for them
been taken to its continuous-trading limit, it would have led to the
Black-Scholes pricing formula."[2] But it did not occur to him to do so.
He had done his warrants paper with Samuelson, and was now focusing
his research energies on the larger and more important problem, as he
saw it, of intertemporal choice under uncertainty, which work was to be
the focus of his PhD dissertation.

He brought to that problem the mathematics of continuous-time
stochastic processes, the first economist ever to do so. In that analytical
framework, it is as if at every infinitesimal instant in time the die that
determines the return on an asset is rolled afresh, so that the return over
any finite interval of time, no matter how short, is always the sum of

many rolls. The very next month, November 1968, Merton presented the first installment of his PhD work to a student seminar at MIT, in a paper that was subsequently published as "Lifetime Portfolio Selection under Uncertainty: The Continuous-Time Case" in the peer-reviewed Harvard journal *Review of Economics and Statistics*. In Merton's mind, this was the important stuff, not warrant pricing.

Somehow Fischer Black learned about Merton's seminar and made his way there. When it was over, he went up to Merton: "I've got a paper on this topic, if you're interested." No doubt the paper was Financial Note No. 6B, "The Time Diversification of Investments," in a revised and corrected version dated November 1, 1968. This is the first time the two men ever met, but nothing came of it. In time the two would come to appreciate one another, and to interact on a broad range of research topics, but back then their styles were just too different.

Meanwhile, Fischer was becoming something of a known quantity around MIT. He had gone to see Samuelson back in the spring of 1967 in preparation for the mutual fund hearings, but the two did not hit it off. Fischer struck Samuelson as overdressed, even prissy, and in this respect reminded him of Julian Schwinger, the Harvard physicist. Worse, Fischer's ideas struck Samuelson as likely originating in a libertarian mind-set predisposed to the view that government has no business interfering in private contracts.

Following in Treynor's footsteps, Fischer had better luck with Franco Modigliani, whose famous Tuesday night finance seminar he had begun attending as a guest. By the time Fischer met Merton, he had already produced the first draft of "Banking and Interest Rates in a World without Money," though it would be another year before he presented it in Modigliani's Monetary Theory Seminar.

For a trained economist (like Merton) it is natural to think of the problem of lifetime portfolio selection as a problem of dynamic programming. We imagine the individual looking forward over his (or her) prospective lifetime, deciding how much income to consume and how much to save, and deciding also how much risk to take with his accumulated financial wealth. We imagine the individual evaluating all the different possible choices available, given his time preference and attitude toward risk, and making a choice that will maximize his "utility."

That's the natural approach for an economist. Fischer, however, took a different tack.

He approached the problem as a matter of diversification. "The principle of time diversification is this: just as the investor should spread his investments across different securities to minimize the risk associated with a given expected return, so also should the investor spread his investments across different time intervals to minimize the risk associated with a given expected return."[3] Recall that the capital asset pricing model (CAPM) treats each stock as if it were a die and urges diversification across all the dice. Black's idea was to treat the market portfolio in each period of time as if it were a single die. Then the lifetime portfolio problem is just a matter of deciding how much wealth to allocate to each of the dice the individual will encounter over the course of his life. The diversification principle leads immediately to the answer that the individual should bet exactly the same amount of money on each die.

The logic is straightforward. If you load up on risk when you are young and then pull back when you are old, as many would advise, then you are adding to your risk without increasing your expected return because there may be a run of bad dice rolls just when you are maximally invested. Just as it is better to spread your wealth across many different risky stocks rather than loading up on a single stock, so it is better to spread your wealth across many different risky time periods rather than loading up on risk at a specific moment in time. In fact, if risk is the same in each time period, then you might want to plan to have exactly the same risk exposure when you are young as when you are old.

The "same amount of money" today and tomorrow means the amount of money tomorrow that would have the same value as the amount invested today. Suppose there is a rate of interest r at which we can turn money today into money tomorrow. Then $1 today is the same as $(1 + r)$ tomorrow, and the principle of time diversification says that if we plan to invest x today we should also be planning to invest $(1 + r)x$ tomorrow. In the real world things are not so simple because of uncertainty, but the same basic logic applies.

In a world of uncertainty we expect our wealth to grow at a rate that depends on the riskless rate of interest, but also on the expected return on the market portfolio and on how much of our wealth we choose to invest in that risky portfolio. If we invest x in the market portfolio and the rest of our total wealth w in the safe asset, then we expect next period's wealth to be greater than this period's by an amount $rw + ax$, where a is the expected excess return on the market portfolio. The principle of time diversification says that if that's the rate at which we expect wealth to grow, then that is the rate at which we should be planning for our risky investment to grow as well. Adding in the final wrinkle that consumption c may change as wealth changes, Fischer derived the following differential equation describing how investment changes with time:

$$x_2 = (r - c_1)x - (wr - c)x_1 - \tfrac{1}{2}s^2x^2x_{11}$$

where s^2 measures the variance around the expected return on the market portfolio.[4] This is the general formula, and it has a fairly complicated general solution. Fischer, however, always focused his attention on the slightly special case when the solution has investment as a constant fraction of wealth:

$$x = bw$$

In this case the individual's problem boils down to the choice of the leverage parameter b, which he holds constant over his lifetime.[5]

An example will help to make the strategy clear. Suppose you have high tolerance for risk so that today, with wealth of $100, you decide to borrow an additional $50 in order to buy $150 worth of risky stock. Then, whatever the dice roll happens to be, tomorrow you plan to allocate your wealth similarly with 150 percent in the risky asset and −50 percent in the safe asset. This means that if the stock goes up you add to your stock holdings, and if the stock goes down you reduce them. Alternatively, suppose you have low tolerance for risk so that today, with wealth of $100, you decide to invest only $50 in the risky stock and to hold the remaining $50 in the safe asset. Then, whatever the dice roll happens to be, tomorrow you plan to split your wealth similarly with 50 percent in the risky asset and 50 percent in the safe asset. This means that if the stock goes up you reduce your holdings, and if the stock goes down you add to them.

As a simple rule of thumb, Fischer concluded that the best thing to do is to choose a leverage ratio based on your tolerance for risk and stick with it. He immediately adopted the strategy for his own family, imagining himself as someone with a high tolerance for risk (a self-assessment he would reevaluate after the stock market declines of the early 1970s). When the Wells Fargo project started up in 1969, it was therefore natural for him to think of a leveraged market portfolio as the kind of product that investors might want. It was what his theory of lifetime portfolio choice said they should want. The constant leverage feature of the Stagecoach Fund has its origin in Fischer's Financial Note No. 6.

We don't know how Black got interested in the warrant (option) pricing problem. Possibly he heard about the Samuelson-Merton paper, which would have been around MIT. Possibly he was thinking about ways to achieve the desirable constant leverage portfolio in a world of borrowing constraints. An option is, after all, like a leveraged holding of stock. We see him thinking in this direction in his unpublished proposal for a new kind of option contract that he called the "variable option."[6] What Black called a "50–50 variable call option" was a perpetual option to buy a number of shares of stock equal to 50 percent of the price of the stock, at a price that is equal to 50 percent of the price of the stock. The holder of a 50–50 variable call option on the market portfolio would essentially own shares in a constant leverage index mutual fund.

Whatever the initial inspiration, the important point is that Black claimed, and no one has ever disputed it, that he achieved the crucial differential equation that characterizes the unique solution to the option pricing problem by June 1969.[7] He got the equation but then was unable to solve it. Had he been a better physicist he would have recognized it as a form of the familiar heat exchange equation, and applied the known solution. Had he been a better mathematician, he could have solved the equation from first principles. Certainly Merton would have known exactly what to do with the equation had he ever seen it. (Mathematically speaking, the key equation was just a special case of the equation Samuelson had solved in his 1965 paper.) But Merton wasn't regularly around the Sloan School until the summer of 1970 when he joined the faculty as assistant professor of finance. And even if he had been, Black likely would have kept the equation to himself. He couldn't solve it, but he could already see that if the equation was correct it meant that the Samuelson-Merton approach, while formally correct, was insufficiently deep. Their formulas all revolved around the expected return on the stock and the warrant, neither of which appeared anywhere in Fischer's equation.

Coming from economics, it was natural for Samuelson, and for Merton following him, to think of the option pricing problem from the point of view of the individual investor considering the range and probability of values that the option might have upon maturity, and then discounting those future values back to the present. From this point of view, it seems obvious that the current price of the option must depend on the investor's attitude toward risk. Even more, since the option is more risky than the stock, it seems intuitive that, if the investor is to hold both the option and the stock, the expected return on the option must be higher than the expected return on the stock. How much higher must depend on both the investor's attitude toward risk and the riskiness of the option, and (just to make things harder) the riskiness of the option changes with the stock price. It seems like a complicated problem.

By contrast, coming from Treynor's CAPM, it was natural for Black to think of the option pricing problem as essentially a matter of calculating exposure to market risk at a moment in time. And it was furthermore natural for him to proceed, following the method of Treynor, by writing down a differential equation describing how the value of the option changes over time. Black's preferred CAPM approach to the problem appears in the published 1973 Black-Scholes article under the heading "An Alternative Derivation," so it needs to be emphasized that this "alternative" was in fact the key that he used to unlock the problem in the first place. In 1969 Black was applying CAPM not only to options but also to lifetime investment strategy, to money, and to business cycles. To understand how he was able to crack open the problem that had so far defeated everyone else, we must start where he started.

Black began by supposing that the formula for the option price w is a function only of the stock price x and time t, $w(x,t)$. He used w to denote the option price because, along with everyone else at the time, he focused his attention on warrants rather than options. Because the option price depends on the stock price, a small fluctuation in the stock price will cause a small fluctuation in the option price, $\Delta w = w_1(x,t)\Delta x$. From this there follows a similar relationship between the market risk in the option (measured by its beta) and the market risk in the stock. Invoking CAPM, Black used the betas to obtain equations for the expected return on the option and the stock.[8] Expanding the term for the return on the option, and working out some simple algebra, he arrived at the crucial differential equation:

$$w_2 = rw - rxw_1 - \tfrac{1}{2}v^2x^2w_{11}$$

where r is the rate of interest and v^2 is the variance of the stock return. (Note the similarity to the time diversification equation on page 126.)

This is the equation that unlocks the secret of option pricing. Although Black was not initially able to solve it, this equation by itself was enough to show that there was more to the problem than Samuelson and Merton realized. In typical laconic understatement, Black commented: "The warrant value did not depend on the expected return on the stock, or on the expected return on any other asset. I found that remarkable."[9]

After "many, many days" trying unsuccessfully to solve the equation, Black put the problem aside. He had plenty of other ideas about how to apply CAPM, and he moved on to them. In Black's mind, just as in Merton's, the warrant valuation problem was simply not that important. It was a kind of ivory tower curiosity, important to some academics but not to the wider world. Who really cared about warrant valuation except for speculators who were attracted to the built-in leverage that gave the potential for huge price fluctuations? Certainly not Fischer. So he put his equation in a drawer and worked on other things.

One day, in summer or early fall of 1969, at one of their regular meetings on the Wells Fargo case at Fischer's office in Belmont, Myron Scholes brought up the topic of options pricing.[10] At MIT, he had been directing a master's student who had some data on options prices that he wanted to analyze for his thesis.[11] Scholes had been reading up on recent work on the topic, most importantly an empirical study by Case Sprenkle published in Paul Cootner's 1964 *The Random Character of Stock Market Prices*. He had been thinking about how to apply CAPM to the problem of pricing options by constructing a zero-beta hedge portfolio of options combined with the underlying stock. When he told Black about this work, Black pulled from his file a single sheet of paper containing the differential equation he had derived, and they began to work together on the options pricing problem.

Scholes brought his own approach to the problem in a number of dimensions. For one, whereas Black's approach was to look for an appraisal price (what the price *should* be), Scholes naturally approached the problem from the perspective of speculative arbitrage. Since the value of the option moves with the value of the underlying stock, one can imagine setting up a hedged position that is long the option and short the stock. If you could get the hedge just right, such a position should have no market risk. It wouldn't be perfectly riskless, Scholes realized, but he reasoned that the remaining risk would be diversifiable and hence not priced. According to CAPM, the position as a whole should therefore have an expected return equal to the riskless rate of interest, and since you know the price of the stock you should be able to back out the price of the option. The problem remains how to determine the appropriate hedge ratio.[12]

The hedge ratio that Scholes needed was of course precisely w_1, defined by the equation $\Delta w = w_1(x,t)\Delta x$. A position that is long one option and short w_1 shares of stock should have an expected return equal to the riskless rate of interest. When you calculate the expected return on this hedge portfolio in terms of the expected return on the option and the stock, and expand the expression for Δw, some simple algebra leads directly to the crucial differential equation. Scholes' risky arbitrage argument was therefore another intuitive way of understanding why the equation held, and so provided confirmation that Black's approach was on the right track. But it got them no closer to solving the equation. Indeed, success cannot have appeared very likely, since Scholes seemed no better equipped to solve the equation than Black.

Nevertheless, working together, they did manage to solve it, and in a most unlikely way. Bringing a number cruncher's practical empiricist approach to the problem, Scholes was naturally attracted to the analysis of Case Sprenkle, a graduate student at Yale who had come up with an incomplete formula for the option price containing parameters that he estimated from the data. Having this proto-formula in mind, Black and Scholes achieved the key breakthrough by thinking not about what had to be in the formula but rather about what had to be absent from it.

Starting as they did from CAPM, both Black and Scholes had expected the formula to be a function of the market risk in the option, which was presumably some multiple of the market risk in the underlying stock. That is why, according to Scholes, "We were both amazed that the expected rate of return on the underlying stock did not appear in the differential equation."[13] In the derivation of the differential equation, the market risk in the stock and the market risk in the option exactly canceled one another. Thinking about Sprenkle's formula applied to a special case where the market risks cancel then provided the opening for Black and Scholes to reason their way to the right conclusion.

Sprenkle had produced a formula for the option price that required the user to provide two inputs: the expected return on the stock, and the discount rate for valuing the payoffs of the option. But Black and Scholes knew from the differential equation that the expected return on the stock could not enter the correct formula. They concluded that, without loss of generality, they could assume that the option was written on a zero-beta stock, which meant they could set the expected return on the stock equal to the interest rate. Further, since the option on a zero-beta stock would have a zero beta as well, they could use the same interest rate as the appropriate discount rate. Plugging these rates into Sprenkle's formula, they got a formula for the value of an option on a zero-beta stock. But the formula also satisfied the differential equation, which meant that it was also the formula for the value of an option on a non-zero-beta stock. The problem was solved.

The Black–Scholes option pricing formula is:

$$w(x,t) = xN(d_1) - ce^{-r(t^*-t)}N(d_2)$$

where $d_1 = [\ln(x/c) + (r + \frac{1}{2}v^2)(t^* - t)]/v(t^* - t)^{1/2}$, and $d_2 = [\ln(x/c) + (r - \frac{1}{2}v^2)(t^* - t)]/v(t^* - t)^{1/2}$. In this formula $N(d)$ is the cumulative normal density function that describes the distribution of the stock price, c is the exercise price, t^* is the expiration date, and t is the current date. From this formula it is easy to calculate the correct hedge ratio as $w_1 = N(d_1)$.

Having solved the pricing problem, Black and Scholes turned to the question of application. Why should anyone care about their formula? Speculators would care, to be sure, as they care about anything that might give them an edge in their competition with other speculators, but what about economists whose concern is, after all, with the general welfare? How does option pricing help? One natural application was to the problem of valuing corporate securities. Back in 1958, Modigliani and Miller had shown that the *total* value of the firm is unaffected by the way it is financed, whether entirely by stock, entirely by debt, or by some blend of the two. What they left unanswered was the question of how the value of the stock and the value of the debt, considered independently, are affected by the way the firm is financed. Fischer would have been aware of this problem from his conversations with John Lintner, and Myron from his conversations with Merton Miller. It seemed that the options formula might provide the answer.

From the point of view of options pricing, corporate bondholders may be viewed as owners of the firm's assets who have issued a call option (the stock), the exercise price of which is just the face value of the bonds. At any date in the future when the firm is liquidated, the bondholders will get paid first up to the face value of their bonds, and stockholders will get everything left over. The Black-Scholes formula can therefore be used to value the stock, leaving the value of the bonds as a residual from the total value of the firm. The difference between this calculated value and the face value of the bonds provides a measure of the discount due to the possibility of default. In this way, the Black-Scholes solution to the options pricing problem seemed to open up a new "contingent claims valuation" approach to traditional problems of valuation in corporate finance.

Black and Scholes went public with their formula and the proposed application to securities valuation at the second Wells Fargo Conference on Capital Market Theory, organized by Myron Scholes at MIT on July 27–29, 1970. The substance of their remarks is contained in the earliest surviving draft of their options pricing paper, "A Theoretical Valuation Formula for Options, Warrants, and Other Securities" dated August 1970.[14] That paper closes with the acknowledgment: "Robert C. Merton has developed the same formula as ours, starting from somewhat different assumptions. The knowledge that his formula agrees with ours gives us greater confidence that we haven't made any substantive errors along the way."

Scholes met Merton for the first time in February or March 1970 when Merton interviewed for a position at the Sloan School, and subsequently began interacting regularly with him, but not about warrant pricing. "I guess we did not appreciate that each of us had an interest in this research area."[15] As Scholes tells the story, it was only at the July 1970 conference that Merton came to know of the Black-Scholes formula. At the very same conference, indeed in an afternoon session on the very same day that Black and Scholes presented their paper, Merton gave his own paper titled "A Dynamic General Equilibrium Model of the Asset Market and Its Application to the Pricing of the Capital Structure of the Firm." In that paper, Merton apparently had the essentials of the contingent claims valuation application of options pricing, but he did not yet have the correct options formula. Indeed, because he had missed the session at which Black and Scholes presented their paper, after the conference he asked Scholes about it. Scholes explained their derivation of the formula but Merton was not convinced. For him, the stumbling block was CAPM.

In Merton's view, CAPM was a very special theory of asset pricing, confined to a one-period static setting with mean-variance utility specification. At best, results from CAPM could be approximately true, at least by comparison to the results he would derive from his own more general intertemporal CAPM.[16] From this vantage point, he was naturally skeptical about the generality of the options pricing formula that Black and Scholes had achieved, simply because they based their derivation on CAPM.

He would have been most skeptical of Black's original derivation of the equation, because it was most explicitly reliant on CAPM in its use of beta to calculate the expected return on the option. But he would also have been skeptical of the risky arbitrage derivation that Scholes preferred because it relied on CAPM for the argument that a zero-beta exposure should have an expected return equal to the riskless rate. One of the most important results of Merton's intertemporal CAPM is that "contrary to the classical Capital Asset Pricing Model, expected returns on risky assets may differ from the riskless rate even when they have no systematic or market risk."[17] Since the Black-Scholes formula appeared to depend on the simplifications of CAPM, that meant there was probably a more general formula still out there to be found. Merton was determined to find it, and claim it for his own.

When Black heard about the conversations Scholes was having with Merton, he was not happy. Immediately, he began thinking with Scholes about a more general approach to the problem that would build on the risky hedge argument but not rely on CAPM. This is the argument that gets central billing in the August 1970 draft written after the conference. But this argument didn't satisfy Merton either. Why ever would you expect the residual risk in a hedged option position to be diversifiable?[18]

Meanwhile Merton was thinking about the problem on his own, and in his own terms. Thinking about the Black-Scholes risky hedge,[19] Merton realized that in his continuous trading framework, you could *exactly* replicate the pattern of returns on an option by taking a position in the underlying stock combined with borrowing, provided that you could costlessly adjust that position at each instant throughout the life of the option. Of course, in the real world instantaneous costless portfolio adjustment is impossible, but in the continuous time mathematical framework it is perfectly possible, and it has a crucial analytical implication. Since you can exactly replicate the returns on an option by dynamic trading in securities whose prices are known, you can exactly calculate the price of an option at any moment in time. The price of the option is simply the price of the replicating portfolio.

To construct the replicating portfolio, all you need to know at each moment in time is the hedge ratio w_1. A call option is then nothing more than a leveraged holding of stock, which is to say w_1 shares of stock at price x combined with borrowing of $w_1 x - w$. This line of reasoning immediately led Merton to the crucial differential equation, and hence to the Black-Scholes formula. One Saturday, sometime in August 1970, Merton called Scholes on the phone: "You're right."[20]

Merton's line of reasoning came to be called the no-arbitrage approach because of the observation that if the option price is not exactly equal to the price of the replicating portfolio then there will be arbitrage profits to be earned by buying the option and selling the replicating portfolio, or vice versa. This argument is of course strictly correct only within the framework of the model, and can only be approximately correct in actual trading environments. Thus, like Black and Scholes, Merton offers a normative theory of rational option pricing in the sense that his theory tells what the option price should be rather than necessarily what it will be on account of the behavior of arbitrageurs. However, unlike Black and Scholes, Merton's derivation depends not at all on CAPM, or any other theory of asset pricing. Further, Merton's idea of pricing complex securities by thinking about what kind of dynamic trading strategy could be used to hedge their risk would prove to be robust and remarkably productive in future years. In this respect, the profession followed Merton, not Black or Scholes.

In 1971, Merton was asked by his senior colleague Paul McAvoy if he might be willing to publish his own derivation of the options pricing result in a new journal he was editing. Merton agreed, but with the proviso that publication be delayed until the Black-Scholes paper appeared. Thus it was not until 1973 that Merton's paper "Theory of Rational Option Pricing" appeared in the *Bell Journal of Economics and Management Science*.[21]

Meanwhile, excited by their results, all three men began buying warrants, using the Black-Scholes formula to identify mispricing, but they lost money. (Black liked to say that he lost less money than Scholes or Merton.) It turned out that the warrant price was different from the formula for a very good reason that the formula did not take into account, namely an imminent corporate takeover. Black drew the lesson that sometimes the market knows more than the formula.[22]

In academia the mechanism through which persuasion takes place is substantially a mechanism of intellectual competition. Such competition is standard practice, but in the case of options pricing there was considerable risk that the process might go astray for the simple reason that Black was an outsider while Merton and Scholes were insiders. The latter had proper academic credentials, proper academic jobs, and powerful established academic supporters. Black had none. In the annals of the history of science, it is not exactly unknown for an outsider to lose out in favor of an insider. (Black would have had in mind Jack Treynor's experience of inventing CAPM only to see others get the credit.) In this case that did not happen. Why not? One reason is that, in a larger sense, all three men were outsiders, battling entrenched opinion within both economics and finance as those fields were then organized.

At that time finance was a field largely outside the rubric of economics. Paul Samuelson has reflected on his own experience: "Finance was my Sunday painting. Sunday painters are not quite in the Club. They publish in unrefereed journals and are not read much."[23] (Samuelson is no doubt referring here to his early papers in the *Industrial Management Review*.) Similarly, Stephen Ross remembers being warned as a graduate student at Wharton in 1970 against switching from economics to finance: "Finance is to economics as osteopathy is to medicine." The newcomers to the field were of course going to change all that forever, but it was hard to get started. Meanwhile, Michael Jensen's *Studies in the Theory of Capital Markets* (1972) provided an outlet for the many good papers in the new finance that the journals were rejecting. Eventually, the *Journal of Financial Economics* would provide a more regular outlet, but the first issue would not appear until 1974.

Black and Scholes discovered just how low was the status of finance among economists when they tried to publish their result in economics journals. In the fall of 1970 their paper was rejected in short order by both the *Journal of Political Economy* and the *Review of Economics and Statistics*, in both cases without even being sent out for referee report. The editors saw the contribution as a narrow technical one at best, but also not really economics, and hence not even worth considering.

They could have tried finance journals, but the kind of finance they were doing was outside the rubric of finance as it was then organized. There was a reason for the economist's low opinion of finance, and that reason was the low analytical level of most of the work being done in the field. Finance was at that time substantially a descriptive field, involved mainly with recording the range of real-world practice and summarizing it in rules of thumb rather than analytical principles and models. In this context, it is not surprising that Black and Scholes never even considered the finance journals. They viewed themselves as part of the larger revolution in finance that was coming in from economics, and that meant they had to convince the economists first. The crucial intervention came from Merton Miller and Eugene Fama, who persuaded the *Journal of Political Economy* to reconsider.

Why did they do it? Scholes was, of course, a former student, but why did Miller and Fama stick their necks out for the unknown Fischer Black? One reason is that he was not unknown to them. They would have met him as early as November 1967 when he and Treynor came to Chicago to present their paper at the CRSP seminar. And they would have met him again at the August 1969 Wells Fargo conference in Rochester, New York. And they would have met him still a third time, in March 1970, when Black came again to Chicago, this time to debate Arnold Bernhard, publisher of the *Value Line Investment Survey*, which produced regular reports ranking stocks on their prospects for outperformance in the next quarter. The title of the session was "Portfolio

Management: Active or Passive," with Black arguing for the passive side. That talk subsequently became "Implications of the Random Walk Hypothesis for Portfolio Management," Black's first article for Treynor's *Financial Analysts Journal*. Even without proper credentials, Black was becoming known and associated with the University of Chicago.

In fact, according to James Lorie, Black's name kept popping up as someone for the appointments committee to consider, and finally they decided to act. Lorie proposed to hire Black as Ford Foundation Visiting Professor of Finance for the academic year 1971–1972. Black traveled to Chicago to give a job talk on May 13, after which he took a few days in Indiana with Mimi for their long-postponed honeymoon. On May 19, the dean telephoned with an offer. Then, in August 1971, the Black-Scholes article was accepted subject to revision, and in September 1971 Black moved with his family to Chicago. Notwithstanding Black's sense of himself as an outsider, he apparently had powerful supporters at Chicago.

Those Chicago supporters had more than altruistic motives; they were at the center of the group that was pushing to establish an options exchange at the Chicago Board of Trade (CBOT), and so had special reason to appreciate the importance of the work Black was doing. As early as July 1969, the CBOT had formed an advisory committee to study the potential impact of an organized options market, and the chair of that committee was none other than James Lorie.[24] Not only that, when the committee hired the consulting firm Robert Nathan Associates to do the study, that firm hired both Lorie and Merton Miller to help prepare its two-volume report, "Public Policy Aspects of a Futures-Type Market in Options on Securities," published in November 1969. That report subsequently became the intellectual core of the case presented to the Securities and Exchange Commission (SEC) on March 30, 1971.

Options pricing may have been a bit of academic exotica in 1968 when Black started working on it, but soon it was going to go mainstream, and the economists at the University of Chicago saw the chance to get in on the ground floor. They had reason to know what few others yet grasped, that options were going to be a big thing. That's why, while other academic institutions were just beginning to take an interest in Black, Chicago moved ahead preemptively. Soon after Black arrived in Chicago, the SEC cautiously approved the new options exchange on October 14, 1971. There was still a lot to be done, but the road was clear. The Chicago Board Options Exchange (CBOE) would eventually open for business April 26, 1973, and the Black-Scholes formula would be published shortly thereafter.[25] Almost overnight the outsiders would become insiders.

Notwithstanding the support he received from Miller and Lorie, Black did not follow them in their enthusiasm for the new options exchange. He continued to think of options on individual securities as just a way of achieving a leveraged position on an individual stock, a goal mainly of interest to speculators who should not be encouraged. The world of CAPM, the ideal world that Fischer always held in the back of his mind, was a world of equity and debt only, no options. In May 1972 at the biannual Center for Research in Security Prices (CRSP) seminar at Chicago, he shocked his new colleagues with a paper titled "A Central Market in Options for Securities: Opportunities and Unrealistic Hopes." He concluded: "Options are an exciting way to gamble, and the Chicago Board Options Exchange wants to act as the gambling house and take its cut. There's nothing wrong with that; but if we are to permit this form of gambling, it seems logical to tax it heavily, as the government taxes betting on horse races."[26]

After the CBOE opened, a student at Chicago, Roger Ibbotson, approached Fischer with a proposal that they buy a seat on the new exchange (then selling for $40,000) and try to make money by trading options using the Black-Scholes formula. Fischer had already been burned once by his amateur trading at MIT, so he declined, but Ibbotson went ahead on his own and he did manage to make money for a while doing arbitrage trades that involved buying and selling mispriced options while hedging out the stock price risk with an offsetting position in the stock or some other option. For the first year or so, this kind of trade produced a considerable amount of profit because there was a great deal of mispricing.[27] The old-timers, accustomed to pricing over-the-counter options using intuition and rules of thumb, stuck to the old ways long enough for the newcomers with their analytical models to take some money away from them. But after about a year the transition was complete, and the transitional arbitrage opportunities largely disappeared.

As Fischer had expected, the formula did not get the correct price all the time, but the real importance of the formula turned out to be something else that he had not anticipated. Traders who used the formula were better able to manage their risk exposure, and that meant they could focus on arbitrage opportunities rather than betting on the direction of a particular stock price move. As a consequence they could take bigger positions safely, and outlast market fluctuations that would wipe out a less sophisticated trader. As the sophisticated newcomers took the place of the old-timers, the Black-Scholes prices increasingly became the market prices. In this respect, what happened when options started trading was a harbinger of what would happen again and again over the next 20 years, every time a new type of security was traded for the first time. The experience of the options exchange proved that the "quants" were the future.

Black missed out on Ibbotson's arbitrage profits because he believed as much in the efficiency of actual market prices as he did in his own CAPM-based model of what those efficient prices should be. Black summed up his position for Ibbotson: "Information is more valuable sold than used." Rather than becoming a gambler himself, he went into the business of selling information to the gamblers. Since the key unknown input into the option pricing formula is a measure of the stock's volatility, he started an options service that sold his own proprietary estimates of volatility. Every month he distributed printed tables showing his own valuation of all the options listed on U.S. exchanges and helpfully indicating which options were overpriced and which were underpriced, always according to the Black-Scholes formula calculated using his own volatility estimates.

Although he would not himself trade, the fact that his clients were all traders forced him to adopt their frame of reference. In order to sell his estimates, he had to suggest how people might use them. Thus, he suggested that people might use his tables of option values to construct a portfolio of options by buying underpriced options and writing (selling) overpriced options. Or they might use the tables to figure when to use options as a cheaper substitute for stock, either on the long side by buying an underpriced option or on the short side by writing an overpriced option. He even suggested a strategy of risky arbitrage by combining underpriced options with a short position in the stock, or writing overpriced calls against a long position in the stock.

Any one of these trading strategies would produce profits provided that Black's estimates of true option value were better than the estimates embodied in market prices. But what is most notable is that none of the strategies involved the kind of speculation that Black continued to abhor. Instead, they were all about exploiting inefficiencies in pricing, which is to say they were all about helping to make prices more efficient. In effect, although Black had opposed the creation of the options market, once it existed he tried to do what he could to make sure that trading took place at efficient prices.

Fischer's involvement with the option pricing problem changed his life forever. When he first started tinkering with the problem, he had no notion of how important the solution would soon be. At the time, he was much more concerned about the application of CAPM to money and to business cycles, and in a way he never changed his mind. Although the options pricing work opened the doors of academia to him, he did relatively little additional work in the area. It was Merton, not Black, who built the edifice of modern finance on top of the original result. Fischer used the opportunity instead to further quite a different agenda.

On May 19, 1971, the very day that he received the offer to come to Chicago as Ford Foundation Visiting Professor of Finance, Fischer Black wrote to James Lorie: "I am enclosing the latest paper on my monetary theory ideas. I'm also enclosing a reprint of my *JBR* paper. If the spirit moves you, I'd appreciate your provoking [Milton] Friedman into giving me comments on them, especially on the latest one."[28] The "latest paper" would have been Financial Note No. 17A, "Dynamic Equilibrium and Monetary Policy." The reprint would have been "Banking and Interest Rates in a World without Money." The Money Wars were about to begin.

▪ Chapter Six ▪

THE MONEY WARS

Merton Miller is a great economist.

He is also a fine warrior. In the 1950s he takes up finance and engineers a stunning campaign that, after a period of years, decisively undermines the Old Guard and installs Modern Finance.

That done, he brings his methods to the Real World, and becomes a strategist for Chicago's commodity crowd in their battles with New York's establishment and Washington's power brokers.

He does all this with such finesse, such humor, and above all, such devotion to economic principle that you reluctantly admire him even as he rides past you to victory.

Here you can learn by example as you study his strategies. You may even learn how to win the war, by adopting public policies that promise the greatest good for the greatest number of people.

Fischer Black in Merton Miller, *Financial Innovations and Market Volatility* (1991, p. vii)

The Ford Foundation Visiting Professorship was for only one year, but Fischer felt sure enough about his future prospects to close down his office in Belmont, sell his house in Arlington, and move to Chicago with his entire family, now enlarged by a second daughter, Melissa, born November 3, 1970. Initially they took a year's lease at 908 Ashland Avenue in Wilmette, a suburb along Lake Michigan to the north of the city. But when the offer of a tenured professorship materialized they bought in the upscale neighboring village of Kenilworth at 244 Oxford

Road, just a few blocks from the lake. It was a nice house, whitewashed brick with a slate roof, similar in vintage and architectural style to Fischer's parents' house in Bronxville. The first thing Fischer did after moving in was to add air-conditioning.

From the point of view of Fischer's new colleagues at the University of Chicago, Kenilworth was a strange choice. "The heart of WASP America," as Merton Miller called it, was no place for a professor. Besides, it was on the opposite side of the city from the university, at least an hour commuting distance each way. Most professors lived in Hyde Park near to the university, and those who preferred a more suburban life usually chose one of the southern suburbs. Instead, Fischer bought himself a Mercedes and timed his commute to arrive at the university before the rush.

That first year he had no teaching responsibilities, so his life continued much as it had been in Boston. His consulting projects for Wells Fargo and other clients continued to occupy half of his time, leaving him free to spend the rest of his time on the intellectual projects that interested him. His research assistant from that first year remembers Fischer as a tall, lanky man with a bemused smile and somewhat regal bearing, who dressed formally in a three-piece suit even while working alone at his desk. He gave the impression of a man of ideas, floating above the fray of ordinary concerns, devoting himself entirely to the thinking of new thoughts. He would request an article from the library, then the bibliography of the article, and so on all the way back as he tunneled into the literature in search of something on which he could build.

Soon Fischer became a regular presence at the weekly workshops around which intellectual life is organized at Chicago. Every week someone, most often someone from Chicago but sometimes an outside visitor, would present a paper they were working on and the audience would discuss it. Sometimes Fischer would ask a simple question that struck people as naive: "What do you mean when you say 'money'?" Sometimes he would make a casual remark that struck people as simply off-the-wall: "I don't think econometrics is valid." And sometimes he would zero in on a single offending passage: "On page 38 you make a fundamental error." At Chicago, it has been said, you don't present a paper, you defend it. Fischer looked and behaved differently from everyone else, but in his love for and commitment to uncompromising intellectual debate he fit right in.

When it came time to present his own ideas, he was unafraid to make strong claims, but also unembarrassed about being shown to be wrong. One day, he asked Professor Arnold Zellner if he could present his ideas on econometrics to the Colloquium on Econometrics and Statistics. So many people showed up that they had to move to a larger room. After 45 minutes of criticizing econometric practice, Fischer sat down. "So what do you propose to do instead?" people asked. "I don't know," he responded mildly, "but I'm open to suggestion." Having stirred up the hornets' nest, he was content simply to take notes on the ensuing discussion.

Fischer provoked people in order to learn from them and at Chicago it worked because of the open intellectual atmosphere characteristic of the place. Fischer remembered himself as having been "obnoxious and abrasive" in those early years, but actually he was no more so than some others.[1] Indeed, unlike others, for whom the battle could all too easily become personal, for Fischer it was always about the ideas. And the ideas he was most interested in exploring were about macroeconomics.

Back in 1968–1969, he had sketched his own macroeconomic theory by thinking about how money and business cycles would fit into an ideal capital asset pricing model (CAPM) world. Now at Chicago he found himself inside academia, with a chance to get a hearing for his theory and to develop it further. Under the leadership of Milton Friedman, Chicago was a place that welcomed critics of the dominant Keynesian orthodoxy. Maybe Fischer's own theory would prove to be the alternative they were looking for?

At the time he arrived at Chicago, Fischer's knowledge of standard macroeconomics would have come almost exclusively from his interactions with John Lintner and Franco Modigliani. Lintner had been a student in the famous Seminar in Fiscal Policy at Harvard back in the early days when Professors Alvin Hansen and John H. Williams were bringing the new Keynesian thinking to a generation of eager graduate students. It was in that seminar that Lintner formed the idea to devote himself to the underdeveloped financial side of the Keynesian model, and so got started on the path that led him eventually to CAPM.[2]

Lintner would have explained to Fischer that, in the Keynesian view of the world, economic fluctuations originate in shocks to the economy coming from outside. What the layperson calls a business cycle is actually the way the economy adjusts dynamically to shocks. Positive shocks cause booms, and negative shocks cause recessions. The magnitude and persistence of fluctuations depend on the economy's "structure, institutional arrangements and behavioral relations," all of which evolve over time. In general these relations are such that "initiating changes gives rise to cumulative expansions or contractions in economic activity which are self-reversing."[3]

The ambition of the Keynesian economists was to describe this process of dynamic adjustment in a collection of mathematical equations called an "econometric model," each equation carefully calibrated to historical data using the most advanced statistical procedures. Using such a model, one could simulate the effect of any given hypothetical shock. Also, and more important, one could simulate the effect of any hypothetical policy intervention, in order to assess its effect on economic performance.[4] The computer made all this possible. For each individual equation, you could investigate many different functional forms to find the one that best captured the observed patterns. And once you had your system of equations, you could investigate the complex pattern of response to any impulse or policy you could imagine. Imagination and computing power were the only constraints.

All this fun and games with computers had a serious object. With the help of large-scale econometric models, it seemed possible to design an economic structure that would not collapse under even the largest shocks, such as happened during the Great Depression of the 1930s. And it seemed possible as well to calibrate monetary and fiscal policy, both automatic stabilizers and discretionary intervention, in order to mute short-run fluctuations. Probably it would be impossible to achieve permanent full employment, given continuing shocks from outside the system and continuing innovation in the internal workings of the system. But considerable stabilization had already been achieved, and further improvement seemed well within reach.

A key leader of the econometric charge was Franco Modigliani, who led the research team that, in the second half of the 1960s, produced the monetary sector of the econometric model that the Federal Reserve used to help it make policy, the so-called FMP model.[5] (The initials stand for the Federal Reserve, MIT, and the University of Pennsylvania, the three institutions where the model was developed.) Modigliani's approach, however, built more on Irving Fisher than on John Maynard Keynes. What Modigliani taught in his classes followed closely the outlines sketched by Irving Fisher in his famous book from 1930, *The Theory of Interest*. In that book Fisher paints a picture of the economy as a system of interacting commodity demand and supply functions, demand being a matter of households maximizing utility and supply being a matter of firms maximizing profits.[6] If prices are just right, then the quantities demanded equal the quantities supplied and we have equilibrium.

Borrowing and lending enter Irving Fisher's framework naturally once we distinguish future commodities and their prices from current commodities and their prices. In each time period, people who spend more than their incomes borrow from people who spend less than their incomes. In equilibrium, the quantity of borrowing must equal the quantity of lending, and the rate of interest is the price that moves to bring about this equality. In a world with a full spectrum of opportunities to borrow and lend at different maturities, there will be not one rate of interest but rather an entire term structure of interest rates. In Irving Fisher's model, the rate of interest in each period depends on the balance between production possibilities and consumption desires in that period. And the interest rate for borrowing that stretches over several periods is just an average of the one-period rates over that longer period.

For the purpose of monetary analysis, Irving Fisher extends this simple general equilibrium model by adding a version of the quantity theory of money that relates the flow of money spending to the value of economic transactions according to the following equation:

$$MV = PT$$

Here M is the quantity of money, V is the velocity of money or number of times per period that a unit of money changes hands, P is the general level of prices, and T is the volume of transactions over the period. Fisher's idea was that, in the short run, changes in M on the left-hand side of the equation cause changes in both P and T on the right-hand side, while in the long run changes in M affect only P.

For Fisher, the difference between the short run and the long run comes from something he called "money illusion," meaning the inability of firms and households to distinguish between nominal and real interest rates. He emphasized that the nominal rate of interest that equates borrowing and lending will normally adjust for any inflation that is expected to reduce the value of money, but that adjustment will usually be incomplete. An expansion of the money supply therefore tends to cause a fall in the real rate of interest (the nominal rate minus inflation) below its equilibrium level, and vice versa for a contraction of the money supply. In Fisher's model, monetary fluctuation causes real interest rate fluctuation, and that's what causes business cycles. He concludes that the right monetary policy can stabilize business cycles by controlling the money supply in order to stabilize the level of prices.

In his own work, Modigliani went beyond Fisher by adding an explicit account of the demand for money balances motivated mainly by convenience in transactions.[7] (Since prices are quoted in units of money, it is convenient to keep some money on hand to make payments.) A household whose income temporarily exceeds its spending has a choice between money and bonds as financial instruments for transferring surplus income into the future. Since, by assumption, money doesn't pay interest, the higher the rate of interest the more attractive are bonds relative to money, so the demand for money falls as the interest rate rises.

Modigliani also went beyond Fisher by providing an explicit account of the money supply. Where Fisher's basic model focuses on government-issued currency, Modigliani's focuses on bank deposits created when banks buy government bonds or make loans. For Modigliani money is therefore always a form of credit, albeit one still under the ultimate control of the central bank. Like Fisher, Modigliani assumes that changes in the money supply are neutral in the long run, in the sense that they affect only the level of prices.[8]

The significant difference from Fisher comes in Modigliani's analysis of the short run, where he disregards Fisher's money illusion and instead posits various price rigidities.[9] If wages and prices are rigid, then they cannot move to bring supply and demand into equality, and consequently short-run equilibrium may involve unemployment. In an unemployment equilibrium, changes in the money supply are not neutral, but rather affect the rate of interest. An increase in the money supply means that interest rates have to fall in order to attract increased money demand, but changes in the rate of interest also affect the level of spending and so also income and employment. According to Modigliani, the right monetary policy can induce the level of spending required for full employment. The right monetary policy means either picking the right quantity of money or picking the right rate of interest.

Operationally, things are not quite as simple as this because the central bank doesn't actually control the money supply or the rate of interest directly, but only the supply of bank reserves and the discount rate at which member banks can borrow from the central bank. And if banks need more reserves, the central bank cannot really refuse to provide them. Says Modigliani: "In the face of an upsurge in commercial loan demand, banks will endeavor to accommodate this demand because of the importance of their commercial loan customers as a source of deposits as well as other business. On the other hand, in the face of a decline in demand, there is rather little they can do to prevent borrowers from reducing their indebtedness. Thus, in the short run, fluctuations in the volume of commercial loans will tend to reflect variations in customers' demand."[10]

What this means is that, in the short run, fluctuations in the quantity of money are endogenous, determined by demand, not by central bank policy. And this is something to worry about because endogenous fluctuations in money have a destabilizing effect on the overall economy. An expanding money supply will exacerbate a boom, and a contracting money supply will exacerbate a recession. The problem is how to rein in this natural tendency toward instability. Modigliani's idea was for the central bank to establish a target for the money supply, and penalize deviations from that target. If banks demand more reserves in order to accommodate burgeoning loan demand, the central bank should go ahead and provide the needed reserves but at a discount rate that is higher than other short-term interest rates.[11]

Putting operational details aside, the job of the central bank is clear. So long as there is unemployment, monetary expansion is appropriate to help restore the economy to full employment. But once full employment is achieved, the central bank appropriately shifts its focus to long-term price stability, which requires that the money supply be expanded in line with money demand. Expand too fast and you'll get inflation, but expand too slowly and you'll get unemployment rather than deflation, since wages and prices are sticky and refuse to fall.

All of this Fischer Black would have been exposed to by sitting in on Modigliani's seminar at MIT. But it didn't make sense to him. Modigliani claimed that he was assuming perfect capital markets, but that didn't seem to be the case when it came to money. How could it be an equilibrium for bank money to pay no interest? Shouldn't competition force banks to pay interest at the risk-free rate?

In 1968 Fischer first attempted to work out his own views on money in Financial Note No. 7A, "Banking, Money, and Interest Rates." In the years to follow, his analysis would undergo considerable refinement, but his conclusion never really wavered from the bold declaration on the first page of that first paper: "The major conclusion of this paper is that monetary policy has virtually no effect, either in the long run or in the short run, on the level of economic activity or on the price level." On March 12, 1970, Fischer presented a revised version of this first paper to Modigliani's Monetary Theory Seminar. Modigliani commented, "Fischer would say the most outrageous things, but always with such a sweet smile."

In this first paper, Fischer's argument is entirely verbal and intuitive. He asks himself not how money and bonds work in the actual world, but rather how they would work in the "simpler world" of true equilibrium (by which he means the CAPM ideal, though he does not say so explicitly). Instead of Modigliani's world of money and government bonds, Fischer imagines a world of bank loans and bank deposits, both of which pay a rate of interest determined by competition among banks. In this world, all payments are made by debiting one bank account and crediting another, and it makes no difference whether the accounts are positive (bank deposits) or negative (bank loans). Individuals face borrowing limits in order to prevent them from deliberately spending their way into bankruptcy, but otherwise they are completely free to use their bank accounts to absorb any difference between their income and their spending. If their average balance is positive, then interest is credited to their account; if their average balance is negative, then interest is charged to their account.

In this simpler world, Fischer asserts, "money does not exist." For him, reasoning in terms of Quine's predicate logic, the assertion of nonexistence undermines all statements that anybody might want to make about money. Since money does not exist, the Federal Reserve (the Fed) cannot be said to control it, and the economy cannot be said to be affected by it. The economists' monetary theory simply has no meaning because it involves statements about something that does not exist. What does exist is short-term credit, and credit demand gets set equal to credit supply by changes in the rate of interest. In Fischer's idealized simpler world, private credit markets take care of everything and there is nothing left for the Fed to do.

If Fischer had confined his conclusions to his abstract simpler world, economists would have had little trouble with them.[12] But from the very beginning Fischer claimed that the conclusions he had reached about his simpler world would hold true also in the more complex real world. Why so? Because if they didn't, that would imply unexploited profit opportunities. And the exploitation of those profit opportunities would tend to change the way the system worked over time, bringing it ever closer to his simpler world. For Fischer, reasoning based on the simpler world was dependable because it was based on equilibrium, whereas reasoning based on any other kind of world was not.

The problem, of course, was how to map between the simple and complex, between his theory and the real world, so that people who were accustomed to dealing with the complexity could see through to the underlying simplicity. People like Modigliani seemed to be convinced that the Federal Reserve controls total bank reserves. And they seemed to be convinced that the quantity of transactions balances has some significance for economic activity. But they also seemed to recognize that there is considerable slippage between total bank reserves and total transactions balances. In an attempt to communicate with people like Modigliani, Fischer initially summarized his views by saying that he believed the slippage was complete. Maybe the Fed controls reserves, but that doesn't mean it controls transactions balances.[13]

In his mature theory, however, he went further, arguing that the Fed doesn't even control reserves, that in practice the Fed operates a "passive monetary policy" of providing all the reserves that banks demand. Maybe the Fed does this deliberately, for example by targeting net free reserves rather than total reserves.[14] Or maybe it is forced to do so by the market, since periodic sales of Treasury bills by the Treasury provide an opportunity for banks to get rid of excess reserves or replenish deficient reserves.[15]

From the beginning, Fischer thought that the Fed did not in practice control the money stock, and thus monetary policy must have almost no effect on economic activity and inflation. Why, then, be concerned? One reason was that government intervention to control bank activity has quite a substantial negative effect on the banks themselves. If banking were deregulated, then commercial banks would do considerably more business, because much of the trade in short-term credit instruments (such as commercial paper) would take place on the balance sheets of banks instead. To practical bankers, Fischer's "simpler world" seemed pretty far from the actual world, but they resonated to his ideas about deregulation. Thus did Fischer's first money paper come to appear in the autumn 1970 issue of the *Journal of Bank Research*, published by the Bank Administration Institute.[16]

The skeptical reception afforded Fischer's first money paper at MIT stimulated him to produce a second, Financial Note No. 17A, "Dynamic Equilibrium and Monetary Policy," in December 1970, in which he tried to frame his argument in the economist's own mathematical modeling language. But this paper didn't get him any further with Modigliani and company than the first paper had done. Fischer's hope in sending both papers to Milton Friedman (via James Lorie) in the spring of 1971 must have been to plant a seed in the presumably more favorable soil of Chicago.

At Chicago, Keynesian macroeconomics had long been under attack by Milton Friedman, who had been using his Workshop in Money and Banking to work out a monetarist alternative.[17] Milton Friedman entered the economics department in 1946, and the very next year joined the Austrian economist Fritz Machlup as one of the founding members of the libertarian Mont Pelerin Society. Called together by the great Austrian economist Friedrich von Hayek, the Mont Pelerin Society had adopted at its initial meeting a Statement of Aims: "Its object is solely, by facilitating the exchange of views among minds inspired by certain ideals and broad conceptions held in common, to contribute to the preservation and improvement of the free society." That was Friedman's project.

The Friedman era did not, however, really begin in earnest until the departure of the Cowles Commission for Yale University in 1953, and it was not completely secure until the arrival of George Stigler in 1958. One sign of consolidation: In February 1962 the Chicago-based *Journal of Political Economy* published a mini-symposium on the Chicago School of Economics.[18] What was this Chicago School?

To the outside world, the Chicago School stood for a set of policy prescriptions, in general pro-market and anti-regulation, that was boldly out of step with the times that had elected President John F. Kennedy in 1960. To the inside world of academia, the Chicago School stood for a set of methodological principles that one observer has called "Tight Prior Equilibrium," principles that notably did not include the two revolutions that gave the mainstream of postwar economics its distinctive cast: Keynesian activist stabilization policy and large-scale econometric modeling.[19] Instead, the intellectual style of the Chicago School involved a strategic retreat to the hard-core economic principles of supply and demand in competitive markets, from which stronghold forays could be mounted against a wide range of applied problems, both economic and noneconomic.

Friedman's special target was interventionist Keynesian stabilization policy. In the 1950s, his main object was to counter the extreme fiscalist view of some Keynesians that would relegate monetary policy to the task of keeping interest rates permanently low. In the 1960s, when more moderate Keynesians like Modigliani began advocating the use of monetary policy to stabilize business cycles, the target shifted. Modigliani's view that monetary expansion was appropriate so long as there was any unemployment at all amounted to an expansionary bias that Friedman felt compelled to oppose.

For Friedman, the important thing about money is that, like gold, it is *not* the liability of any private individual. If we want to think of it as a form of credit, we should think of it as a liability of the government, a form of borrowing that has perennially attracted profligate kings because it pays no interest. From this point of view, the essential message of the quantity theory of money concerns the limits of this apparently costless source of government finance. If the government issues more money than people want to hold, so supply exceeds demand, then the price of money will tend to fall. A fall in the price of paper money relative to commodities is the same as a rise in the price of commodities expressed in money. In short, overissue causes inflation.

Friedman's famous proposal that the government should increase the money supply by a fixed percentage every year, say 3 percent, was intended first and foremost to place a limit on government's use of money issue to finance its spending. (The reason for choosing 3 percent rather than zero is to allow for growth in money demand as the economy expands.) If the government wants to spend more, then it will have to rely on taxation or on explicit borrowing in the bond market, and in both these channels the cost of government finance will be plainly visible.

A secondary benefit from a fixed money growth rule is a kind of automatic business cycle stabilization. A fixed growth rule will inevitably lead to cyclical imbalances between supply and demand since demand will rise faster than 3 percent in booms and slower in recessions. In Friedman's view these monetary imbalances will serve as an automatic stabilizer to hold back growth during expansions and encourage it during recessions. The automatic character of this effect is its greatest virtue since attempts by central bankers to do better by using their own discretion have not generally been successful. In Friedman's view, the political system has tended to bias central banks toward expansion, so that they tend to exacerbate booms rather than stabilize them, and then reverse themselves too late and with too much force, so that they exacerbate the downturn as well.[20]

The divergence between Friedman and Modigliani on practical policy should not be allowed to obscure their underlying agreement on matters of monetary theory. Both Friedman and Modigliani accepted the quantity theory of money as applicable in the full-employment long run. Both also accepted that money has effects on income in the short run. Their only dispute was around whether monetary authorities could improve on a constant money growth rule. Do we know enough about the mechanisms involved? And can we trust central bankers to implement an improving policy? Modigliani answered yes to both questions, while Friedman answered no.

Given the methodological predilections of the Chicago School when they set out to build a new program in finance, it was natural for them to focus attention on understanding the fluctuation of stock prices as the operation of the supply and demand mechanism in a competitive market system. The problem was that, before CAPM, no one knew how to extend the economics paradigm to finance. All they had was the 1958 paper of Franco Modigliani and Merton Miller and the 1959 portfolio choice theory of Harry Markowitz, and Milton Friedman had reservations about whether Markowitz was even economics.[21] Modigliani was of course a Keynesian, and so he went to MIT. Merton Miller was not, so in 1961 the Graduate School of Business hired him and the project of building the finance program got started in earnest.

Efficient markets theory was the first step, and CAPM was the second, but by the late 1960s Miller was on the lookout for the next new step. One day in 1970, he circulated a memo to the business school faculty. He was not going to teach the old macroeconomics anymore, and he was looking for allies to help develop a different approach. Charles Upton, a junior professor at the time, raised his hand and together with Miller began the project that would result in the 1974 textbook, *Macroeconomics: A Neoclassical Introduction*. They summarize their approach in the preface: "[Traditional] macroeconomics comes through essentially as a course in economic therapy stressing how the government can keep an inherently dysfunctional economy alive by a nicely timed sequence of transfusions and bleedings. We believe that the course in macroeconomics should emphasize rather that a market economy left to its own devices will settle into a full employment equilibrium."[22]

Believing in markets as they did, Miller and Upton were nevertheless not trying to reform macroeconomic theory, but only to write a textbook that shifted the emphasis of existing macroeconomics from therapy for a sick economy to laissez-faire for a healthy one. The usual textbooks focused most of their attention on the problem of unemployment and how to use fiscal policy and monetary policy to solve it, leaving to the last chapter any treatment of long-run growth. Miller and Upton reversed the emphasis. Their first 15 chapters all concern economic growth under conditions of full employment, while only the final two chapters concern unemployment and what (if anything) to do about it.

Needless to say, Miller and Upton's idea of applying equilibrium concepts to macroeconomics was very much to the taste of Fischer Black. But Fischer's connection with Miller went deeper than that. More than anyone else at Chicago, Miller was Fischer's mentor in the ways of academia. Indeed, even before he went to Chicago, Fischer had identified Miller as someone he wanted to engage more deeply.

In April 1971 Fischer produced Financial Note No. 21A, "Taxes and Capital Market Equilibrium," which argued, against conventional wisdom, that the 1958 Modigliani and Miller results about capital structure irrelevance extend also to a world with taxes. In Miller's 1976 Presidential Address to the American Finance Association, he would single out this paper and its subsequent extension to the case of uncertainty (Financial Note No. 21B) as key influences on his own thinking—"papers still unpublished but whose contents were communicated to me, sometimes in very forceful fashion, in the course of many arguments and discussions."[23]

Ten years later, Fischer would write: "Merton Miller is, in my opinion, the best scholar in finance today. He is creative, productive, critical, and limits closely the time he devotes to outside activities. . . . His book with Upton on macroeconomics is the best introduction I know of, and is a significant research volume at the same time."[24] Merton Miller was, it is clear, the kind of scholar that Fischer himself wanted to be. An understanding of how Fischer Black viewed the academic world of finance and economics must begin with Merton Miller.

Above all, Merton Miller believed in markets. If one person wants to buy and another person wants to sell, then both are better off when they trade. Markets make trade possible, hence markets are good. Indeed, the higher the volume of trade, the more good the market must be doing. If a market attracts very little trade, then probably it doesn't do much good and we shouldn't mind if it closes down. But if a market attracts a lot of trade, then it must be doing a lot of good and we should mind a lot if it closes down.

One reason that markets close down, or never open in the first place, is government interference through regulation. Since markets are good, regulation that interferes with the working of markets must be bad. That doesn't mean, however, that government has no useful role to play in economic life. Says Miller: "We are not anarchists! We obey traffic signs! We believe, in fact, that the coercive powers of the state—for that is what regulation ultimately comes down to—are a precious natural resource. And, like all such other natural resources, that coercive power must be husbanded, and used sparingly only when the evidence shows overwhelmingly that the available noncoercive alternatives, essentially private contracting and competitive discipline, will lead to vastly inferior social outcomes."[25]

As an undergraduate economics major at Harvard, Miller had been on the scene at the birth of Keynesianism, but the lesson did not take. Instead, Miller's intellectual roots were laid during his graduate student years at Johns Hopkins University as a student of the great Austrian economist Fritz Machlup.[26] Machlup himself had grown up in Vienna during the 1920s, where intellectual debate counterposed socialism and state control on the one side with the free market and human action on the other. To Machlup, the rise of Keynesianism in the United States looked like a recapitulation of much the same threat to human liberty. Arriving at Johns Hopkins in 1947, and following the example of his teacher Ludwig von Mises, Machlup devoted himself to teaching his students about the virtues of the free market and the dangers of state control. In 1949, Merton Miller became one of those students.

Miller's path to the University of Chicago began with Machlup, but his big break came when, as a lowly assistant professor at the Carnegie Institute of Technology (now Carnegie-Mellon University), he shifted from the economics department into the business school, and from public finance to corporate finance. To facilitate this change, he began sitting in on Franco Modigliani's graduate course in "Money and Macroeconomics" until one day in 1956 when Modigliani tossed out to the class an idea he had been working on. Modigliani recalled, "I didn't really believe my result and [thought] there probably was something wrong."[27] But Miller did believe the result, and his subsequent collaboration with Modigliani produced the 1958 Modigliani-Miller paper that made him famous. One of his first acts after arriving at Chicago was to edit a collection of Fritz Machlup's *Essays on Economic Semantics,* published in 1963.

Miller met Fischer for the first time in 1968 when he came to MIT to give a talk. Miller remembers, "Fischer had read one of my books, and after that we corresponded regularly." Probably the book was the Machlup volume, which Fischer would have found congenial first of all for its emphasis on clear expression. Miller writes in the preface, "By forcing ambiguities, sloppy reasoning, and implicit theorizing out into the open, Professor Machlup has alerted his own students and the profession at large to the tyranny of words."[28] But the volume would also have opened Fischer's eyes to the existence of theoretical traditions and approaches alternative to the Keynesian orthodoxy that at that time dominated intellectual discourse in Cambridge. It is perhaps no coincidence that, when Fischer started writing papers for publication, the first papers he wrote were about monetary theory and business cycle theory.

That is not to say that Fischer ever became an Austrian economist, self-consciously building on the monetary theory of von Mises or the business cycle theory of von Hayek. No, in 1968 his starting point was Treynor's CAPM, and that never changed. Nor did Fischer immediately adopt the libertarian political ideology of Mont Pelerin. In 1968 he believed in equilibrium, not markets. This is the difference that explains Fischer's initial divergence from Miller on the question of the desirability of an options exchange. But the seed was planted, and as Fischer came to learn more about markets, the seed would grow.

When he arrived at Chicago, Fischer's mind was not on markets but on the theory of money. Having cut his eyeteeth on Modigliani's neo-Keynesian monetary theory, he was now looking forward to taking on Milton Friedman's monetarist version. Into the essen-tially fraternal debate between Keynesians and monetarists, Fischer would bring a completely different approach to the theory of money. He would explain to Friedman: "The points I make are in the context of a 'modern credit economy' in which the government has both interest-bearing and non-interest-bearing liabilities, and in which there are smoothly functioning private credit markets and financial intermediaries. My model says, in essence, that income (and wealth, and other variables) determines money, rather than the other way around."[29] From Fischer's point of view, the dispute between the monetarists and Keynesians was largely irrelevant, because in a modern credit economy the central bank must be largely irrelevant.

Even before Fischer arrived, Milton Friedman responded to the arguments in Fischer's papers. In a letter of August 6, 1971, he opens: "I enjoyed reading it and am glad to report that in my opinion its conclusions are utterly fallacious." The same letter closes: "Your model, therefore, assumes expectations to be formed irrationally, assumes market[s] to be continually in disequilibrium, and conflicts with a great mass of empirical evidence. With respect to your so-called passive monetary policy, here you are simply falling into a fallacy that has persisted for hundreds of years. I recommend to you Lloyd Mints' book on *The History of Banking Theories* for an analysis of the real bills doctrine which is the ancient form of the fallacy you express. Do let me urge you to reconsider your analysis and not let yourself get misled by a slick argument, even if it is your own."[30]

For Friedman, and indeed for most American economists, the fault lines of monetary debate had been laid down long before in the arguments leading up to the establishment of the Federal Reserve System in 1913. When Friedman writes that he detects the real bills doctrine in Fischer's theory, he is linking Fischer with J. Laurence Laughlin, an archconservative professor at the University of Chicago who had led the opposition to centralized banking and active money management. In Laughlin's view, the problem was not with money but with credit, and the solution was to privilege productive business credit over unproductive government and speculative credit. This he proposed to do by making business credit (real bills) eligible for "discount," in effect making business credit a form of money, at least potentially.[31] That is the real bills doctrine that concerned Lloyd Mints, who succeeded Laughlin as professor of money and banking at the University of Chicago, and that is the real bills doctrine that concerned Milton Friedman, who succeeded Mints.

The problem with tying money to business credit is that business credit tends to expand during booms and contract during recessions.

Laughlin's real bills doctrine would therefore exacerbate business fluctuation by expanding money during booms and contracting it during recessions. The real bills doctrine was, from this point of view, an automatic *de*stabilizer. In fact, according to Friedman, the Great Depression of the 1930s was the result of just such a policy. Informed by the real bills doctrine, the central bank allowed the money supply to contract in line with contracting business credit, and the result was depression. This was one of the bogeymen that Friedman saw behind Fischer's theory. The other bogeyman was inflation and hyperinflation, caused by central banks monetizing credit expansion during a boom or a war.

Friedman's opening blast did not discourage Fischer. Rather, it sent him to the library for an education on the history of monetary thought. There he found the 1970 article of Thomas Humphrey, an economist at the Federal Reserve Bank of Richmond, on "The Monetarist-Nonmonetarist Debate." Following the leads in this article, Fischer decided that his view was closer to the "reflux" doctrine than to real bills, which amounts to claiming an intellectual ancestry older than Laughlin, all the way back to John Fullarton in his 1845 book *On the Regulation of Currencies*. Fullarton had argued that an overissue of bank notes or deposits was simply impossible because people can always get rid of any excess by repaying their bank loans. Fischer adapted the argument for modern times, arguing that an overissue of government currency and bank reserves is simply impossible because people can always get rid of any excess by using it to buy a Treasury bill at one of the regular T-bill auctions.

Fischer's research took time, so he didn't respond to Friedman's letter until January 5, 1972:

> It is the "reflux" doctrine that comes closest to my view, not the real bills doctrine. . . .
>
> In the U.S. economy, much of the public debt is in the form of Treasury bills. Each week, some of these bills mature, and new bills are sold. If the Federal Reserve System tries to inject money into the private sector, the private sector will simply turn around and exchange its money for Treasury Bills at the next auction. If the Federal Reserve withdraws money, the private sector will allow some of its Treasury Bills to mature without replacing them.

But claiming Fullarton rather than Laughlin as his intellectual ancestor cannot have helped Fischer's case very much. Quite the contrary, it must have confirmed Friedman's impression that what was at stake was one of the oldest divisions in monetary theory, that between the "currency principle," which sees money as a form of paper gold, and the "banking principle," which sees money as a form of inside credit. Fullarton had been writing in opposition to proposals that sought to fix the quantity of currency issued by the Bank of England. Friedman's proposal to fix money growth at 3 percent was a modern version of those ancient proposals. Realizing that he and Fischer were on opposite sides of an ancient debate, Friedman drew the conclusion that convergence could not be expected. He sent Fischer's response back with handwritten comments: "Nonsense," "Utter nonsense," and "The convergence on the first round is so minute that I doubt that continued correspondence can be justified as an efficient technique for achieving agreement."[32] Thus ended the first round, but Fischer was not so easily put off.

Friedman's Workshop in Money and Banking was the most famous workshop at Chicago, and special rules applied. You had to have Friedman's permission to attend, and one of the requirements for attendance was to offer work of your own for discussion by the other members of the workshop. Furthermore, in Friedman's workshop presentation was limited to just a few minutes at the beginning. Everyone was expected to have read the paper already, and to have come prepared to discuss it. Friedman himself always led off the discussion, framing the issues that he thought most needed attention.

Into the lion's den went Fischer, with the very paper that Friedman had dismissed as fallacious.[33] Jim Lorie recalls, "It was like an infidel going to St. Peter's and announcing that all this stuff about Jesus was wrong." Friedman led off the discussion: "Fischer Black will be presenting his paper today on money in a two-sector model. We all know that the paper is wrong. We have two hours to work out why it is wrong." And so it began. But after two hours of defending the indefensible, Fischer emerged bloodied but unbowed. As one participant remembers, the final score was Fischer Black 10, Monetary Workshop 0.[34]

And the next week, Fischer was back again, now forcing others to defend themselves against his own criticisms. If it was a theoretical paper, he would point out the profit opportunity implied for anyone who understood the model. If it was an empirical paper, he would point out how the correlations were consistent with his own theory as well as the quantity theory. "But, Fischer, there is a ton of evidence that money causes prices!" Friedman would insist. "Name one piece," Fischer would respond. The fact that the measured money supply moves in tandem with nominal income and the price level could mean that an increase in money causes prices to rise, as Friedman insisted, but it could also mean that an increase in prices causes the quantity of money to rise, as Fischer thought more reasonable. Empirical evidence could not decide the case.

All the while he was taking on Friedman, Fischer was also pressing hard on Merton Miller and Charles Upton to treat their subject more fundamentally in their macroeconomics book. Miller and Upton alert their readers to Fischer's influence: "The cognoscenti will also detect the strong influence of that rapidly growing body of work in the field of finance under the heading of the 'efficient markets hypothesis.' We have tried to purge basic macroeconomics of all results that would seem to leave opportunities for individuals to earn above-normal returns from mechanical trading rules or chart-reading (including charts of the money supply or of the National Bureau's leading indicators). We regret that we have not been as successful in this purging as we had hoped, but at least we have tried. Our colleague, Fischer Black, has been particularly helpful in keeping our attention focused on this class of problems and in suggesting ways out of the difficulties when we stumbled into them."[35]

The chapters that would have most concerned Fischer were those on money where Miller and Upton hew closely to Milton Friedman's quantity theory of money. Miller remembered Fischer fondly as someone who had 10 ideas every day, nine of them completely crazy, but the tenth pure genius. Was Fischer's view on money crazy, or genius? In their chapter on money and banking, Miller and Upton explicitly recognize that "a cashless society in which commercial bank deposits are used to the exclusion of currency is completely conceivable." This is exactly the world that Fischer had treated. But according to Miller and Upton it is not the world we actually live in, and they alert the reader that "this chapter may be skipped without loss of continuity."[36]

Apparently Fischer did not convince Miller, but then neither did

Miller convince Fischer. After the clash with Friedman about Financial Note No. 17, Fischer tried a second time to rephrase his ideas in the accepted mathematical modeling language of economics in Financial Note No. 27, "The Uniqueness of the Price Level in Monetary Growth Models with Rational Expectations." But this second modeling effort was no more successful in winning over the academics at Chicago than the first had been at MIT. The experience apparently left Fischer loath to try again. From then on he would prefer to write in his own idiom.

The end result was that Chicago became famous for two different alternatives to Keynesian orthodoxy: Friedman's quantity theory of money in the economics department, and Fischer Black's efficient markets theory of money in the Graduate School of Business. Friedman saw money as essentially paper gold. Starting from CAPM, Fischer saw money as a form of credit arising from riskless borrowing and lending between individuals. Everyone else at Chicago arrayed themselves on the intellectual map bounded by these two positions. Merton Miller adopted a position close to Friedman's end. Arthur Laffer was probably the closest to Fischer's end. Eugene Fama tried to stake out a position somewhere in the middle between Friedman and Fischer, but in the end he achieved only a formal integration of what are in fact fundamentally different conceptions of the nature of money.[37]

In 1971, when Fischer was first trying to engage Friedman, a revival of the banking school approach to money cannot have seemed destined for much success. Everyone knew that the big debate was between the monetarists and the Keynesians, between Friedman and Modigliani, and both sides of that debate followed the currency school tradition. In 1971, Fischer's was therefore more or less a lone voice in the halls of academe. It is true that his theory had found some resonance among practical bankers, but that was probably more for its support of deregulation. Twenty years later, at Goldman Sachs, Fischer's theory would find its deepest resonance among practical traders for his suggestion that central bank intervention creates profit opportunities by distorting asset prices. In 1993 Fischer wrote: "In trying to influence the economy, central banks drive down some interest rates and drive up other interest rates. Traders can earn expected profits by lending wherever rates are artificially high and borrowing where rates are artificially low. . . . Central banks lose what currency (and bond) traders make."[38] But that was 20 years later.

In the meantime, since he had managed to attract the attention of practical bankers, Fischer continued to work out the implications of his theory for them. In Financial Note No. 30, prepared for the Wells Fargo Conference on Capital Market Theory held July 25–27, 1973, Fischer sketched his ideas about "Bank Funds Management in an Efficient Market."[39] "Banking," he reminded his audience, "is probably the most regulated business in the United States." Banks are regulated in the kind of assets they can hold, and the kind of liabilities they can issue. They are limited in the rate of interest they can charge on loans, and limited also in the rate of interest they can pay on deposits. They are restricted from doing business in geographical areas other than their home territory, and restricted from entering businesses unrelated to banking. That's the bad news.

The good news is that regulation, to the extent that it distorts banking practice, creates inefficiency, and inefficiency is a potentially rich source of profit opportunity for a competitor that can see how to exploit it. Taking the world of uncontrolled banking as his ideal, he proceeded to suggest practical ways of getting around regulatory obstacles, while continuing to satisfy the letter of the law. In effect, he argued, banks *can* behave as though they were uncontrolled, and those that do so behave can expect to reap higher profits than those that continue on with banking in the traditional way.

Instead of allowing their behavior to be directed by regulation, banks should think about their business as if they were uncontrolled. And when they do, they will realize that banking is essentially two different businesses, loan administration and funds transfer processing. Banks that focus their attention on those two core businesses can expect to earn higher profits than banks that continue to view their business as providing liquidity by issuing bank deposits, and providing loans to people who have access to no alternative source of credit. Twenty years later, in an academic context, Fischer would draw the same contrast between what he called the "finance" view and the "economics" view of banking.[40]

In the 20 years after Fischer first broached these new ideas, there was almost no progress in academic thought about banking, but there was tremendous progress in the way banking was done. Back in the early 1970s, Fischer envisioned a future world in which deposit accounts and long-term home mortgages would both pay a rate of interest tied to the short term wholesale rate of interest, namely the federal funds rate. This is more or less what happened, although it took a while and the evolution continues. He also envisioned a world in which the Depression-era restrictions of Glass-Steagall were relaxed, and a world in which truly national banks would offer a full range of financial services. This, too, has happened, even if more slowly.

The pace of evolution toward Fischer's simpler world was slower than Fischer anticipated, for the very good reason that it takes time to learn new ways, especially for regulators who do not have the profit motive to spur them on. Indeed, the whole rationale for regulation, from an economic point of view, stems from a view that the profit motive cannot be relied upon to produce socially optimal outcomes. The Glass-Steagall regulatory framework was a response to the collapse of the banking system in the 1930s, a collapse that had contributed to the depth of the Depression even if it was not the prime cause. The prospect of uncontrolled banking was, from this point of view, something to be resisted by any means possible, and so it was resisted. That is why the change was so slow in coming.

But Fischer was right about the essential point. There were ways for sophisticated banks to evade regulations without breaking the letter of the law, and they could make money doing so; and so they did. Once someone was doing it, regulators faced a choice. They could impose a new regulation to block the apparent loophole, or they could relax existing regulations in order to allow other less sophisticated players the freedom to pursue the same profit opportunities. In practice, regulators did a little of both, and over time the banking industry was transformed.

In the early 1970s, however, all this was in the future and advocates of bank deregulation faced a very hard sell. In the culture of the times, to be in favor of deregulation was practically to be in favor of bank failure and depression. What the advocates of deregulation needed was a positive message of rational regulation, to supplement the negative message of deregulation. As Miller would say, "We are not anarchists!" Some forms of regulation make economic sense even in a perfectly efficient market. Here Fischer made a further contribution, this time in collaboration with Merton Miller and Richard Posner (1978). (The latter, now a famous libertarian judge and author, was at that time a professor in the University of Chicago Law School. Coincidentally, like Fischer, Posner began his intellectual career at Bronxville High School.)

In a world of risky borrowing and lending, any lender is wise to require assurances that borrowers will not act in such a way as to increase the probability of default. To achieve this end, lenders typically require borrowers to maintain a certain level of equity as a cushion against default. By analogy, bank depositors might be expected rationally to require similar assurances before lending their funds to a bank. And a government that insures bank deposits might be expected rationally to require such assurances on the depositors' behalf. The best assurance is a requirement that the bank maintain an adequate equity buffer, thereby ensuring that the bank's stockholders absorb the lion's share of any default risk so that bank deposits can be largely risk-free. Fischer had in mind a fairly large equity buffer, perhaps even as large as the entire deposit liability. Clearly that is not what has happened, but the regulatory shift toward risk-based capital requirements is a step in the direction he anticipated.

The larger point is that many of the developments in practical banking could be foreseen in the early 1970s, but only if you looked at the world in the right way. Fischer tried hard to get his academic colleagues to see the future as he did, but without much success. Try as he might, he could never really think like they did, and of course they could never really think like he did. In the end, of course, it didn't matter because the world changed anyway. And as the world changed, economists began to change as well.

In 2003, Michael Woodford, professor of economics at Princeton University, published his magnum opus *Interest and Prices*, in which he develops a theory of "monetary policy for a cashless society." It's not yet Fischer's "Banking and Interest Rates in a World without Money," since Woodford's goal is to construct a theory of how monetary policy affects economic activity and inflation in such a world. Nevertheless, Fischer would write to Woodford in 1994 that "the views in your letter are closer to mine than any other views I have seen."[41] The world had changed, and ideas were coming around.

In fact, by the time Fischer wrote to Woodford, his own ideas had changed somewhat as well, no doubt partly as a consequence of his shift from academia to Wall Street. At Goldman Sachs he came to accept that there were sufficient frictions in the economic system to give the central bank the ability to distort interest rates if it wanted to. Indeed, these were exactly the distortions that Fischer encouraged the traders at Goldman Sachs to exploit. In 1993 he would share his 20-plus-year view with Goldman Sachs: "I believe that central banks have little control over economic activity and inflation. . . . Eventually, they may realize that they have little power and may abandon their futile attempts to fine-tune the economy. For the foreseeable future, though, they will continue to push interest rates and currency rates around, and thus to create opportunities."[4]

■ Chapter Seven ■

GLOBAL REACH

In my view, financial futures represent the most important and far-reaching financial innovation of the last 20 years. They have changed forever, and for the better, the way business firms here and throughout the world manage and control the exchange-rate risks, interest-rate risks, and portfolio risks they face. The times were indeed ready for just such an innovation as foreign currency futures in the early 1970s.

Merton Miller, "Introduction" to
Bob Tamarkin, *The Merc* (1993, p. viii)

On May 16, 1972, the International Monetary Market (IMM) opened for business in Chicago, trading futures contracts in seven major currencies: British pounds, Canadian dollars, Deutsche marks, Italian lira, Japanese yen, Mexican pesos, and Swiss francs. The IMM began as a spin-off from the old Chicago Mercantile Exchange, and was the centerpiece of a far-ranging revitalization effort imagined and directed by the Merc's energetic new chairman, Leo Melamed. He got the idea, so the legend goes, from a story that Milton Friedman liked to tell about his attempt in the fall of 1967 to sell the British pound short in anticipation of an imminent devaluation. At that time, the only way to bet on exchange rates was to enter into a forward exchange contract with a dealer at one of the big banks. But no bank in Chicago or New York would accommodate him. The banks thought of themselves as providing foreign exchange "cover" for the legitimate business needs of their international corporate clients who were looking to hedge their exchange-rate risk exposure. From the banks' point of view, Friedman had no legitimate business need. He was just a speculator.

Speculation was the business of the Mercantile Exchange. Founded in 1919 out of the remnants of the Butter and Egg Board, from the beginning the Merc played second fiddle to the larger and more prestigious Chicago Board of Trade, where the more important grain contracts were traded. In 1958, the Merc nearly went out of business for good when scandal roused Congress to ban trading in the lucrative onion futures contract, and reduced the Merc back to its original eggs. By January 1969, when Melamed became chairman, contracts in pork bellies and live cattle had been added, but nonetheless the Merc remained "a roughhouse of trading cliques known not so fondly among outsiders as the Whorehouse of the Loop."[1] Determined to change this casino image, Melamed pushed for the adoption of stricter trading rules, initiated plans to move the exchange to a new building, and began to look around for new market opportunities. Melamed remembers the idea behind the IMM: "My strategy was to attract a new legion of traders who would fashion a financial image unencumbered by the history of agricultural futures."[2]

The idea to trade currencies made sense only if exchange rates could fluctuate, but in the 1960s the fixed exchange rate system that had been established at Bretton Woods in the closing days of World War II was still in force. In December 1968 Milton Friedman wrote to the newly elected President Richard Nixon urging him to use his inaugural address to announce a switch from the fixed exchange rate system to a new flexible exchange rate system, but Nixon did not heed his advice.[3] Friedman forecast that the Bretton Woods system would eventually collapse, but for the next few years he expected only to see more and more frequent adjustments of the fixed parity. That wasn't enough fluctuation to support a speculative market. As proof, on April 23, 1970, the International Commerce Exchange in New York listed nine currencies, but failed to attract significant trading volume. Melamed drew the conclusion that the prospects for futures markets in currency were excellent, but that the time was not yet ripe. Then he got lucky.

On August 15, 1971, after Germany and Japan abandoned their parity with the dollar, President Nixon announced that the United States would no longer exchange dollars for gold at the fixed price of $35 per ounce. The collapse of the fixed exchange rate system seemed to be happening ahead of schedule, and Melamed responded by accelerating his plans. His first call was to Friedman, whom he commissioned to write a paper on "The Need for Futures Markets in Currencies" as the intellectual backing for the new markets he would propose. With Friedman's paper in hand, he was ready when, on Friday, December 18, 1971, President Nixon announced the new Smithsonian Agreement to raise the price of gold to $38 (thereby reducing the value of the dollar) and to stabilize the major currencies within a band of 4.5 percent around the dollar. In Melamed's judgment, the band was wide enough to support a speculative market. Two days later, he held a press conference to release Friedman's paper and to announce plans to introduce new futures markets for trading currencies.

The problem the Merc faced was that speculators alone would not make a successful market. Experience showed that futures markets are not successful unless they attract business from hedgers, but the needs of the hedgers were already being met by the big international banks. Viewing the IMM as competition, and rather unsavory competition at that, the banks initially refused to use the new markets and, as a consequence, the futures prices established by the speculators at the IMM at first deviated from the forward price established in the interbank market. So long as the interbank forward market remained the better indicator of the true price, there was no reason for hedgers to switch. Melamed's solution was to create a special Class B membership in IMM for firms that would arbitrage between the two markets, and so keep the IMM price tied to the world price. The profits earned by these Class B members became a powerful argument to convince the banks to do business directly with the IMM.

Another argument was increased exchange rate volatility. As it happened, the attempts to patch up Bretton Woods did not work, and after March 1973 exchange rates floated. Mark Powers, the Merc's first economist, had anticipated what would happen if exchange rates ever became truly flexible. "I'd be surprised to see the banks continue to carry on their exchange operations as they do now. I suspect it would be too risky for their conservative nature and they would as soon give it up as to take the risk."[4] In the event, what happened was that the banks themselves became hedgers, covering their forward exposure to business clients in the IMM futures market. Friedman's assessment in 1971 that the interbank market lacked the necessary breadth, depth, and resilience to do the job turned out to be exactly correct.[5]

Even so, the time required for banks and other hedgers to learn how to use the new markets meant that it took three or four years before the IMM was truly accepted. Melamed points to September 1975 as the critical turning point, when trading continued on the IMM during the Mexican peso crisis even while the interbank forward market shut down. Building on that success, the IMM went on in January 1976 to introduce the first interest rate futures contract on the 90-day Treasury bill. Five years later, in September 1981, it would introduce the first cash-settled futures, a contract on three-month Eurodollar deposits. It was only 10 years from maverick idea to indispensable institution.

Fischer Black's involvement in these developments came most directly in his seminal 1976 article on "The Pricing of Commodity Contracts," which used the capital asset pricing model (CAPM) to develop a pricing formula for forward contracts and sorted out the difference between forwards and futures. The same article also developed a formula for pricing options on commodity futures along the same lines as the Black-Scholes formula for pricing options on securities.[6] In 1976 there were no commodity options because Congress had banned them. But the Merc, in conjunction with its new regulator, the Commodity Futures Trading Commission, was trying to get Congress to exempt dealers from the ban. Notwithstanding Fischer's lucid theoretical explanation, Congress turned the proposal down flat.

Probably Fischer was not disappointed by the result. Futures markets exist, he said, because they are an inexpensive way to transfer risk, and because people like to gamble. "Neither of these counts as a big benefit to society."[7] In time, Fischer would come to appreciate the social benefits of gambling as a source of market liquidity, but not yet. In his 1976 article, the biggest benefit of futures markets is the information provided by the prices that they generate—this was always Merton Miller's main argument in favor—but even that side benefit arises only if markets are efficient. As in the case of the Chicago Board Options Exchange, Fischer's role was to provide a rational formula to guide a speculative market in establishing efficient prices. These markets were going to exist whether Fischer wanted them or not, so he might as well help them to produce as much benefit to society as possible.

In 1976, Congress was not ready to lift the ban on commodity options, but it was only a matter of time before it would. Finally in January 1983 the Merc traded its first option contract on a commodity futures. The contract in question was the S&P 500 Stock Index, which happened also to be the Merc's first futures contract on an index. Introduced the previous April 1982, this "ultimate contract," as Melamed would call it, capped a decade of financial innovation and set the stage for the derivatives revolution on Wall Street that Fischer would watch from his perch at Goldman Sachs. In the early 1970s, however, all this was very much in the future and perceived only dimly, if at all.

When Fischer arrived in Chicago in the fall of 1971, the big issue on everyone's mind was not the future of futures but rather the collapse of Bretton Woods. Downtown the Merc was inventing a new financial instrument for transferring exchange rate risk, but in Hyde Park the focus of academic discussion was largely elsewhere. The academics were busy inventing new theories of international trade and finance for the brave new world of flexible exchange rates that seemed to be unfolding. The opportunity to be in the center of that intellectual ferment had been a central factor in Fischer's decision to come to Chicago in the first place, and he jumped in with both feet.

The center of the ferment was the Workshop in International Trade, where everybody talked the new language of the "monetary approach to the balance of payments" developed by Robert Mundell, who did the pioneer work while on the staff of the International Monetary Fund (IMF) before coming to Chicago in 1966. (He would be awarded the Nobel Prize for it in 1999.) By the time Fischer arrived, Mundell had just left but his students and colleagues remained behind. A cross section of the work they produced was published in 1976 in a volume edited by Jacob Frenkel and Harry Johnson under the title *The Monetary Approach to the Balance of Payments.*

The essence of the monetary approach is to understand the flow of international reserves as the symptom of an imbalance between the supply and demand for money. An outflow of reserves indicates excess supply, and an inflow excess demand. From this point of view, reserve flows function as an automatic mechanism to distribute money across countries according to their need for it. Given the world supply of money (the sum of each nation's individual supply), the quantity of money in any one country is endogenously determined by that country's demand for money. Given the world demand for money (the sum of each nation's individual demand), the world supply of money determines the world level of prices, and hence the purchasing power of money in each individual country.

Sometimes called international monetarism, the monetary approach was actually developed mainly by Keynesians. Mundell himself was trained as a Keynesian at MIT, where he earned his PhD in 1956 under the economic historian Charles Kindleberger, famous outside academia for his 1978 history of financial crises, *Manias, Panics, and Crashes*. At the time, the Keynesian-monetarist debate was largely about whether fiscal or monetary policy was the better tool for stabilization. In this debate the monetary approach to the balance of payments tended to strengthen the Keynesian view, since it concluded that the use of monetary policy for domestic stabilization purposes is "incompatible with the proper functioning of a system of fixed exchange rates."[8] In Mundell's view, monetary policy should ideally be assigned to the balance of payments, allowing fiscal policy to focus on domestic income stabilization. Whereas Milton Friedman's domestic monetarism urged an exogenously fixed money growth rule to stabilize business fluctuation, Mundell's international monetarism favored allowing international reserve flows to produce endogenous domestic money supply fluctuations.[9]

Mundell developed the monetary approach in an attempt to understand and then to counter the forces that were already beginning to rip apart the Bretton Woods fixed exchange rate system. He saw the Bretton Woods system as similar to the nineteenth-century gold standard, with the dollar, New York, and the Federal Reserve System standing in the place of the pound, London, and the Bank of England.[10] What had worked before could work again. The whole idea of the Bretton Woods system had been to provide a stable framework for the recovery of world trade, and eventually world capital flows as well.

The central role assigned to the U.S. dollar under the Bretton Woods system was not so much a deliberate choice as it was a simple recognition of reality. The United States was the dominant economic power, and it had emerged from the war holding the lion's share of the world's gold. Over time gold could be expected to distribute itself more evenly, although in order for the gold to flow out, the United States would have to run balance of payments deficits. In fact, given the fixed world stock of gold, the only way for international reserves to continue to increase in line with world economic growth was for the United States to run permanent balance of payments deficits. Mundell developed the monetary approach in an attempt to support the Bretton Woods system by explaining to all participants the constraints on domestic economic policy that had to be respected in order for the system to function.

Unfortunately, before policy makers could absorb the lesson, gold outflows combined with apparently permanent U.S. deficits to undermine the credibility of the dollar. Given the peg to gold, there was no way for failing credibility to be reflected in a falling value of the dollar. Instead, for the decade of the 1960s, the monetary authorities focused their efforts on supporting the value of the dollar by various ad hoc measures. The so-called interest equalization tax was supposed to prevent capital outflows by taxing domestic purchases of foreign securities. The rise of the Eurodollar market was supposed to forestall attempts to convert dollars into gold by ensuring that foreigners could earn a competitive interest rate on their dollar reserve balances. The introduction of the IMF's Special Drawing Rights was supposed to create an artificial international reserve currency whose supply would not be subject to the vagaries of the U.S. balance of payments. These measures succeeded in delaying but not preventing the collapse of the Bretton Woods system.

It is thus fair to say that the world backed into its experiment with floating rates, but it was an experiment that had long been urged by voices within academia, most prominently by Milton Friedman in his classic essay "The Case for Flexible Exchange Rates" (1953). The fixed rates that the architects of Bretton Woods (and Robert Mundell, following them) had seen as providing a stable framework for world trade, Friedman and others saw as no better than a price fixing scheme. Like all other price fixing schemes, the attempt to peg exchange rates was bound to require intervention to handle the inevitable imbalance of supply and demand. In Friedman's account, such intervention was the real threat to world trade. Indeed, the very existence of a balance of payments problem owes to fixed prices, and would disappear if exchange rates were allowed to find their own level.

Although Mundell himself always favored fixed rates,[11] as Bretton Woods moved toward collapse others began to use his monetary approach to advocate for flexible rates. For example, Mundell's Chicago colleague Harry Johnson pointed out that, with exchange rates free to fluctuate, *both* monetary and fiscal policy would be free to address domestic stabilization goals.[12] The only worry was that instability of flexible rates might raise the cost of international trade.

Milton Friedman wasn't worried. In his mind, exchange rates were simply a reflection of the price levels in different countries, and different price levels were simply the reflection of different money supplies. This way of thinking about exchange rates dates to the celebrated discussion of "purchasing power parity" (PPP) by Gustav Cassel, the great Swedish economist and pioneer of general equilibrium theory. Writing in the period immediately after World War I, and anticipating a postwar revival of international trade and capital flows, Cassel had been concerned with the problem of where to fix exchange rates. He reasoned from the quantity theory of money that we can use the change in each country's money supply as a measure of the likely change in that country's price level. And he proposed that we can use the difference between the changes in two countries as a measure of the likely change in the equilibrium rate of exchange between the two currencies.

Cassel summarized his theory in the simple equation: $P = eP^*$. Here P and P^* are the price levels in two countries and e is the exchange rate between their currencies, so eP^* is the foreign price level expressed in domestic currency. Since price levels are fairly stable variables, Friedman drew the conclusion that the exchange rate should also be a fairly stable variable, at least in the long run. (Both purchasing power parity and the quantity theory of money are theories about the long run.) For the short run, Friedman argued that speculation would correct deviations from equilibrium by buying in anticipation of a rise and selling in anticipation of a fall. Not everyone was so sanguine. The worry remained that exchange rate instability might raise the cost of international trade.

The Austrian economist Fritz Machlup was not worried, and neither was Egon Sohmen, who, like Mundell, was a student of Kindleberger, but whose views on exchange rates stemmed more from his undergraduate training at Harvard under Gottfried Haberler.[13] Forward exchange markets, they argued, can be expected to provide as much exchange stability as any individual firm could want, even if the actual exchange rate moves around a lot. If Company A is worried about the value of a payment that it expects to receive in foreign currency, all it needs to do is to arrange for some of its debt to be denominated in that foreign currency. If Company B is worried about the value of a payment that it expects to make in a foreign currency, all it needs to do is to arrange for some of its financial assets to be denominated in that currency. Observe that A and B can both achieve their hedging objectives simply by borrowing and lending between themselves. In fact, they can leave their debts and assets just as they are, and instead enter into an equivalent forward exchange contract. B arranges to buy from A the foreign currency that B expects to need, and A arranges to sell to B the foreign currency that A expects to receive, at a price fixed now for delivery at a specified date in the future.[14]

In practice the way the exchange market actually worked was that A and B typically did business not with each other but with a dealer, generally a bank. Once A and B do their separate deals with the bank their problems are over, but the bank's problem has just begun because, inevitably, the exposures to A and B do not exactly offset. Thus the exchange dealer himself is exposed to exchange risk. It stood to reason that if dealers were going to expand their book of forward contracts to meet an expanded demand for forward cover, they would need to find a way to hedge their own risk exposure. In fact, what they needed was a currency futures market, although it would take some time for them to realize it. Until then, they would continue their usual practice of hedging forward exchange risk in the spot market.[15]

Fischer's introduction to the debate between the fixed and flexible rate camps came while he was still in Cambridge, hanging around MIT. Franco Modigliani had a plan for international monetary reform that he had drawn up with his student Hossein Askari and was circulating for comment.[16] The plan envisioned an enlarged role for the IMF's Special Drawing Rights, which would continue to be firmly tied to gold, while the parity of the dollar would change over time in response to changes in the dollar price of internationally traded commodities. In this respect, Modigliani's plan was strikingly similar to Irving Fisher's 1920 proposal for *Stabilizing the Dollar*. Both plans were attempts to conceive of an international system that would allow the United States freedom to use monetary policy for domestic stabilization. The difference lay in the specifics. Fisher wanted to link the dollar price of gold to the domestic price index, while Modigliani preferred a link to an international price index.

July 15, 1971, exactly one month before the United States would go off gold, Fischer Black commented on the Modigliani-Askari plan. "I start with the view that the best international monetary system is one in which exchange rates are flexible between all pairs of countries, in which there is no international monetary authority, and in which gold has no monetary role. In addition, I believe that barriers to trade, barriers to international movement of capital goods, and barriers to foreign ownership of a country's assets are all serious deficiencies in an international economic system."[17] To Modigliani, this must have sounded like Milton Friedman. In fact, however, it was Fischer's intuitive extension of his CAPM-inspired "world without money" to the world as a whole.

How would Fischer's "best international monetary system" work? Each individual country would have its own banking system making loans and issuing deposits, both of which would pay the risk-free interest rate denominated in the country's own unit of account. Because deposits are all short-term, interest rates would be able to adjust fully for any expected price inflation internally, and also for any expected exchange rate depreciation externally. Thus, despite the multiplicity of national units, there would be essentially a single world market for risk-free borrowing and lending, and a single risk-free rate of interest. Similarly, there would be a single world capital market, a single world market portfolio of risky assets, and a single world price of risk. In such a world, some (risk-averse) countries might be net lenders, while other (risk-tolerant) countries might be net borrowers, but no more economic significance would attach to either position than would attach to lending by risk-averse individuals and borrowing by risk-tolerant individuals.

That's what true international equilibrium would look like.[18] Different countries might well use different national units of account, so we

Golden anniversary of Stanley and Marianna Fischer Black at the family home in Bryson City, North Carolina, June 1951. *Front row*: Peter Cox, Wilkes Black, Louis Black, Marianna Black, Stanley Black Sr., Blakeney Black, Stanley Black III, Fischer Black Jr.; *Second row*: Warren Cox, Louise Cox, Elizabeth Black, Ellen Winston, Julia M. Black, Julia Black; *Third row*: Fischer Black Sr., Oscar Cox, Chester Fischer, Louis Fischer, Richard Winston, Stanley Black Jr. *Courtesy:* Stanley Black III.

Above: Fischer and Blakeney at the family home in Falls Church, Virginia, circa 1945. *Courtesy:* Blakeney Black.

Left: Fischer with Blakeney and Lee in the backyard of the family home in Bronxville, New York, circa 1948. *Courtesy:* Blakeney Black.

Fischer and Tinna wedding, Scarsdale, New York, July 1958. *Courtesy:* Blakeney Black.

Fischer and Mimi wedding, Arlington, Massachusetts, July 1967. *Courtesy:* Alethea Black.

Fischer and Cathy at the wedding of Cathy's son Kevin, Mount Kisco, New York, March 1993. *Courtesy:* Beverly Hall, photographer.

Fischer as a freshman at Harvard College, 1955. *Courtesy:* Harvard Yearbook Publications.

Fischer as a professor at MIT, 1975. *Courtesy:* MIT Museum.

Fischer as a partner at Goldman Sachs, 1991. Reprinted by permission. Copyright 1991 by Goldman, Sachs & Co.

Young Robert Merton at MIT with President Jerome Wiesner, Paul Samuelson, and Howard Webber, Director of MIT Press, June 1972.
Courtesy: MIT Museum.

Myron Scholes at MIT, 1970.
Courtesy: MIT Museum.

Questions – Empirical.
At the time of his death, Fischer was working on a paper "Sufficient Conditions for the Fisher Effect." *Courtesy:* MIT Archives/Estate of Fischer Black, Alethea Black.

Questions – Empirical

Can we take seriously the Wainwright relation between interest rates and expected inflation?

What are the effects of timing problems in measuring the rate of inflation?

How do you deal with the existence of assets in different tax brackets, with possible changes in tax bracket over time?

If the real rate is not constant, how do you estimate the Fisher effect?

What if changes in the real rate are correlated with changes in the actual or expected inflation rate?

Can you estimate the biases as price controls are put on and taken off?

Is there a better estimate than the actual inflation rate of the expected inflation rate?

Did Nelson + Schwert use ex post data in their test, as Stan Fischer suggest?

Fama says a transaction weighted price index won't be affected by price controls, because there will be few transactions at the fixed prices. Who uses such an index? What about [?]?

Questions – Theoretical

Need uncertainty to get equity expected returns higher than debt, but might not need that.

Inelastic supply of housing: all in price?

What if the industry that produces housing is taxed like other capital?

What if short and long term supply elasticities of housing are different?

Is there a change in the mix of land and buildings? Does transportation cost or distance come in?

How does the size of the housing sector affect things? Is it subsumed by [?] elasticity?

What about personal taxes?

Do we need a theory of optimal capital structure? (with uncertainty?)

If other things are risky, can we take housing to be riskless? Does it matter?

Does the demand elasticity of housing matter?

What about the cost of moving money into or out of the corporate sector? Do we need uncertainty to model that properly?

Questions – Theoretical.
Courtesy: MIT Archives/Estate of Fischer Black, Alethea Black.

Fischer with Alethea as a toddler, 1971. *Courtesy:* Alethea Black.

Fischer's girls. From the top, Melissa, Alethea, Ashley, and Paige, December 1978. *Courtesy:* Paige Black.

Fischer eating cereal with cold orange juice instead of milk, at his parents' house in Tampa, 1993. *Courtesy:* Alethea Black.

Fischer with Mori (Mamoru) Ogata and Eric Fortier at Goldman Sachs, 1989. Reprinted by permission. Copyright 1989 by Goldman, Sachs & Co.

Fischer receiving the Financial Engineer of the Year award, December 1, 1994. Robert Merton is clapping. Photograph courtesy of John F. Marshall, Ph.D., Executive Director, IAFE 1992–1998. Copyright 1994 IAFE.

Jack Treynor memorializing Fischer at the International Association of Financial Engineers (IAFE) conference, September 1997. Photograph courtesy of John F. Marshall, Ph.D., Executive Director, IAFE 1992–1998. Copyright 1998 IAFE.

Franco Modigliani grips Jack Treynor at the IAFE conference. Photograph courtesy of John F. Marshall, Ph.D., Executive Director, IAFE 1992–1998. Copyright 1998 IAFE.

have to use exchange rates to translate from one set of accounts to another, but that's a detail. There is no particular reason to expect the exchange rate to remain constant over time, nor is there any particular reason to want it be constant, but if nonetheless we do want to keep it constant, it should be relatively easy to do. The way to keep a currency from depreciating, Fischer says, is not to rely on reserves that will eventually be exhausted, but rather to sell domestic bonds and capital at a more attractive price. Thus, from the beginning, it seemed to Fischer that both fixed and flexible exchange rates should be compatible with international equilibrium. He had no dog in the fixed versus flexible exchange rate fight.

Therefore, he focused his attention instead on the question of whether the actual world is in equilibrium, because if not, then there should be a profit opportunity somewhere waiting to be exploited. Suppose, for example, that countries impose a tax on holdings of foreign assets. (It doesn't have to be a literal tax, maybe only a psychological aversion to foreign investment.) Equilibrium asset returns will be distorted by the tax, and anyone clever enough to figure out the distortion need only find a way around the tax (or a way to overcome the aversion) in order to earn excess returns.

Once you do the math, it turns out that such a tax produces an alpha effect very much like the one Black and Scholes had earlier found in the data and tried to exploit at Wells Fargo. However, if the source of the distortion is barriers to international investment, then what we want is not a leveraged low-beta fund, but a fund that enables investors to break through the barriers to foreign investment.[19] Given the fate of the Stagecoach Fund, Fischer must have felt that there was not much practical chance of constructing an international fund. Instead, his vision of international capital market equilibrium provided the vantage point from which Fischer engaged in discussions about the monetary approach to the balance of payments.

Like CAPM, the monetary approach was explicitly an equilibrium theory, and Fischer liked that. In fact, in one sense the monetary approach seemed more general than CAPM, since it typically included explicit treatment of the market for goods. In another sense, however, the monetary approach seemed less general, because it typically took the world supply of money as an exogenous variable determined by world central bank policy. For Fischer, monetarism at the level of the world was no more acceptable theoretically than monetarism at the level of an individual country. Put another way, if the domestic money supply responds passively to domestic money demand (as Fischer thought it did), then no flows of international reserves should be necessary to equate supply and demand, and the money supply should be endogenous at the world level as well as the national level.

The big problem with Fischer's theory of passive money is that it provides no explanation for the level of prices or for inflation, and hence no explanation for exchange rates, either. Indeed, from the standpoint of standard economics, Fischer's theory hardly even qualifies as a monetary theory since the whole point of standard monetary theory is to explain these prices. In his earliest work, Fischer finessed the issue by saying simply that he was taking the level of prices to be fixed exogenously. Since Keynesians were using the same finesse for their own purposes, Fischer got away with it, more or less. But in an international setting, where the debate focused on alternative explanations of exchange rates, the same finesse was impossible and Fischer was forced to confront the problem head on. In a world of endogenous money, what determines the price level, inflation, and exchange rates? Under the gold standard, the value of gold provides the answer to all three questions, so that is where Fischer started.

At Chicago, the young economic historian Donald N. McCloskey and the finance economist J. Richard Zecher were circulating a controversial paper called "How the Gold Standard Worked, 1880–1913." It was supposed to be an application of the monetary approach to economic history. "The theory assumes that interest rates and prices are determined on world markets, and that therefore the central bank of a small country has little influence over them and the central bank of a large country has influence on them only by way of its influence over the world as a whole." The important point is that these assumptions were more or less what McCloskey and Zecher found to be the empirical fact of the matter for the United States and Britain during the gold standard period. Stated positively, they found that during that period world commodity and capital markets were unified. Price changes for individual goods across the two countries were just as closely related as price changes across different regions of the United States. "There appears to be little reason to treat these two countries on the gold standard differently in their monetary transactions from any two regions within each country."[20]

Fischer was captivated by the McCloskey-Zecher results, in much the same way as he had earlier been captivated by Jensen's results showing that no mutual fund beat the market. Jensen's results had suggested that CAPM equilibrium was not just a theory about how financial markets might work, but also a positive description of how they actually do work. Now McCloskey and Zecher seemed to suggest that equilibrium, not just in financial markets but also in goods markets, was a positive description of how the international system had actually worked once upon a time. And if it worked that way under the primitive transportation and communication technologies available back then, it only stood to reason that it must work that way today as well. Once again the idea of equilibrium proved to be a powerful lens for revealing previously unsuspected structure in the world around us.

McCloskey and Zecher saw their result as a consequence of international arbitrage in goods markets, a kind of extension of the law of one price to nontradable goods, so they interpreted it as a confirmation of purchasing power parity. Fischer saw the same result as a consequence of international equilibrium that extends from financial markets down into commodity markets, so he interpreted it as a confirmation of what he called "the law of one equilibrium," which says that market forces determine the relative prices of all goods independent of monetary factors. For Fischer, the purchasing power parity relationship was merely a corollary of this more fundamental law.

In Fischer's reading, Cassel's PPP equation says in effect that the relative price of different national *bundles* of goods is independent of monetary factors.[21] There is, of course, no reason to expect the relative price of national bundles to remain constant over time as the forces of supply and demand evolve, and anyway tariffs and taxes may distort the equilibrium. The important point is that, at any moment in time, there is only one equilibrium and it is independent of monetary factors. In effect, purchasing power parity provided the model of international commodity market equilibrium that Fischer needed to complete his international extension of CAPM. And the gold standard provided the model of how the variables left unexplained by CAPM and PPP might be determined.

Suppose that what we mean by the gold standard is a world in which currency is literally gold coins. Then we can define the money supply as the quantity of gold coin, and we can define the balance of payments as the flow of gold coin in and out of the country. In Fischer's mind, the monetary approach to the balance of payments is best suited for this gold currency world.[22] The total supply of gold coin relative to demand determines the world price level, and that total distributes itself across different countries in accordance with the distribution of demand. However, that's not the world we live in. The Bretton Woods system is not a system of gold currency but rather a system of national currencies, all tied to a single national target currency, the dollar.[23]

In fact, the idealized gold currency world is not even the world of the historical gold standard. The way the gold standard actually worked, much of the world's monetary gold was held by national central banks as reserves, which Fischer preferred to call "government inventories." The purpose of the inventories was to defend the gold value of the national currency, and it was the inherent weakness of that inventory defense mechanism that led to the failure of the gold standard. Put simply, finite inventories ran out. Instead of selling gold from an inventory, they would have been better off selling capital, meaning stocks and bonds. In this way, the domestic price of capital, not the domestic price of goods, would have been the variable that adjusted in order to maintain the exchange rate target. If we want to have a gold standard, Fischer argued, then instead of the gold coin system or the government inventory system we should have a "fiat gold standard." Countries would peg their currency to gold, but hold no inventories of gold.

Fischer's proposal for a system of zero reserves shows clearly that he viewed the nominal exchange rate not so much as the relative price of two different national baskets of commodities, but rather as the relative price of capital in two different national accounting systems. Starting as he did from CAPM, this financial point of view was entirely natural to Fischer, as natural to him as the commodity basket view was to the economists. The consequence of the finance view was, however, far-ranging. First of all, unlike commodities, financial capital is homogeneous in a unified world market, and the two prices of capital—the riskless rate of interest and the price of risk—are therefore the same everywhere. Furthermore, the price of financial capital can and does jump instantaneously to maintain equilibrium. Asset prices are, in this respect, fundamentally different from goods prices, and thinking about the exchange rate as a relative asset price is therefore fundamentally different from thinking about it as a relative commodity price. For Fischer, unlike Friedman, the nominal exchange rate is not a slow-moving variable like the price level, but rather a fast-moving variable like the stock market.[24]

This means that if we leave the nominal exchange rate free to float, it is likely to fluctuate quite a lot. But these fluctuations convey no real information, and therefore something like a gold standard may be a good idea after all, especially if we adopt the no-inventory fiat gold standard system. Of course, pegging to gold would mean that the domestic commodity price level would fluctuate with the relative price of gold and, given the existence of long-term contracts, people might experience that fluctuation as risk. Very well, says Fischer, if you want a stable domestic price level, you can get it even while you peg to gold, provided you change the peg in line with the domestic price level. "When the price level starts to rise, the price of gold is dropped; and when the price level starts to fall, the price of gold is raised."[25] By fixing against gold rather than another currency, a country can avoid the characteristic Bretton Woods problem of importing inflation or deflation from another country. By adjusting the price of gold according to the desired price index, a country can avoid importing inflation or deflation from gold itself.

Thus Fischer wound up advocating for a system quite similar to that proposed by Irving Fisher back in 1920 (and Modigliani in 1971), but for almost exactly opposite reasons. Reasoning from the quantity theory of money, Irving Fisher wanted to use control of the domestic quantity of money to stabilize domestic prices, and he was looking for a way to weaken the discipline of the gold standard in order to make room for his domestic stabilization goals. By contrast, Fischer Black, reasoning from his theory of passive money, proposed to use a peg to gold to control the domestic price level directly, while allowing the domestic quantity of money to fluctuate endogenously. Irving Fisher imagined a system of fluctuating gold inventories in order to buffer the domestic system from gold standard discipline. Fischer Black imagined a system of zero inventories in order to ensure the most direct contact between the different national capital markets.

In December 1981, Fischer seems to have thought that this completed his theory of money. Now he had a story about price levels, inflation, and exchange rates that was consistent with his theory of passive money. In his early work, he had treated the price level as a variable fixed exogenously, and argued that the money supply would expand endogenously to meet money demand at that exogenous price level. Now he had a theory of how that price level was fixed exogenously by exchange rate policy. And it wasn't just a theory about how the world might work. In Fischer's mind, it was how the system actually did work, more or less. Policy makers may talk the language of controlling money supply in order to control prices, but what they actually do is to control exchange rates. In fact, in a world of developed financial markets, that's about all they can do. Fischer thought that his work on the fiat gold standard completed the puzzle, but in fact there was one piece of the puzzle remaining.

In a world of gold currencies, it wouldn't matter whether you did your accounting in pounds or dollars or gold, you would come out with the same answer. If you were holding the world market portfolio, as CAPM tells you to do, you would see the same return whether you lived in Britain or the United States. If you combined that risky portfolio with borrowing or lending in order to achieve your desired risk exposure, it wouldn't matter whether you were borrowing pounds or dollars, you would borrow the same amount.

But suppose instead a world of national currencies pegged to gold at a price depending on an index of domestic prices, so that exchange rates between any two currencies fluctuate over time. In this world, the currency in which you do your accounting makes a difference. And that difference will be compounded by your choice of which currency to use for borrowing and lending to achieve your desired risk exposure. The question is, Does that difference affect your investment decision? One way to think about the problem is to observe that you can hedge your foreign exposure completely, and so can your foreign counterparts. People in country A who expect to receive payments in the currency of country B can hedge by writing forward currency contracts with people in country B who expect to receive payments in the currency of country A. In this way all currency risk can be eliminated, and for investment purposes we are essentially back in a single-currency world. Since you can do it, it seems intuitive that you *should* do it; at least that's how it seemed to Fischer at the time he left academia for Goldman Sachs. When clients asked how much of their foreign currency exposure they should hedge, he would say 100 percent.

At Goldman Sachs, the question of optimal hedging arose because institutional investors were dipping their toes into the water of international investing in search of an improved risk/return trade-off. In effect they were starting to overcome the barriers to international investment that Fischer had in 1974 identified as a force distorting asset returns. Investors could see the opportunity for excess returns, and new derivatives products such as swaps and index futures were making it increasingly easy to overcome any explicit barriers in the form of taxes or regulations. American pension funds were investing in the British stock market, and their experience of the volatile dollar/pound exchange rate made them wonder whether and how much to hedge currency risk.

Having told clients to hedge 100 percent, Fischer decided to do the math to check whether his intuition was correct. He tells the story: "Between Christmas and New Year's in 1988 I went away to a quiet place and started writing out formulas. I started Monday morning and had the answer that evening: but it seemed wrong. The formula I found said you should hedge less than 100 percent of your foreign currency risk."[26] What he had found was what he would call his "Universal Hedging Formula":

$$\text{Fraction of exchange risk hedged} = (\mu_m - \sigma_m^2)/(\mu_m - \tfrac{1}{2}\sigma_e^2)$$

where μ_m is the expected return on the world portfolio in excess of the riskless rate, σ_m^2 is the variance of that excess return, and σ_e^2 is the variance of the exchange rate, all three quantities calculated as averages across all countries.

The key to Fischer's result is that people in different countries use different price indexes to measure their wealth. As a consequence, "real" (inflation-adjusted) returns are different depending on which currency we use to do our figuring. This difference creates the opportunity for a free lunch. In a world of uncertainty, people who do their figuring in different currencies can completely insure one another against currency risk, but that's not the free lunch. The free lunch comes because currency risk has a positive expected return in equilibrium, so people can do even better if they *don't* completely insure one another.

The reason is something Fischer liked to call "Siegel's paradox" to give credit to his Chicago colleague Jeremy Siegel, who would go on to write the best-selling book *Stocks for the Long Run*, used by professional and individual investors alike. Siegel pointed out that, mathematically speaking, expected changes in currency values between two countries do not add up to zero across the two countries.[27] The deeper economics underlying this result is that people who measure risk and return using different measuring rods can shift risk to the person who measures it the smallest, and shift return to the person who measures it the largest. In other words, the underlying reason why there are different currencies is the very same reason why currency risk has a positive expected return. Says Fischer: "If everyone in the world eventually consumes the same mix of goods and services, and prices of goods and services are the same everywhere, hedging will no longer help."[28]

The consequence is that the ideal world market portfolio contains, in addition to a value-weighted cross section of all stocks and bonds, also a value-weighted cross section of currency risk exposures. One way to implement this would be for the investors of each country to lend in their own currency to the investors in every other country. An equivalent but possibly cheaper way is by using forward and futures contracts.[29] When full international capital market equilibrium is achieved, everyone will hold this world market portfolio. Until then, there are excess returns to be earned by those who move first, possibly very large excess returns.[30]

Ideas about an international extension of CAPM crystallized in the early 1970s, in the work of Fischer and others, long before the relaxation of capital controls and the development of exchange markets made possible the reality of an international CAPM.[31] Black's universal hedging version of international CAPM came, however, after the reality was already well on its way, and that timing affected the reception of his new idea. In 1988, when Fischer first got his result, discussion about optimal hedging was driven largely by practical and empirical concerns, not abstract and theoretical concerns. Given the historical volatility of certain individual British stocks and of exchange rates between the pound and the dollar, and given the historical covariance between these series, clients wanted to know what hedge ratio would provide the greatest reduction in volatility for each stock. It's an empirical question, and it generates an empirical answer, in fact a different answer for each stock.[32]

Fischer took the same question and asked what the answer would be in full international CAPM equilibrium in a world with multiple currencies. It's a theoretical question and it generates a theoretical answer. He discovered that the optimal hedge has nothing to do with the volatility of individual stocks, or individual exchange rates, or even the covariance between the two. In fact, the optimal hedge is the same for all British stocks, and the same for Japanese stocks and for the stocks of any other country as well. It is a *universal* hedge.

To many a practitioner, indeed to many an academic, Fischer's result seemed to rest on too many unrealistic assumptions about the world, number one being the assumption that the world is always in full international CAPM equilibrium.[33] Fischer's Goldman colleague Bob Litterman reminds us that "since the world is not in equilibrium and most investors do not hold market capitalization weighted portfolios, the universal hedging percentage does not generally apply as a portfolio prescription."[34] For Fischer, however, the result was essentially a matter of logical deduction from a relatively few fundamental principles. The world may not literally be in equilibrium, but the ceaseless search for profit is always pushing in that direction, and the assumption of equilibrium is therefore both realistic and practical.

Fischer got the formula because, unlike everyone else, he thought about the problem in equilibrium terms, but that's not all. He got the formula also because of his earlier thinking about how to price futures and forwards, and about the monetary approach to the balance of payments, and about how a fiat gold standard might work, and about why there are different currencies in the first place. Probably not all of this was strictly necessary background to solve the problem at hand, but it was the background that Fischer brought when he sat down to think about the problem. And it was the background that made Fischer able to recognize the solution, and interpret its implications, when he found it.

With the theory of universal hedging, the final piece of Fischer's monetary theory fell into place. As proof that the puzzle was complete, the final implication of the theory was a simple formula that showed how to make everyone in the world better off. Said Fischer in 1989, "Options don't help anyone get a more efficient portfolio, but this does."[35] It had taken 20 years, but it was worth the effort.

Fischer had been attracted to the University of Chicago by the intellectual opportunity it afforded, and he was not disappointed. Secure at the Graduate School of Business, under the protective wing of Merton Miller and James Lorie, he ventured forth to explore what was happening in economics elsewhere in the university. Safe inside his office on the third floor of Rosenwald, with Myron Scholes on one side and Eugene Fama on the other, he constructed within his own mind an alternative intellectual universe, unconstrained by what anyone else thought. At Chicago, Fischer could be a maverick without bearing the costs that everywhere else are imposed on those who refuse to conform to societal norms. He loved it.

The one downside was the obligation to teach. No one was ever better than Fischer at working one-on-one with a student, but the subject had to be one that he was interested in learning about himself. And the student had better be interested in solving the problem, not just in finishing the degree requirements. And the student had also better be prepared to defend his proposed solution against alternatives, even alternatives that no one except Fischer was prepared to consider. For him, the whole point of academic life was to think new thoughts, and he was interested only in interacting with people who shared that commitment. The word got around that he was a good person to talk to, but you didn't want him on your dissertation committee for fear he might not sign off on the end product.

Standard classroom lecturing about matters that Fischer thought had already been resolved was simply a bore, and Fischer was lousy at it. He recalled: "I was terrible, judging by the ratings my students gave me. I thought lectures were a waste of time for me and for my students (especially when the material is in a book). I looked for every possible excuse to cancel classes. One thing I did was to fill some classes with reviews of past exams. That worked well, so gradually I started doing more of it. Eventually, I worked out the following system.

"I handed out lists of questions and packets of readings at the start of each semester. In each class we would discuss three or four of the questions. They would give their views and I would give my views. The students liked it, and I liked it. My ratings went from the bottom to the top, and I'm sure they learned more than when I was lecturing."[36] Students would recall of his "Fifty Questions" course that every year the questions stayed the same, but the answers always changed. In effect, Fischer handled teaching, which he hated, by turning it into research and intellectual dialogue, which he loved.

There was only one other downside to life in Chicago. Fischer's wife Mimi hated it. Left alone for most of the time in Kenilworth with two small children, she missed the support of her family in Boston. People said that she read the Boston newspapers and kept her watch on Boston time. She had pushed Fischer to take the Ford Foundation Professorship, but had not anticipated a longer stay, nor had she anticipated how absorbing Fischer would find academic life. No one produces that amount of work without spending long hours at the desk, away from wife and family. When Mimi married Fischer, he was a business consultant, and so were most of his friends. Now suddenly he was a professor, and most of his friends were scruffy academics. It wasn't the life she had thought she was going to have. Attempts to build a social life around Fischer's academic friends were not a success, and were not repeated. These friends all saw Fischer's devotion to his work as quite appropriate, and Mimi's life in posh Kenilworth as nothing to feel sorry for.

In fact, the trouble with the marriage went deeper than Chicago versus Boston, or academia versus business. Married life had been calmer when Fischer was at Arthur D. Little, but even then Mimi had been frustrated by what she saw as Fischer's passivity and lack of ambition. She had pushed him to ask for a raise, and when the raise was not forthcoming, had pushed him to start his own consulting business, going so far as to hire the secretary and rent the office. From her perspective, Fischer was completely impractical and quite incapable of managing his own career, so she had to do it for him. She saw "Fischer drifting in a lifeboat with only one oar, an inadequate person with no street smarts, very stupid about anything regular . . . a sad person, like a street person."[37] In effect, she agreed with Fischer's father, who criticized him for simply "floating" through life without any clear direction.

To make matters worse, although Fischer was not conventionally ambitious, he was clearly quite driven by the need to prove himself on intellectual grounds. The problem was that neither his wife nor his father put much value on such achievement. Fischer would put on a front of not caring what other people thought of him, and sometimes he may even have succeeded in convincing himself that the front was real. But he did care what his father thought, and he did care what his wife thought, and it pained him that neither one thought that his intellectual work was worth very much. Mimi would dismiss him as "a madman scribbling formulas in the middle of the night," and his father would ask, "When are you going to get a real job?" It just made Fischer more stubbornly determined to show them. In doing so, however, he withdrew even further from them, in order to work even harder.

In Fischer's mind, he was prepared to do anything for Mimi except neglect his work. In her mind, he wasn't prepared to do even the minimal things any normal person would do. They were at hopeless cross-purposes. Divorce was one way out, but Fischer ruled it out on account of the children. Moreover, he didn't think they needed a divorce. He was happy to leave Mimi alone to do her job, raising the children, and asked only that she leave him alone to do his job, thinking and writing. They could be, he reasoned, like partners in a firm. When he required less demanding female companionship, he could and did find it readily enough outside the marriage by placing personal ads in the local paper, and he encouraged Mimi to do likewise. For Fischer, such an accommodation was nothing more than an alternative lifestyle, but of course for Mimi it made her situation even more intolerable.

One final attempt to square the circle was to find a way for Mimi herself to join the academic life. In March 1973, Lorie arranged for Mimi to talk with a dean at the Medical School about taking science classes toward an eventual degree, but she decided it was too late to be thinking about going back to school. Instead, by the fall she was pregnant again, with Ashley, born May 4, 1974. Soon thereafter she packed up the kids and returned to Boston for good. Realizing that Fischer was never going to be the normal husband and normal father that she wanted him to be, she returned to Boston where she would at least have her own parents to help her.

Fischer went to see Lorie. "Jim, I don't know what I'm going to do. Either I'm going to have to move back to Boston or get a divorce." "Fischer, I have enormous confidence in you. I predict you'll do both." For the time being, however, Fischer left the Kenilworth house empty and rented an apartment near the university. He took his meals at the nearby Billings Hospital cafeteria, and on weekends flew back to Boston. Melissa remembers her mother tying a yellow ribbon on the front of their house whenever Fischer was expected. It was the symbol of welcome for a returning prisoner made famous in the 1973 hit song "Tie a Yellow Ribbon Round the Ole Oak Tree."

■ Chapter Eight ■

STAGFLATION

Perhaps in most cases where we seek in vain the answer to a question, the cause of the failure lies in the fact that problems simpler and easier than the one in hand have been either not at all or incompletely solved. All depends, then, on finding out these easier problems, and on solving them by means of devices as perfect as possible and of concepts capable of generalization.

David Hilbert, "Mathematical Problems" (1902)

As news of the Black family drama traveled the academic grapevine, the Sloan School at MIT recognized an opportunity. They could never pay Fischer what he was making at Chicago, but they could eliminate the intercity commute and the cost of dual residence. It seemed like a good chance to woo Myron Scholes as well, who had left MIT for Chicago in 1973, so they got approval from the dean to make an offer to both men. In the event, Scholes decided to stay at Chicago, but Fischer accepted immediately. His only conditions were a secure steel office door and stationery with his name on it, both of which he needed for his options service.

In the fall of 1975 he moved into his new office on the second floor of the Sloan Building, E52-243E in MIT lingo. As office mates, instead of Scholes and Fama, now he had Robert Merton on one side and on the other the corporate finance expert Stewart Myers. Unlike Chicago, there was no Merton Miller or James Lorie to protect him or show him the ropes, but maybe that wouldn't matter. The senior figure in the department was Franco Modigliani, but he split his time among the economics department and myriad outside commitments, so the younger faculty were left alone to run the program as they saw fit. That meant that Fischer was largely free to do his own thing.

As for the family, they moved into a new house at 20 Amberwood Drive in Winchester, just a block away from the local public school that Fischer's girls would attend. Although Fischer continued to spend long hours at work, his commute was a lot shorter and he spent more time at home, albeit most of it in the home office he set up in the basement. In this way, his life stabilized for several years, interrupted now and again by a few nights in a hotel when Mimi threw him out. But always she took him back, and they even had another child, Paige, born November 2, 1978.

At MIT, intellectual life revolved around the Tuesday night finance seminar, which began after dinner and continued on until it finished, often as late as 10:30 at night. MIT seminars were open to everyone, and everyone came to this one. Typically the discussion would find Franco Modigliani on one side of the argument, Fischer on the other, and Bob Merton in the middle trying to keep the peace and make sure the presenter got to say what he came to say. In Merton's view, the job of the audience was not to test the presenter's defenses, but rather to try to understand what he was saying and to help him improve his argument. It was all much more polite than the Chicago rough-and-tumble, and at first Fischer's aggressive Chicago style stuck out.

In time Fischer learned to yield on style, but never on content, and that's where the trouble started. He was used to being in the minority at Chicago, given his fundamental disagreement with Milton Friedman on the subject of money. But at Chicago he could always depend on a shared pro-market worldview as common ground. At MIT, by contrast, economics was defined by the neo-Keynesian troika: Paul Samuelson, Robert Solow, and Franco Modigliani. In this context, Fischer would always remain an outsider.

At MIT, the market was generally a good thing, but subject to specific failings that require focused intervention to correct. Deviation of social cost from private cost and social benefit from private benefit means that public goods (such as education) tend to be undersupplied and public bads (such as pollution) tend to be oversupplied by the private market. Further, the market power enjoyed by large firms means restricted production, high prices, and excessive profits at the expense of the consumer. And, most important of all, wage and price rigidity means that the supply side of the economy adjusts only very slowly to fluctuation in aggregate demand. Persistent unemployment is the consequence, and the solution is government intervention to stabilize aggregate demand using fiscal and monetary policy.

At MIT, the purpose of economics, broadly speaking, was to bring all these imperfections to light in order to provide the intellectual basis for governmental intervention to counteract them. For the MIT economists, economics was in effect a kind of engineering science in the service of the public interest. At MIT, by contrast to Chicago, the government was seen not as the natural enemy of the market, but rather as the natural client of the economist engineer. The special purpose of academic economics was to develop the basic science behind the eventual engineering, and to train the basic scientists who would then advise the eventual engineers.

For Paul Samuelson, the acknowledged leader of the neo-Keynesian troika, the challenge of developing the basic science was fundamentally about bringing mathematical methods to bear on the development of economic theory. Just as in physics, "capture by mathematics" could confidently be expected to produce a flowering of basic theory, simply because mathematics was so much more convenient than natural language for drawing out a chain of deductive reasoning. By choosing mathematics as the language for economic theory, Samuelson argued, we can practically guarantee efficient and correct deduction of conclusions from premises.

Of course there is nothing in the convenience of mathematics to save us from big mistakes if we base our deductions on false premises. "Where the really big mistakes are made is in the formulation of premises."[1] Nevertheless for Samuelson, and for the department he built around himself, the focus was on the deductions, not on the premises. At least to begin with, he was willing to take as given the standard economic idea of modeling consumer behavior as the maximization of utility, firm behavior as the maximization of profit, and macroeconomic behavior as the interaction of aggregate demand and aggregate supply. Using mathematics, he could be sure of doing the economics better than previous generations, and so be sure that his efforts would result in improvement of economic theory. The underlying idea was that better theory would then translate into better engineering and hence improved economic performance.

Samuelson's conceptualization of the problems of economic theory as a series of mathematical problems carried with it a set of further implications about intellectual strategy. An analogy that would have been in Samuelson's mind, whether consciously or not, was the famous 1900 Paris Lecture of the mathematician David Hilbert in which he laid out some 23 unsolved mathematical problems as possible foci for further development of the field. Hilbert recommended a strategy of building up to the solution of these difficult problems by starting with the solution of simpler ones. Just so for Samuelson, because general equilibrium problems seem to be more difficult than partial equilibrium problems, it made sense to start with the latter. The famous model of general equilibrium achieved by Leon Walras in 1874 under the very special conditions of perfect competition and perfectly flexible prices can stand in our minds as the kind of theory we might one day achieve for more realistic premises. But right now we need to focus our attention on simpler models that we know how to solve.

One such simpler model that attracted enormous attention in the 1960s was the growth model of Robert Solow in which he constructs an entire theory of economic growth around the simple idea of an aggregate production function:

$$Y_t = A_t f(K_t, L_t)$$

where Y is output, K is capital, L is labor, and A is a technology factor.[2] This idea becomes a theory of growth when we assume that a certain proportion s of output gets added to the capital stock, and that both labor and the technology factor grow at exogenous and constant rates over time. Then the equation describing the growth of the capital stock is just

$$K_{t+1} = K_t + sA_t f(K_t, L_t)$$

Of particular interest to Solow was the "balanced growth steady state equilibrium" in which capital, labor, and output all grow at the same constant rate, a rate that surprisingly turns out to depend only on the rate of population growth and technological change. (In the Solow growth model, the savings rate affects the *level* of capital and income for given labor, but not the growth rate.) This image of a steady growth path became, for the MIT economists and the generations of students they trained, the mental image of long-run equilibrium toward which the economy tends and around which it fluctuates.

The study of this model, and others like it, formed the core of economics teaching at MIT. Whereas Chicago admitted large numbers of students and washed most of them out with tough qualifying exams, MIT admitted only a carefully selected few, and then worked hard to supply them with the analytical tools they would need for carrying further the MIT agenda of developing basic economic science. What the professors taught, and what the students learned, was how to adapt a variety of workhorse models to new problems. At MIT, the first step in any analysis was to go to the blackboard and write down a model as the framework for thinking and talking about the problem.

The essential difference between the economics department and the business school at MIT was that in the latter the imagined client of economic science was business, not the government. At the Sloan School, the idea was to transfer basic economic knowledge into practical business applications. Stewart Myers, for example, built on the fundamental work of Modigliani and Miller to draw out insights for the traditional problems of corporate finance. Bob Merton, another example, developed the theory of continuous time finance to "stock the shelves" with ideas for new financial products and businesses that might one day be useful to the growing industry. As in the economics department, teaching was seen as an important way to spread new ideas. Stewart Myers' textbook *Principles of Corporate Finance* (with Richard Brealey) became the standard reference in the field, and Robert Merton's papers elaborating the continuous-time finance model, collected in *Continuous-Time Finance*, built the edifice of modern asset pricing theory.[3]

In one respect, Fischer was a good fit for the Sloan School. Ever since Treynor had turned him on to the capital asset pricing model (CAPM), he had been interested in working out practical applications of the new theory. In this vein, during his years at MIT, he developed a proposal for how corporations should fund their pension liabilities, a proposal for fundamental reform of business accounting, and a practical way to value uncertain investment projects by using conditional rather than unconditional forecasts. All three of these projects were about using economics to help business do its job better. (See Chapter 9.)

The MIT style of teaching was a harder fit. Fischer was always more interested in the next new thing than in providing a systematic account of the state of knowledge so far achieved. And even his conception of what had been achieved was different. Finance, he thought, was not so much a collection of academic papers ringing the changes on a set of workhorse models. Rather it was more like a language, and learning finance was essentially about learning to construct grammatical sentences in the language of finance. His impulse, when faced with a new problem, was not to go to the blackboard and write down a mathematical model, but rather to talk around the problem, approaching it simultaneously from as many different angles as possible, and almost entirely with words, not mathematics. Formal modeling would come later, if at all, and only after the problem had been essentially solved.

The reason for emphasizing verbal treatments was to maintain maximal flexibility of mind. Once you write down a model, you freeze the problem into a given intellectual framework and it becomes very difficult to consider alternative frameworks. Within the framework of a given model there is plenty of work to do—you can fiddle with the underlying assumptions, or investigate the consequences of changing a significant parameter—but all your work will be for naught if you have the wrong framework to start with. In Fischer's view, finance was a very young field, not yet sufficiently mature to be a promising candidate for formalization. And economics was similarly immature, notwithstanding its lengthy history. Maybe he was wrong about that, but the important point is that such a methodological stance made Fischer the odd man out at MIT.

Indeed, Fischer's intellectual strategy for developing new economic theory was almost exactly the opposite of Samuelson's. Not mathematical problems but practical problems were the focus of his attention. And his approach to solving them was not to build up from simpler specific problems but rather to build down from the solution of more general problems. The general equilibrium model is sufficiently general, he would insist, to be consistent with almost any data we might observe.

The challenge of theory is to construct a stripped-down example of the more general model that reveals the significant factors at work in specific instances of interest.

Given his educational background, Fischer also probably knew about Hilbert's 1900 Paris Lecture. But the message he would have taken from it was not about the power of specialization but rather about the power of generalization, to which Hilbert also refers. Says Hilbert, "If we do not succeed in solving a mathematical problem, the reason frequently consists in our failure to recognize the more general standpoint from which the problem before us appears only as a single link in a chain of related problems. After finding this standpoint, not only is this problem frequently more accessible to our investigation, but at the same time we come into possession of a method which is applicable also to related problems."[4]

Fischer's more general standpoint was of course general equilibrium, which he understood as a generalization of the capital asset pricing model he had learned from Treynor. For Fischer, general equilibrium was not complicated but simple, expressible not in thousands of equations describing supply and demand for myriad individual goods, but rather in one simple equation expressing asset price equilibrium:

$$ER_i = R_f + (ER_m - R_f)\beta_i$$

This general equilibrium equation is the starting point for Fischer's theory of economic growth. He only needs to add the further supposition of a constant rate of consumption γ out of total capital value, a supposition analogous to Solow's supposition of a constant rate of saving s out of income, in order to achieve his fundamental growth equation:

$$K_{t+1} = (1 + R_i - \gamma)K_t$$

Here the return R_i is a random variable reflecting the risk/return choices of the society in question.[5]

Fischer's organizing image of how the economy moves through time is thus not Solow's balanced-growth steady-state path, but rather a nonstationary geometric random walk. In Fischer's conception, unlike Solow's, economic growth depends on patience, which keeps the rate of consumption below the return on capital. It also depends on risk tolerance because higher tolerance means a higher expected return. And it also depends on luck because the actual rate of return may be higher or lower than expected.

Despite the different images of growth, the difference between Fischer and his MIT colleagues was not so much about the nature of the world outside the window as it was about the most effective scientific approach to learning more about that world, and how best to use such knowledge once achieved. Much like John Maynard Keynes himself, Fischer was fascinated by the "dark forces of time and uncertainty" that seemed to be driving the world around him. But Keynes famously saw those forces as an urgent threat to be met by enlightened governmental intervention. Following Keynes, the neo-Keynesian vision of steady-state growth is best understood as an image of the ultimate goal to be achieved by active management. Fischer saw the same forces out there in the world, but he saw them not as threats but as opportunities, both for the individual and for society. Risk is just the cost of reward, and instability the cost of growth. What we need is not government intervention to eliminate risk, but development of financial theory, and institutions and markets, to help us live in a world of risk.

Could all this ever be adapted for the MIT environment? The neo-Keynesian commitments of his MIT colleagues meant that intellectually Fischer could not expect much positive intellectual support, however much his colleagues might like him personally or respect his achievements in financial theory. Fischer adapted to the resulting sense of intellectual isolation by embracing a certain degree of physical isolation as well. He stayed in his office with the door shut, and did not respond to knocks. Although his window looked out over the Charles River, he kept the blinds closed, his file cabinets arrayed in front of the blinds, and his back to the window. He maintained a large stock of cookies for energy and water to wash them down, and he worked alone at his steel desk, cleared of everything except a pad, a pencil, and a telephone that he used to interact with the outside world, even with his own secretary, who sat just outside the door. Alone in his office he might have been anywhere. With isolation came intellectual freedom.

Anyone who was working in an area that interested Fischer could count on receiving a phone call. "This is Fischer Black. I've been reading your paper and on page 12 you say something I'd like you to explain." There was never any small talk, and once he got what he was looking for, he would hang up. Most often it was a one-sided conversation, with Fischer initiating the call, asking questions, and getting answers. But he always offered to reciprocate and would write at the bottom of his own papers: "If you have any questions or comments, please call me at 617-253-6691, or write me at 50 Memorial Drive, Cambridge, MA 02139."

From time to time, a research conference would tempt Fischer from his MIT lair. He would always arrive having read and prepared written comments on all the papers that would be presented, regardless of whether he was on the program as a formal discussant. In an even more striking breach of usual academic practice, when editors asked for his candid opinion on papers submitted for publication, Fischer would always insist that they keep his name on the report he prepared for the author. In this way he took advantage of every opportunity for focused intellectual exchange. He needed the friction of dialogue to spark his own work.

Apart from the Tuesday night seminar, Fischer's only regular foray into the halls of MIT was to meet his teaching commitments, which he seems to have approached as a further opportunity to engage with minds potentially open to his own way of thinking. Starting with the Fifty Questions approach he had invented at Chicago, Fischer developed his course into a training ground where he would teach students his own idiosyncratic approach to solving problems. To this day, many former students remember the course as a key influence on their thinking, so much so that some took it more than once.

Consistent with Fischer's conception of finance as a language, the essential text for his course was "Fischer Black's Glossary for Finance," which ran 51 pages from "Accounts payable" to "Yield," and the "Supplement," which ran an additional 35 pages from "After-tax discounting" to "Unemployment." The typical entry was a paragraph of prose discussing the concept and its connection to other concepts. The purpose of the glossaries was to provide a bridge between the natural language that students already spoke and the special language of finance that they would find in the professional literature, most notably in the unpublished work of Fischer Black that comprised the bulk of the reading list.

As Fischer conceived the course, class time was an opportunity for students to construct their own finance sentences in the presence of a native speaker. The exercise of answering the Fifty Questions gave them something concrete to talk about. It also required them to think from the beginning in the terms of the new language, rather than translating back and forth into more familiar natural language or mathematics. Students would talk, and Fischer would write whatever they said on the board without comment until the board was full. Then he would comment on each of the answers, in effect correcting the students' usage. Once in a great while the rhythm would be broken when something a student said caused Fischer to take out his gold mechanical pencil and write a note to himself while the class fell silent. Remembers one student, "We lived to be the person who would cause Fischer to stop and pull out his pencil."

In the fall term the course was targeted to the MBA students and called "Problems in Finance." In the spring term the course was targeted to the PhD students and called "Advanced Topics in Financial Markets and Institutions." The Fifty Questions were the same in both courses, but the second course covered more of them and at a higher level. There were nine categories of questions: Capital Market Equilibrium, Corporate Finance, Accounting and Economic Earnings, Underwriting, Trading and Investment Companies, Options and Futures, Corporate Assets and Liabilities, Banking and Monetary Theory, and International Economics. The course thus covered almost all of finance, but in a way that made clear the unity of the subject and, most important, the utility of the finance language for talking your way through concrete problems.

For 25 years, from 1948 to 1973, economic growth in the United States had been strong and economic fluctuations relatively shallow, though inflation began to creep up in the late 1960s and early 1970s. In about 1973, however, everything changed. The recession of 1974–1975 was the deepest yet seen in the postwar period. And within a few years, even that would be exceeded by the double-dip recession of 1980–1982, which saw unemployment rising briefly above 10 percent. In retrospect, the year 1973 marked the end of prosperity and the beginning of the era of so-called stagflation, a word coined to combine "stagnation" and "inflation," the two outstanding economic facts of the decade.

The stock market saw it coming. From January 1973 to September 1974, the S&P 500 index fell 42 percent. In fact, over the entire decade from 1965 to 1974, stocks returned on average only 1.2 percent per year, compared to an average return on Treasury bills of 5.4 percent. Nevertheless, writing in February 1976, Fischer Black summed up his view of the future: "Thus today's investor may have about the same wealth, and may face about the same volatility and difference between stock returns and bond returns as the investor of 10 years ago. Such an investor may decide to keep in stocks the money he currently has in stocks."[6] In investment terms, the previous 10 years had been a lost decade, but there was no reason to be pessimistic about the next 10 years. Things could easily turn around.

The rational basis for Fischer's sangfroid was the efficient markets idea that returns are, to a first approximation, independent random variables from one year to the next. The fact that returns have been low does not mean they will continue to be low. Indeed, if anything, the recent experience of low returns might lead one to anticipate higher returns in the future. Why so? Fischer reasoned that since, empirically, volatility tends to decrease as stock prices rise and since, theoretically, expected returns should be correlated with volatility, it follows that expected returns should be high when prices are low and low when prices are high.

Fischer had discovered the empirical relationship between price and volatility in work he did at Chicago looking for better ways to estimate the volatility input into the options formula. It was the only empirical regularity concerning volatility in which he had any confidence. He would say, "One of my problems is that I am unwilling to write down any definite model of the general process by which volatilities change, and then use statistical methods to estimate the numbers that appear in the model. I can't imagine having enough confidence in any model to use statistical methods in this way."[7] Because of the volatility effect, Fischer thought that stock returns were probably mean reverting, but in 1976 he apparently didn't think the effect was sufficiently reliable to bet on. He did not suggest that people increase their stock holdings, but only that they to hold on to what they already had.

One reason for his caution was that no one was quite sure what was causing the stagflation, and what, if anything, could be done about it. The simultaneous appearance of unemployment and inflation was particularly troubling for the neo-Keynesians since their basic model suggested a trade-off between unemployment and inflation. One way to explain the facts was to emphasize exogenous increases in prices, for example the 1974 oil price increase. Another way was to emphasize that the supposed trade-off between unemployment and inflation was only ever meant to hold in the short run, so maybe what was happening was that the long run was catching up.[8] Keynesians took the first tack, while monetarists took the second, but Fischer had a different idea. Fischer's idea was that the economy could be understood as being in full general equilibrium all the time, even in the middle of stagflation.

It is important to appreciate how radical this idea was at the time. Practically everyone else, Keynesians and monetarists alike, viewed business cycles as short-run deviations from long-run equilibrium, so academic discussion was largely confined to questions about the possibility and desirability of correcting deviations by explicit policy intervention. Keynesians were, of course, more optimistic about the possibility than monetarists, and during the years of prosperity their policy optimism had captured the imagination of the majority of economists. But as the years of stagflation wore on, the monetarist policy pessimism gained more and more adherents, and the MIT neo-Keynesians found themselves increasingly on the defensive.

Into this fractious debate stepped Fischer Black with the suggestion that it might be possible to understand business fluctuation as an equilibrium. Uncertainty, not disequilibrium, was the source of business fluctuation, according to him. In the context of the mainstream debate, Fischer's suggestion seemed not only a little bit crazy, but even more than a little bit dangerous. Even the monetarists had never gone so far as to claim that the business cycle was an equilibrium. The great Austrian economist Friedrich von Hayek had tried to propose some such theory way back in the early years of the Great Depression, but he had been vanquished by Keynes himself, not to mention the lived experience of the Depression. To argue that the Depression could be understood as an equilibrium seemed tantamount to arguing that nothing should be done about it, and that was simply unacceptable. Equilibrium theories of the business cycle fell into disrepute in the 1930s from which they never recovered, at least not until Fischer Black.

Fischer was not, however, trying to revive von Hayek. In origin, Fischer's theory was nothing more than an extension of Irving Fisher's model of general equilibrium to the case of uncertainty. Irving Fisher had not himself treated the case of uncertainty, mainly because he lacked the necessary analytical tools. He wrote: "To attempt to formulate mathematically in any useful, complete manner the laws determining the rate of interest under the sway of chance would be like attempting to express completely the laws which determine the path of a projectile when affected by random gusts of wind. Such formulas would need to be either too general or too empirical to be of much value."[9] But Fischer Black did have the necessary analytical tools, namely the capital asset pricing model, so he thought he might be able to do what Irving Fisher could not. In fact, Fischer thought he had already done so in his Financial Note No. 8, "Equilibrium in the Creation of Investment Goods under Uncertainty."[10] Now his idea was to use that early work to provide an explanation for stagflation.

The basic cause of business fluctuation, Fischer came to think, is a mismatch between the pattern of production and the pattern of demand, a mismatch that can arise even in full general equilibrium because investments must be made on the basis of only very limited knowledge about the future world in which they will be producing output. Keynes had built his macroeconomic theory around a mismatch between aggregate investment and aggregate saving. For Fischer the important thing was not the aggregates but rather the detailed sectoral pattern of production and demand. Writing in March 1976, Fischer asks: "Why do human capital and business have ups and downs that are largely unpredictable? I think it's because of basic uncertainty about what people will want in the future and about what the economy will be able to produce in the future. If future tastes and technology were known, profits and wages would grow smoothly and surely over time."[11]

This way of thinking about business cycles put Fischer at odds with his MIT colleagues, much as his way of thinking about money had earlier put him at odds with his Chicago colleagues. The idea that the problem was in the details of the sectoral match did not necessarily rule out a role for government, but it definitely ruled out the kind of aggregative fiscal and monetary policy interventions that were the focus of traditional macroeconomic debate. If Fischer's theory was right, then intervention could be effective only to the extent it was able to help the private sector get the match right, in detail, which was a tall order to say the least. The word got out that Fischer was absolutely first-rate in the specialized subfield of finance, but quite out of his depth when it came to general economics. As always, the negative reaction made Fischer all the more determined to develop his ideas further.

In developing his theory of business cycles, Fischer started from Irving Fisher's 1930 book *The Theory of Interest as Determined by Impatience to Spend Income and Opportunity to Invest It*. As the seminal text for post–World War II American economics, it was a logical place to start. Notwithstanding his lack of formal training, Fischer had every reason to think that by engaging the work of Fisher he would automatically be engaging modern economics. He also had special reason to find Irving Fisher's work a congenial starting point since Fisher, like himself, came to economics from mathematics and physics. Irving Fisher was a kindred spirit.

Fisher's 1930 treatise was actually a combination and revision of two earlier books, *The Nature of Capital and Income* published in 1906 and *The Rate of Interest* published in 1907. It is the material in the second book, with its mathematical structure of utility-maximizing individuals and profit-maximizing firms, that would become central to postwar economics education and thinking. By contrast, the material in the former, essentially an economic theory of accounting, had been rejected by most economists. But Fischer Black didn't reject it. Indeed, his entire approach to economics was based on it.

In the 1906 book, Irving Fisher paints a picture of the economy as a stock of wealth moving through time, throwing off a flow of services as it goes. In Fisher's formulation, all wealth is capital, not just machines and buildings, but also land and even human beings. Indeed, for Fisher human beings are the most important form of capital because they are the most versatile. Thus, at the highest level of abstraction, there is no distinction between the traditional categories of labor, capital, and land. All produce a stream of income (services) so all are capital, and their income discounted back to the present is their capital value. Similarly, at the highest level of abstraction, there is no distinction between the traditional categories of wages, profit, and rent. All are incomes thrown off by capital; hence all are forms of the more general category of interest, which is the rate at which income flows from wealth.

Fisher summarizes this worldview in the following diagram:[12]

	Present Capital		**Future Income**
Quantities	Capital-wealth	$\rightarrow$	Income-services
			$\downarrow$
Values	Capital-value	$\leftarrow$	Income-value

The first arrow indicates the transformation of present capital wealth into future income services by means of *technology*. The second arrow indicates the transformation of diverse specific services into money values by the process of *exchange*. The third arrow indicates the transformation of anticipated future money values into a present money capital-value by the process of *discounting* using the rate of interest. Think of a factory producing a stream of goods spread out over several years in the future. Those goods have a money value equal to their selling price. Fisher's point is that the value of the factory today derives from the value of the goods it will produce in the future, and the key link is the rate of interest.

For Irving Fisher, the quintessential form of capital was the factory, but for Fischer Black it was the human being. Human capital was not only the largest fraction of his own personal wealth, but also the largest fraction of the wealth of the economy at large. We don't see this fact in the standard economic statistics because we don't buy and sell human beings so there is no market price of human capital. But we do see the payments made to human beings for the work they do (wages), and when we compare that number with the payments made to physical capital for the work it does (profits), we get some idea how much human capital there is. Says Fischer: "Even if we add real estate and other personal property to the value of business capital, the value of human capital is probably well over half of the total. So if we have to think of capital as being either physical or human, we're better off thinking of it as human."[13]

The fact that so much of wealth is unobservable poses a problem since we'd like to be able to measure the total. Why so? Says Fischer Black: "Wealth and welfare are not the same. I claim, however, that as a practical matter, an increase in wealth normally means an increase in welfare."[14] Irving Fisher held a similar view and for much the same reason. If wealth is just the present value of future income flows, then an increase in wealth must mean an increase in some income flow, and hence an increase in welfare for someone.[15] It follows that, as a general rule of thumb, we should adopt economic policies that increase wealth. But how can we do that if we can't measure human capital, which is the largest fraction of wealth? Fischer Black says that we can use the stock market as a proxy, because the values of different kinds of capital tend to move together. The reason is that physical capital and human capital are complementary inputs into production. When stocks go up, probably the value of human capital goes up, too, and when stocks go down, so does human capital.

For Irving Fisher, the key economic variable is the rate of interest that measures the sustainable rate of income flow from the current stock of capital. In his theory of interest, he explains how this rate of interest is determined by utility-maximizing individuals choosing a time path of consumption (his "First Approximation") and by profit-maximizing firms choosing a time path of production (his "Second Approximation"). However, he can solve the problem only for the case where all time paths are known with certainty. In his "Third Approximation to the Theory of Interest" he talks about the case of uncertainty, but cannot derive a mathematical formula.[16]

Reading Fisher through the lens of Treynor's CAPM, Fischer Black saw how to do what Fisher could not. In his Financial Note No. 2, he had helped Treynor work out the mathematics involved in applying CAPM to the capital budgeting problem of the firm. And in his Financial Note No. 6 he had himself used CAPM to treat the problem of "Individual Investment and Consumption under Uncertainty." These were the first two approximations of Irving Fisher, but now done for the case of uncertainty. All that remained was to put them together. In Financial Note No. 8 Fischer did just that, albeit for very special assumptions about technology. The result was his wheat model of business fluctuation.

The standard CAPM starts with an exogenously given supply of various different securities, and proceeds to work out a theory of market-clearing security prices given the risk preferences of wealth holders. In equilibrium everyone holds the market portfolio and adjusts risk exposure by borrowing or lending at the risk-free rate. What Fischer did in his wheat model was to conceive of the assets in CAPM as real rather than financial, specifically as varieties of wheat in a one-period agricultural cycle, which moreover become assets endogenously because someone chooses to plant the wheat rather than consume it. In equilibrium, both the market portfolio of wheat varieties and the price of that market portfolio are determined, so the model is about general equilibrium not just security price equilibrium. Even so, the model inherits the essential feature of CAPM that the prices of all capital goods derive from just two fundamental prices of capital, the rate of interest and the price of risk. These two prices, and two prices only, are sufficient statistics that summarize production opportunities and investor preferences throughout the entire economy.[17]

For Irving Fisher, thinking about a world of certainty, the rate of interest was the sustainable rate of income flow from the current capital stock. For Fischer Black, thinking about a world of uncertainty, the rate of interest was simply the realized return on the stock of capital, a number, moreover, that was a random variable fluctuating over time. What we see as fluctuations in aggregate income are thus, at the highest level of abstraction, merely the fluctuating return on capital.

One problem with the simple wheat model is that it doesn't really tell us anything about unemployment, which is the main reason that most people care about the business cycle in the first place. But we can expand the model to treat unemployment by bringing in multiple goods and roundabout production using labor (or better, human capital). Then a boom is a period when the pattern of production is a good match for the pattern of demand, and a recession is a period when the match is bad. When the match is bad, that means people are working in the wrong economic sectors, producing the wrong mix of outputs. A bad match means that prices and wages will shift in order to encourage workers to shift from one sector to another, but those shifts take time since they typically involve accumulation of sector-specific capital. The mismatch theory of cycles in output is thus also a theory of cycles in employment.

If the business cycle is nothing more than the fluctuating value of capital, it follows that if we want to understand what causes business cycles, what we actually need to understand is why the value of capital fluctuates as it does. The salient fact is that it fluctuates a great deal, as we know because we observe one measure of that fluctuation in the stock market. Sometimes the return on stocks is even negative. What explains such dramatic volatility?

One potential culprit can be dismissed immediately. The wide fluctuation of the stock market cannot be fluctuation in the expected return, which is the sum of the risk-free rate and a risk premium. There is simply not enough variation in either one to account for the swings we see in capital valuation. Indeed, as a first approximation, Fischer thought that both numbers should be treated as constants.

Another possible culprit is speculation that causes stock prices to fluctuate in a wide band around their fundamental value. This was and remains a rather prevalent view among economists, as for example Robert Shiller, the 1972 PhD student of Franco Modigliani who would become internationally famous for his book *Irrational Exuberance*.[18] If we think of the economy as a stationary stochastic process evolving over time, then the stock market fluctuates too much; hence investors must be irrational.

Fischer had a different view. The volatility of stock prices makes perfect sense if the world is nonstationary, as he believed it was. In a nonstationary world, the range of possible futures that investors need to assess in order to form estimates of current value is much wider than in a stationary world. In a nonstationary world, prices won't be very good estimates of value, but they will probably be the best estimates we have, and maybe even the best estimates we *can* have. Since discount rates don't vary much, the reason that capital values are so volatile must be that expectations of future income values shift around a lot. It's just the dark forces of time and uncertainty at work.

In a nutshell, Fischer's view is that the return on capital fluctuates so much because future income values are so uncertain, and future income values are so uncertain because the details matter. Firms know that people in the future will want food, and housing, and transportation services, but they don't know exactly what kind. Firms must make investment and production decisions without knowing the details that they would have to know in order to be sure they were doing the right thing. If they are lucky, they will turn out to have guessed right, so they'll be able to sell what they produce, and income values will be high. If they are unlucky, they will turn out to have guessed wrong, so they won't be able to sell what they produce, and income values will be low. In the meantime, individual capital values will fluctuate because new information keeps coming in that causes us to change our estimates up or down. And the total value of capital will also fluctuate because new information tends to affect all individual values in the same direction. New information either increases or decreases the probability of a good match between production and demand in the future.

The mismatch idea was in Fischer's mind at least as early as March 1976, but it was two years before he produced what he considered to be a proper academic treatment, "General Equilibrium and Business Cycles" (April 1978). He had high hopes for the paper, as he took it around the academic seminar circuit to workshops at Carnegie-Mellon University, the Federal Reserve Bank of Minneapolis, MIT, Stanford University, the University of California at Berkeley and at Los Angeles, the University of Chicago, the University of Pennsylvania, and the University of Southern California. In September 1978 he produced a revised draft, with a long footnote thanking 46 individual people for comments. But he was unable to find a reputable academic journal willing to publish it.

In 1979, he managed to get some of his ideas out in a long interview with the business magazine *Fortune*.[19] In 1981 the *Financial Analysts Journal* published a popular version under the title, "The ABCs of Business Cycles." But for an academic audience, the best that Fischer could manage was publication as Working Paper No. 950 (August 1982) in the National Bureau of Economic Research series. The *American Economic Review* rejected the paper outright. It was a discouraging experience for Fischer. What was the problem?

One problem certainly was the high level of abstraction from which Fischer approached the question of business fluctuation. Notably, his theory made no contact with the actual data of business cycle fluctuation. Indeed, Fischer actively resisted any contact that would involve econometric techniques he considered to be fatally flawed. Moreover, his theory also made no contact with the models that economists already used to talk about business fluctuation, models that typically did make contact with the data even if they did not provide fully satisfactory explanations of it. All such models, Keynesian and monetarist alike, included monetary fluctuation as an important part of the explanation of output fluctuation, but of course this mechanism was completely absent from Fischer's theory, consistent with his unorthodox views on money. Fischer's theory thus offered no point of traction where traditional macroeconomists, of whatever stripe, could connect with Fischer or he with them. The result was that it was not Fischer Black, but rather Robert Lucas, who ushered in the revolution in macroeconomics that took place in the late 1970s.

Born in 1937, Lucas came to economics late, after a BA in history, but in time to earn his PhD in economics from the University of Chicago in 1964. By his own reckoning, his key intellectual influences were Milton Friedman, as conveyed in the graduate classroom, and Paul Samuelson, as conveyed in his classic 1947 book of mathematical economics, *Foundations of Economic Analysis*. After spending the first decade of his career at Carnegie-Mellon, Lucas returned to Chicago in 1974 as Ford Foundation Visiting Research Professor and stayed on permanently for the rest of his career. In 1995 he would be awarded the Nobel Prize for work he did in the 1970s that "developed and applied the hypothesis of rational expectations, and thereby . . . transformed macroeconomic analysis and deepened our understanding of economic policy."

The hypothesis of rational expectations was for macroeconomics what the hypothesis of efficient markets was for finance. It said that, as a matter of theoretical discipline, economists ought to model agents (both firms and consumers) as making the best use of whatever information they have about their environment, specifically so when forming expectations about the future to guide their behavior in the present. If as economists we posit a world with certain features, then we ought to assume that behavior in that world takes into account all the same features in some optimal way. It doesn't sound like such a radical idea, but in fact it had very radical consequences because it meant that every model that made some other assumption about how expectations were formed had to be revisited. The hypothesis of rational expectations thus undermined existing models, but in a way that made maximal contact with those models. Economists did not have to throw out what they knew, but only to change one underlying assumption and work out the changed consequences.

The work of Lucas formed the core of an intellectual movement that Yale economist James Tobin would call Monetarism Mark II, the successor to Milton Friedman's Monetarism Mark I.[20] Whatever the name—the movement called itself "new classical macroeconomics"— the key idea was captured in the title of a famous paper by Lucas published in 1975, "An Equilibrium Model of the Business Cycle." In his subsequent 1977 manifesto, "Understanding Business Cycles," Lucas went even farther, explicitly endorsing the economic research program of Friedrich von Hayek, the great Austrian anti-Keynesian. Says Hayek: "The incorporation of cyclical phenomena into the system of economic equilibrium theory, with which they are in apparent contradiction, remains the crucial problem of Trade Cycle Theory."[21] That's the problem that Lucas said he was trying to solve. It was also the problem that Fischer was trying to solve.

Fischer knew the work of Lucas quite well. The two men had met in the early 1970s when Lucas came to Chicago to give a paper in Friedman's Monetary Workshop, and they had subsequently overlapped on the Chicago faculty for a year before Fischer left for MIT.[22] In early drafts of his own theory, Fischer refers to the work of Lucas as closer to his own than that of any other economist. The problem was that Lucas didn't go far enough, because the Lucas models were not really full equilibrium models. In the model of his 1975 paper, for example, Lucas had business fluctuations being driven by exogenous fluctuations in monetary policy, which Fischer had long before decided was inconsistent with equilibrium. Fischer presented his own work as doing better than Lucas by explaining business cycles without introducing any disequilibrium elements at all.

But Lucas was not convinced. Most important, he was unwilling to give up the quantity theory of money. In the end Fischer was forced to conclude that "the rational expectations theories are really cleaned-up monetary theories. No amount of cleaning, though, can disguise the fact that all these theories are disequilibrium theories. In every one of them there is a way for individuals to profit if the world works as the theory says it does."[23]

In effect, Fischer came to see Lucas as Mark II monetarism, much as Tobin did. But unlike Tobin he thought that the Keynesian theories were equally problematic. Says Fischer: "That's why my theories are anti-Keynesian. . . . Keynesians assume that people act against their own interests in systematic and massive ways."[24] With views like that, it is no wonder that Fischer had trouble publishing. There was simply no academic constituency for a theory that both Keynesians and monetarists saw, quite correctly, as providing aid and succor to their intellectual opponents. Fischer had been rejected before, many times in fact, but always he had found a way back in. Now he began to consider that maybe he didn't want back in.

Fischer's last years at MIT were full of rejection, but it wasn't personal. Indeed, it is fair to say that the mainstream of macroeconomics hardly even noticed him. Practically everyone except Fischer was lined up on one side or another of the increasingly fractious debate between the Keynesians and monetarists, a debate in which the monetarists had been steadily gaining ground through the 1970s. At the end of the decade the monetarist side got an extra boost when the outside political world quite suddenly tipped over from policy optimism to policy pessimism.

First to go was the United Kingdom, as Margaret Thatcher was elected prime minister. Soon thereafter, monetarism became the official monetary policy of the United States after Paul Volcker was appointed chairman of the Federal Reserve System. Then in November 1980, conservative Republican Ronald Reagan was elected president in a landslide over incumbent Democrat Jimmy Carter. True to form, in this sea change election Fischer identified politically with neither the Democrats nor the Republicans. He supported John Anderson, the failed third party candidate who ran on the National Unity Party ticket.

In the narrower world of macroeconomics there was another third party getting organized, alternative to both Tobin and Lucas, and Fischer took an interest. Two papers, one by Finn Kydland and Edward Prescott (Carnegie-Mellon and University of Minnesota respectively) and a second by John Long and Charles Plosser (both at the University of Rochester), launched what would turn out to be the next big thing in academic macroeconomics.[25] In just a few years it would sweep traditional monetarism and Keynesianism both off the academic stage, and in 2004 Kydland and Prescott would share the Nobel Prize for it. The title of Long and Plosser's paper gave the movement its name: "Real Business Cycles." The idea was to see how far one could get in explaining business cycles with a simple general equilibrium model without any money. The basic idea sounds like what Fischer had proposed years before, but the implementation followed rather different lines.

In brief, the idea was to build on the neoclassical growth theory that Robert Solow had developed around the concept of an aggregate production function. Solow had used the construct to draw attention to the large portion of output growth that cannot be attributed to growth in either capital or labor, a "residual" that he attributed instead to technological change. The idea of real business cycle (RBC) theory was to use the same construct to draw attention to the large portion of output *fluctuation* that cannot be attributed to fluctuation in either capital or labor, and then to attribute the residual to technological fluctuation. According to Kydland and Prescott, exogenous technology shocks explain most of the business cycle fluctuations we observe.

Fischer didn't think much of this line of argument. Because the real business cycle authors emphasize aggregate shocks, unemployment in their model takes the form of intertemporal substitution of leisure for work. To Fischer, this just didn't sound right, but he made no headway in persuading them to follow his alternative mismatch theory.[26] More generally, Fischer's criticism of the nascent RBC movement was the same as his criticism of the new classical movement that had preceded it. Both were moving in the direction of full general equilibrium, but both also held fast to special assumptions and restrictions that had no place in the most general model. In the case of Lucas, the problem had been a prior commitment to the quantity theory of money. In the case of the RBC school, the problem was a prior commitment to an overly aggregative formulation of market equilibrium, and also to econometrics.

Instead of estimating individual equations as the Keynesians liked to do, the new RBC school preferred to "calibrate" an entire simple equilibrium model to match selected key features of the data.[27] But Fischer had no more use for RBC econometrics Mark II than he had for Keynesian econometrics Mark I. In an apparent attempt to nip the new econometrics in the bud, in 1982 Fischer chose finally to publish his long-standing views on the subject. The "Trouble with Econometric Models" that he identified at the very beginning of his academic career was now taking a different form, but it was the same basic trouble. As he would later write, "They have some success at this, but I don't see what we learn from it. . . . Successful calibration does not imply that a model has correct structure any more than correlation implies causation."[28]

The end result was that the emerging RBC school did not provide sufficient incentive to tempt Fischer to stay in academia. When colleagues asked why he was leaving, Fischer would say that he felt his creativity had been flagging. These were strong words coming from a man who valued creativity above all else, and yet rather oblique coming from a man who believed, ever since his undergraduate encounter with the young Jerome Bruner, in "Creativity as a Process." If his creativity was flagging, it was because something had gone wrong with the process.

Given the direction in which macroeconomics was apparently heading, the opportunity for conversations that would stimulate the economic side of his intellectual interests seemed to be narrowing. Since that was the way he developed his ideas, he drew the conclusion that he could not expect from himself any more creativity along those lines.

Fortunately his human capital was fairly well diversified. He could simply shift his emphasis from economics to finance, just as his economist critics had been urging him to do all these years. At the same time, he could also shift from the abstract theory favored by academics to the practical application favored by business, much as his wife and father had been urging him to do all these years. Anyway, he knew from experience that it was just as easy to have good conversations about financial problems outside of academia as inside, maybe even easier.

Put another way, it could be said that Fischer left academia because it was no longer the setting in which his human capital had the highest expected return. Long years before, he had placed his bets and arranged the sectoral allocation of his human capital with a different end in mind. He had tried to use finance to foment an intellectual revolution in macroeconomics. But luck was not with him and the match he had imagined did not ultimately work out. Instead, Robert Lucas was the one producing the product that the market wanted. There was nothing left to do but to accept the market's verdict, and bear the cost of a sectoral switch. Years before Fischer had left consulting in favor of academia when his experience at Wells Fargo made him realize that the practical world of business was not yet ready for his ideas. Now the practical world of business seemed more ready than academia, so he switched back.

Appendix 8.A   THE CAMBRIDGE CAPITAL CONTROVERSY

Suppose we buy Irving Fisher's idea that the value of wealth is a good proxy for social welfare, and suppose we buy Fischer Black's idea that the level of the stock market can be interpreted as a good proxy for wealth even though most wealth is unmeasured human capital. We still have a problem. How do we know that an increase in the dollar price of stocks is an increase in real wealth? Irving Fisher worried about just this problem, and he advocated for a stable dollar because otherwise the dollar value of future services might go up even as the real quantity of services was going down, simply because of price inflation.

Unlike Irving Fisher, Fischer Black was not concerned about inflation,[29] but he did worry about another measurement problem. Ideally we'd like a way to measure the quantity of capital separate from the price of capital, just as we measure bushels of wheat separately from the price of wheat. Unfortunately, and somewhat surprisingly, what we want turns out to be impossible—as Fischer well knew, since, just about the time he was getting interested in economics, a long-standing controversy on exactly this question was finally getting resolved.

Called the Cambridge capital controversy because it involved mainly economists at Cambridge University in England on one side arguing with economists at MIT in Cambridge, Massachusetts, on the other side, the argument was about whether the concept of a quantity of aggregate capital made logical sense. Finally everyone agreed that, as a matter of strict logic, it did not, although argument continued about whether that logical problem has any very significant empirical consequence.[30] As a student of Quine, Fischer was naturally inclined to accept the logical argument as definitive. He is referring to the logical result when he writes in 1975: "It's not clear to me whether you can distinguish between an increase in the value of a unit of capital and an increase in the number of units. If you can, I'm not sure how. You certainly can't count the units."[31]

In 1975, he recognized the problem involved in measuring capital but hadn't yet determined how to handle it. In his wheat model he had simply sidestepped the measurement problem by making convenient assumptions.[32] Eventually he would arrive at the idea that the market value of capital is already a measure of the quantity of capital, in efficiency units, so we don't need to go behind market value to distinguish the units from their value.[33] Meanwhile, the most important point is that the market value of capital fluctuates very widely, and almost all of that fluctuation must involve changing values, not changing units.[34]

■ Chapter Nine ■

CHANGING FIELDS

When things go badly, some people react by doubling their bets. They in-crease their exposure to risk in hopes of recouping their losses. On the other hand, when things go well they may reduce their exposure to risk so they can't lose what they have won. It's a very common gambling strategy and it's a very common philosophy of life.

Fischer Black, "Why and How Does an Investor Diversify?" *Fischer Black on Markets,* Vol. 1, No. 5 (1976, p. 6)

The rejection of Fischer's business cycle theory placed additional stress on a marriage that already had its share of trouble. Mimi no doubt hoped that Fischer would finally give up his quixotic academic quest and focus instead on his family, maybe switching over to a more lucra-tive career path. She was, understandably, tired of raising four children more or less by herself and with not much money. Meanwhile Fischer likely hoped that Mimi would finally recognize the importance of what he was doing and provide him with the kind of supportive family life he needed to do his best work. He told a favorite student, "Long ago I realized that I could be a great husband or a great scientist, but not both. I've made my choice." They were at hopeless cross purposes.

As the marriage deteriorated, Fischer's office became in effect his home. He would arrive before anyone else, as early as 6:30 A.M., and was often the last to leave, as late as 11:00 P.M. Finally, sometime in late 1981, Mimi threw Fischer out again and this time he decided not to go back. Instead he answered an ad and rented a room in the house of Bill and Mary Clinton at 103 Ronald Road in Arlington. For the next few years the Clintons and their two children provided a kind of adopted family for Fischer, a home where he could come and go, engage and disengage, at a rhythm of his own choosing. In the summer of 1983, when the Clintons bought a larger house at 241 East Emerson Road in Lexington, Fischer moved with them, buying a half interest in the property. The idea was to have a place where he could bring his four girls after the divorce, which would become final in November 1983.

Meanwhile, Wall Street was beginning to discover the value in academic finance, hiring finance professors as consultants and recruiting master's students as permanent employees. At first the academics had been isolated in special research departments away from the business of the firm, but by the early 1980s that was beginning to change. Consulting for Goldman Sachs, Robert Merton convinced Robert Rubin, then head of the Equities division, that there might be a place for a finance person at a high level within the firm, where he could infuse the ideas of academic finance into all the various business areas. Back at MIT, Merton told Fischer about the opportunity and asked which of their students he should recommend. After thinking about it for a while, Fischer came back to Merton: "Bob, I'd be interested in that job." This was December 1983, in the middle of the academic year.

And so it happened that, in February 1984, Fischer moved to New York to start a new life at Goldman Sachs. He rented a small apartment in Battery Park City so he could walk to work, but mainly he lived at his office. On weekends he drove his Roadmaster station wagon to Boston to see his daughters, keeping himself company with audiotapes of Broadway shows and lectures of Friedrich von Hayek. It wasn't an ideal arrangement, but it did provide the respite he needed. Away from academia, and away from Mimi, he started to put his life back together again.

After a few years, when he became president of the American Finance Association, he took the opportunity to collect all of his economics papers, most of them unpublished and unpublishable during his sojourn in academia, in a book he titled *Business Cycles and Equilibrium*. He arranged the articles chronologically, and published them exactly as he had written them, with no reference to any more recent developments in economics. It was his swan song to economics. Looking back in 1995, he would recall: "I have found Goldman better for learning than a university, partly because the firm's business requires continual learning as it adapts to new conditions."[1]

It is clear, then, why Fischer left academia for Goldman Sachs, but why did Goldman Sachs hire Fischer out of academia? Certainly not for his unorthodox macroeconomics. Nor were they probably much interested in his demonstrated achievements in academic finance, all of which were anyway available for free in the public domain. No, what made the fit was Fischer's unusually deep and intellectual approach to the practical problems of everyday business finance. The Fischer that Goldman hired was not the tenured professor at the University of Chicago and MIT, but the young man who learned finance from Jack Treynor and honed his skills consulting for Wells Fargo. The Fischer they wanted was the author of *Fischer Black on Options* and *Fischer Black on Markets*, two newsletters that he distributed in 1976–1977 to subscribers of his options service and others.

More immediately, what must have appealed to Goldman Sachs was not Fischer's theory of money, but rather his work on pension fund investment policy, the theory of business accounting, and practical methods of capital budgeting. In this work they could see how Fischer might add value by helping their clients think more deeply about the practical problems they were encountering in everyday business. In fact, all three of these projects have their origin in conversations with Treynor way back at the beginning of Fischer's career in finance. In academia they were side projects. At Goldman Sachs they, and projects like them, would be at the center of Fischer's attention.

Writing in 1972, Jack Treynor sounded an alarm. Corporations were promising pension benefits to their employees, but taking no very substantial steps to ensure their ability to fulfill on their promises. "Ultimately many pension beneficiaries are going to wake up to find that their investment losses have deprived them of their main source of support in retirement."[2] Treynor urged that promised pension benefits be recognized as proper liabilities of the firm, and hence as claims not just to specifically designated pension fund assets but also to the general assets of the firm itself. In his mind, the ambiguous status of pension benefits served to disguise a fundamental conflict of interest. If the firm did well, shareholders enjoyed the upside, while if the firm did poorly, pension beneficiaries absorbed the downside.[3] The ambiguity served to increase current stock value to the benefit of shareholders, but only to the extent that pension promises were a fraud.

On Labor Day 1974, President Ford signed into law the landmark Employee Retirement Income Security Act (ERISA), which addressed exactly Treynor's problem, but not to his satisfaction. The Act required corporations to fully fund vested pension benefits, but did little more to ensure the security of those benefits than to insert a new government agency, the Pension Benefit Guaranty Corporation (PBGC), between the shareholders and pensioners. The conflict of interest thus remained, but now with the government absorbing (some of) the downside losses that formerly fell on the shoulders of individual pensioners. Like deposit insurance for banks, the PBGC effectively gave firms an option—heads I win, and tails you lose—that would encourage them to take even more risk with the assets in their pension plans.

For Treynor, a better way would have been to require firms to maintain sufficient equity so as to be able to meet accumulated pension liabilities even in bad times. Just like any other creditor of the firm, pension beneficiaries should be able to force reorganization and recapitalization whenever the equity buffer falls short. That was Treynor's preferred approach but, as he always noted, there was also another way.

The alternative was to require firms to set aside pension assets that exactly matched their accrued pension liabilities. If we think of vested benefits as a promise to make a definite set of cash payments, then this alternative approach calls for pension assets to be invested in fixed income instruments with the exact same pattern of cash flows. In this way, benefits could be made completely secure quite independent of the equity of the sponsoring firm. Treynor himself did not pursue this line, but Fischer Black did.

Instead of emphasizing conflict between shareholders and pensioners, Fischer emphasized the common interest that derived from the special tax status of pension fund assets. Suppose the firm faces an unfunded pension liability of $100 million. It can meet that obligation by issuing $100 million of its own bonds, transfer the proceeds to the pension fund, and then use the funds to buy a diversified portfolio of bonds with risk similar to that of its own bonds. If we think of pension assets as assets of the firm, this funding operation changes nothing on the combined balance sheet. The beauty of it comes later because the interest the firm pays on the bonds it issues is tax deductible, while the interest it receives on the bonds it holds in the pension fund is not subject to tax. In effect, what Fischer proposes is a simple tax arbitrage that makes both shareholders and pensioners better off at the expense of the government, which will collect fewer taxes. The real beauty of the arbitrage is that it gives pensioners exactly what they want, namely guaranteed pension benefits.

Fischer first broached the proposal as early as July 1973, well before it was clear what ERISA would do, and then first published it in the *Financial Analysts Journal* in 1976 under the title "The Investment Policy Spectrum: Individuals, Endowment Funds, and Pension Funds."[4] The proposal was only a few paragraphs in a much longer article covering many other matters. Probably Fischer thought the financial incentive was so large that he had only to point it out and eager corporate treasurers would immediately adopt his plan. But that's not what happened. A few years later he tried again, this time with a stand-alone article with an unambiguous title, "The Tax Consequences of Long-Run Pension Policy," published again in the *Financial Analysts Journal* in 1980. "My message is simple: Almost every corporate pension fund should be entirely in fixed dollar instruments."[5] By this time, his voice had been joined by others, but even so without much effect on pension fund investment practice.[6]

The main problem, as he came to understand, was that almost no one in the business world looked at the problem the way he and Treynor did, by viewing the firm and its pension fund as a single entity. The typical corporate financial officer tended to see any proposal for the firm to issue $100 million in bonds as a dangerous increase in firm leverage. And the typical corporate pension fund manager tended to see any proposal to invest pension assets entirely in bonds as a dangerously conservative policy likely to produce insufficient return to meet pension obligations. In his next version of the plan, "A New Investment Strategy for Pension Funds" (prepared with the help of one of his MIT students, Moray P. Dewhurst), Fischer did his best to meet the former leverage objection by emphasizing explicitly how, once you include pension assets, leverage does not increase.

One person who was not convinced was Peter Glasser, a "member of the post-ERISA enfant terrible school of pension administrators," according to *Institutional Investor*, who had been appointed assistant treasurer of Cyclops Steel at only 34 years old.[7] Having just convinced his CEO to keep the firm's pension assets in stock despite the dismal performance record of the 1970s, he was not happy to hear Fischer's advice that he should be completely in bonds, and he fired off a critical letter to Fischer at MIT. In the subsequent exchange of letters, the "prudent man" standard promulgated by ERISA emerged as the principal bone of contention.[8]

Glasser argued that the legal standard requires maximizing the likelihood that pension obligations will be met, which implies investment in securities with high expected return (and hence high risk). Fischer argued to the contrary that the standard requires maximizing the present value of promised pension obligations, which implies investments in bonds with low risk (and hence low expected return). Fischer welcomed the exchange, since Glasser was exactly the kind of person he hoped to reach. He arranged for their correspondence to be published in the *Financial Analysts Journal* with the hope of reaching other open-minded treasurers, and began flying around the country at his own expense to promote the strategy to anyone who would listen.

When Fischer took his idea on the road, he had the thought that, quite apart from it being a good idea, he might make some money from it. As an investment adviser to the pension funds that might decide to follow his strategy, he stood to make a percentage of all the assets under management. Pension money was big money, and getting bigger every day as a result of ERISA. Even a tiny percentage of such a big number would still be a big number, certainly enough to replace his increasingly unsatisfactory academic salary, and maybe even enough to save his marriage. But he couldn't get anyone interested. Fischer was, as usual, too far ahead of his potential clients.

At Goldman Sachs, however, with an entire investment bank behind him, he thought he might have better luck. At least he would have the opportunity to present his proposal to clients as one of a number of alternatives for them to consider. In an unpublished 1987 memo titled "Managing Pension Assets: Four Views," he presents his own view ("the most comprehensive view") as the final one. While recognizing that a case could be made for investing pension assets in stock, Fischer continued to insist that "the firm's strongest protection against a recession will be a pension plan invested entirely in cash, since short-term fixed income securities are the best defense against possible disaster."[9] In 1995, in one of his very last memos, published in abbreviated form as "The Plan Sponsor's Goal," Fischer continued to hold fast to his original position. "Because the pension plan is a con-duit rather than an individual, I question the usual formulation of the plan sponsor's goals."[10]

In fact, by 1995, the usual formulation of the plan sponsor's goal had become largely moot, but for a very different reason. Back when Treynor and Fischer were getting started, before ERISA changed the landscape, the typical corporate pension plan promised benefits tied to the employee's time in service and salary, and not tied at all to the returns realized on the assets set aside to fund those benefits. Under such a so-called defined benefit plan, the corporation shouldered the burden of investment risk, including the responsibility to make up the difference in case of poor performance. Fischer's proposal showed how to eliminate that risk by careful asset allocation. But corporations found an easier way.

The same ERISA that required corporations to fully fund their traditional defined benefit pension plans also provided an alternative, the so-called defined contribution plan colloquially known today as a 401(k) plan after the relevant section of ERISA. In such a plan, employers make cash contributions to the pension fund, and that is the end of their financial obligation. All investment risk is borne by the employee, not the firm. The problem of ensuring pension benefits thus becomes a problem of lifetime individual investment, not a problem of corporate finance.

As a partner at Goldman Sachs, Fischer necessarily held most of his personal wealth in the firm, where it was exposed to very considerable risk. He was, however, free to invest the rest of his wealth any way he wanted. He had long taken the position that "pension liabilities should be funded with the safest instruments available—perhaps insurance contracts."[11] And that is exactly what he did with his own wealth, putting all of it in guaranteed investment contracts, which are short-term instruments issued by insurance companies. They were, he thought, even safer than Treasury bills because of the provision that you could redeem them from the issuer for full face value even before the stated maturity. As always, Fischer practiced what he preached.

In 1972, Jack Treynor sounded another alarm in an article titled "The Trouble with Earnings." This time his target was the accountant, "the oldest of the professionals in the investment industry," and therefore the one most resistant to replacing craft with science, and the one most insistent on holding fast to "accounting ritual" in the face of rational judgment. The problem was that the most important output of the accounting ritual, namely a measure of "accounting earnings," bears no very close relationship to the "economic earnings" that the security analyst wants for his calculation of the value of the firm.

In Treynor's view, the security analyst poses a deadly threat to the accountant, since the security analyst's modern and scientific method of judging the worth of a company is demonstrably superior. What the world wants to know is the value of the firm, not the change in value with which the accountant is obsessed. There is no room for both the analyst and the accountant, because one is rational and the other is ritual. The best thing would be for the accountant to disclose as much information as he (or she) knows about the firm, with as little ritualistic processing as possible, and leave the rest up to the analyst.

Fischer's lifelong engagement with the problems of accounting starts here, but characteristically he finds a more positive approach. Although there could be no question that the theories of modern finance require far-reaching changes in accounting practice, there could also be no question that at the end of the day the role of the accountant would remain important and distinct from that of the security analyst. Simple disclosure could not be the answer, because anything disclosed to the analyst is also disclosed to competitors. In this respect, "an accountant's job is to conceal, not to reveal."[12] Even more, because the accountant is privy to a great deal of proprietary information inside the firm, he should in principle be able to produce a better estimate of the firm's value than the analyst. The goal should therefore be not to replace the accountant but to redirect his attention toward the task of estimating value.

In fact, existing accounting practice already manages to convey some pretty useful information about firm value, albeit in somewhat garbled form, as Fischer had reason to know from his study of Value Line. The fact that Value Line was able, using only publicly available accounting data, to predict dependably which individual stocks will outperform and which underperform, could only mean that there is information in accounting data that is not yet in the market price.[13] Of course Value Line has to do a number of transformations on the data in order to produce their own estimates of value, but that is just the point. Wouldn't it be better to have the accountants themselves, inside the firm, doing the transformations needed to report the firm's value, rather than concentrating so much on measuring earnings?

According to Fischer, what the security analyst really wants is an earnings number that he (or she) can multiply by a standard price-earnings ratio in order to get the firm's value. To the extent that the accountant responds to the needs of the analyst, he will therefore be driven to report as earnings something that is *already* a measure of value, even though historical precedent keeps him talking about that number as if it were the change in value from one period to the next. In fact, actual earnings numbers are pretty close to being a random walk,[14] which is to say that they already behave as if they were asset values in an efficient market. And earnings are also already more highly correlated with market value than any other accounting aggregate, including book value.[15] So accountants are already implicitly reporting value in the guise of earnings. Imagine how much better accountants could do if they embraced the goal of estimating value explicitly. In an issue of his newsletter published in July 1976, Fischer proposed that accountants explicitly treat "earnings as a measure of value, not change in value."[16]

Treynor and Fischer were, of course, not the only people thinking about the implications of modern finance for accounting standards. In November 1978 the Financial Accounting Standards Board (FASB) weighed in with a document that would be seen as a watershed for the subsequent evolution of the profession. Its Statement of Financial Accounting Concepts No. 1, titled "Objectives of Financial Reporting by Business Enterprises," stated:

> Financial reporting should provide information that is useful to present and potential investors and creditors and other users in making rational investment, credit, and similar decisions. . . .

"Investors" and "creditors" are used broadly and include not only those who have or contemplate having a claim to enterprise resources but also those who advise or represent them.

On the face of it, FASB was directing accountants to provide the information that analysts find useful. The Chicago-trained economist William Beaver, in his best-selling 1981 textbook *Financial Reporting: An Accounting Revolution*, would characterize the 1978 document as marking the shift from a focus on "stewardship" of the firm's assets to a focus on "information" about the future prospects of the firm as an entity.

But in the very same document FASB also reiterated the traditional focus of accounting practice: "The primary focus of financial reporting is information about earnings and its components. . . . Financial accounting is not designed to measure directly the value of a business enterprise, but the information it provides may be helpful to those who wish to estimate its value." Suffice it to say, in 1978 the accounting profession was still in play. The 1978 FASB report was not the end of the revolution in accounting, but the beginning.

Fischer's response to FASB 1978 was to elaborate further his idea that accountants should adopt rules to make their measure of earnings into a measure of value. In a famous article titled "The Magic in Earnings,"[17] he proposed that the goal of accounting should be to come up with a number that the analyst needs only to multiply by a constant, say 10, in order to arrive at an estimate of value. In effect, the goal is to internalize within the firm all the various adjustments that the analyst sitting outside the firm would do himself if he had access to the detailed information available to the accountant. There is no need for the accountant to disclose detailed information that might be helpful to the firm's competitors. All he needs to disclose is aggregate earnings.

In effect, Fischer sees the accountant and the analyst doing the same thing but in very different institutional settings and with access to different data. Both are trying to estimate value, using the best methods they can find. And both are critical for ensuring the efficiency of pricing for firms with traded stocks. Indeed, accountants are even more critical for firms without traded stocks, since value is a critical guide to the efficient allocation of resources.

Fischer's idea that accounting values and market values are two separate attempts to measure the same thing suggests a practical method for improving accounting rules. If the stock market is efficient, we should be able to test different accounting rules by seeing how well their estimates correlate with the stock price. Our goal should be to come up with a set of rules that makes the price-earnings ratio as stable as possible, both over time and across firms. Working with one of his MBA students, Stephen Stickells, Fischer measured the co-movement of various accounting measures with stock prices, and confirmed earlier work that suggested the closest correlation was with primary earnings before extraordinary items.

Having thus arrived at what he thought was a satisfactory conceptual basis for a new theory of accounting, Fischer set himself the task of learning the details of existing accounting practice. In fall 1980, he volunteered to teach for the first time a class in accounting, and he spent the semester working his way through the standard textbook with the students. By the end of the semester only three students remained in the class, but Fischer didn't mind. He wasn't trying to teach so much as he was trying to learn.

What he learned was that the biggest concrete challenge for his goal of treating earnings as a measure of value was to find rules to prevent earnings from showing a negative value in a bad quarter. After all, it makes no sense for a firm to have negative value. "Creative accounting" was the answer. Accountants were long accustomed to receiving pressure from management to find ways to make bad quarters look better, and sometimes they even succumbed to that pressure, albeit with trepidation about possible violation of professional standards. Now comes Fischer telling them that they should have no such trepidation, and that creative accounting is potentially a good thing provided that it is disciplined by a focus on the estimation of value. For Fischer, the purpose of creative accounting is not to lie about the condition of the firm, but rather to tell the truth. The purpose of creative accounting is, or rather should be, to make accounting earnings more closely reflect firm value.

Having given the accountants what he thought they needed, namely permission to indulge in creativity within clearly defined bounds, Fischer moved on to other things. Probably he expected accountants to pick up the ball and run with it. But ten years later he checked back in and found, after a comprehensive review of the literature, that the accountants had not picked up the ball, so he decided to do so himself.[18] An update of his earlier empirical work showed that the primary earnings number was still more highly correlated with stock price than other possible accounting measures (including book value, which, unlike earnings, is actually supposed to measure value). So the question was how that primary earnings number might be improved.

Fischer's idea was a simple one. Observing that a company's stock can be viewed as an option (with strike price equal to the face value of outstanding debt), it follows that if earnings is to be a measure of value, then earnings, too, must be an option. So he proceeded to calculate the option value of accounting earnings by treating fixed costs (such as interest and depreciation) as the strike price. The resulting options-adjusted earnings number had the attractive feature that it was always positive since, even when an option is far out of the money (when unadjusted earnings are negative) there is always some probability that future good luck will bring it back into the money. And it had the further attractive feature that it correlated even better with the stock price than did unadjusted earnings.

So there it was, a simple adjustment that anyone could do. "Option valuation is challenging, but so is the reality the firm is trying to describe. I think it's time to add option theory, which is now part of the mainstream, to the language of accounting." It was just a first step, and no doubt other people could do even better. The important thing was to get the process going.

That's what Fischer had been trying to do back in 1980 when he published "The Magic in Earnings." For Goldman Sachs, an economist interested in the fundamentals of accounting was the kind of intellectual firepower they wanted on their team. Even if their clients weren't interested, they could use him for their own internal purposes, if only to stimulate others within the firm to do better.

The third line of Fischer's work that would have interested Goldman Sachs also has its origin in Jack Treynor, this one all the way back with the capital budgeting problem that stimulated Treynor to produce his capital asset pricing model (CAPM) in the first place. The problem, it will be recalled, was how to discount uncertain future cash flows back to the present in order to calculate the value of a project the firm might be contemplating. Treynor managed to solve the problem for a single period—that was CAPM—but the extension to multiple periods defeated him. That was where matters stood until he met Fischer and showed him the problem. Fischer took an interest and managed eventually to solve the problem.

The relevant paper was Financial Note No. 2, "Corporate Investment Decisions" (September 12, 1967). The first version had a mathematical mistake that Fischer corrected in the second version (May 29, 1969). Though it was not published until 1976, well after the options paper that established his reputation, this joint paper with Treynor was actually the first substantive paper Fischer ever wrote in finance. Like everything Fischer wrote, the intuition is very strong, and the verbal account quite simple and compelling. But the mathematical model in this earliest paper is highly complex, indeed quite unsuitable for practical use, as Treynor and Black themselves freely admit. "The practical use of the value equation is severely limited by the difficulty of estimating cash flows as a function of economic variables, and, even more important, by the difficulty of estimating covariances between changes in information variables and changes in the market. The farther in the future the cash flows get, the more difficult these factors are to estimate."[19]

In practice, people handled capital budgeting problems simply by extending the familiar method for calculating present values under the assumption of certainty.[20] For a project with a stream of known future cash flows C_t, people were accustomed to calculating $PV = \Sigma C_t/(1 + R_f)^t$, where R_f is the risk-free interest rate. For a project with a stream of uncertain cash flows C_{it}, they learned to calculate $PV = E\Sigma C_{it}/(1 + R_i)^t$, where $R_i = R_f + \beta_i(ER_m - R_f)$, the expected return on an asset with the same beta as the project under scrutiny, given the expected risk premium $(ER_m - R_f)$. It's a lot simpler than the formula Treynor and Black had proposed.

But it's still not simple enough. Even this simpler formula requires that we know three things, all of which are difficult to estimate: the expected cash flow, the beta of the project, and the expected risk premium. Our investment decisions can only be as good as our estimates of these three numbers, which means they probably can't be very good.[21]

Is there a way we can do better? In November 1981, Fischer produced the first draft of his alternative, "A Simple Discounting Rule."

Instead of forming unconditional expectations about future cash flows, he suggests, why don't we focus our effort on forming expectations about a single future scenario in which the return on the market is exactly equal to the risk-free rate. In that case the risk premium is zero, so the project's beta doesn't matter, and the discount rate is just the risk-free rate. We still need to estimate cash flow, but that's one number, not three. So if it is not much harder to form conditional expectations than it is to form unconditional expectations, our estimates of present value should be better, and that means our investment decisions will be better. And if it is actually easier to form conditional expectations, the improvement can be quite large.

In seminars where he first broached this idea to his academic colleagues, Fischer would begin by asking them a question: "Is it easier to form conditional or unconditional expectations?" Put another way, is it easier to think about how your project will perform in a specific economic scenario or how it will perform on average across all possible economic scenarios? After letting them chew on the question for a while, eventually convincing themselves that conditional expectations were actually easier, Fischer would pull the rabbit out of the hat. If conditional expectations are easier, that means there is an easier way to calculate the value of an uncertain future cash flow. Once you have the conditional expectation fixed in your mind, just discount it by the market return under that same conditional expectation.

Building on this simple intuition, Fischer wrote what was in effect a manual for practical decision making, "Corporate Investment and Discounting Rules" (February 1983). "The rules in this paper are designed to take some of the mystery and complexity out of the process of making corporate investment decisions." The first of the 11 rules was "Discount Conditional Cash Flows at the Interest Rate." In a classic Fischer move, the last of the 11 rules undermines the first. "Use Pro Forma Earnings Statements Instead of Discounted Cash Flows." Apparently, Fischer viewed his theory of accounting as a deeper approach to the problem of capital budgeting than his simple discounting rule.

When Fischer traveled down to New York to meet Robert Rubin in December 1983, all his ducks were in line. On the personal front, his divorce was now final, so his only tie to Boston was his four girls, whom he was going to be able to see only on weekends anyway. On the professional front, he had spent the last three years developing three different projects, each of which demonstrated a different dimension of what he could bring to a firm like Goldman Sachs. And there was more as well: the first few issues of another newsletter, *Fischer Black on Taxes* (January and February 1981); a memo on "Four Uses of Underwriters" (March 1982); and a paper on "The Future for Financial Services" (October 1982). He was ready for Rubin, and he was ready for Goldman Sachs.

In retrospect, the academic years would seem to him like a long hiatus, an interesting detour on the road from consulting for Wells Fargo in San Francisco to consulting for Goldman Sachs in New York. Whether he consciously planned it or not, it is certainly no accident that when he felt himself coming to the end of the road in academia he reached back into his past. Reviving the lines of research he had begun in those years, he revived as well the excitement that he had felt in those years. The options pricing coup had made possible the detour into academia. But without the options pricing coup, his consulting work at Associates in Finance might well have led him to Goldman Sachs sooner or later anyway.

One person who was especially gratified with Fischer's move was his father. Finally his son had a real job. He welcomed the prodigal son with open arms, and Fischer found that he was glad to be back. Every day he would phone his parents from the office at 11 o'clock.

Another person who was especially gratified was Mimi. The divorce settlement meant that she got 40 percent of Fischer's new higher income. (Fischer had insisted on the unusual terms, in line with his conception of the marriage as an economic partnership.) Indeed, for a while it seemed like the new job might also bring the possibility of reconciliation. Fischer and Mimi went away together on a Caribbean vacation to try it out, but nothing came of it. Fischer had a new job and a lot more money, but he was still very much the same person.

Appendix 9.A   NEWSLETTER CHRONOLOGY

Fischer Black on Options, Volume 1

No. 1: "What to Do When the Puts Come" (February 9, 1976).

No. 2: "All That's Wrong with the Black–Scholes Model" (February 23, 1976).

No. 3: "The Long and the Short of Options Trading" (March 8, 1976).

No. 4: "The Long and the Short of Options Trading (Conclusion)" (March 22, 1976).

No. 5: "Why and How Does an Investor Diversify?" (April 5, 1976).

No. 6: "What Happens to Stocks When Options Start Trading" (April 19, 1976).

No. 7: "Who Should Worry about Diversification?" (April 26, 1976).

No. 8: "One Way to Estimate Volatility" (May 17, 1976).

No. 9: "What Stop Loss Orders Can and Can't Do" (June 14, 1976).

No. 10: "How We Came Up with the Option Formula" (June 21, 1976).

No. 11: "How We Came Up with the Option Formula (Conclusion)" (July 5, 1976).

No. 12: "What Should We Do about the Fools and the Gamblers?" (July 19, 1976).

No. 13: "Speculation, New Ventures, and the Economy" (August 9, 1976).

No. 14: "Stock Price Volatility Changes: Initial Tests" (August 23, 1976).

No. 15: "Stock Price Volatility Changes: Delays and Causality" (September 13, 1976).

No. 16: "Screening Options" (September 20, 1976).

No. 17: "Screening Spreads" (October 1976).

Fischer Black on Options, Volume 2

No. 1: "The Search for Put Option Values" (June 1977).

Fischer Black on Markets, Volume 1

No. 1: "Is This the Time to Switch to Bonds?" (February 17, 1976).

No. 2: "Inflation and How to Deal with It" (March 1, 1976).

No. 3: "Human Capital and Investments" (March 15, 1976).

No. 4: "Ups and Downs in Human Capital and Business" (March 29, 1976).

No. 5: "Why and How Does an Investor Diversify?" (April 12, 1976).

No. 6: "Who Should Worry about Diversification?" (April 26, 1976).

No. 7: "How Passive Monetary Policy Might Work" (May 10, 1976).

No. 8: "What a Non-monetarist Thinks" (May 24, 1976).

No. 9: "What Stop Loss Orders Can and Can't Do" (June 14, 1976).

No. 10: "The Accountant's Job" (June 28, 1976).

No. 11: "The Magic in Earnings" (July 12, 1976).

No. 12: "What Should We Do about the Fools and the Gamblers?" (July 19, 1976).

No. 13: "Speculation, New Ventures, and the Economy" (August 9, 1976).

No. 14: "Stock Price Volatility Changes: Initial Tests" (August 23, 1976).

No. 15: "Stock Price Volatility Changes: Delays and Causality" (September 13, 1976).

No. 16: "The Effects of Restricting Credit" (September 27, 1976).

■ Chapter Ten ■

WHAT DO TRADERS DO?

In this world, there will be no need for securities firms. Nonfinancial firms will issue their securities directly to investment firms. Individuals will adjust their borrowing and lending to match their spending needs, and will buy or sell shares of investment firms when they want to take more or less risk. Individuals will have no reason to own or trade in the shares of non-financial firms.

Fischer Black, "The Future for Financial Services"
(1985, p. 224)

The presidential address is the final official act of the yearlong term of president of the American Finance Association. Usually it is scheduled as the last session on the second day of the annual conference, but in 1985 the decision was made to schedule it instead for early-morning breakfast on the third day, Monday, December 30. That year the president was Fischer Black, Vice President of Trading and Arbitrage at Goldman, Sachs & Co., and the meetings were held in New York City, at the Sheraton Hotel in midtown Manhattan. The change was made with the idea that it would open the event to finance professionals on their way to work.

As breakfast was served, Robert Merton, incoming president of the Association, made the introduction. "In a series of self-administered word association tests with the name Fischer Black, I kept hitting on the same three: creative, prolific, and unorthodox." Unorthodox career path, unorthodox views on macroeconomics, and unorthodox teaching style. "As I need hardly mention, being different does not always mean being better. But in Fischer Black's case, the research record is clear." The Black–Scholes option pricing theory could serve as exemplar of the ideal research protocol that gives rise to the ideal research outcome.[1]

After Merton's introduction, Fischer stood up and the audience settled in for the usual 45 minutes to an hour. But after only 15 minutes Fischer sat down. Was he finished? Yes, he was. The audience was stunned, and not just by the unexpected hole now open in their schedule. Fischer's words rang in their heads: "We might define an efficient market as one in which price is within a factor of 2 of value; i.e., the price is more than half of value and less than twice value. By this definition, I think almost all markets are efficient almost all of the time. 'Almost all' means at least 90 percent."[2]

It was Fischer's way of getting people to talk, and talk they did. What stunned them was not the idea that price can deviate quite far from value, but the fact that Fischer Black of all people should now be promoting the idea. Hadn't he been arguing the other side for his entire academic career? Had only two years on Wall Street been enough to change his mind?

In fact, Black had been thinking along these lines well before he came to Wall Street. As early as 1982, in work he was doing with James M. Stone, then commissioner at the Commodity Futures Trading Commission but a friend of Fischer's since the early 1970s, Fischer had already been thinking about a world in which "noise traders" (who trade on noise as if it were information) have the effect of adding random noise to market prices. The noise in prices attracts other "information traders" who trade on actual information, but even after they come into the market some noise will remain. The net effect of noise trading is therefore to make prices less informative for the producers and consumers who use them to guide their economic decisions. Even though markets might be financially efficient, in the sense that there exist no opportunities for net trading profits, they may not be economically efficient because prices send the wrong signal.[3]

This distinction between financial efficiency and economic efficiency is the origin of the distinction between price and value that Fischer would make in his presidential address. His rough estimate of the scale of mispricing (the factor of 2) left the door open for those, like his friend Stone, who might want to explore the possibility of regulation. But Fischer himself was more interested in understanding mispricing as an equilibrium phenomenon. In equilibrium the noise in prices should reflect a balance between the forces making prices more noisy (the noise traders) and the forces making prices less noisy (the information traders).

Viewed against the background of Fischer's previous work, what is most notable about the noise trading idea is not any switch of sides in the great efficient markets debate, but rather the acceptance of a role for uninformed speculation even in equilibrium. "Noise makes financial markets possible, but also makes them imperfect," he says.[4] Ever since he had first learned the capital asset pricing model (CAPM) from Treynor, Fischer had thought that a world of mutual funds selling shares in a diversified equity portfolio, and banks providing elastic borrowing and lending facilities, would provide just about all we need in the way of financial services. In such a world, there would be practically no trading in individual shares, and that would be a good thing. Instead of fluctuating at the whim of "fools and gamblers," prices would be established by professional security analysts (joined by professional accountants) forming their own scientific estimates of value.

In addition to scientific finance theory, from early days Fischer thought that technology would be another force for progress, specifically the new technology of electronic computing. Hired by the New York Stock Exchange in 1970 to consult on "Helping the Specialist," Fischer produced a report advocating an electronic order book and a new type of more flexible limit order, a "participating buy order" to buy at the specialist's bid price and a "participating sell order" to sell at the specialist's asked price.[5] In effect, Fischer's idea was to help the specialist right out of a job by using computer technology "to reduce or eliminate the need for specialists, market makers, and block positioners."[6]

In all these ways, a common theme that runs throughout all of Fischer's early work was the elimination of uninformed speculation. The only exception was when it came to individual investors, the fools and gamblers who insist on trading despite the fact that doing so both increases their risk and reduces their expected return. Fischer reasoned that, since their trading hurts only themselves, we should do nothing about it and rely instead on experience to teach them the error of their ways. Says Fischer in 1977, "All the traders, even those that lose money, help investors and society generally by helping to make securities correctly priced."[7] Here he is reasoning that uninformed noise trading will wash out in the aggregate, while providing liquidity that the informed traders need to help establish the correct price. It is exactly this line of reasoning that Fischer would reconsider in his work with Stone, and by the time of his presidential address he had changed his position completely. "Noise trading actually puts noise into prices," he says.[8] But he doesn't say anything about eliminating the noise traders. Why not?

Even though the effect of noise trading is to cause market price to deviate quite far from value, it is not clear that we can do anything about it that information traders are not already doing. In an ideal world, where information is freely available, there would be no room for noise traders, or indeed for any trading at all, and price would always equal value. But in our imperfect world, where information is costly, noise traders keep the information traders in business by providing the expected profits that encourage them to gather information in the first place. In such a world price deviates from value, but it is hard to see how that consequence can be avoided. In a world where information is costly, maybe the best we can do is to help the information trader.

The big question raised by this new point of view is, Why do noise traders trade in the first place? Since they are bound to lose money to more informed traders, it makes no economic sense for them to trade, but they do so anyway. Says Fischer, "Perhaps they think the noise they are trading on is information. Or perhaps they just like to trade."[9] Either way, accepting noise traders into the theory of equilibrium is tantamount to accepting a certain kind of irrationality, which is a huge step for an economist, but one that Fischer was apparently prepared to take. In fact the groundwork for this additional bold step had also been laid years before he stood up to give his address.

In early 1982, the editor of the *Journal of Financial Economics* had sent Fischer a paper to referee, "Explaining Investor Preference for Cash Dividends" by Hersh Shefrin and Meir Statman, both economists at Santa Clara University in California. Fischer was the natural choice because of his 1976 paper drawing attention to the "dividend puzzle" as something that needed to be explained. Given the unfavorable tax treatment of dividends, it makes no economic sense for firms to pay them, but they do so anyway. Shefrin and Statman explained that, although a preference for dividends is inconsistent with economic rationality, it is perfectly consistent with the results of modern psychological studies into the way actual people make decisions under uncertainty.[10] Fischer began his referee report, "This paper is brilliant. It rings both new and true in my ears." On Fischer's recommendation, the paper was published.[11]

Shefrin and Statman were pioneers in the application of psychology to finance that would, over the next decades, grow into a separate subfield called behavioral finance, and Fischer's support for their first paper was instrumental in getting the new field off the ground.[12] His help did not stop there. As incoming president of the American Finance Association, Fischer had responsibility for organizing the program for the annual meeting in December 1984, and he called upon Shefrin to organize a session on behavioral finance. Only about 25 people showed up, but Fischer made sure that the papers were included in the published proceedings, and he specifically drew attention to them as one of two "areas that I think deserve more attention in the future."[13] The next year, in his presidential address, he would state simply, "I think we must assume that investors care about dividends directly."[14]

Given this background, when Fischer says that noise traders are people who just like to trade, it is clear what he means to do. He means to open the door for a behavioral explanation of trading, much as he had earlier done for dividends. He is not, however, in any sense giving up the notion of equilibrium and efficiency, as some of the more extreme behavioral finance people were urging.[15] Quite the contrary. In fact, Fischer is giving up economic rationality at the level of individual behavior precisely in order to save the notion of equilibrium at the level of the economy as a whole. His conception of equilibrium in "Noise" (1986) uses costly information to make room for individually irrational behavior that doesn't all wash out in the aggregate and so affects asset prices. But equilibrium with costly information is still equilibrium. Some people might say that the resulting equilibrium is inefficient, but not Fischer. In a world of costly information, that's what efficiency looks like.

As a follow-up to his work with Stone, in October 1982 Fischer wrote a paper on "The Future of Financial Services" to spin out the practical consequences of his new line of thinking.[16] For most of his academic career, Fischer had been thinking about the properties of an ideal world without frictions, a world in which there is no need for securities firms. But in the actual world frictions are significant—costly information, costly management, and costly selling—and these frictions make room for securities firms that specialize in "helping individuals reduce costs and avoid unnecessary risks." Having come to this conclusion, Fischer was well prepared when, a year later, the opportunity arose to join the securities firm Goldman Sachs. The decision to leave academia thus involved as much pull as push. Thenceforth, instead of producing theories about an ideal world not yet achieved, Fischer would be producing business products to move the actual world closer to the ideal.

At the time Fischer joined the firm, Goldman Sachs did basically two things: investment banking and trading. Investment banking means corporate finance, helping corporate clients with their financing problems whatever they may be: mergers and acquisitions, bond underwriting, and general advice on regulatory, accounting, or tax matters. Trading means acting as broker or dealer in the market for a particular financial instrument, or proprietary trading on the firm's own account.

Goldman Sachs had always been a great trading firm, and in 1981 it had expanded that dimension by acquiring J. Aron, then the premier firm trading commodities and currencies. But almost immediately the type of riskless arbitrage for which J. Aron was famous, the near simultaneous buying and selling of the same commodity at slightly different prices, lost its profitability. Robert Rubin, a partner at Goldman Sachs since 1971, was sent in to fix the problem.[17]

The solution he found was to shift toward more risky forms of arbitrage, to find analogues to the risk arbitrage that Goldman Sachs was already doing in other markets. The idea was to extract profit from more subtle forms of mispricing by buying underpriced assets and selling other overpriced assets, and holding the position until prices correct. Because such trades involve exposure to risk, the key to making them work is to hedge out all the risk that is correctly priced in order to focus your exposure on the mispricing opportunity.

Rubin's own career at Goldman had been built on just this kind of risk arbitrage, most recently in the market for traded options. A founding member of the Chicago Board Options Exchange in 1973, Rubin had been making use of the Black-Scholes formula even before it was published. He thus had reason to know the commercial value of the kind of analytical firepower that Fischer could bring to bear in support of the trading side of the business. By 1984, when Rubin hired Fischer, there were throughout the firm a few others of the new breed of quantitatively oriented traders, most notably Mark Winkelman and Jon Corzine. They were as yet very much in the minority, but they were clearly the future. The example of Salomon Brothers, where John Meriwether had built the premier fixed income trading operation on Wall Street, was a constant reminder of how far they had yet to go.

The new breed of traders all realized the importance of analytical support for the kind of trading they were doing. Put simply, you need a model of some kind in order to calculate the correct hedge for any given risk exposure. However, no one knew better than the traders themselves the vast distance between abstract finance theory and practically usable models. Probably only at Goldman Sachs would the idea ever have occurred that someone like Fischer Black could help them. But Goldman Sachs has a culture that believes in intellectual firepower as its competitive edge. Get the brains first and then figure out how to make money from them. There was no question about Fischer's brain, but what to do with it?

Rubin remembers that there were two ideas in mind when Fischer was hired. The main idea was that Fischer would be a resource helping to apply financial theory not just in trading but all across the firm. He would look at a business anywhere in the firm, consider from a theoretical standpoint why it made money, and make suggestions about how it might be generalized or expanded. In this latter respect, Fischer fit into Rubin's ambition to grow the firm and transform it into the premier investment banking firm in the world. Rubin recognized that Black was unlikely to make a big contribution to the business right away, but he was prepared to wait. He soothed his more skeptical partners: "We will learn from Fischer, and he will learn from us."

Meanwhile, Fischer would lead a narrower effort to use computer technology and financial theory to make money trading equities and equity options. This was the second idea about how to use Fischer. He would build analytical capacity in the Equities division in much the same way that Stanley Diller, formerly of the Business School at Columbia University, had been doing over in the Fixed Income division. It was just the kind of arrangement that always suited Fischer. Close to the action but off to one side, he would have the freedom to watch and learn.

Over the course of the next decade, Fischer would have three careers at Goldman Sachs. He started out directing the Quantitative Strategies Group in the Equities division, and that's where he made the contributions that would earn him a partnership in the firm. Then in February 1990 he moved over to join the Fixed Income Management Group in Goldman Sachs Asset Management (GSAM). Two years later, in December 1992, he moved back to the main office to join Fixed Income Research.

As Fischer moved through the firm, his many contacts formed divergent impressions of him. Some, perhaps even most, couldn't see that he added much value. Where were the deals he landed, or the trading coups he engineered? Nowhere. It didn't help that Fischer apparently viewed his job at Goldman Sachs as a way of supporting the research interests that were his real passion. Indeed he had negotiated as part of his contract that he would have one day a week completely free to work on his own projects! That was one day of a five-day workweek, but Fischer also worked weekends, so in the end he was able to preserve almost half of his time for himself.

And even when he was ostensibly working for the firm, he seemed to be able to work on anything that caught his interest. Uniquely, he seemed to have no boss and to face no daily profit and loss statement. Essentially he had an academic life, but with a Wall Street salary and no teaching responsibilities. He was, said a former student from Chicago days who also wound up on Wall Street, the only person who ever had fun working on Wall Street. He enjoyed an enviable position, and people who were working harder than he was naturally resented it.

Other Goldman colleagues, while noting the lack of any direct contribution, point to the indirect value of having the name Fischer Black on the firm's roster. If your job was to sell fancy derivative products, it helped to have in your corner the great Fischer Black, whose impenetrable formula unlocked the mystery that made such products possible. When Goldman Sachs expanded its operations in Japan, they quite deliberately used Fischer as a draw in high-profile publicity events. His elementary talk on "Development of Option Price Theory" in June 1989 filled a room of 500 seats at the ANA Hotel Osaka.

But the sales staff learned to be careful how they used Fischer. He could just as easily queer a deal as clinch it. If you let him talk about what he thought pension fund managers should be doing, he would trot out his idea that they should be investing entirely in bonds. And in communicating his ideas, he often seemed unable to connect with the concerns of the typical client, whose understanding of the issues at stake was many levels below his own. He would tell them the truth as he saw it, with no regard for what they needed to know or were able to absorb. Fischer's managers learned to save him for select, quantitatively oriented, clients.

A third point of view about Fischer, quite definitely a minority view but held by the minority that really counted because they ran the firm, was that Fischer in fact contributed tremendous value. Fischer was the first "quant" at Goldman, during a time when the firm was seriously committed to building up the quant side of its operation but still unsure what kind of a quant operation would fit with the Goldman culture. They started with Fischer, and then added others. Alan Shuch, who worked closely with Fischer during his years at Goldman Sachs Asset Management, sums it up: "We used him to help recruit other quants and to vet them. There was not one instance where Fischer had reservations and we hired the person anyway. He had that much credibility." And after the new quants were hired, Fischer continued to make himself available to them. "It is as if he said to all quants, 'Just consider me your assistant.' Many of them thought they were going into research in academia, but a visit to Fischer showed they were going to be in the flow, part of the action."

As the first Goldman quant, Fischer invented and then modeled the kind of contribution that quants could make to the firm. Traders who had to face him in the postmortem conference after a losing trade learned the advantage of facing him before putting on the trade in the first place. Deal makers who anticipated dropping the Fischer Black name learned the advantage of soliciting his candid view before taking him out on a sales call. In both dimensions, the analytical discipline of quantitative finance in the style of Fischer Black gradually seeped into the general culture of the firm, just as Rubin had foreseen.

It worked because in many respects Fischer was the very model of what Goldman says it wants its people to be: team-oriented, unselfish about credit, honest, client-focused, and intellect-driven. Indeed, this is exactly what Fischer liked about Goldman. "Goldman is different. It hires talented, driven people, but only if they seem willing to work for the good of the whole firm. It finds ways to make teamwork a reality, partly by sharing the gains from success widely among all who contribute. In a business full of ethical challenges, Goldman consistently serves client interests. It makes room for unusual views like mine, even when they conflict with conventional wisdom. Because everyone reviews everyone, the management process is unusually dispassionate and sensible."[18]

In other ways, however, Fischer was entirely atypical of what Goldman people actually are. He was a terrible manager and worse salesman, largely unable to participate in the intensely collaborative culture inside the firm, and unwilling to nurture client relationships outside the firm. Left to his own devices, he would never have gotten anywhere. It took work by other people, people like Robert Rubin who had the vision and understood the value of someone like Fischer, to draw him out of himself and involve him in the business of the firm. Rubin remembers, "It was good to have someone thinking about these things, to warn us if he sees something."

Mark Winkelman sums it up: "He was a puzzler, always searching in his own very deliberate and disciplined way for another piece of the puzzle." When he found one, he would point it out to other people, but would make no particular effort to ensure that the firm exploited its implications. People could use it if they wanted to, or not, and Fischer was largely indifferent between the two. He would not sell his point of view, perhaps because he could not. Rather he left the ideas to sell themselves, or not, as the case may be. (Possibly he agreed with Treynor that markets are more efficient when there exist a diversity of views, even if all of them except for one are wrong.)[19] In any event, after pointing out the new piece of the puzzle, he would go back in his office and search for another. In his office he kept a poster of a man running down a country road: "The race is not always to the swift but to those who keep running."[20]

Fischer often said that Goldman never really figured out how best to use him, and that rather passive way of putting the matter points exactly to the problem. Most people, faced with an incentive structure that says you will be paid depending on your contribution to firm profits, can be expected to work pretty hard figuring out how the firm can best use them. But unlike most people, Fischer didn't use money as a yardstick by which he measured his success. Jon Corzine remembers, "He was the easiest partner in the world when it came to discussions about money, his share and compensation. Basically he didn't care." "He had a different scale, and never switched," comments Mark Winkelman.

Fischer's first office was on the 29th floor of the main Goldman Sachs building at 85 Broad Street, three blocks south of Wall Street. He sat right next to the trading floor, but he might just as well have been in a different building since he rarely left his office. Never could he be found prowling the trading floor, looking over shoulders, asking questions or making suggestions, driving the troops to greater effort on the firm's behalf. Nor was he keeping tabs on them from inside the office, which he had specially sound-insulated to his specifications so he could not even hear what was happening outside. Instead he spent most of his time alone with his computer, a Compaq Deskpro 386 running DOS, not Windows, with a monochrome (amber) monitor that had a character generator but no graphics capability. His keyboard was attached with an extra-long cord, but no mouse. A good typist, he worked without taking his hands off the keyboard or his eyes off the screen.

He did almost all of his work in an outlining program called Think-Tank, which he used as a kind of external associative memory to supplement his own. Everything he read, every conversation he had, every thought that occurred, all got summarized and added to the database that swelled eventually to 20 million bytes organized in 2,000 alphabetical files. And many of the electronic files referred to further paper files that eventually filled seven three-drawer lateral file cabinets outside his office. Reading, discussion, and thinking that Fischer did outside the office were recorded on slips of paper to be entered into the database later. Reading, discussion, and thinking that took place inside the office were recorded directly. While he was on the phone, he was typing. While he was talking to you in person, he was typing. Sometimes he even typed while he was interviewing a prospective job candidate, looking at the screen, not the candidate.

ThinkTank was not only Fischer's memory, but also Fischer's interface with the outside world. Wherever an outline mentioned a specific person, perhaps the author of a paper that Fischer had found useful, he included also that person's phone number. He had a piece of computer code written that allowed him to dial a number from within the outline simply by highlighting it. Waving his hand to indicate this elaborate office setup, he would say, "This is what I think is artificial intelligence!"

Plugging in to his computer, Fischer became a thinking machine dedicated to solving problems in finance, and not just for Goldman Sachs. Many people have the memory of getting a phone call from Fischer, often at odd hours of the morning or night or even on a weekend. "This is Fischer Black. I've been reading your paper and it seems to me that the second sentence on page 3 is completely wrong." Others have the memory of phoning him to ask a question. "I may not be the best person to help you, but you might want to read a paper on the subject by so-and-so whom you can reach at such-and-such number." On the other end of the phone was Fischer, and ThinkTank.

So well did the system work for him that he hated to unplug. He even communicated with his secretary, whose office was close by, almost entirely by sending out notes. Most days, he ate lunch at his desk, and the same lunch every day, broiled fish that he would drown in fresh lemon juice and wash down with liters of bottled water that he kept in his office credenza under lock and key. It was brain food, fuel for the organic component of the man-machine symbiosis. Fischer was never happier than when he was solving problems, and he organized his life around that activity. But of course he also had a job to do.

The job of head of Quantitative Strategies was to find ways for the firm to earn excess returns by trading in the market. For Fischer, this posed a curious challenge since he tended to believe that markets were sufficiently efficient that there was no way to earn excess returns. Now his job was to test market efficiency in real time, with real money, backed by all the resources of Goldman Sachs. He would later say, "Markets look a lot more efficient from the banks of the Charles than from the banks of the Hudson." But it was by no means easy to make money. Three weeks after he arrived at Goldman, Fischer told an academic colleague that he had just lost a half million dollars for the firm.[21] He took the lesson that he could not himself beat the market, but maybe there was something else he could do to help the traders.

Although he could not himself do what the traders did, he found himself strangely fascinated by them. In a sense they were doing in the markets for securities what Fischer himself had spent his life doing in the market for ideas. Like him, the traders were looking for inefficiencies and how best to exploit them. The psychological stresses and pleasures of going against conventional wisdom were common ground in their two very different worlds. Another common ground was an addiction to video games, Fischer to Mario Brothers on his Game Boy, and the traders to the game unfolding on their trading screens. The disciplined life and mental habits that Fischer had adopted for himself were his way of managing the bohemian rebel that was such an integral part of his character. It occurred to him that if he could help the traders achieve even some part of his disciplined approach to problems, they might have the success in their world that Fischer had enjoyed in his. Anyway, it was worth a try.

At the time, the quantitative trading strategies used at Goldman and elsewhere fell into two general categories. There were technical trading strategies that looked to exploit trends or other patterns in price movements. And there were fundamental strategies that used company-level research to pick out underpriced stocks, or economy-level research to time fluctuations in the market as a whole. In an efficient market neither strategy should make money, and the evidence of academic studies convinced Fischer that markets were at least that efficient. It followed that anyone adopting either of these strategies was likely to be a noise trader, and so likely to be losing money systematically to any true information trader. One way Fischer could help traders was by preventing them from trading on noise. He began by confiscating books on technical trading that he found around the trading floor.

In a similar vein, Fischer made a habit of challenging any and all traders' folk wisdom that did not comport with rational economic analysis. The only thing that should matter to a trader, he would always insist, is prospective total return given current market conditions. In general that means treating trades with negative carry (negative immediate cash flow) just the same as trades with positive carry, treating short positions the same as long positions, and treating illiquid markets the same as liquid markets. Traders should be just as prepared to hold a position with unrealized gains as a position with unrealized losses, and just as prepared to hold old positions as new ones. Of course it does no good to exhort traders to change their behavior if the performance measures that determine their compensation encourage something else. So Fischer began criticizing performance measures as well. The overarching idea was to reward traders for their skill, not their luck.[22]

But even if you get the incentives right, the psychological literature tells us that human beings are simply not very good at making decisions under uncertainty. The simple commonsense model of probability that we all carry around with us involves systematic biases that will trip us up if we let it infect our trading decisions. Fischer's way of combating these biases was to make $100 bets with the traders. A favorite was "Let's Make a Deal." Suppose there are three closed doors and you are told there is a prize behind one of them. After you choose door number one, one of the other doors is opened to reveal no prize, and you are then offered the opportunity to change your choice to the remaining unopened door. Should you switch or stand pat?

Strange as it may seem, you should switch. Here's why. If the prize is behind the first door, then you lose by switching. If it's behind the second, so the third door gets opened, then you win by switching. If it's behind the third, so the second door gets opened, then again you win. You are twice as likely to win by switching as by standing pat. Got it now? You owe Fischer $100.

Other distortions creep in from other sources, most importantly the tendency of human beings to have excessive faith in the results of complicated calculations rather than asking whether and how they make sense. A case in point is the Black-Scholes options formula. When options first started trading in 1973, the Black-Scholes model helped to make markets more efficient by providing an analytical basis for pricing. But one set of persistent deviations of market prices from the Black-Scholes formula puzzled Black. Options with low exercise prices tended to be underpriced, while options with high exercise prices tended to be overpriced, so that so-called "money spread" trades often seemed to make sense. And options with a short time to maturity tended to be overpriced relative to longer-term options, so that so-called "time spread" trades also often seemed to make sense. Even though there were plenty of professionals trading these spreads, the deviations of market prices from their theoretical values continued to persist. Maybe the formula was wrong and the market was right, but what precisely was wrong?[23]

Fischer came to think that the problem was that the formula treated volatility as constant over the life of the option, even though it clearly wasn't. And the formula treated the stock price as changing continuously over time, even though it sometimes would jump discontinuously. In the tables Fischer produced for his clients, he worked out ad hoc adjustments to take account of these factors.[24] In effect, he was doing what he could to ensure the efficiency of options prices, even if that meant encouraging systematic deviation from the Black-Scholes formula. Consequently he was amused to discover at Goldman Sachs that markets often seemed to follow Black-Scholes even when there were good reasons not to. The formula had become a source of noise.

But if prices were following the formula when they shouldn't, that meant there were trading profits to be earned. Black dusted off his 1976 memo, "All That's Wrong with the Black-Scholes Model," and put the Goldman Sachs traders to work. In time, he would publish the memo, first under the title "The Holes in Black-Scholes," and then in revised form with the even stronger title "How to Use the Holes in Black-Scholes."[25] The point was not so much to get the one correct model as it was to help the trader. The attraction of Black-Scholes was that it was simple enough for traders to understand how a change in the underlying assumptions would cause a change in the calculated option price. The important thing was the traders' ability to use the model to help them think.

To help traders use the model intelligently, Fischer focused attention on their interface with the computer. Working with H. S. Huang, he completely redesigned the computer program that Goldman traders used to value options. He wanted something that traders could run interactively on their individual PCs, in order to build their intuition about how changes in the model's assumptions would change the calculated price. He insisted that all words on the screen be spelled out completely (no abbreviations), that everything fit on a single screen, and that calculation be as fast as possible. That meant replacing the Black-Scholes formula in the original program with the simpler formula proposed by John Cox, Stephen Ross, and Mark Rubinstein, a formula they derived from the assumption that the underlying stock price moves either up or down by a fixed amount in each discrete period over the lifetime of the option. Not only was Cox–Ross–Rubinstein faster for the computer, it was also more intuitive for the human user.[26] The overarching goal was to use man–machine symbiosis to reduce noise trading at Goldman Sachs and so to improve profitability.

Fischer also had ideas about ways to increase the information content of trading. Suppose that it is true, as Fischer believed, that there are strong forces tending to push toward efficiency. It follows that, if we want to earn excess returns, we have to look for situations where, for one reason or another, these forces are blocked or otherwise not operative. It's not enough to find situations where prices look funny. We must also have some idea about what is causing them to look funny. And, no small task, we must have some idea about why we are able to overcome that cause. In other words, we have to have an edge.

Fischer thought that Goldman's edge could be financial theory combined with computer technology. Computers were already used fairly widely within the firm, but essentially as fancy calculators to back up technical trading and fundamental trading strategies. Fischer's idea was different. He wanted to use the computer actually to trade. Fischer's idea was to use the computer to automate the mechanics of trading and so make trading strategies possible that would be too burdensome, just in terms of paperwork, under a nonautomated system. If you could get ahead of the curve on trading technology, you could exploit arbitrage opportunities that existed because no one else had figured out how to exploit them.

That was the idea, but how to implement it? Fischer himself was clearly the wrong person to do it. He was a terrible manager of people, and had no real interest in getting better at it. He was also far too much the big-picture thinker to ever concern himself with the nitty-gritty of software development that was needed to make the strategy a reality. Nevertheless, he seems to have convinced Rubin to give him a chance anyway. He would hire people fresh out of school so they would be cheap, and he would set them loose to see what they could do.

In June 1985, Fischer hired Jeff Wecker, recently graduated from Princeton University with an undergraduate degree in civil engineering, a degree involving lots of statistics and probability mathematics but no finance. Wecker remembers that Fischer was most interested in his programming skills and experience. Soon after, Fischer hired Wecker's friend Michael Dubno, a computer wizard and college dropout whom Wecker described as "the fastest hack he ever met." People at Goldman would call them Fischer's "graduate students." With Fischer backing them, they thought they were going to inherit the world.

The first day of work Fischer handed Wecker the textbook *Options Markets* by John C. Cox and Mark Rubinstein. "Read this and ask questions. If you understand this book, you'll know more than I do." For the first six months, Wecker's job was simply to learn, and learn he did, spending hour after hour talking with Fischer and others in Equities. After a while he began to get anxious to do something, to make some money for the firm. It was only then that Fischer pointed him in the direction of the Value Line futures contract, which had been trading in Kansas City since 1982 but at what seemed to be the wrong price.

Apparently the market did not appreciate the fact that the Value Line index was a geometric average, not an arithmetic average, and, since the former is always less than the latter, they were overpricing the futures contract. For example, the geometric average of 2 and 8 is $(2 \times 8)^{1/2} = 4$, but the arithmetic average is $(2 + 8)/2 = 5$. "So, what do you want to do about it?" asked Fischer. "I guess I want to sell the futures contract and buy the stocks in the index," answered Wecker. The idea was to buy in the cheap market and at the same time sell in the expensive one. That way you gain if, as you expect, the prices in the two markets converge, and at the same time you are hedged against movements in the overall level of prices since what you lose on your long position in stocks you gain on your short position in futures, and vice versa. Said Fischer, "Okay. How do you want to do it?"

The idea was to use the Direct Order Trading (DOT) system that had recently been introduced by the Securities Industry Automation Corporation (SIAC) to trade a list of stocks all at once rather than one by one, but that was just the start. When they started to think about it, it became clear that they didn't want to be trading all the stocks in the index since transactions costs would eat up the profits. Instead they chose a subset of stocks that was highly correlated with the index, and periodically updated that subset to take account of changing correlations. But even that smaller subset generated more trades than the Goldman Sachs operations system could handle, so they had to automate operations as well. The whole thing was a programming nightmare, but when they were done they had the first program trading system on the Street. And it made money.

In June 1986, the futures price started to move toward the correct theoretical price and by summer's end the move was complete. At the peak, when they accounted for fully a third of the open interest in Value Line index futures, the size of the position attracted the attention of Goldman Sachs management. Robert Rubin came down to investigate. "What's the biggest risk you face, and can you quantify it?" he asked Wecker and Black. "Maybe the futures price just won't converge," suggested Black. "Maybe the locals on the other side of the contract won't be able to take the losses and so will default," suggested Wecker. Rubin was satisfied and they left the trade on.

As it happened, one of the biggest positions on the other side was held not by any local Kansas City speculator but by a group of young finance professors. They knew quite well that Value Line was a geometric index, but they were focusing their attention on a different apparent price inefficiency variously called the small firm effect or the January effect. For some years, the stocks of small firms had been exhibiting excess returns in January. Nobody was sure exactly why this happened, but the professors were betting that the pattern would continue. For that bet, the Value Line index seemed to be just what they needed because it was an equally weighted index so that small stocks were overweighted relative to a capital-weighted index like the S&P 500.

The professors' arbitrage called for a long position in the Value Line futures and a short position in the S&P 500, whereas Fischer's arbitrage called for a short position in the Value Line futures and a long position in the stocks underlying the index. Two players, both of them confident that they held the winning hand, made for high stakes, until halfway through the summer of 1986 when the professors realized their mistake as prices began to move against them. Years later, they discovered who had been on the opposite side of their losing bet. One of them wrote a rueful postmortem, "How I Helped to Make Fischer Black Wealthier."[27] The professors had thought they were information traders, when in fact they were actually noise traders. Got it now? You owe Fischer $100.

Anyway, once the price converged, the Value Line trade was done, and Fischer's group moved on to the next arbitrage, and the next one after that. At the peak, Wecker had as many as 20 programmers working for him, grinding out the code for the next arbitrage, but it all developed from that first Value Line trade. Wecker remembers, "The only way we could make money was to take the theory and crunch through the software." It was a new way of trading and Goldman got there first. Soon others wanting to do similar trades came to Goldman and for a while it became the top house for doing basket trading. The same software that made it possible to trade the Value Line basket of stocks also made it possible to trade any other basket, and so opened up a whole new class of arbitrage opportunities.

Before Fischer joined Goldman Sachs, the only active trader he knew at all well was Jack Treynor. Way back when they were both unknowns at Arthur D. Little, Fischer had decided to devote himself to working out the consequences of assuming that markets were efficient, and that life project took him into consulting and then academia. Treynor had gone the other direction, devoting himself instead to working out the consequences of assuming that markets were inefficient. That life project took him to Merrill Lynch, then editorship of the *Financial Analysts Journal*, and then into full-time investment management.

Treynor's path involved a career spent asking the question: How might an analyst add value in an efficient market? There are only two ways. Either he uses superior information or he applies superior reasoning to existing information. In his 1981 article "What Does It Take to Win the Trading Game?" Treynor writes: "Although the market is highly competitive, market efficiency as such should not prevent active investors from outperforming the market, by capitalizing on either inefficiencies in the propagation of information or inefficiencies in valuation."[28] "Information-based traders" exploit the first inefficiency by focusing their efforts on "investigation," which means gathering superior information. "Value-based traders" exploit the second inefficiency by focusing their efforts on "analysis," which means superior reasoning. For his own investment practice, Treynor saw greater opportunities in value-based trading. In his view, systematic errors in conventional asset valuation provide regular opportunities to earn excess returns.

In line with this view, Treynor's favorite way to test an investment idea was to tell other people about it. If they understood the idea easily and agreed that it was a good idea, he would know that the idea was probably already reflected in the price and would move on to the next one. If they found the idea incoherent or unsound, then he would know that the idea was not in the price, and conclude that it was worth more careful study. (In the world of academia, Fischer adopted a recognizably similar approach to testing his own intellectual ideas by laying his outrageous views open for scrutiny in academic seminars.)[29]

Treynor always emphasized that the stock market game is zero-sum, like poker, in the sense that one trader's profit is another trader's loss. Value-based traders establish the bid price at which they are willing to buy and the ask price at which they are willing to sell, setting the spread wide enough to compensate for the risk of losing to an information-based trader with superior information. In Treynor's world, this spread can be quite wide, as much as 30 to 40 percent of the price, so price can deviate rather far from value. Most of the time the price lies inside the spread, so value traders don't trade. Whenever price reaches the spread, however, money flows from information traders to value traders. The point is that the true cost of trading faced by the information trader (and by anyone else who wants to trade quickly) is not the visible spread offered by dealers, but the largely invisible and much wider spread offered by the value trader.

In this way of thinking, the value-based trader, *not* the dealer, is the ultimate source of liquidity in the market. "Although the securities market ostensibly involves the exchange of securities for cash, it actually involves the exchange of money for time, with securities serving as incidental vehicles."[30] Value-based traders choose the price of the trade, while information-based traders choose the time of the trade. In effect, the former are selling time while the latter are buying it, and the price of time is the value-based traders' spread. "On every trade, time is either worth more than it costs, or less."[31] What one side wins, the other side loses. For Treynor, the key to success for an active investor is the decision about which side to be on. He favored the value-based strategy on the view that information-based traders tend systematically to underestimate what they pay for time. Time tends to cost more than it is worth.

All of these ideas about the trading game would have been in Fischer's mind when he arrived at his new job at Goldman Sachs and faced the task of helping the trading side of the firm to make money. But they didn't help him very much because, unlike Treynor, Fischer saw no reason to expect systematic overpricing or underpricing of time in equilibrium. That's why he focused his initial efforts on helping to eliminate noise. Whether Goldman traders decide to pursue an information-based trading strategy or a value-based trading strategy, certainly the odds of their making money would be increased if he could ensure that their information and valuation procedures contained as little noise as possible. But even as he helped the traders, Fischer kept coming back to the more fundamental question whether trading of *any* kind could be relied upon as a permanent source of profit for the firm. A strategy of reducing noise and exploiting arbitrage opportunities was fine for the short run, but seemed to be inherently limited as a source of profit in the long-run efficient equilibrium. Or was it?

As he thought about the problem, eventually Fischer concluded that there were at least two sources of trading profit that would survive even in full equilibrium. One involved taking advantage of central bank intervention, either in currency markets or in credit markets. Central banks are willing to lose money in the cause of the presumably higher good of economic stabilization. Central banks attempt to lower the short-term interest rate in order to stimulate the economy in a time of business downturn, but they can only succeed in doing so if they are prepared to lend to all comers at the new low rate. As a consequence, traders can make money by borrowing at that low rate and lending in some other market. "When a country like the U.S. makes its short rate artificially low, while a country like Germany makes its short rate artificially high, traders can borrow at the U.S. short rate and lend at the German short rate. This combination of borrowing and lending is like buying the deutsche mark against the dollar, so a trader can take this position in the forward market without actually borrowing or lending."[32]

The other reliable source of trading profit is "flow" trading. Simply by participating in a market, traders obtain information about the sources of supply and demand, and that information allows them to anticipate price movements. For Fischer, this source of profit was potentially a very big thing. He urged devoting more of the firm's resources to it, and less to the more glamorous proprietary trading where he doubted that Goldman had any very dependable information advantage. "In general I think we underestimate how much we earn from flow trading."[33]

But why should this source of profit persist permanently? After all, the whole point of active trading is to beat the market, so if Goldman is winning then its counterparties must be losing, and if its counterparties know they are losing, won't they avoid trading or at least insist on a discount to cover themselves for the risk? Either way, the long-term profitability of the strategy appears to be in jeopardy. Just so, when Fischer had been consulting for Wells Fargo, he devised strategies to reduce transactions costs for the new passive mutual fund strategy that Wells Fargo was trying to launch. Now at Goldman Sachs he found himself on the opposite side of the very same transactions. Wells Fargo's transactions cost was Goldman Sachs' trading profit. Why can't passive traders simply drive trading profit to zero, or even negative as a charge for the liquidity service that they provide?

Fischer's thinking about this problem went through many iterations, stretching over his entire career at Goldman, starting with his earliest ruminations about noise and continuing until just before his death when he asked the *Financial Analysts Journal* to publish his latest draft.[34] As a stimulus to his thinking, he presented his evolving drafts regularly on the academic seminar circuit where, after the stock market crash of October 1987, there was a great deal of interest in understanding the trading process. Indeed, a huge academic finance literature built up in a very short time, and Fischer presented his work as a contribution to that literature.[35] However, whereas most of that literature focused on understanding how the existing set of institutions worked, Fischer (as usual) was trying to imagine a possible world that might lie in the distant future.

One constant throughout the evolution of Fischer's thought was his focus on trading as a game played between active and passive traders, which is to say between the informed or "news" traders (such as Goldman Sachs) and uninformed noise or "nice" traders (such as Wells Fargo). Treynor's conception of the trading game, by contrast, had pitted against one another the two different styles of active traders (information-based and value-based). (Treynor assumed that dealers capture all the profit opportunities of trading with noise traders, which they use to offset the losses involved in trading with information traders.) Fischer thus conceived of the problem more broadly than Treynor did, but eventually he came to see that the central issue was the price of time, just as Treynor had said. Some traders are buyers of time, and others are sellers, and their interaction determines the price of time.

The problem was how to conceive of the price of time in an equilibrium setting. Fischer found his way into the problem by thinking about an equilibrium in trading methods. Instead of taking as given the existing market and limit orders, and the existing institutional role of dealers, he asked what kind of orders would exist in an unrestricted competitive equilibrium. Suppose there were many competing exchanges, each trying to offer a trading environment that would attract business away from the other. What kind of environment would they offer?

The answer is by no means obvious. News traders who are in a hurry want average price market orders and deep markets. Nice traders who are patient want limit orders and shallow markets. But a separating equilibrium, in which each kind of trader trades with others of its own kind, will not be sustainable so long as each can bluff by pretending to be the other kind. And anyway, there might be some news traders whose news is not perishable (such as traders following Treynor's value-based strategy), and there might be some nice traders who are sufficiently unhappy with their current position that they want to trade quickly. So news traders may be selling time and nice traders may be buying time. In an anonymous market, it will be impossible to tell who is news and who is nice.

Here's what Fischer thought exchanges might look like one day. There will be no market orders or limit orders of the kind we are familiar with, nor will there be any dealers or other specialized market makers. Instead there will be a new kind of limit order that he called an "indexed limit order" with a price that changes with general market conditions. (In Fischer's world, the specialist survives not as a market maker but only as the "price adjuster.") This indexed limit order is the very same kind of special limit order that Fischer had advocated back in 1971 under the name "participating order," but with one difference. Now he imagines that there will be a range of indexed limit orders, each with its own specified "urgency," or rate of execution. Exchanges set the price impact for each level of urgency in order to balance supply and demand.

The way an equilibrium exchange will work, according to Fischer, it will cost more to trade quickly than to trade slowly, because very urgent orders will have a large price impact while less urgent orders will have a small price impact. The price of a security is therefore not a single number, but an entire schedule depending on trading urgency. Similarly, the price of time is not a single bid-ask spread, but an entire schedule. In this world, news traders make money, whether their news causes them to trade quickly or slowly, and nice traders lose money. The reason is that in an anonymous market there is no way to distinguish news traders from nice traders since they all trade the same way. The only way for outsiders (or even the traders themselves) to tell the difference between news and nice is to watch who is making money on average and who is losing it.

For a firm like Goldman Sachs, one message of Fischer's paper is that the information advantage derived from flow trading can be depended upon to remain profitable more or less permanently. Another message is that, in order to exploit that information advantage most effectively, you want to be the equilibrium exchange. Fischer had done what Rubin brought him in to do. He had looked at the firm's trading business, asked how it made money, and made suggestions for ways to make more money from it. By the time Fischer understood trading to his satisfaction, Rubin had left Goldman Sachs in order to serve as Secretary of the Treasury under President Bill Clinton, and Fischer had been diagnosed with the cancer that would soon end his life. But what Rubin had predicted had come true. "We will learn from Fischer, and he will learn from us." The biggest thing that Fischer learned at Goldman was about trading.

■ Chapter Eleven ■

EXPLORING
GENERAL EQUILIBRIUM

One final caution: with so many ways to use options, it may seem that options are for everyone. But they aren't. There are many people who would be better off buying a portfolio of stocks and holding on to it, or buying mutual fund shares, or just lending.

Fischer Black, "The Long and the Short of Options Trading," *Fischer Black on Options,* Vol. 1, No. 4 (1976, p. 6)

There are so many ways to use derivatives that I'm almost surprised when someone doesn't use them. Producers and consumers, investors and issuers, hedgers and speculators, governments and financial institutions: almost everyone can use them.

And there are so many kinds of derivatives: futures and options, embedded and free-standing, listed and unlisted, swaps and swaptions. The variations are endless: and for each kind, you can choose the long side or the short side.

Fischer Black, "The Many Faces of Derivatives" (1995)

It was options more than anything else that got Fischer a tenured job at the University of Chicago. And it was options again, or rather derivatives more generally, that got him the private sector equivalent of tenure, namely an invitation in October 1986 to join Goldman Sachs as a full partner. One of the first memos Fischer had written at Goldman was to point out a potentially lucrative tax arbitrage using term structure swaps. It was enough to convince the corporate finance side of Goldman about the potential contribution Fischer could make to their business. From then on, he served as a kind of internal consultant, helping the firm to think about potential uses for each new derivative product as it began to trade.

Fischer's interest in finding ways to profit from distortions caused by the tax and regulatory structure goes all the way back to his days at Chicago. There was always a part of him that took satisfaction from beating the system while playing by the system's own rules. He loved to tell students the story "How I Got Free Life Insurance from TIAA" by borrowing out all the cash value of the policy. One part of the story was about taking advantage of the tax deduction for interest paid on the borrowing while allowing the cash value of the policy to grow at a pre-tax rate. Another part of the story was about exploiting regulatory restrictions that prevented the insurance company from charging more than 5 percent on its cash value loans. Fischer concluded his analysis, "I only hope that writing this paper does not cause changes that reduce the value of my life insurance policy."[1]

The primitive tax treatment of options opened further opportunities to make money at the expense of the IRS, and Fischer got a kick from figuring out how best to exploit them. In another early memo for students, titled "Saving Taxes with Options," Fischer shows how "the [IRS] ruling makes an option worth more to a tax-exempt investor than to a taxable investor." As a consequence, if taxable investors write options and tax-exempt investors buy them, then both can win, even if they both hedge completely with offsetting positions in the underlying stock.[2] Ten years later Fischer's first proposal to Goldman Sachs involved a similar idea. The 1984 memo, titled "Term Structure Swaps," shows how a swap contract between a taxable and a tax-exempt investor could produce gains for both, gains large enough to leave room for Goldman Sachs to profit by charging a fee for arranging the swap in the first place.[3] This was the kind of thing that got him tenure at Goldman Sachs.

Having secured his job, Fischer turned his attention to his private life. His attempts at reconciliation with Mimi having failed, now he signed up with a dating service, and before long got matched up with Cathy Tawes, herself recently divorced from a partner at Goldman

Sachs. They began dating in June 1986, and moved in together in her home at 5 Stornowaye in Chappaqua in 1987. Eventually they married, in February 1993, and bought a new house together at 103 Clearview Lane in New Canaan, Connecticut. Cathy had two children of her own from her first marriage, so there was never a question of raising children together. Rather, the relationship would be about Fischer joining her pre-existing family, which was exactly the arrangement that had always worked for him.

Cathy could not have been more different from Mimi, shorter, plainer, and quieter, with brown hair not blonde. No one would call her stunning, but she had the essential quality that Mimi never had. She understood who Fischer was and what he needed. She appreciated his fine qualities and was prepared to compensate for his deficits. A social worker by training, she understood Fischer's personality not as anything abnormal that needed to be fixed, but rather as an extreme case within the range of normal human variation.

As mature adults coming together, Cathy and Fischer had enough in common to understand one another, but also enough difference to help one another. On the Myers-Briggs Type Indicator test, he was an "INTJ" while she was an "ISTJ."[4] Stripped of psychological jargon, what that means is that both of them were most comfortable spending time in the inner world of thoughts and ideas (I), and preferred a disciplined and organized approach to the outer world of experience (TJ). The difference was in how they preferred to gather information. Fischer was the intuitive one (N), always seeing the big picture, relationships between things, and deeper meanings. Cathy was the sensing one (S), always seeing the concrete facts of the matter. She could keep him grounded because she understood who he was, and because she herself was a naturally grounded person.

Cathy understood that Fischer's work was his life, and she never interfered with that. If he wanted to work 12-hour days, even on Saturday, and then drive round-trip to Boston on Sunday to see his girls, that was fine with her. What she added to the rhythm of his life were periodic breaks for vacation, in the Berkshires during the summer, at the Boulders resort in Arizona during the winter, and other places in between. Fischer could bring his work, but they would be together, enjoying one another's company in beautiful surroundings. For Fischer, all the pieces were finally in place. Finally he was in the right job, and with the right wife.

The irony of Fischer's life is that all the important career opportunities were opened up by his work on options, even though options had no very important place in the ideal CAPM world that he always held in the back of his mind. The capital asset pricing model (CAPM) envisions a world of debt and equity, and that is all, but in the real world derivatives were increasingly all the rage. The world in front of Fischer's eyes thus seemed to be moving farther and farther from the ideal world inside his head. It was a puzzle, but then Fischer always liked puzzles.

A significant fraction of Fischer's work for the corporate finance side of Goldman concerned potential applications of one or another new derivative financial instrument. How will the new instrument work? How should it be priced? How can we use it to make money? These questions provided more than ample fodder for the evaluative external dimension of Fischer's mind but also, and ultimately more important, for the creative internal dimension since Fischer could not help looking through to the deeper underlying questions. It was easy enough to see the immediate reason why someone might want to issue or buy some derivative or another. But from a deeper point of view, it was not so obvious why the need arises in the first place. A CAPM world without derivatives is entirely possible, so why do we have derivatives?

Merton Miller had always emphasized misguided regulation and distortionary taxes as the stimulus for financial innovation, including the burgeoning derivatives market.[5] The glee with which Fischer devised strategies for making money at the expense of the IRS was, in this respect, more than adolescent pleasure at outwitting the adult fuddy-duddies. It was also a mature appreciation for the way that exploiting loopholes in the system could, in time, cause it to change. Indeed, and here Fischer went beyond Merton Miller, the problem is not just with regulation and taxation, but with the very accounting system that generates the numbers that government, and the private sector, uses. Given the craziness of accounting rules, as Fischer believed, he had no qualms about using derivatives to manipulate reported earnings. Accounting earnings should be a measure of the capital value of the firm, not its change in value, and derivatives could be used to move toward such a positive end goal.[6] So for Fischer the initial stimulus for the derivatives revolution was evasion of regulation, taxation, and accounting rules, but that left open the question of why derivatives continued to flourish even after the initial stimulus was muted.

Probably the most common answer is that derivatives help people to hedge risk,[7] but Fischer never found this answer to be very convincing. The problem is that most of the risks that people want to hedge are, when you look at them closely, risks that other people have created. Says Fischer, "Most of the risks we worry about are man-made." Not to put too fine a point on it, the basic fact is that people like to speculate. They could hold index funds, but instead they choose to place their money with managers who try to beat the market by exposing them to diversifiable risk. They could finance their house purchases with floating-rate debt, but instead they choose fixed-rate callable debt that exposes them to interest rate risk, and the result is that someone else must be persuaded to take the other side of their bet. Given that some people want to speculate, other people must be persuaded to take the other side of these man-made risks, and that is where financial institutions come in. "Financial institutions can spread them around, using diversification, syndication, derivatives, and all the other tools in our bag of tricks."[8]

From the fact that most derivatives concern the distribution of man-made risks, it follows that derivatives must not be very important for things that really matter, but Fischer came to think that in the future they could become more important. These same derivative instruments, developed to shift around man-made risks, could potentially be used to hedge true risks, which are located mainly in productive firms, not households. Firms could potentially hedge out the myriad specific risks they face—asset risk, liability risk, and business risk—by issuing complex derivatives customized to their needs. And here there is a clear role for a firm like Goldman Sachs to act as intermediary, by taking the other side of the derivatives, pooling the risk, and issuing other derivatives to hedge what remains. That's what Fischer thought the corporate finance side of Goldman was doing, among other things, and he approved of it and tried to help.

But in his mind all of that was just the early stages of a transition to an ideal future world where all the complexity might simplify. In the future world as Fischer envisioned it, individual firms might eliminate the risk of bankruptcy and default simply by buying put options on their own stock price with a face value equal to the value of their debt.[9] In this world, corporate debt would become the riskless borrowing envisioned by CAPM. The only difference from the ideal CAPM world would be that individual wealth holders would hold in their market portfolio, alongside the debt and equity emphasized by CAPM, also some small piece of all the put options issued by firms.[10] It doesn't look exactly like the CAPM world of debt and equity, but deeper down it is exactly the CAPM world that Fischer held in his mind ever since his 1969 wheat model. By holding the puts as well as equity and debt, individual wealth holders would, in effect, hold a market portfolio of the underlying real capital stock of the nation.

Thus Fischer came to see the proliferation of derivatives not as a deviation from his original ideal but as the road leading toward it. Much had to change before the ideal could be realized, and derivatives were proving to be an indispensable tool for that change. The shift in Fischer's attitude that is evident in the parallel quotations that head this chapter reflects, therefore, no shift at all in his underlying worldview. The CAPM ideal is front and center throughout. What Fischer learned at Goldman was to view derivatives as part of the solution, not part of the problem. It turned out that, not for the first time in his life, the markets knew more than the model. The markets recognized the potential contribution of derivatives, and the markets were right.

In 1986, the markets taught Goldman Sachs an important lesson about the risk side of risk arbitrage as losses in the Fixed Income division mounted to $100 million. Robert Rubin and Stephen Friedman, newly appointed co-heads of the division, finally located the problem in the behavior of implicit interest rate options embedded in many fixed income products. As interest rates fell, homeowners were refinancing their mortgages, and corporations were exercising call provisions that allowed them to refinance their bond debt. The effect was that if you had a long position in these assets, it didn't rise in value as much as you might have been expecting. Meanwhile, if you were hedging with a short position in Treasury securities, you took the full brunt of the price rise as a loss. The bottom line was that Goldman needed better models of the embedded bond option.[11]

The problem came to Fischer's attention during the postmortem meetings Rubin would hold on Saturdays to figure out why yet another trade had not worked out as planned. Everyone would have his say while Fischer listened from the edge of the room until finally Rubin brought him in. "Fischer, you've been pretty quiet. Is there anything you'd like to add?" It was clear that they weren't valuing the implicit bond option correctly, but it wasn't exactly clear how they should be valuing it since the Black-Scholes formula was about options on stocks, not bonds. Fischer went back to his desk and, working with Bill Toy and Emanuel Derman, put together a simple model of the term structure that could be used to value any fixed income derivative product. This was the famous Black-Derman-Toy (BDT) model, not published until 1990, but essentially finished by late 1986.[12]

BDT was a computer model intended from the beginning for practical use. Fischer had already become convinced about the superior practical utility of the binomial tree framework of Cox-Ross-Rubinstein for valuing equity options. The Black-Derman-Toy model used the same simplified framework to value bond options. It worked, where Black-Scholes didn't, because it allowed you to treat the essential feature of bonds that distinguishes them from equity, namely the fact that at maturity their value is known with certainty (abstracting from default). The link between BDT and a proper formal theory of the term structure would only get worked out later.[13]

For Fischer, always having in mind the ideal CAPM world of riskless short-term borrowing and lending, it was natural to think of the entire pattern of fixed income prices as being driven by the single stochastic process for the short-term riskless rate of interest. From this point of view, long bond prices and their volatility must reflect market consensus about the future path of the short-term riskless rate and its volatility. The great thing about fixed income securities is that we know their price at maturity, and that fact allows us to read the market's mind by translating the existing yield curve and volatility curve into a consistent pattern of future short-term interest rates and volatilities.[14] We can then use that pattern to price any other fixed income security, including derivative securities. By construction, all such prices will be consistent with current bond prices, and with each other. This was the original Black-Derman-Toy model.

One reason that Fischer and his team were able to produce BDT so fast is that Fischer had been thinking about the underlying theory of the term structure for a long time, indeed ever since his days at Arthur D. Little when he began hanging around MIT and attending Franco Modigliani's Tuesday night seminars. Modigliani was then building an econometric model of the monetary sector of the U.S. economy for the Federal Reserve System. A key issue in the project was the link between short-term and long-term interest rates, since standard theory says that monetary policy affects the short rate but that private spending is more sensitive to the long rate. Unfortunately, existing theory didn't speak very clearly on the question of how the two rates were linked.

Modigliani had claimed in 1966, "There is by now general agreement that in an ideal world of no transactions costs or taxes, rational behavior and certainty (about future rates), the maturity structure must be controlled by the simple principle that *all outstanding instruments, regardless of maturity, must produce identical returns over any given interval of time*—where the return is defined as the sum of cash payment plus any increase (or minus any decrease) in the market value of the instrument. . . . There is unfortunately much less agreement as to the determinants of the yield structure in the 'real world.'"[15] Stated simply, in an ideal world the return on short-term bills should be equal to the return on long-term bonds, but we don't really know how these two numbers should be related in the real world.

According to Modigliani, the most important feature of the real world missing from the ideal model was uncertainty. In general, you would not expect two instruments to have identical returns unless they also have the same risk. So the question became how to measure risk. Suppose you are trying to shift purchasing power from the present to a period one year from now. Then a one-year Treasury bill has very little risk because its price at maturity is fixed, but a 10-year Treasury bond has a lot of risk because its price a year from now will depend on economic conditions a year from now. Suppose, though, you are trying to shift purchasing power 10 years into the future. Then the 10-year bond has less risk than the one-year bill because the short-term interest rate can change a lot over that horizon. Modigliani reasoned that, depending on your preferred time horizon, you will perceive risk differently.

His idea was that people will prefer to hold bonds with maturities that match their time horizons, and will switch into other maturities only if the yield differential is attractive enough to encourage speculation. If the yield differential is high enough, people will even be willing to engage in arbitrage by going short their preferred maturity and long the less preferred maturity. Given the pattern of demand for preferred maturities and the supply of bonds of different maturities, some pattern of interest rates will bring demand into line with supply. This "Preferred Habitat Theory," as Modigliani called it, was supposed to provide the missing link between short rates and long rates.

None of this seemed right to the young Fischer. CAPM said that the right way to measure risk was simply covariance with the market portfolio. Thus it seemed to him that, to paraphrase Modigliani, the maturity structure must be controlled by the simple principle that all outstanding instruments, regardless of maturity, must produce identical *risk-adjusted* returns over any given interval of time. In other words, expected returns on short-term bills should be exactly equal to expected returns on long-term bonds.[16] In February 1970, Fischer wrote: "The expected one period return on any debt security, gross of transactions costs, depends only on the market risk in the security. . . . Until it is proved otherwise, I suspect that the market risk in a debt security is not significantly different from zero. . . . The expected one period returns on all debt securities, gross of transactions costs, are equal."[17] This was Fischer's starting point in thinking about the term structure of interest rates.

Fischer's idea that bonds have no market risk does not mean that they are riskless. Quite the contrary. They are quite full of default risk and interest rate risk. Fischer's only point was that these risks should be diversifiable, and hence not priced in equilibrium. Thinking in this way, it was natural for Fischer to consider also the conditions under which the potential diversifiability of these risks would actually be realized. The key, as he came to think, was somehow to separate out these risks so that they could be traded separately. So we find him, as early as 1970, imagining some financial institution going into the business of selling guarantees against default and guarantees against price fluctuation. "Thus a long term corporate bond could actually be sold to three separate persons. One would supply the money for the bond; one would bear the interest rate risk; and one would bear the risk of default."[18]

What Fischer was thinking about was a way to make long-term risky corporate bonds into short-term riskless assets, much like the revolving loans in the simple CAPM world. He talks about "guarantees," but we recognize that what he means is "options." (The Black–Scholes formula, which he and Scholes would announce a month later, showed how to think about pricing these guarantees.) Today, it is conventional wisdom that any financial asset is just a bundle of risk exposures that you can price and sell separately. Back then, it was a visionary leap with no hope of immediate practical application. Fischer made one attempt to develop the idea a little bit further, by using options theory to price the default risk in corporate bonds.[19] But he did not then pursue the idea of using options to hedge interest rate risk. As a consequence, he had nothing much to say at first when the problem of pricing bond options arose at Goldman Sachs.

Instead, the most immediately useful contribution came not from Fischer but from Richard Roll, hired into Goldman Sachs out of academia in 1985 to build a Mortgage Security Research capability within the Fixed Income division. A student of Eugene Fama, and a classmate of Myron Scholes and Michael Jensen, Roll had written his thesis applying the efficient markets model to Treasury bill rates, and he had followed up with a paper making use of the Sharpe-Lintner CAPM to adjust for market risk. Empirically, he found that the betas for bonds were, for the most part, near zero.[20] It was exactly the finding that Fischer had expected on theoretical grounds but Roll, an empiricist at heart and by training, was after something else. Roll was trying to use CAPM to build a model of observed term premiums at various horizons, premiums that previous theorists had attributed to liquidity factors. By contrast Fischer, always more the theorist, having convinced himself on logical grounds that the liquidity premium at any horizon must be zero, was left with a bold theoretical formulation that could not easily explain why the term structure tends in practice to slope upwards.

Fifteen years later, when the two men met at Goldman Sachs, both were still approaching the problem of modeling the term structure from their own preferred methodological stance. Roll's approach was to fit an empirical model that captured as much of the variation in prices as possible. Fischer's approach was to build a theoretical model of the underlying equilibrium structure of prices. That was BDT. The problem with BDT was that, from a trader's perspective, it didn't do demonstrably better than other models that used multiple underlying factors and did not assume equilibrium. It didn't do demonstrably worse, either, but for traders the *assumption* of equilibrium is both extremely strong and prima facie implausible, since their entire livelihood is based on finding and exploiting deviations from equilibrium. Indeed, as Fischer admitted, his model could not fit data in which there were opportunities for riskless arbitrage! So the traders never switched over to BDT.

The real contribution of the BDT model for traders was not in identifying profitable trades, but in providing an intuitive understanding of the term structure. The contribution of BDT to the firm as a whole was in pricing custom options for clients, and in calculating the appropriate hedge for the firm's portfolio of fixed income derivatives, such as the term structure swap book. In subsequent versions of the model, Fischer would work to make it more flexible and realistic. Eventually he was even willing to consider adding a second factor.[21] It is significant, however, that his second factor was the drift, or rate of change, of the short-term rate of interest. Fischer continued to hold fast to the idea that it is the short rate of interest driving everything.

And he continued to hold fast to the idea that the term structure we observe can always be understood as an equilibrium, even though that made it hard to explain the persistent upward slope. In an attempt to explain the slope of the term structure, in one of his very last papers, "Interest Rates as Options" (1995d), Fischer zeroed in on the fact that the riskless short rate can be viewed as the sum of a riskless real rate of interest and the expected rate of inflation, two factors that in principle can move independently of one another. The important point is that there is no economic reason to expect either of these numbers necessarily to be positive, and yet we nevertheless expect their sum, the nominal interest rate, always to be positive because investors can always choose to hold currency that pays a zero yield.

Thus it is theoretically possible that the nominal interest rate we actually observe may not be equal to the "shadow" nominal rate that would clear markets in a world without currency. Fischer had long hypothesized that such a "currency trap" might have been a significant cause of the Great Depression of the 1930s.[22] Now he added the idea that the possibility of such a currency trap at some time in the future, even if it doesn't actually come to pass, has the effect of raising the long-term interest rate, so tending to produce a positively sloped term structure. The idea of viewing interest rates as options thus may help to explain why the term structure tends to slope upward. What economists identify as a liquidity premium may instead be a consequence of the option character of interest rates in a world with zero-yielding currency.

October 19, 1987, Black Monday, is a date etched permanently in the memory of a generation of Wall Street denizens. People remember exactly where they were, who they were with, and what they said and did as the Dow Jones Industrial Average plunged 508 points, losing 22.6 percent of its value, the largest percentage drop in a single trading day on record. Rob Jones, a young trader who began his career at Goldman Sachs as one of Fischer's "graduate students," remembers never before seeing so many of the firm's partners on the trading floor, all of them looking over his shoulder at the Quotron screen where they could see the firm's capital, and their own personal wealth, disappearing before their eyes. From his point of view, Monday was actually a better day than the previous Friday when for a while markets stopped working, and a trainee fainted dead away from the tension in the air. Jones remembers running into Fischer's office to let him know what was happening, "I put in an order to sell at market and it never filled!" "Wow, really!" Fischer was fascinated. "This is history in the making!" he exclaimed gleefully, clapping his hands together.

As fast as stock prices were falling, futures were falling faster. If you could have bought the futures while simultaneously selling the stocks, you could have made a lot of money on Monday, but it wasn't easy to do. One major problem was the New York Stock Exchange rule that bars selling a stock short except when its last change was an uptick. But that was only part of the problem. Fischer later remembered: "Because volume was high, investors had trouble reaching their brokers, brokers had trouble reaching the exchanges, and everyone had trouble keeping track of trades. People even had trouble making payments through their banks, especially via the Federal Reserve wire system. Part of the problem was that computers were unable to handle the volume smoothly. Queues built up, printers broke down, and people had to stop putting in certain kinds of orders because the computers were overflowing."[23]

The most important consequence was that derivatives came "un-hitched" from their underlying stocks, and that made things worse because a fractured market is less liquid than a unified market, and lower liquidity makes for lower prices. "Whatever the original reasons for the crash, it frightened people. The sharp decline, the high volatility, the mispriced securities, and the congestion caused people to withdraw from the market. This led to a decline in the equilibrium level of the market that was greater than the decline a model would have figured—unless it accounted for the psychological factor."[24]

For Fischer, trading congestion and its effects on market psychology were sufficient to explain the mechanics of the crash, and so to counter other proposed explanations and their associated remedies. Some people said the market went down too quickly, while others said that it was too volatile. Some blamed so-called program trades that triggered sell orders after an initial decline, or leverage that triggered margin calls on the way down. Many people seemed to think that increased government regulation was the answer. The Brady Commission recommended "circuit breakers" to halt trading after large downward price moves, and increased government control over margin requirements in the derivatives markets.[25] But Fischer had a different view.

Fischer thought that the Brady proposals would probably not help and might even hurt by making markets less liquid. Investors, dealers, and exchanges were already responding to what they learned on October 19 by changing their investment strategies, computer programs, and business practices. What was needed was less government regulatory interference, not more. "The only changes that make sense to me are to move margin-setting authority away from the Federal Reserve Board to the private sector, and to get rid of the uptick rule."[26] Fischer's idea, apparently, was to focus on changes that would prevent a recurrence of congestion when prices drop sharply.

Unlike most other commentators, Fischer was, by and large, completely unconcerned about preventing the price drop that caused the congestion in the first place. Everyone else took it more or less for granted that such a large price drop could never be consistent with equilibrium, but Fischer had a different view. The underlying cause of the price drop, he said, was a change in investor taste for risk that had been happening throughout the years preceding the crash, but without being fully recognized by market participants and so without being reflected in market prices until the crash. This, in a nutshell, is Fischer's "Equilibrium Model of the Crash" (1988a).

In fact, Fischer had been noticing the changing taste for risk even before the crash. In early 1987, unusually, volatility began to rise along with prices, instead of the usual inverse relationship. What could be causing it? In June Fischer wrote a memo on "Stock Market Volatility," pointing out that "people who increase their use of portfolio insurance will cause the market to go down more than it would otherwise go down, and will cause the market to go up more than it would otherwise go up. They will increase volatility."[27] By "portfolio insurance," Fischer meant any dynamic trading strategy that involves buying when prices go up and selling when prices go down. But he also meant the product being marketed under that name by the firm of Leland, O'Brien, Rubinstein Associates (LOR), a product that had by 1987 attracted $60 billion under management.

The LOR business had grown out of Leland's academic work, which used the Black-Scholes option pricing formula to develop dynamic trading strategies that would produce a pattern of returns similar to a put option on a portfolio of stocks.[28] Leland's idea was to provide an instrument that would allow institutional investors such as pension funds to ensure that the value of their portfolio would never fall below a specified floor. If the value of the stocks fell, then the put option would come into the money and so buffer the decline.

The business opportunity came from the fact that in general there was no traded put option available for investors to buy. Instead LOR would use its expertise to create a dynamic trading strategy, tailor-made for each client's portfolio, that would replicate as closely as possible the payoff from the appropriate put option. The Black-Scholes formula showed how, over any small interval of time, the return on a stock option is like the return on a portfolio of stocks and bonds, where the proportion of stocks to bonds is called the delta hedge ratio. Black and Scholes had used this idea to fix a rational price for an option given the observable prices of stocks and bonds. LOR simply reversed the logic by using the delta to form the replicating portfolio dynamically over time.

At Goldman Sachs, the success of LOR had stimulated pressure to develop their own version of portfolio insurance, and Fischer was naturally at the center of that attempt. Working first with Rob Jones (who had not yet been bitten by the trading bug), Fischer developed what they would call constant proportion portfolio insurance (CPPI). The key insight goes all the way back to Fischer's earliest work in Financial Note No. 6, "Individual Investment and Consumption Strategies under Uncertainty." Constant proportion portfolio insurance is essentially the investment policy Fischer had proposed for individuals and tried to implement at Wells Fargo two decades before.[29] Only the letters used to signify the variables are changed: $e = mc$, or Exposure equals Multiple times Cushion.[30] The obvious reference is to Einstein's relativity formula, $E = mc^2$. It is meant to be a joke that helps you to remember the formula.

The way it works is quite simple. First you specify a floor value below which you want to ensure that the portfolio never falls. That gives you your Cushion as the difference between the current portfolio value and the floor. Then you specify the Multiple in accordance with your tolerance for risk, and the formula tells you how much of your portfolio to invest in the risky asset. Having chosen your risky portfolio, you then hold the rest of your wealth in the safe asset. Over time, as the portfolio value changes, your cushion changes, and you continue using the formula to reallocate between the risky and safe assets. In order to reduce trading costs, you will want to specify the percentage move that triggers a trade, but that's all there is to it.

The beauty of the formula is in both its simplicity and its generality. Because it is simple, you can easily understand how it works, and so customize it for your own needs or preferences by specifying your own floor, your own multiple, and your own trigger percentage move. And you can change any of these over time as your needs or preferences change. Instead of producing something that was more elaborate or technically sophisticated than LOR, Fischer produced something that was simpler and also, as he proceeded to argue, better.[31] But it was all to no avail. Goldman was late to the market, and then after the crash the market dried up completely so the product went nowhere.

The intellectual effort involved had, however, prepared Fischer to understand why volatility was increasing in the months before the crash. Essentially people were adopting trading strategies that increased price volatility by increasing buying pressure when prices rose and increasing selling pressure when prices fell. The same intellectual effort also prepared the groundwork for Fischer to understand why prices fell so far during the crash. Essentially, given the increased demand, the "cost" of portfolio insurance had to rise in order to equilibrate markets, and that meant that equilibrium mean reversion of asset prices had to rise. (The cost of portfolio insurance is the loss from selling low and buying high as required by the dynamic trading strategy.) But mean reversion is not something that investors can readily observe, so for a while their behavior continued to reflect the historical lower rate of mean reversion. The result was that, as prices rose, investors miscalculated the degree to which expected return was falling. By October 19, enough investors had become aware of the true state of affairs to calculate correctly, and prices fell until expected return was high enough that investors were willing to hold the existing quantities of stock.

In effect, Fischer concluded, the crash was caused by noise. If investors' beliefs about mean reversion had kept up with the changing facts about mean reversion, prices would never have risen so far, and so would not have had to fall so far to get back into line. Even so, prices never got even close to a factor of 2 deviation from value, and probably even the one-day fall of 22.6 percent overestimates the extent of the deviation because on that day price changes were exacerbated by congestion and psychology. In Fischer's mind, the crash was well within his new broadened conception of equilibrium with costly information and noise traders.

"What makes you think that an econometrician has something to contribute on Wall Street?" In 1986, Fischer was interviewing Bob Litterman, a 1980 PhD in economics from the University of Minnesota, for a job in Fixed Income Research. Long before, Fischer had formed his own conclusion that "The Trouble with Econometric Models" was likely fatal, and decided that exploring the logical consequences of equilibrium theory was more likely to provide genuine insight into the world, while econometrics was more likely to discover patterns that would prove to be spurious. At Goldman Sachs, talking now to practitioners rather than to academics, Fischer reiterated his view: "Certain economic quantities are so hard to estimate that I call them 'unobservables.' Two of these are the expected return on the stock market and the risk premium on bonds."[32] Nevertheless, Fischer did not stand in Litterman's way, and he was hired.

Three years later, in 1989, Scott Pinkus, the head of Fixed Income Research, came back from the Tokyo office in Japan with the commission to build an asset allocation model that clients could use to guide their efforts to diversify internationally. He gave the task to Litterman, but wanted to involve Fischer also, given the enthusiastic reception Fischer had received in Japan. Thus were the theorist and the econometrician forced to work together for the good of the firm. The result was the Black-Litterman asset allocation model, which would eventually become the centerpiece of the distinctive approach to investment management pursued at Goldman Sachs Asset Management (GSAM).[33]

Quite apart from his methodological objection to econometrics, Fischer cannot have been initially very keen on the project. Given his equilibrium mind-set, Fischer's inclination would have been to recommend that clients simply hold a market index fund, with the quantity of bonds from each country chosen to match the quantity issued by each country. The only interesting theoretical question was how much to hedge the currency risk, but by the time Pinkus approached him Fischer had already sorted out that problem to his own satisfaction. Under a number of simplifying assumptions, his Universal Hedging Formula showed that one should hedge only a fraction of the risk, indeed the same fraction for each exposure.[34] In Fischer's view, a global bond portfolio was better than a domestic bond portfolio not so much because of improved diversification but because of the opportunity to make excess return from bearing currency risk. In his mind the problem was solved, so why do we need an asset allocation model?

The reason is that clients are not content simply to hold the market portfolio. They want to try to beat the market by shifting their holdings away from the market portfolio, and they want a quantitative model to help them do so in a disciplined way. In effect, clients believe that current asset prices reflect deviations from true equilibrium, deviations that create opportunity to earn excess return by overweighting their portfolio with the underpriced bonds and underweighting with the overpriced bonds. Clients have views, but they are not sure how to translate those views into optimal asset allocation decisions. That's why they need an asset allocation model.

Once the problem was framed that way, Fischer could see it as essentially the same problem that he and Treynor had grappled with long ago in their paper on "How to Use Security Analysis to Improve Portfolio Performance." They had proposed separating portfolios into a passive and active part, and shifting funds between the two parts over time depending on whether the active part proved genuinely able to beat the market or not.[35] In effect, the challenge posed by Goldman's Japanese clients was to improve on Treynor-Black. Put that way, the project seemed worthwhile.

As Litterman tells the story, once receiving the assignment from Pinkus, he started working from the portfolio theory of Harry Markowitz, a theory that tells how to derive optimal portfolios provided the clients are willing to formulate their views on expected returns and covariances for every asset under consideration. But he soon found that the Markowitz procedure didn't work very well for bonds. Because the returns on bonds are so highly correlated, very small differences in expected returns imply very large shifts in portfolio allocation. If German bonds are expected to outperform U.S. bonds by only 20 basis points, the Markowitz procedure can very easily suggest that you arrange your portfolio as a very large long position in German bonds combined with a very large short position in U.S. bonds. This might make sense for a trader engaged in risk arbitrage, but it makes little sense for a long-term investor. What long-term investors want is a way to choose the optimal tactical deviation away from their long-term strategic portfolio allocations.

The idea of Treynor-Black had been to blend the passive with the active based on the *ex post* realized performance of particular analysts or portfolio managers. The idea of Black-Litterman was to blend the passive with the active based on *ex ante* expected deviation of performance from equilibrium. To estimate the *ex ante* equilibrium expected returns, Fischer proposed to use his international CAPM (with universal hedging) to calculate what expected returns would have to be in order for investors using the Markowitz procedure to select the world market portfolio as an optimum.[36] In effect, the idea was to use empirical methods to estimate the covariance matrix, and then to use theory to derive the implied expected returns.

The remaining problem was how to blend the theoretical equilibrium returns with the client's views in order to calculate optimal portfolio allocations. Litterman's first idea was to average the two and then use the Markowitz procedure to calculate the optimum portfolio, but the deviation from equilibrium prices was still enough to cause wide deviations of the calculated optimum from the market portfolio. The solution was to treat both equilibrium returns and client views as independent measurements of an unknown parameter, each one measured subject to error, and then to calculate the best combined estimate. When the resulting set of expected returns is used to calculate the optimum portfolio, it will tend to be close to the market portfolio for two reasons. First, the client typically expresses views on only a subset of available asset returns, and so implicitly accepts the equilibrium views on everything else. Second, the client's expressed uncertainty about his own views lowers the weight of those views relative to the equilibrium view.[37] Thus the resulting portfolio is a combination of the passive market portfolio and an active view portfolio, just as in Treynor-Black, but now with a more sophisticated algorithm for choosing the optimal combination.

The natural home for the Black-Litterman model inside Goldman Sachs was the Asset Management division, then in the early stages of development and looking for a distinctive approach that it could develop as a source of competitive advantage in the market. (In 1976 Goldman had opted out of the asset management business on the view that it didn't want to compete with its clients, so they were entering the market late.) Not only did GSAM want the Black-Litterman model, but they also decided that they wanted Black himself since their chief investment officer was just leaving. And so it happened that, in February 1990, quite suddenly Fischer picked up and left his home at 85 Broad and moved to 32 Old Slip, just a few blocks away.

Initially, GSAM focused only on bonds, and the first version of Black-Litterman was therefore just for bonds. But by the time Fischer moved over, GSAM was also attracting some equity money, and so Fischer worked with Litterman to extend the model to include equities.[38] Even so, the overall approach proved to be too new to attract sufficient business, and anyway GSAM itself was yet unsure exactly what direction it wanted to go. In time the equilibrium approach would become the centerpiece of investment management at GSAM, but not in the early 1990s. Instead, in December 1992, Fischer moved back to 85 Broad, now to join Fixed Income Research, which had become the center of quantitative finance at the firm.

There, Fischer and Litterman continued to develop the model and to find new uses for it. One idea was to run it backwards. Rather than taking as input the portfolio manager's views about mispricing and generating as output the optimal portfolio allocation weights, the model could just as easily take as input the actual portfolio weights and generate as output the views that would have to be held in order for that portfolio to be optimal. The idea was that if these implicit views turned out to be surprising, as most often they were, the manager might want to change the portfolio allocation. One famous case of this happened in 1993, when they ran the model for Mike O'Brien in the London office to reveal an implicit negative view on U.S. Treasuries.[39] When the market started to move against him, O'Brien used this information to construct a massive hedge by buying Treasuries, and wound up making $100 million rather than losing.

Another idea was to use the model as a tool for risk control by calculating how much each position in a portfolio is contributing to the overall risk in that portfolio. This idea emerged from the work Fischer and Litterman were doing as part of the continuing education program for the Fixed Income division. Once a month, 100 employees would gather at the Short Hills Hilton for a three-day refresher course in the basics. After outlining the fundamental points of modern portfolio theory, Fischer went on to talk about risk control, emphasizing the control of major risks. What he worried about was the perfect storm, which he envisioned as an unusually large negative shock, or collection of shocks, that hit the entire portfolio at once. To get the students thinking in the right way, he challenged them to "list gains and losses from a world market crash that is not reversed."

This was in 1993, a time when it was not easy to get people to think about the possibility of catastrophe, much less to take steps to hedge against it. It was a banner year for Fixed Income and for Goldman Sachs as a whole (Goldman posted an unprecedented $2.6 billion in pretax profits). And it was a banner year for Fischer as well. He got married for the third time, and used his annual bonus to buy a new house. But 1994 would bring reversal. It turned out that the profitability in 1993 had been due "in large part to substantial and concentrated fixed income, currency, and commodities positions that benefited from declining interest rates and the decline in relative value of certain European currencies."[40] In 1994, interest rates moved the other way and the firm got caught in a worldwide bear market for fixed income.

In September Stephen Friedman, who had been managing the firm as sole senior partner since Robert Rubin left at the end of 1992, stepped down and Jon Corzine took his place. In October, Bob Litterman was made partner and put in charge of devising a firmwide risk management system. For Litterman, as for Fischer, the natural approach was to treat the entire firm as a portfolio, and to investigate the main sources of risk in that portfolio.[41]

Fischer played only a supporting role in the firm's response to the losses of 1994, because by this time he was struggling with problems of his own. On Valentine's Day in 1994, he had had trouble buttoning his shirt collar and joked with Cathy about a possible tumor. He put off going to the doctor for a while as he tried to research it himself. Finally he went to the Mount Sinai Hospital to have it checked out. It was throat cancer, it was serious, and he would need an immediate drastic surgery to have any chance at all. Notwithstanding all of his special efforts to ward off fate, Fischer's bad genes had caught up with him. He burst into spontaneous laughter when the doctor told him the news.

After the diagnosis, Fischer's focus shifted to summing up his life's work. He didn't know how much time he had left, but he was clear on one thing. The most important thing was the book he had been working on ever since he moved over to GSAM. Fortunately he had spent much of the previous year preparing a revised draft, so he was nearly done. Bob Merton agreed to take charge of final publishing details in case the operation did not go well, but Fischer did recover sufficiently to take care of the final details himself. And he survived long enough to see the book, titled *Exploring General Equilibrium*, in print in June 1995.

It's a strange book in many ways, but as in everything Fischer ever wrote, form was carefully chosen to follow function. The book represents Fischer's return to unfinished business with economics that he had put behind him when he left academia, for good as he thought at the time. His 1987 book, *Business Cycles and Equilibrium*, was supposed to be his swan song to economics, but after it was published he found that he could not keep away. Even though economics had rejected him, he was still interested in the problems it treated.

The coincidence of publication of his first book with the October 1987 crash seems to have spurred him on. Paul Samuelson remembers receiving his complimentary copy of the book on the very day of the crash, a juxtaposition that confirmed for him the limitations of the equilibrium point of view. Fischer, of course, had a different view. The crash was certainly a challenge, but one that he thought the equilibrium approach could face. Having in mind the scanty information on which expectations about the future must necessarily be based, Fischer had always thought that volatility was more or less exactly what one should expect. Now the search for a fuller explanation of the crash reinvigorated his research into the theory of business fluctuation.

Having developed by 1988 his theory about how the widespread adoption of dynamic trading strategies had changed the mean reversion properties of expected market returns, Fischer continued on to understand what had caused people to adopt such strategies in the first place. Way back at the beginning of his career he had been led to propose a dynamic trading strategy as a way of achieving time diversification of risk. Now, 20 years later, he worked to embed the individual's problem in a proper general equilibrium framework, using the accepted modeling strategies of economics as he understood them. The result was his paper on "Mean Reversion and Consumption Smoothing."[42]

In this paper, he tried hard to play by the economists' rules. Economists seem to be interested in simple aggregative models that match a set of stylized facts about aggregate data. In fact, two empirical puzzles had come to preoccupy macroeconomists, the high average return on equities relative to riskless instruments, and the very smooth time series of aggregate consumption. Neither fact was consistent with standard economic models. In an attempt to engage with economists, therefore, Fischer developed an aggregative version of his general equilibrium theory of business cycles that was able to match these stylized facts.[43] But economists weren't having any of it, and Fischer found that the economics journals were still closed to him. Rejection only made him more determined.

Fortunately, the move to GSAM left him with time to spend on his own projects, and that is exactly what he did. The very first memo Fischer produced after the move was "An Input-Output Model of Business Cycles," a sketch of what would become the core of the eventual book.[44] The memo amounted to a restatement of his sectoral mismatch theory of business cycles, but now framed explicitly as an alternative to the version of real business cycle (RBC) theory that had captivated economists over the past decade.

Says Fischer: "The standard neoclassical growth model is not, in my view, well suited to the study of business cycles. It emphasizes flows rather than stocks and has too much certainty. It glosses over important differences among workers and among machines that help explain fluctuations. It artificially assigns all uncertainty to technology and none to tastes. It has no human capital and makes no distinction between durables and non-durables." As he expanded this first memo into a book, his bill of particulars against standard economics would only lengthen, and his determination to confront the economists on each point only strengthen. In the published book there would be 14 items on his list of "the features of RBC theory that seem arbitrary and unmotivated."

To make doubly sure that his readers didn't miss the point, he devoted 45 pages of the book to "issues in the literature, and my responses," organizing the 106 issues alphabetically from "Adjustment costs" and "Aggregate demand" to "War" and "Worker-specific capital." It seems a strange way to organize a book, but he was actually only following the model of the Glossary for Finance that he had produced for teaching at MIT. He was trying to teach his readers how to speak the language of finance as he understood it.

To make triply sure that his fellow researchers didn't miss the point, he devoted 125 pages of the book to specific comments on their papers, again organizing the 308 papers alphabetically, this time by author from "Abel" to "Zarnowitz." This also seems strange, but here again Fischer was only following the model of the referee reports that he had long produced for journal editors. Already famous for insisting that editors leave his name on referee reports, in his final book he went one step further by sending each comment to the author before the book was published, and asking for reaction.

The point of it all was to make his readers feel as acutely as he did the inadequacy of existing answers to the questions he thought were most important, in the hope that they would engage more seriously with the alternative answers he offered in his own treatment. By the time he was done, the scope of his alternative theory had swelled far beyond its humble origins as a restatement of his mismatch theory of business cycles. At the top of the list of stylized facts that Fischer now wanted to explain are "unlimited growth," "persistent inequality," and "growing specialization." His ambition now was nothing less than explanation of the grand dynamics of economic growth.[45]

The overarching argument of *Exploring General Equilibrium* is that it is possible to explain more or less all of the economic facts we observe in the world as consequences of general equilibrium. We don't need any special assumptions about price rigidities, externalities, or imperfect markets. We do, however, need a very general form of the general equilibrium model, more general than standard RBC specifications of production functions and utility functions allow. Specifically, Fischer insisted on generalizing the standard model in at least two dimensions: sectoral disaggregation and roundabout production (and consumption).

In his theory there are billions of sectors producing highly differentiated outputs with highly specialized inputs in order to meet highly differentiated final preferences. Further, the flow of output at any moment in time depends on a sequence of inputs stretching back into the past, even the distant past, inputs that potentially continue to contribute to outputs on into the future, possibly even into the distant future. Likewise, the flow of final utility from consuming current output depends on consumption in the past (the utility function is time-inseparable), and current consumption continues to contribute to utility in the future.

The result is that the current flow of output (and consumption) in any one specific sector is linked both cross-sectionally and cross-temporally with the flow of output in every other sector in the past and the future. From this point of view, economic growth appears as a process of increasing sectoral differentiation and increasing temporal roundaboutness, a process with no apparent end in sight. What we observe as accumulation of capital, both physical and human, is just the form that the process takes.

What did the economists make of all this? Robert Lucas might have been speaking for the profession when he responded to Fischer's draft comment on one of his own papers. "No, no response to your October 15, [1993] letter. I think specific, simulatable models are a good thing to have, and am in the business of producing them. You are doing something different, which I leave you to define. So we are not going to have a meeting of minds."[46] But Fischer didn't give up. "I like [specific models] too, so long as we call them 'examples' and so long as we don't try to fit them to data." Lucas didn't give up, either. "But why does this follow? What else but 'examples' can we use to fit the data?" Fischer took the last word: "I like fitting examples to stylized facts, as I think you do, but not to an array of alleged numerical features of the economy."

At the heart of Lucas' criticism lies the conviction, completely at odds with Fischer's view, that the general equilibrium model with no restrictions is so general that it is vacuous. Since it is consistent with practically any set of facts, it can hardly be said to explain any specific set. Indeed, since it is impossible to disprove the model with evidence, it hardly even qualifies as a theory.[47] Fischer apparently saw this methodological argument as the most serious challenge to his viewpoint, and took considerable pains in the book to confront it by laying out his alternative methodological justification.

For him, the starting point of all useful analysis is some stylized empirical fact the researcher is trying to explain. That is why his book begins with a list of 23 such facts that he proposes to explain. "They are my observations, derived from everyday experience, from reading newspapers and magazines, and from studying technical publications." Ideally we would like to explain each of these facts by some kind of general equilibrium theory, he says, even if other kinds of theories are possible, because general equilibrium theories usually imply fewer profit opportunities.

Explanation of a fact, for Fischer, involves creating a specific and simple model that incorporates only "the most basic economic processes." It means revealing the underlying economics so we understand what the fact means. Explanation is about passing from the general to the specific, from the abstract to the concrete, and mostly it is a matter of thinking, not a matter of econometrics. We already know the facts, and we already know the general class of theories that would provide the most satisfying explanations. What we are looking for is a specific example focused on explaining a specific fact.

Fischer calls this process "exploring general equilibrium," and contrasts it with what he sees economists doing. Apparently they begin with a simple model whose chief attraction is that they know how to solve it, and then they test the model using data whose chief attraction is that it is available. The inevitable rejection of the model then starts a process of adding complexity, patchwork style, until the model more or less fits the data. Even if the starting point was a specific example of general equilibrium, the patches quickly cause the theory to deviate. The process keeps economists employed, and the pages of their journals filled, but it typically adds more noise than information.

As an aid to identifying theoretical noise, Fischer includes in his book a list of common economists' assumptions that are inconsistent with general equilibrium. The list, titled "What Doesn't Matter," has 13 entries including fixed factors, economies of scale, externalities, non-convexities, and adjustment costs, every one of them a basic tool in the economist's standard toolbox. These contrast with a parallel list, titled "What Matters," of 12 "key features" that are fully consistent with general equilibrium and that Fischer promises to use repeatedly in the pages that follow. Compare and contrast these two ways of doing economics, Fischer seems to be saying, and see if you don't find my way more satisfying.

Having established the general workability of the approach, as he thought, and shipped the book off to MIT Press for publication, Fischer's next move was to establish the specific workability of the approach for one of the most topical issues of the day, namely the economic growth experience of the 1980s. Fischer determined to enter that debate with a paper arguing that all the relevant facts can be explained simply as a consequence of unusually rapid but neutral technological change, change that took the form of unusually rapid sector-specific accumulation of both physical and human capital over the 1980s. Fischer's plan seems to have been to use this new paper, in combination with the book, to engage with the economists once again. Probably this would have meant leaving Goldman Sachs where, before he got sick, rumblings had begun about asking Fischer to retire.

Instead, in March 1995 his cancer returned, and this time there was really no reasonable hope for recovery, so Fischer refused further treatment. On May 1, 1995, he sent his paper "Interest Rates as Options" to the *Journal of Finance*. "I would like to publish this, though I may not be around to make any changes the referee may suggest." And then, on May 3, he sent "Equilibrium Exchanges" to the *Financial Analysts Journal*. "Barring a miracle, this is my last submission. My association with the *Journal* has been long and satisfying. Keep up the good work." Having thus cleared the decks, the next few weeks he devoted to producing a plausible draft of "Neutral Technological Change," which he now knew would be his last paper.[48]

After that, the last months of his life were spent putting his personal affairs in order. He arranged for his own hospice care, selected his own casket, and phoned up old friends. Meanwhile, two of his oldest friends kept him company on his bedside table: Van Quine's *Quiddities: An Intermittently Philosophical Dictionary*, and Noam Chomsky's *Knowledge of Language: Its Nature, Origin, and Use.* He was thinking back to 1962–1963 when, free from both Tinna and Harvard, he had begun to put in place the strategies of research and communication that had made possible his life's work. As the end approached, he stopped taking food and refused intravenous feeding in an effort to hasten the inevitable. He died on August 30, 1995.

After his death, Fischer's secretary at Goldman Sachs sent his last paper to Ed Glaeser, a young economist at Harvard who had provided extensive comment on an early draft of Fischer's book, along with a letter from Fischer that he had written back in May.

Dear Ed:

This is my last paper. I haven't finished the references section. I may or may not be able to do more work on it.

If you think a journal would find it interesting, please send it in. If you like the thrust of it and want to share authorship, feel free. Please do not feel any special obligation. I doubt the major journals would accept it even with the references completed.

The check is toward submission fees.

Sincerely,
Fischer

■ Epilogue ■

NOTHING IS CONSTANT

I start with the view that nothing is really constant. Volatilities themselves are not constant, and we can't write down the process by which the volatilities change with any assurance that the process itself will stay fixed. We'll have to keep updating our description of the process.

Fischer Black, "Studies of Stock Price
Volatility Changes" (1976, p. 177)

W hen Fischer's cancer came back, his MIT colleague John Cox, along with Jon Corzine at Goldman Sachs and Robert Merton now at the hedge fund Long-Term Capital Management (LTCM), rushed to put together a fitting tribute only a month before Fischer died. There were three dimensions to it, and they described each in a letter they wrote to Fischer.

First was the endowment of a Fischer Black Visiting Professorship of Financial Economics at MIT. "Holders of the Chair should exemplify the research qualities of its eponym: originality, curiosity, dedication to scholarship, intellectual honesty, and the courage to challenge the status quo." Second was a Fischer Black Prize to be awarded by the American Finance Association. Third was the publication of Fischer's scientific papers, along with commentaries by peers "that trace the intellectual development of the ideas, identify patterns of continuity, both across subject matter and through time, pointing out instances of fundamental changes in thought. They will include reflections on the self-integrated perspective provided by your two books."[1]

Fischer was stunned, and deeply appreciative. "As you know, I like the idea of mixing basic and applied research. I think the best pure science grows out of efforts to solve applied problems; and sometimes the best applied science grows out of simple intellectual curiosity. . . . This award is unique. I'd rather have this than any other prize out there. I hope it helps to spread my enthusiasm for finding useful truths."[2] The "other prize out there" was of course the Nobel Prize, which Fischer knew he was in line to receive for his work on options, but which he also knew is never awarded posthumously.

After his death there was a further outpouring of appreciation, beginning with a service at Memorial Church at Harvard University in October 1995.[3] The list of speakers was a veritable who's who of the financial revolution that had swept through America and then the world.

Douglas Breeden, professor at Duke University, spoke first, remembering his first contact with Fischer, which came when Fischer wrote a note of appreciation for an early paper of his.[4] It was typical of the man. "He listened to ideas, not reputations." Before he died Fischer sent Breeden a copy of his own last book, *Exploring General Equilibrium*, with a handwritten inscription: "Isn't it fun to develop and apply financial theories!"

Jon Corzine, representing Goldman Sachs, spoke of Fischer's rare combination of conceptual brilliance and practical application. "Fischer was simply the best. Giants without arrogance are rare." Fischer stood out for his unflinching honesty and integrity, both personal and intellectual, and for his commitment to excellence. But he also cared about others, and he knew how to have fun.

Michael Jensen spoke about his first meeting with Fischer in a hotel room at the Chicago airport, where they met with Bill Sharpe to discuss mutual fund performance. The result was a 29-year friendship. The man Jensen knew was never petty, never angry, never emotionally out of control. He was a model scholar, always learning and teaching, in life as well as finance.

Robert Merton, representing MIT, spoke of the "majestic colleague and dear friend" who fascinated his colleagues with his insights and questions, not least in his famous Fifty Questions course. Merton read from the tribute to Fischer that he had put together with Corzine and

Cox, and from Fischer's letter in response, "Someone out there seems to know me."

Merton Miller, representing the University of Chicago, told how Fischer had come to be appointed professor of finance without having published much of anything. "Anyone who knew Fischer could recognize that there was no risk at all." For the next 20 years, if the phone rang at 11 P.M., it was probably Fischer with a criticism of one of Miller's papers. The Graduate School of Business would do its own tribute in the form of two Fischer Black Research Fellowships, in recognition of the role Fischer had played in stimulating student research.

Fischer's brother Lee read the remarks of Myron Scholes, who could not attend in person. Scholes remembered meeting Fischer back in 1968, a man then full of excitement about both finance and life, with a mind bubbling over with ideas and a pen busy writing them down in the middle of the flow. On a personal level, he was also great fun to be with, and Scholes cherished happy memories of vacationing together on Cape Cod with their young children. Somehow Fischer made an impression that stayed with you. Even today, whenever a new intellectual problem comes up, Scholes finds himself asking, "What would Fischer say?"

Jack Treynor marveled at the large number and wide range of people who regard knowing Fischer as one of the most important things in their lives. And then he reached for words to characterize the man he had known longer than anyone else speaking that day. "For most people, ideas scarcely exist until they are reduced to symbols—to words or mathematics. But Fischer's greatest contributions were in a far country beyond symbols. For him research meant abandoning the comfortable, familiar forms rather than merely refining or extending them—letting go of the old, in order to grasp the new. Research was a lonely journey into that far country—a journey from which one can never really go home again." Death did not frighten him. "For Fischer, death was just another journey."[5]

Alethea Black, Fischer's eldest daughter, spoke last. The father she had known worshipped at the altar of logic, but at his desk he sought the sublime, and found it. As a young man, life was for him a search for meaning; as an adult an appreciation of beauty; and as a mature man a source of joy. "Time exists as a continuum that we don't understand." A budding writer herself, she concluded by reading a poem she had written for one of her short stories, "Poem Hidden in a Book to a Future You."

The eulogies attest to the range of Fischer's influence, and begin to reveal the common thread running throughout his life. Who was Fischer Black? He was the man from Mars who looked at finance, and economics, through fresh eyes. He was the Zelig who managed always to be in the center of the intellectual action, even as that center moved from the world of business into academia and then to Wall Street. He was the visionary prophet who saw how the new ideas in finance would lead to a sea change, not just in the world of practical finance but also in our everyday lives. And he was the extraordinary man who lived his life as if that sea change had already happened.

In all investment, the biggest source of risk is time. The world around us is always changing, so it is impossible to know what the future holds. If we project the past into the future and make our plans accordingly, we will almost certainly be wrong, most likely far wrong. Usually tomorrow is a lot like today, but the more distant future is beyond our reach. And even in the short run, discontinuous jumps are entirely possible. Given all that changeability, it is not at all obvious that we can even hope to understand fully the problem we face, much less to solve it in any reasonably complete way. Nevertheless this is the problem we face, and the problem we must attempt to solve.

Classical economists such as Adam Smith faced an easier problem than we do. They lived in a world in which the present was largely determined by the known past. Their goal was to recruit the power of human reason to safeguard the precious achievements of that past, mainly against the depredations of mankind itself. The principle of parsimony was always in conflict with the principle of profligacy, and not at all certain to win out. Economic theory, the product of human reason, was all about identifying the laws of motion of the economic system, the better to achieve this goal.

Only in the twentieth century did economists such as John Maynard Keynes start to face the problem of the uncertain future, but they couldn't see how to solve it. Given the inaccessibility of the future to the power of human reason, Keynes famously distinguished between speculation (bad irrationality that causes waves of stock market fluctuation) and animal spirits (good irrationality that causes capital investment despite the impossibility of calculating profitability). Individual reason cannot be depended upon, he concluded, but maybe collective reason can. Government could devise methods of social control consciously to direct the evolution of economywide aggregates so as to produce certainty and security in a future otherwise subject to the "dark forces of time and ignorance."

As the twenty-first century approached, Fischer Black had a different view. Like Keynes, he faced squarely the problem of a radically uncertain future. Like Keynes, he wanted to take maximal advantage of the opportunity offered by an open-ended future, while at the same time implementing methods of risk control to channel the realization of that opportunity within manageable bounds. Also like Keynes, he recognized the inaccessibility of the unknown future to individual human reason, and placed his faith instead in collective human reason. Unlike Keynes, however, Fischer Black saw the best agent of collective human reason as the market, not the government.

Market equilibrium, as Fischer conceived it, is all about producing two numbers, the rate of interest and the price of risk, that summarize our collective tolerance for risk as a guide for our individual choices. For Fischer, speculation and animal spirits are much the same thing, neither one good or bad, but just how people psychologically handle the unknown future. The important thing is to offer them a better way. Given the collectively determined rate of interest and price of risk at each moment in time, the capital asset pricing model (CAPM) shows how people can deliberately choose their risk exposure to match their own risk tolerance, and how they can formulate plans for dynamically altering that exposure over time. CAPM does not eliminate uncertainty, but it does show how to live with it.

It is important to emphasize that Fischer's conception of CAPM equilibrium is only an instantaneous balancing of forces at a single moment in time, and a balance that is moreover constantly shifting from moment to moment. The legendary speculator George Soros famously criticized the economists' conception of equilibrium: "Equilibrium analysis eliminates historical change by assuming away the cognitive function."[6] Possibly that criticism is apt for classical economists like Adam Smith, but not for twenty-first-century thinkers like Fischer Black. Indeed, for Fischer, the cognitive function is at the very center of the conception of equilibrium. Market prices are as volatile as they are mainly because people's understanding of the situation they face, and will face in the future, is constantly changing.

In Fischer's world, the future is unknown, and it is probably not even stationary, so knowledge of the past is not much help to us. To make matters worse, of the two prices that guide individual choices, we actually observe only the rate of interest, not the price of risk. As a consequence, Fischer's conception of equilibrium lacks any sense of balancing over time, a feature that is central to the concept of equilibrium held by most economists, classical as well as modern. In Fischer's world, we can't observe the price that links today with tomorrow, so we can't hope to optimize over time. What we observe is the market price of current wealth, and all we can choose is how to allocate that wealth today.

Simply put, radical uncertainty about the future means that human reason is insufficient to determine behavior, and it is that indeterminacy that makes room for psychology and persuasion to make a difference. The same indeterminacy is the source of what George Soros has called the alchemy of finance. Mere ideas about the future become realities in the present when enough people become persuaded. Fischer's life was devoted to persuading people of one big idea, the big idea embodied in the capital asset pricing model, and its manifold ramifications. To the extent he could persuade people to think about the world in a CAPM way, he could make the CAPM ideal a reality. Ideas would change institutions, and institutions would change ideas, in a process of co-evolution toward CAPM.

When Fischer first encountered CAPM, he thought he could see the future. And in his youthful excitement, he thought he could short-circuit the process of evolution toward that future by jumping in with a second-generation product, the Stagecoach Fund, before first-generation products such as the simple index fund had been introduced. The leap didn't work, and from its failure Fischer learned an important life lesson. In an evolutionary process it is important to be ahead of the curve, but not too far ahead; and to get the pace right you need to be engaged in the day-to-day flux. That's the truth behind Fischer's statement that he found Goldman better for learning than a university. At Goldman he was in the flux where the evolution was taking place; client concerns kept him grounded in reality rather than jumping ahead. Even in academia, Fischer preferred to work on applied problems not just because he wanted to feel useful, but more important because doing so kept him in touch with the current stage of the evolutionary process in the outside real world.

Fischer wasn't interested merely in understanding the world; he wanted to change it. Living as he did in the world of ideas, he thought that he could most effectively change the world by changing ideas about the world. Because of noise, natural selection doesn't work very efficiently to weed out bad ideas, nor do human cognitive powers work very efficiently to mutate good new ideas. There was therefore every reason to suspect that the world of ideas must be rife with inefficiency. Fischer devoted his life to intellectual creativity and arbitrage in that inefficient world of ideas.

A naturally risk-averse person, Fischer chose to take all of his risk in a world where he saw high reward (eventually) for being right, and not much cost for being wrong. As he assessed the opportunities available to him, the highest risk-adjusted return came from investing his time and energy in the production of new knowledge, so that is what he did. As in all risky investments, the return was not guaranteed. The key was therefore to prepare oneself, psychologically as well as financially, to accept the fluctuations of fortune with equanimity, and keep rolling the dice. Fischer just kept reminding himself that what matters is not the realized historical return but the expected future return.

As he worked to generate new ideas, and to find effective ways to insert them into the evolutionary flux, Fischer gave surprisingly little thought to the likely consequences of his new ideas, supposing they were to be adopted. If people adopted his proposal for dynamic trading, would that not change the dynamic behavior of asset prices, perhaps making them more volatile? (Think about the role of portfolio insurance strategies in the crash of October 1987.) If people adopted his theory of accounting, would that not open up new possibilities for manipulation of numbers by those interested in lying rather than telling the truth about firm value? (Think about Enron and its demise in 2001.) If people adopted his pension funding proposals, would not Congress simply change the tax law to eliminate the arbitrage he was trying to exploit?

Because he didn't consider the likely consequences of his proposals, Fischer could seem wildly irresponsible, and in a sense he was, but that's not how he saw himself. From his point of view, the economic system is an evolving process in which each new solution inevitably generates new problems that call for yet another round of new solutions. At any moment in time, the system is in equilibrium, but over time its behavior is changed by evolution, the precise course of which is impossible to foretell. His attitude was that we can't really know the effect of any change unless we actually try it, so why don't we try it and see?

This pragmatic, experimental attitude found more favor in the world of practical business than it did in academia. His idea that central banks should stop trying to manipulate interest rates, and that business cycles should be allowed to run their course, seemed to academic macroeconomists not only irresponsible but also actively dangerous. The entire field of macroeconomics had arisen, after all, in response to very real disturbances such as the Great Depression that had given rise to very real social configurations like fascism and communism. Mere macroeconomic intervention, whether of the Keynesian or monetarist variety, seemed infinitely preferable. What sane person would propose that we try Fischer's ideas and see how they work out? We did try them, and we did see, and the result is the economics that is accepted today.

It is certainly true, Fischer might have answered, that the economics of today is in some kind of intellectual equilibrium with the economic experience of yesterday, but there are forces at work changing both. When he proposes one of his outrageous ideas, he does not expect the current intellectual equilibrium suddenly to shift over to his position. He is planting a seed for the future, and meanwhile trying to shift the current equilibrium of ideas marginally in his own direction. The way you change business practice, Fischer learned through experience, is by proposing something rather close to existing practice that people can actually implement. The way you change ideas, Fischer also discovered through experience, was very different. When he tried to frame his ideas in terms close to existing academic practice, he was ignored. He had more success in shifting the equilibrium when he staked out a position rather far away from it, and defended that position consistently and tenaciously.

Fischer's strategy for changing the thinking in academic economics and finance was not only to stake out extreme positions, but also to solicit support for those positions from outside academia. His reason for publishing in the *Financial Analysts Journal* was not only that he found the standard economics journals largely closed to him, but also that the *FAJ* had a circulation 10 times that of even the best journals. The circulation did not include very many academics, to be sure, but it did include almost every important practitioner. By changing ideas on the ground, Fischer hoped eventually to change ideas in the ivory tower as well. Academia would follow where practice leads.

Such a rhetorical strategy could be viewed as highly irresponsible. What if everyone behaved as Fischer behaved, staking out extreme positions and seeking support from the public before their theories have been properly vetted and approved by the established academic authorities? The result surely would be intellectual anarchy, distraction of impressionable youth, and regression of scientific knowledge. Maybe so, but Fischer never thought of himself as setting an example for others to imitate, even if they could. He was an original, and he knew it. There was no chance that everyone would behave as he behaved. The real problem was not too many Fischers, but too few.

The twenty-first-century worldview that faces squarely the extent of our uncertainty about the future also raises deep questions about the very possibility of a truly scientific understanding of the world around us. If nothing is constant, there are no unchanging laws of motion to be found, and we waste our time if we insist on looking for them. From a scientific point of view, formal mathematical theories that rely on assumptions of stationarity in order to find determinate solutions to the optimizing problem of the firm or the household simply assume away the essential core of the problem. Elaborate statistical analyses of mountains of historical data rely similarly on assumptions of stationarity, and so, from a scientific point of view, it is similarly hard to learn much about our true problem in this way. Thus the two predominant research methodologies in economics and finance, methodologies that had been developed and refined over centuries past, were closed to Fischer.

Says Fischer, "I do not fully understand some of the tools and concepts used by those who have had training in economics or finance."[7] Actually, of course, he understood them all too well, just as well as those who used the tools and concepts understood Fischer's criticisms of them. The limitations of formalism and econometrics that Fischer pointed out were not news to any good practitioner, but what other choice did they have? The world may not be stationary, but that doesn't mean we cannot progress toward understanding it by understanding first a world that is more tractable. The tools and concepts that we develop for that tractable world can then, in some future time, be extended to incorporate more realism. And meanwhile the process of developing those tools and concepts helps us to learn more about the real world. It gives us models we can actually solve and match up to data that we can actually collect using statistical methods we can actually implement. Doing so, we learn about the world, and in that way we make scientific progress by increments.

Such a defense of the methodological status quo wasn't good enough for Fischer. When he says that he doesn't understand the standard tools and concepts, he means to question whether those tools and concepts can be depended upon to produce more information than noise, given the nature of the system we are trying to understand. And he means to suggest that maybe the standard tools and concepts are not so much helping us to progress by increments as they are holding us back from progressing by leaps. Maybe we need to step back first in order to find solid ground from which we can leap forward. In this regard, CAPM was the only solid ground Fischer ever found, and he kept his feet planted firmly on it for his entire career. Denying himself the false psychic comfort of mathematical modeling and econometrics, he adopted instead a more direct and elementary approach that admits, indeed embraces, the extent of our ignorance. Everything he subsequently achieved was more or less a direct consequence of looking at the world through CAPM glasses.

Are markets efficient as Eugene Fama insists, or excessively volatile as behavioral economist Robert Shiller insists?[8] From Fischer's point of view, the question is ill-posed. Certainly he believed that the collective wisdom embodied in market prices is usually much better than any individual guess. But he also says, "Given the volatility of expectations, I'm surprised that markets are not more volatile."[9] At any moment in time, markets are about as efficient as they can be, given current conditions. But market prices are also not as a volatile as they should be, given ideal conditions. As markets become more efficient, we should expect them also to become more volatile. For Fischer, efficiency and volatility are not alternatives but complements.

Is CAPM dead? After the initial wave of excitement about the empirical success of CAPM, it became increasingly clear that measured

CAPM betas were not very good predictors of the cross section of stock returns.[10] In response, empiricists like Eugene Fama turned away from CAPM in favor of so-called factor models. And theorists like Stephen Ross developed the explicitly multifactor arbitrage pricing theory (APT) as an alternative to CAPM. Not Fischer. For him CAPM was right in the pragmatic sense that really mattered. It had produced usable insights into how the world works, and it continued to do so. In a world that was infinitely changeable, CAPM remained always the pole star for this explorer of uncharted economic lands.

Colleagues of Fischer often remark that you never could predict what his position would be on any issue under discussion. The very same colleagues also often remark on his steadfast, not to say rigid, attachment to CAPM. But what none of his colleagues fully grasped was the connection between these two dimensions of the man. It was Fischer's insistence on looking at the world through CAPM glasses, without the noise added by formalism and econometrics, that produced his unique insights time after time. It was his grounding in CAPM that freed him to indulge in flights of pure intellectual fancy. CAPM gave Fischer a way to be in the daily flux while still maintaining a critical perspective outside of it.

With CAPM as his pole star, Fischer made himself into a point of intellectual calm and constancy in all the various settings in which he participated. As the fashion in academic finance swung from efficient markets to behavioral explanations of excessive volatility, Fischer kept his footing. As the fashion in academic economics swung from Keynesianism to Monetarism Mark I to Monetarism Mark II, Fischer kept his footing. And similarly in the practical world, the crash of 1987 and the super profits of 1993 both left him unmoved. Neither the bad times nor the good times would last, he thought, and he turned out to be right.

In February 1994, the hedge fund Long-Term Capital Management commenced operations with $1 billion in capital, and with a star-studded cast of principals led by fabled Salomon Brothers bond trader John Meriwether and including also the future Nobelists Robert Merton and Myron Scholes.[11] Fischer Black had been invited to join, but declined. Given the mounting campaign at Goldman to encourage him to retire, and the unprecedented 1993 bonus payout, you might have thought that Fischer would welcome the opportunity to try something different, but he wanted no part of it. "They are loading up on risk," he told Cathy.

The principals at LTCM didn't think so. Their core idea was to exploit some rather simple arbitrage opportunities that were more or less sure to make money provided only that they were prepared to hold the position for as long as six months to two years. There was no very fancy mathematical or econometric modeling involved in identifying the opportunities. The technically most sophisticated part of the strategy was the system for risk control, where they took elaborate precautions to lock in long-term financing and to control their exposure to short-term asset price fluctuation using "value at risk" estimates based on past patterns of price movement. The LTCM partners thought they had a low-risk, high-return strategy, and for a while it worked like a charm. They made so much money, in fact, that in December 1997 their original capital had grown to $7.5 billion and the firm decided to return $2.7 billion to the original investors.

But by August 1998, the firm's capital was down 40 percent, due to a series of historically unprecedented market moves for which their risk control system had not prepared them. They still had plenty of capital, much more than they had started with, but their attempt to raise new capital in September was unsuccessful, and further unprecedented market moves brought the firm to the brink of failure. On September 23 William J. McDonough, president of the Federal Reserve Bank of New York, brokered a meeting between LTCM and its largest creditors. The result was a deal in which the creditors accepted ownership of the remaining assets of LTCM rather than forcing immediate liquidation. The partners and investors were left with only $400 million.

In all investment the biggest source of risk is time. In effect, the core of the LTCM strategy was the idea that time tends to cost more than it is worth, a difference between price and value that they tried to arbitrage in a myriad different ways. The principals didn't think they were loading up on risk, but as it turned out they were. If they could have held their positions for six months to two years, they were guaranteed to make money, but as it happened they were unable to hold on, notwithstanding a risk control system that was state-of-the-art. Fischer Black's prescience in this regard kept him from joining the principals for the glory days when they earned 40 percent returns for a strategy that seemed quite conservative. But it also kept him safe from the eventual denouement, though of course by that time he was not around to see it.

What did Fischer see that no one else did? First, he always emphasized the limitations of the "value at risk" methodology, and urged instead a focus on the major risks that could bring down the entire operation. The fact that something had never happened in prior historical experience was no reason at all to rule it out as a possible future event. Second, the idea that time tends to cost more than it is worth is an idea that markets are inefficient in a way that can be exploited for systematic profit. Fischer had met this idea long before in Treynor's view that a value-based trading strategy is superior to an information-based strategy, but he never succeeded in convincing himself of the merit of Treynor's view.

As always, Fischer thought it was safer to assume that markets were efficient unless there was a strong argument for believing otherwise. The problem is that the theory doesn't say very much about what time should be worth. The simple CAPM, for example, has no answer at all. CAPM is about equilibrium at a moment in time and has nothing to say about how that equilibrium changes through time. In Fischer's mind, the principals of LTCM were loading up on risk because CAPM provided no convincing reason to think that time was systematically priced higher than its value.

Most of Fischer's colleagues never could understand why he held onto CAPM and resisted the apparent scientific progress of the field. They put it down to sheer stubbornness. They similarly could not understand Fischer's simultaneous willingness to entertain the most outlandish ideas. They put that down to lack of training that left him lacking in sound judgment. The apparent paradox of simultaneous rigidity and flexibility that Fischer presented to his colleagues thus usually got explained away as nothing more than a set of personality quirks. But from a deeper point of view there was no paradox. Having found as he thought the only secure anchorage available, namely CAPM, Fischer could entertain any idea, no matter how outlandish, without any fear of losing his moorings.

Fischer was an original, but it was Jack Treynor who set his originality on the path of exploring the revolutionary idea of finance by introducing him to CAPM. Fischer did the work that Treynor never could, but it was Treynor more than anyone else who showed him what needed to be done. For Treynor, as well as Fischer, CAPM was about much more than finance, and it was about much more than economics, too. It was also about life, and it was also about politics.

Awarded the Chorafas Prize in April 1994, and anticipating that his surgery would make it impossible for him to travel to Berne in Switzerland to accept the prize, Fischer prepared a speech on "Equilibrium and Politics" that expressed his libertarian political views more sharply than ever before. "As I have studied markets over the years, I have become more and more impressed with their resilience. I believe that both financial and economic markets work, almost all the time, without the intervention of government. Indeed I think the government's influence is almost always to interfere with the proper workings of the market. Once the government stands ready to act, people apply pressure to make it act in their interest. The public interest is quickly forgotten."[12]

The evidence suggests that Fischer came to these mature libertarian views reluctantly, and only over considerable time. He was a supporter of Kennedy in his youth and John Anderson in his middle age. Was it his experience on Wall Street, a world where libertarian sentiments are the common culture, that changed him? To the contrary, the evidence suggests that it was his experience in academia. Says Fischer: "Government influence in teaching and research is enormous. It leads, I believe, to a great loss of welfare." Always more a man of ideas than a man of action, Fischer's libertarianism was first and foremost about the free marketplace of ideas. The obstacles he had confronted in academia were, he came to conclude, a result of government influence on the organization and functioning of the university, combined with "slowly changing university traditions. I see many of these traditions as outdated."[13]

Chosen as Financial Engineer of the Year by the International Association of Financial Engineers, and having recovered sufficiently from his operation, Fischer attended their annual meeting in October 1994 and used the opportunity to share his views on "Doctoral Education, the Business School, and the University." "I see our university system as similar to the former Soviet empire, and as having similar problems . . . teaching and research are too uniform. They do not respond quickly to shifts in tastes and technology. (In fact, they try to make this into the virtue of preserving traditional values and avoiding fads.) And, most important, teaching and research simply cost too much. . . . In my view, the basic problem with research in business (and economics) is not that it's too theoretical, or too mathematical, or too divorced from the real world (though all of these are indeed serious problems). The basic problem is that we have too much research, and the wrong kinds of research, because governments, firms, foundations, and generous alumni support it."[14]

The way to create a more free marketplace of ideas was, Fischer continued, to stop subsidizing the production of new ideas. Professors, he said, should be paid for their teaching only, since the ones who are not interested in research will stop producing it, and the ones who are interested in research will do it anyway. The result will be a net gain for society. Fewer noise traders relative to information traders in the marketplace of ideas can be expected to increase efficiency in that market.

The academics in Fischer's audience were appalled. Fischer was talking about them! And he was telling their deans to stop rewarding them for research! Once again Fischer succeeded in getting people to talk. But of course what they talked about was themselves, missing as they did so one important dimension of what Fischer was saying. Here, amongst his fellow financial engineers, and facing the likely end of his life, Fischer was actually talking about himself.

Long ago, as an undergraduate at Harvard, Fischer had decided that he didn't much care what he did to make his living, teaching in a university or working in industry, provided it left him time and energy to do the research that he wanted. And from then on that is how he lived his life. He moved from industry (Arthur D. Little and Associates in Finance) to the university (Chicago and MIT) and back to industry (Goldman Sachs), but no matter how he made his living, he always made time for the work that was his life. Even more, the intellectual projects that he began in one setting continued to unfold even as the setting changed.

It was an intellectual strategy that worked very well for him. Beholden to no one, he was free to choose his own problems and work on them using the methods that seemed to him the most likely to succeed. He had no boss but himself. Notwithstanding personal trials that would have diverted anyone less focused, and notwithstanding intellectual rejection that would have crushed anyone less self-reliant, he managed to live the life he wanted to live.

Fischer Black was many things. But first and foremost, from beginning to end, through thick and thin, he was a man of ideas. And the big idea that occupied his mind, first and foremost, from beginning to end, through thick and thin, was CAPM, the revolutionary idea of finance.

Notes

PROLOGUE   The Price of Risk

1. Paul Samuelson, "In on the Creation," unpublished mimeo (September 22, 1997).
2. Samuelson (1962).
3. See Chapter 3 for an investigation of the rumors.
4. Treynor and Black (1973).
5. Derman (2004) provides a fascinating memoir of a leading financial engineer who worked closely with Fischer Black at Goldman Sachs.
6. Treynor (1996) was the concluding article in a special issue of the *Journal of Portfolio Management* published as a tribute to Fischer Black.
7. Treynor (1990, 4).
8. Black (1981b, 14).
9. Treynor (1996, 93).
10. Treynor (1996, 94).
11. Black (1995b, xi).
12. Black interview with Zvi Bodie, Boston, July 1989.
13. Derman (2004, 168).
14. Fischer Black Papers. Institute Archives and Special Collections, MIT Libraries, Cambridge, Massachusetts. Box 10, Folder "How to Look at a Fixed Income Portfolio."
15. "Unobservables" (February 1988). Fischer Black Papers, Box 25.
16. Black (1970, 10).
17. Fischer Black Papers, Box 23, Folder "Sermon on the Mount."
18. Treynor (1996, 94).
19. Simonton (1988, 252).

CHAPTER ONE   Thou Living Ray of Intellectual Fire

1. Gersh (1959).
2. The inspiration for the name was probably the American Society of Composers, Authors, and Publishers.
3. *Bronxville Mirror*, April 15, 1954, p. 5.
4. William Falconer, "The Shipwreck" (1762), Canto I, lines 104–105.
5. Kephart (1913).
6. In these positions she went by her married name, Ellen Winston. See Woofter and Winston (1939).
7. There was a change in leadership at the parent company, McGraw-Hill, but there was also a looming Congressional investigation into price fixing in the industry. See Herling (1962, 250–251).
8. Kirkland and Kennedy (1905) provide the official history of Camden.
9. Carpenter (1954, 1955).
10. Black Family Papers. FB to "Gamma," November 5, 1955.
11. Black Family Papers. FB to parents, November 13, 1955; October 8, 1955.
12. In his application to Bolt Beranek and Newman in summer 1962, Fischer refers to this course as the highlight of his undergraduate career. Fischer Black Papers, Box 2, Folder "Biographies."
13. Bruner (1960, 13, 58). Fischer asked his grandmother to give him Bruner's book for Christmas 1960.
14. Bruner (1962, Ch. 2).
15. Black Family Papers. FB to Elizabeth Black, November 22, 1956.
16. Clifford Geertz, Lecture 31, *Lectures in Cultural Ecology* (spring term, 1957). Thanks to Karl Reisman for providing this document.
17. Black Family Papers. FB to parents, May 9, 1957.
18. Black Family Papers. FB to parents, November 19, 1958.
19. Black Family Papers. FB to parents, n.d. [summer and fall 1960].
20. Edwards (1996, 222–235) provides an account of Miller's seminal role in cognitive psychology.
21. Miller, Galanter, and Pribram (1960, 42).
22. Division of Engineering and Applied Sciences Records. Fischer Black folder. The other members of the committee were George Miller, Van Quine, and the computer scientist Peter Calingaert.
23. Leary (1983, 78).

24. Fischer Black Graduate Student Records. Memo from RHP to JPE, May 2, 1961.
25. Black Family Papers. FB to parents, October 16, 1962.
26. Black Family Papers. FB to parents, August 26, 1961.
27. Black Family Papers. FB to "Gamma," July 31, 1961.
28. Black Family Papers. FB to parents, November 21, 1961; September 15, 1962.
29. Black Family Papers. FB to parents, May 3, 1962; July 13, 1962.
30. Black Family Papers. FB Jr. to FB Sr., March 27, 1962.
31. Black Family Papers. FB to parents, February 4, 1963.
32. "A Syntax Directed Compiler Based on a Macro Assembler," November 30, 1964. Fischer Black Papers, Box 15, Folder "My Programming Language—History."
33. On Licklider, see Hafner and Lyon (1996, 24–39), Edwards (1996, 262–271), and Waldrop (2001).
34. Licklider (1960).
35. Licklider (1965, 28, 126).
36. Minsky (1968) includes McCarthy's 1958 proposal as Section 7.1.
37. Licklider (1965, 190).
38. Black Family Papers. FB to parents, March 8, 1963. MIT has no record of any official enrollment.
39. Black Family Papers. FB to parents, March 8, 1963; April 1, 1963.
40. Bell (1995).
41. Black (1965, 97).
42. A revised version of the thesis was published as Black (1968).
43. Crevier (1993).
44. Black Family Papers. FB to parents, March 14, 1964.
45. Bell (1997).
46. Black Family Papers. Hans R. Stoll to FB Sr., September 4, 1995.
47. Black Family Papers. FB to parents, March 13, 1964.

CHAPTER TWO   An Idea in the Rough

1. The official history of ADL, published to celebrate its centenary year, is Kahn (1986).
2. The official cause of death on April 27, 1966, was stated as "pulmonary edema."

3. Treynor and Vancil (1956).
4. Black (1981b).
5. Treynor and Vancil (1956, 29–30).
6. Treynor (1962, 20). In the 1961 draft (p. 23), the discussion concludes similarly with these words:

   > We see that the risk premium μ_i exacted by the market on ba-
   > sis investment (i) with uncertainty E_i equals $2/\lambda$ times the co-
   > variance of E_i with total market uncertainty E^*. The same
   > statement naturally holds true for any investment with general
   > uncertainty.

   In both cases Treynor emphasizes the essential insight that the correct measure of financial risk is covariance, not variance. But in
   1961 he is thinking about pricing the basic risk factors, while a year
   later he is thinking about pricing shares.
7. Not until it was too late. See Treynor's appendix to Good, Ferguson,
   and Treynor (1976).
8. "Investment Fund Management, Report to Yale University" (July
   1966), p. 75. I thank Jack Treynor for providing me with a copy of
   this document.
9. The first comprehensive *Study of Mutual Funds (1962)* was commis-
   sioned by the SEC from the Wharton School of Finance and Commerce. The immediate background to the 1967 legislation was the
   SEC report *Public Policy Implications of Investment Company Growth*
   (1966).
10. Jensen (1968) cites an unpublished preliminary draft of his thesis,
    dated July 1967, and titled "Risk, the Pricing of Capital Assets, and
    the Evaluation of Investment Portfolios." The published version ex-
    tends the analysis back to 1945.
11. Samuelson (1965a), Mandelbrot (1966).
12. Roberts (1959), Fama (1965).
13. Kendall (1953, 11, 13).
14. Black Family Papers. FB to parents, April 3, 1967. The memo was
    Working Memorandum No. 1, Case #69154; Fahey Papers.
15. Even more, Fischer insisted to Fahey that ADL had a responsibility to
    Yale University, whose program of active investing to beat the mar-
    ket Fahey and Treynor had blessed only a year before. He drafted a
    letter that then went out from Fahey reversing their previous advice.

"What we find upon closer examination is this: that we are unable to demonstrate that professional fund managers (as we find them in the mutual fund industry) of *any* style are able to outperform the market as a whole with any consistency." Fahey to John Ecklund, May 25, 1967; Fahey Papers.

16. Douglas (1969).

17. Samuelson (1965a). Page 370 in *Mutual Fund Legislation of 1967*, Hearings before the Committee on Banking and Currency, United States Senate; Ninetieth Congress, First Session, July 31–August 2, 1967.

18. He never published the first, but Note No. 2 eventually became Treynor and Black (1976).

19. Cary and Bright (1969).

20. Fischer's underlying idea was the same as Treynor's, to compare a managed portfolio with a hypothetical unmanaged market portfolio leveraged up or down in order to have the same market risk. Sharpe had criticized the Treynor measure for neglecting the independent risk that comes from the inevitable lack of perfect diversification in a managed portfolio. Fischer's proposed index is essentially Treynor's, but with a correction for independent risk as well.

21. Financial Note No. 4A, "How to Use Security Analysis to Improve Portfolio Selection" (February 1, 1968), p. 2.

22. Treynor and Black (1973, 67).

23. Treynor was trying to do much the same in-house at Merrill Lynch. Fischer's Financial Note No. 4A concludes, "This model, and the resulting equations, are the work of Jack L. Treynor. My contribution is primarily that of authorship."

24. In 1945, the New York Society of Financial Analysts began publishing what was then called the *Analysts Journal*. In 1947, the National Federation of Financial Analysts Societies formed out of a number of regional societies, and in 1954 it took over the journal. In 1960, the organization renamed itself the Financial Analysts Federation and renamed its journal the *Financial Analysts Journal*. Finally, in 1990, the Financial Analysts Federation and the Institute of Chartered Financial Analysts joined together to form the current Association of Investment Management and Research.

25. Molodovsky (1974).

26. "Editorial Viewpoint," *Financial Analysts Journal* 27 (No. 2), p. 7.
27. "Editor's Comment: The Parable of the Blacksmiths," *Financial Analysts Journal* 32 (No. 1, January/February 1976), p. 4.
28. Glenelg P. Caterer, "Editorial Comment: The Parable of the Horses," *Financial Analysts Journal* 32 (No. 2, March/April 1976), p. 4. Caterer is listed among the 268 "founding fathers" who passed the first CFA exam in 1964.
29. William Sharpe, "Editor's Comment: The Parable of the Money Managers," *Financial Analysts Journal* 32 (No. 4, July/August 1976), p. 4.
30. Originally Financial Note No. 28 (July 1973).
31. Black's article won the Graham and Dodd award for an unprecedented fourth time.

CHAPTER THREE   Some Kind of an Education

1. Treynor (1962), French (2003).
2. Lintner (1965b), Sharpe (1966b), and Fama (1968). More generally, and rigorously, see Stone (1970).
3. Bernstein (1992, 60). Probably Friedman's objection echoes earlier battles between himself and the Cowles Commission, where Markowitz first developed the idea, stimulated by Tjalling Koopmans and Jacob Marschak. After the Commission had migrated to Yale, under the research directorship of James Tobin, Markowitz would spend a year there turning the dissertation into the first draft of what would eventually become the 1959 book.
4. Bernstein (1992, 209). Interview with Jack Treynor, March 23, 1990. Bernstein Tapes, Cowles Research Library, Yale University.
5. Butters and Lintner (1945).
6. Lintner (1948); Butters, Lintner, and Cary (1951).
7. Lintner (1971) is the definitive statement of Lintner's version of the theory.
8. Lintner (1965b, 32), Lintner (1969).
9. This emphasis on the importance of the entrepreneur likely originates in Lintner's classroom encounters with "the great Joseph Schumpeter," as Lintner invariably referred to him. See Schumpeter (1934).

10. Lintner (1956, 1965b).

11. "Standards for Judging New Capital Investments." Lintner Papers, Baker Library Historical Collections, Harvard Business School Archives, Carton 4, File 17.

12. Lintner (1959).

13. "Normative Criteria for Dividend Payouts in Large Listed Corporations" (December 28, 1957). Lintner Papers, Carton 3, Files 72–73.

14. Lintner Papers, Carton 3, File 16.

15. Lintner (1963, 1964) sketch the implications of the theory before Lintner (1965b) tackles the theory itself.

16. Farrar (1962).

17. Lintner (1964, 50).

18. "Decisions under Uncertainty Seminar." Lintner Papers, Carton 4, File 47.

19. Lockwood Rianhard Jr., "On Selecting Leveraged Portfolios" (November 5, 1962); Robert B. Wilson, "A Simplicial Algorithm for Concave Programming," DBA thesis, June 1963. Chapter 23D in Pratt, Raiffa, and Schlaifer (1965) concerns "The Portfolio Problem."

20. "Portfolio Analysis Notes." Lintner Papers, Carton 2, File 37.

21. Lintner (1981).

22. "Security Prices and Risk: The Theory and a Comparative Analysis of AT&T and Leading Industrials" (June 24, 1965). Lintner Papers, Carton 4, File 13. See also Douglas (1969).

23. Markowitz (1959, 96–101).

24. See also Sharpe (1963).

25. Sharpe (1961, 89).

26. Sharpe (1964, 438, footnote 22).

27. Fama (1973).

28. The dissertation was published as "Market and Industry Factors in Stock Price Behavior" (King 1966).

29. Fisher and Lorie (1964, 17).

30. The unpublished 1963 dissertation, titled "The Distribution of the Daily First Differences of Stock Prices: A Test of Mandelbrot's Stable Paretian Hypothesis," had a somewhat narrower focus than the revised 1965 published version, titled "The Behavior of Stock-Market Prices."

31. Mandelbrot (1963, 1967) were portions of a larger unpublished manuscript dated March 26, 1962. See Mandelbrot (1997, 417–418) for publishing details.
32. Mitchell (1915), Mills (1927).
33. Cootner (1964, 337).
34. Arbitrage ensures not full statistical independence, but only some kind of martingale (Samuelson 1965a, Mandelbrot 1966), and maybe not even that (Mandelbrot 1971).
35. Mandelbrot and Hudson (2004) provides a usefully accessible summary of the subsequent dispute between Mandelbrot and the mainstream of academic finance.
36. Samuelson (1965a), Mandelbrot (1966).
37. Fama (1965, 1971); Fama and Roll (1968, 1971).
38. Fama (1991), Black (1993a).
39. Treynor (1961, 18, equation 30).
40. Roll and Ross (1980, 1074). Treynor's (1993) "In Defense of CAPM" concludes: "APT joins the idea of specifying security risk in terms of a factor structure . . . with Modigliani and Miller's arbitrage argument. Some may argue that, in effect, APT substitutes systematic risk *factors* for Modigliani and Miller's risk *classes*." I read this passage as autobiographical, substituting Treynor (1961) for APT.
41. According to contemporary news reports, the speech was called "Development of Option Price Theory," and was held on the afternoon of June 5, 1989, at the ANA Hotel Osaka.
42. Black (1985b).

CHAPTER FOUR   Living Up to the Model

1. Scholes (1972); Miller and Scholes (1972, 1978, 1981, 1982).
2. The dissertation, modeled on Fama, Fisher, Jensen, and Roll (1969) and published as Scholes (1972), was one of the first of what would become a huge literature of event studies.
3. The most comprehensive accounts of the Wells Fargo experiment are Jahnke (1990) and Bernstein (1992, Ch. 12). Black and Scholes (1974b) and Booth (1973) provide contemporaneous postmortems of the Stagecoach Fund episode.

4. Myron Scholes and Fischer Black, "Applications of the Capital Asset Pricing Model to Portfolio Management: Research Findings," December 1, 1969. Fischer Black Papers, Box 28.

5. Miller and Scholes (1972).

6. Ibid., page 17.

7. David E. Besenfelder and Wayne H. Wagner, "Low-Risk Portfolios Levered to Market Risk: July 1945–June 1970," March 19, 1971.

8. Bernstein (1992, 250).

9. Roll (1969). From this perspective, attempts to concentrate the portfolio in low-beta stocks will produce inefficient portfolios with excess variability that is not compensated by any extra return.

10. Bagehot (1971), Black (1971b).

11. Scholes favored negotiating each trade individually. See page 7, Myron Scholes and Fischer Black, "Applications of the CAPM to Portfolio Management: Implementation," January 8, 1971. Fischer Black Papers, Box 28.

12. Cuneo and Wagner (1975, 7).

13. Fischer thought that in the longer run there was considerable market opportunity for "Expanding the Market for Short Term Securities." Financial Note No. 10 (November 26, 1969).

14. J.A. McQuown and W. H. Wagner, "Providing Leverage for Efficient Market Portfolios: From a Banker's Point of View," unpublished mimeo, May 17, 1971.

15. This idea is implicit in Black's idealized "world without money" (Black 1970).

16. Black and Scholes (1974b, 407).

17. The 1969 proposal suggested a weighted portfolio of all the stocks in the universe, using $-\log \beta_i$ as the weight on stock i. The idea that you want to choose the weights to minimize portfolio variance would come later.

18. Black (1972b).

19. In Financial Note No. 15A (August 26, 1970), the first draft of what would become the zero-beta model, Black thanks John Long and Robert Merton for drawing his attention to this fact.

20. Mayers (1972). Roll (1977) suggests that all tests of CAPM are misspecified since, practically speaking, it is impossible to measure the complete market portfolio.

21. Black and Scholes (1974b, 405).

22. Black and Scholes (1974a); see also Black and Scholes (1972).
23. Black (1973, 10).
24. Black (1976a, 1980a, 1993b). See Chapter 9.
25. "The Trouble with Econometric Models," Appendix B in "The Impact of Administration Proposals on the US Financial System," by Myron Scholes and Fischer Black (June 1974). Fischer Black Papers, Box 27. A revised version of this paper was eventually published as Black (1982).
26. "Managing Traders," unpublished mimeo, December 21, 1994.

CHAPTER FIVE   Tortuous Economic Intuition

1. Samuelson (1968, 1049).
2. Merton (1997, 21).
3. Financial Note No. 6A, page 2. On page 24, Fischer notes that Tobin (1965, 43–47) investigates a similar idea in a model where the rate of interest is zero.
4. The notation here assumes that $x = x(w,t)$ a function of both wealth and time, so x_1 is the derivative with respect to wealth and x_2 is the derivative with respect to time.
5. Fischer published the analysis supporting a constant leverage strategy only in 1988, when similar strategies came into vogue as forms of "portfolio insurance." Fischer's version for Goldman Sachs, which they marketed as "constant proportion portfolio insurance" (Black and Perold 1992), has its origin in Financial Note No. 6.
6. Financial Note No. 11.
7. "How We Came Up with the Option Formula," *Fischer Black on Options*, Vol. 1, No. 10 (June 21, 1976), p. 4.
8. The relationship between fluctuations in the option price and the stock price implies that $\beta_w = (xw_1/w)\beta_x$. The capital asset pricing model then implies that the expected return on the option can be written as $E(\Delta w/w) = (r + a\beta_w)\Delta t$, or $E(\Delta w) = (rw + axw_1\beta_x)\Delta t$, where a is the excess return that compensates for bearing market risk.
9. "How We Came Up with the Option Formula," *Fischer Black on Options*, Vol. 1, No. 10 (June 21, 1976), p. 6.
10. Scholes (1998).

11. The student was David S. Wilburn, and the thesis "A Model of the Put and Call Option Market" (June 1970). Wilburn's data was subsequently the basis of Black and Scholes (1972).

12. Thorp and Kassouf (1967) had proposed something like this hedge. Because they thought that warrants tended to be overpriced, they favored a hedge that was short the warrant and long the stock. But they could not figure out the appropriate theoretical hedge ratio, and instead proposed rules of thumb based on supposed empirical regularities.

13. Scholes (1998, 354).

14. This is not the first draft, but it is notably earlier than the October 1, 1970, draft, which is the earliest Black himself had available when he wrote his 1976 account. The October draft is labeled Financial Note No. 16B, so it is a second version. Bernstein (1992, 220) mistakenly refers to the October draft as the first draft.

15. Scholes (1998, 353). Scholes places the initial meeting in spring 1969, but this appears to be a mistake.

16. Merton (1973a).

17. Merton (1973a [1990, 475]). In an intertemporal framework, CAPM appears as a special case that holds only when the rate of interest (or the investment opportunity set more generally) is expected to remain constant over time (Fama 1970b).

18. In the subsequent formal treatment, it turned out that they needed another technical condition for the result to go through, namely joint normality of all asset returns. See Black and Scholes (1973, 643, footnote 7). But that's no more than a technical fix since one would not generally expect the return on an option to be normally distributed.

19. In his Nobel autobiography, Merton credits Black and Scholes for "the rigorous foundation underlying that formula which includes the key hedging insight" (Merton 1997, 21).

20. Bernstein (1992, 217).

21. Merton (1973b).

22. See also Black and Scholes (1972).

23. Bernstein (1992, 121).

24. This paragraph summarizes information contained in William D. Falloon (1998), Ch. 9, pp. 207–227.

25. Black and Scholes (1973).

26. Fischer Black Papers, Box 21, Folder "Options—Exchange—Paper," p. 172.
27. Galai (1975).
28. Milton Friedman Papers, Box 20, Folder 50, Hoover Institution Archives.

CHAPTER SIX   The Money Wars

1. Zvi Bodie interview of Fischer Black (July 1989).
2. Lintner (1947).
3. Lintner (1965c, 388).
4. Duesenberry et al. (1960, 1965).
5. Modigliani (1972).
6. Franco Modigliani, "Lecture Notes on Metastatic Analysis and the Term Structure of Interest Rates," unpublished mimeo (April 1965).
7. Modigliani explicitly recognizes his debt to Fisher by calling his approach Neo-Fisherian (Modigliani 1968, 398). See also Paul Samuelson (1967, 23–24).
8. Modigliani (1963, 88).
9. This is Modigliani's interpretation of Keynes, expressed first in his PhD thesis (Modigliani 1944) and reiterated at the end of his life (Modigliani 2003).
10. Modigliani, Rasche, and Cooper (1970, 181).
11. Modigliani (1971). The same general idea is at the heart of Modigliani's proposal for international monetary reform (Modigliani and Kenen 1966). He proposes creation of a new currency, the Medium for International Transactions (MIT), each country to have its own target (fixed by formula), and deviations from the target beyond a certain amount to be penalized.
12. The idea of starting one's theorizing from a pure credit world is familiar to economists from the work of Knut Wicksell and Ralph Hawtrey, among others.
13. Financial Note No. 7A.
14. Net free reserves are excess reserves (over and above required reserves) minus borrowed reserves (from the discount window).

15. Fischer Black Papers, Box 25, Folder "Research—Monetary Theory—Talk 2."

16. The editorial board of the journal included both James Lorie and John McQuown, both of whom Fischer thanks in his acknowledgments.

17. The edited volume *Studies in the Quantity Theory of Money* (Friedman 1956) consists of papers developed during the early years of that seminar.

18. Miller (1962), Stigler (1962), Bronfenbrenner (1962).

19. Reder (1980).

20. This is a judgment from history, based on his own work in Friedman and Schwartz (1963). It is also a judgment from practice, based on his observation of the central bank in action in Friedman (1968a).

21. See note 3, Chapter 3.

22. Miller and Upton (1974, vii).

23. Miller (1977, 267). The influence of Miller is the likely origin of Fischer's subsequent occasional interest in tax questions, such as the 1981 NBER Working Paper No. 631 "When Is a Positive Income Tax Optimal?" and the unpublished July 1989 paper "Optimal Taxes with Proportional Government Spending."

24. Fischer Black Papers, Box 14, Folder "Merton Miller."

25. Miller (1997, xi).

26. Dreyer (1978).

27. Modigliani (1988, 149).

28. Miller (1963, v).

29. FB to Milton Friedman, January 5, 1972. Fischer Black Papers, Box 10, Folder "Friedman, Milton."

30. Milton Friedman Papers, Hoover Institution, Box 20, Folder 50.

31. See Mehrling (2002) for an account of monetary debate circa 1913.

32. Fischer Black Papers, Box 10, Folder "Friedman, Milton."

33. Probably this workshop was sometime in spring 1972. In July 1972 Fischer produced a revised version of the paper, and in September it was published in the *Journal of Finance* under the title "Active and Passive Monetary Policy in a Neoclassical Model."

34. Interview with Richard Zecher, January 30, 2003.

35. Miller and Upton (1974, x).
36. Miller and Upton (1974, 297 and 294).
37. Laffer (1970), Fama (1980, 1983, 1985).
38. "How to Trade Currencies" (December 15, 1993). Fischer Black Papers, Box 12.
39. Black (1975a) is the published version.
40. Black (1993d).
41. FB to Michael Woodford, April 13, 1994.
42. "How to Trade Currencies" (December 15, 1993).

CHAPTER SEVEN   Global Reach

1. Tamarkin (1993, 168).
2. Melamed (1996, 188).
3. Reproduced in Melamed (1988, 429–438).
4. Quoted in Tamarkin (1993, 192).
5. Quoted in Tamarkin (1993, 185).
6. Cox, Ingersoll, and Ross (1981) generalize the results for futures and forwards to a world of stochastic interest rates.
7. Black (1976e, 176). Fischer recognized that futures were also used to avoid taxes and regulation, but his equilibrium pricing model abstracted from both taxes and regulation.
8. Swoboda (1973, 153).
9. Mundell (1968a), reprinted in Frenkel and Johnson (1976, 87).
10. Mundell (1968b, 143).
11. Mundell (1973); also Laffer (1974).
12. Johnson (1969).
13. Machlup (1970), Sohmen (1961, 1970).
14. The forward price is fixed by covered interest parity.
15. Batt (1970) and Reichers and Cleveland (1970). The spot hedge is inferior to the futures hedge because of exposure to so-called basis risk. Basis risk arises from the possibility that spot exchange rates and forward exchange rates do not rise and fall together.
16. Modigliani and Askari (1971).
17. FB to Franco Modigliani, July 15, 1971. "Comments on 'The Reform of the International Payment System' by Franco Modigliani

and Hossein Askari." Modigliani Papers. Rare Book, Manuscript, and Special Collections Library, Duke University.

18. "Rational Economic Behavior and the Balance of Payments" (Black 1987, Ch. 3). This chapter was originally Financial Note No. 26, the first draft of which was probably written in spring 1972.

19. Black (1974b, 1978b).

20. McCloskey and Zecher (1976, 358, 379). Fischer wrote a review of an early draft, "Review of McCloskey and Zecher" (October 1973). Fischer Black Papers, Box 27.

21. Black (1987, Ch. 5). This chapter was originally written in April 1974.

22. "Problems in the Economics of the Gold Standard" (September 1981), 8, footnote 8. Fischer Black Papers, Box 19.

23. The consequence is that whenever the U.S. price level rose, for whatever reason, foreign price levels had to rise as well in order to keep relative prices in equilibrium. See Black (1978a), and Laffer (1976).

24. See also Kouri (1976); McCulloch (1988).

25. Black (1987, 118). The original paper, "A Gold Standard with Double Feedback and Near Zero Reserves," dates from December 1981. Fischer Black Papers, Box 19.

26. Black (1990b, 62). Fischer says that his starting place was a paper by Perold and Schulman (1988) that argues for 100 percent hedging. Black (1989e) describes universal hedging for practitioners. Black (1990a) goes into more analytical detail for academics.

27. Siegel (1972).

28. Black (1989e, 21).

29. In fact, what the theory says you want is exposure to real exchange rate risk, not nominal currency risk. What you'd really like is inflation-adjusted borrowing and lending, or the forward contract equivalent.

30. Black and Litterman in "Global Asset Allocation and the Home Bias" (March 18, 1993) estimate an expected yield pickup of 188 basis points for switching from domestic bonds to foreign bonds, and 441 basis points for switching from domestic stocks to foreign stocks.

31. See Black (1974b), Solnik (1974), Grauer, Litzenberger, and Stehle (1976), Sercu (1980), Stulz (1981), and Adler and Dumas (1983).

32. Fischer Black and Ramine Rouhani, "Hedging Currency Exposure in British Stocks" (April 8, 1988). Fischer Black Papers, Box 11.

33. Solnik and Adler (1990); Adler and Prasad (1992).
34. Litterman (2003, 56).
35. Zvi Bodie interview with Fischer Black, July 1989.
36. "My Experience with Teaching." n.d. Thanks to Beverly Bell for providing this document.
37. Interview with Miriam Black, May 30, 2001.

CHAPTER EIGHT   Stagflation

1. Samuelson (1952, 63, 64; 1972).
2. Solow (1956, 1957).
3. Brealey and Myers (1981), Merton (1990).
4. Hilbert (1902).
5. Black (1995b, 24–25).
6. "Is This the Time to Switch to Bonds?" *Fischer Black on Markets*, Vol. 1, No. 1 (February 17, 1976).
7. Black (1976f, 178).
8. Friedman (1968b), Phelps (1968).
9. Fisher (1930, 316), quoted in Black (1972c, 249).
10. The earliest surviving draft is numbered 8B and dated October 23, 1969.
11. "Ups and Downs in Human Capital and Business," *Fischer Black on Markets*, Vol. 1, No. 4 (March 29, 1976). Published as Ch. 6 in Black (1987).
12. Fisher (1907, 14). A similar diagram is presented in Fisher (1930, 15) using the terms "capital goods" and "flow of services" instead of capital wealth and income services.
13. "Ups and Downs in Human Capital and Business," *Fischer Black on Markets*, Vol. 1, No. 4 (March 29, 1976), 4. Published as Black (1987, 80).
14. "The Return on Capital" (October 1975), p. 3. Fischer Black Papers, Box 22.
15. This connection between wealth and welfare is one possible reason for Fisher's unusual definition of income that economists have rejected. See Mehrling (2001).
16. Fisher (1907, Ch. 11 and Appendix; 1930, Ch. 9 and Ch. 14).

17. Fischer always thought of Robert Merton's 1973 intertemporal extension of CAPM as a better model of business cycles than the one-period CAPM of Treynor, Sharpe, and Lintner. He was, however, never successful in getting Merton to accept that interpretation of his paper.
18. The scholarly work behind the bestseller is collected in Shiller (1989).
19. "In Praise of Business Cycles," *Fortune* (October 22, 1979).
20. Tobin (1980, 21). Other major contributors to the movement include Thomas Sargent, Neil Wallace, and Robert Barro.
21. Hayek (1933, 33n), quoted in Lucas (1977). Hoover (1988, Ch. 10) emphasizes the differences between Hayek and Lucas.
22. According to Lucas, the earlier paper was Lucas (1972).
23. Black (1981a; 1987, 107).
24. "In Praise of Business Cycles," *Fortune* (October 22, 1979), 156.
25. Kydland and Prescott (1982); Long and Plosser (1983).
26. Kydland and Prescott (1982, 1368) misunderstand Fischer as introducing a cost of adjustment that slows convergence to the optimal aggregate capital stock. Long and Plosser (1983, 42) more correctly view Fischer as emphasizing the point that consumers optimally choose to bear risk even when no-risk alternatives are available, but seem not to appreciate the difference between Fischer's first-order risk and their second-order risk.
27. Lucas (1976) provided an early and lasting critique of Keynesian econometric practice.
28. Black (1995b, 63).
29. "Inflation and How to Deal with It," *Fischer Black on Markets*, Vol. 1, No. 2 (March 1, 1976).
30. See Cohen and Harcourt (2003) and their references for the complete story. For a contemporary account see Samuelson (1966).
31. "The Return on Capital" (October 1975). Fischer Black Papers, Box 22.
32. Because all varieties of wheat are the same from the point of view of the consumers, and because the time pattern of all production is the same single agricultural period, aggregate quantities can all be measured in bushels of wheat.
33. For those who insist on decomposing market value into separate series for units and unit value, Fischer proposed using a standard

method from the theory of index numbers (Black 1995b, 38). For each period, subtract the value of new units of capital from the market value of total capital in order to get a market value of old capital at new prices that we can compare with last period's market value of old capital at old prices. This allows us to calculate the change in unit value, and what's left must be the change in units.

34. This statement is more obvious for short-run business cycles than for long-run growth. Fischer gets the long-run result by classifying all technological change as a change in value.

CHAPTER NINE   Changing Fields

1. "Goldman Sachs," unpublished mimeo (May 18, 1995).
2. Bagehot (1972, 81).
3. Treynor suggests using options valuation theory to calculate the amount by which the market value of pension liabilities falls short of what is promised, a value that accrues to shareholders. Treynor, Regan, and Priest (1976, Appendix E).
4. The original paper was Financial Note No. 28, "The Investment Policy Spectrum: Individuals, Endowment Funds, and Pensions" (July 1973), published as Black (1976d).
5. Black (1980b, 21).
6. Black and Dewhurst provide references to Tepper (1981), OBrien (1980), Surz (1981), and Ehrbar (1981).
7. Molly Brauer, "Understanding Cyclops," *Institutional Investor* (May 1981): 111–112.
8. Black and Dewhurst (1981), Black and Glasser (1982).
9. Black (1989d, 12).
10. Black (1995f, 7).
11. Black and Dewhurst (1981, 34, footnote 2).
12. Black (1976a).
13. Black (1973).
14. Lintner and Glauber (1972) is a classic reference.
15. Beaver and Dukes (1972).
16. *Fischer Black on Markets*, Vol. 1, No. 11 (July 12, 1976).
17. Black (1980a).

18. Fifteen pages of a 40-page draft of "Choosing Accounting Rules" (March 11, 1992) are devoted to one-paragraph summaries and critiques of 90 different papers.
19. Treynor and Black (1976, 326).
20. The following draws from Myers (1996).
21. Fama (1977) and Myers and Turnbull (1977) both elaborate on the difficulties of the accepted procedure.

CHAPTER TEN   What Do Traders Do?

1. "Introduction to Fischer Black's Presidential Address." Fischer Black Papers, Box 16, Folder "Presidential Address."
2. Black (1986, 533).
3. "The Microeconomic Impact of Futures Speculation," by Fischer Black and James M. Stone, mimeo, n.d.; Fischer Black Papers, Box 18, Folder "Futures Markets and Public Policy." "Futures Markets and Public Policy," by Fischer Black and James M. Stone, mimeo, February 1982; Fischer Black Papers, Box 27, Folder "Futures Markets and Public Policy."
4. Black (1986, 530).
5. "Helping the Specialist" (February 17, 1970). Fischer Black Papers, Box 28, Folder "Research Memos." February 8, 1971, was the first day of trading for the new National Association of Securities Dealers Automated Quotation system (Nasdaq).
6. Black (1971b, Part I, 29).
7. Black (1977, 71).
8. Black (1986, 532).
9. Black (1986, 531).
10. Kahneman, Slovic, and Tversky (1982).
11. Shefrin and Statman (1984).
12. Shefrin (2000) and Shleifer (2000) provide good introductions to behavioral finance.
13. Black (1985c). The papers for the session were published as Shefrin and Statman (1985) and DeBondt and Thaler (1985). The reaction of the profession was immediate. In October 1985, a conference was held at the University of Chicago on "The Behavioral Foundations

of Economic Theory," with proceedings published the next year in a special issue of the *Journal of Business* (October 1986).

14. Black (1986, 535).

15. For example, DeBondt and Thaler (1985), and Shiller (1989).

16. Published as Black (1985b).

17. This paragraph and the next draw on Rubin (2003).

18. "Goldman Sachs," unpublished mimeo (May 18, 1995).

19. Treynor (1987).

20. Bernstein (1992, 210).

21. Kotlikoff (1996, 127).

22. "Managing Traders," unpublished mimeo (December 21, 1994).

23. Black (1975b).

24. In 1976, John Cox, Stephen Ross, and Robert Merton showed formally how the Black-Scholes formula could be adapted to take account of these features of the world.

25. Black (1988b, 1989b).

26. Cox, Ross, and Rubinstein (1979). The new model and its interface are described in two long memos: "A Valuation Model for Options, Warrants and Convertibles," by Fischer Black and H. S. Huang (September 26, 1988), and "Valuing Options, Warrants and Convertibles: User Manual," by Fischer Black and H. S. Huang (October 28, 1988). Fischer Black Papers, Box 25, Folder "Value Program."

27. Ritter (1996).

28. Treynor (1981, 57).

29. Treynor (1989) describes this test.

30. Treynor (1983, 560).

31. Treynor (1994, 74).

32. "How to Trade Currencies" (December 15, 1993).

33. "Managing Traders," unpublished mimeo (December 21, 1994), p. 4.

34. It appeared under the title "Equilibrium Exchanges" (Black 1995a). Early titles included "Bluffing" (November 8, 1990); "Trading in Equilibrium with Bluffing, Credits, and Debits" (April 4, 1991); and "Exchanges and Equilibrium" (September 27, 1991).

35. The initial key papers were Grossman and Stiglitz (1980), Kyle (1985), and Glosten and Milgrom (1985). O'Hara (1995) provides a good introduction to the market microstructure literature.

CHAPTER ELEVEN   Exploring General Equilibrium

1. "How I Got Free Life Insurance from TIAA" (August 1974), p. 7. Fischer Black Papers, Box 27.
2. "Saving Taxes with Options," unpublished mimeo (August 1974). Thanks to Bill Margrabe for providing this document.
3. "Term Structure Swaps" (April 13, 1984). The cash flows in a term structure swap are determined by the difference between a fixed long-term interest rate and a variable short-term interest rate. Suppose long rates are higher than short rates; then the swap will typically involve initial cash outflows from the party paying fixed and receiving variable, followed by cash inflows in the opposite direction. If the initial cash outflow is tax deductible for a taxable corporation (like Goldman Sachs), then the instrument can be used as a kind of "corporate IRA" because the initial funds (the cash outflow) accumulate at the pretax rate of return.
4. See Lawrence (1993) for details of the Myers-Briggs measure of psychological type.
5. Miller (1997, 6), Black (1995c).
6. Black (1995e, vi).
7. Miller (1997, Ch. 8), Merton (1990, Ch. 14).
8. Black (1995c, 7).
9. Black (1997).
10. Anticipating that conservative wealth holders might balk at the prospect of writing puts, Fischer worked on alternative roads to the same end. One other way is so-called reverse convertible bonds that convert into equity as the stock price falls. Another way is a credit swap. "Reverse Puts and Reverse Convertibles," unpublished mimeo (May 16, 1990); "Credit Swaps," unpublished mimeo (April 29, 1993).
11. Rubin (2003, 99).
12. Derman (2004, Ch. 10) contains a fascinating account of the technical details of the model, and Derman's role in its development.
13. This involved reformulating BDT in the framework proposed by Cox, Ingersoll, and Ross (1985). See Hull and White (1990).
14. Black, Derman, and Toy (1990).
15. Modigliani and Sutch (1966), my emphasis.
16. Financial Note No. 7A, "Banking, Money, and Interest Rates" (September 5, 1968).

17. Financial Note No. 14A, "The Term Structure of Interest Rates" (February 6, 1970).

18. "Fundamentals of Liquidity" (June 1970), 5.

19. Black and Cox (1976). Black's contribution grew out of two earlier papers: "How to Use the Option Formula in Pricing Corporate Bonds," *Proceedings of the Seminar on the Analysis of Security Prices* 19 No. 2 (November 1974): 61–70, and "More on the Pricing of Corporate Bonds," *Proceedings of the Seminar on the Analysis of Security Prices* 20 No. 1 (May 1975): 1–9.

20. Roll (1970, 1971).

21. Black and Karasinski (1991), and "A Two-Factor Model of Interest Rates" by Fischer Black, Emanuel Derman, and Iraj Kani (November 6, 1992), Fischer Black Papers, Box 23, Folder "Simplest Two Factor Model."

22. The first reference goes back to the 1976 "Ups and Downs in Human Capital and Business," published as Ch. 6 in Black (1987). The last is in his final book, Black (1995b, 82).

23. "What Should We Do about the Markets?" (January 28, 1988). Fischer Black Papers, Box 25, Folder "What We Can Do."

24. Black (1988a, 274).

25. Brady Commission, *Report of the Presidential Task Force on Market Mechanisms* (January 1988).

26. "What Should We Do about the Markets?" (January 28, 1988).

27. Fischer Black Papers, Box 24, Folder "Stock Market Volatility."

28. Leland (1980, 1985).

29. The 1969 paper was finally published as Black (1988c). Equation (33) contains the essence of what he would later dub CPPI.

30. Black and Jones (1987, 1988), and Black and Hakanoglu (1989).

31. Work with Ramine Rouhani refined the basic CPPI to reduce volatility cost in "Constant Proportion Portfolio Insurance: Volatility and the Soft-Floor Strategy" (March 1988), and to compare the performance of the refined CPPI with standard portfolio insurance (Black and Rouhani 1989). Work with Andre Perold established the theoretical properties of CPPI (Black and Perold, 1992), which turns out to be equivalent to a perpetual American call.

32. "Unobservables" (February 1988). Fischer Black Papers, Box 25.

33. Litterman (2003, xii).

34. See Chapter 7.
35. See Chapter 2.
36. Black (1989e).
37. Only in the limit, where the client has views on everything and expresses maximal certainty about them, will client views dominate the equilibrium view.
38. Black and Litterman (1991, 1992).
39. Endlich (1999, 182).
40. Endlich (1999, 195), quoting 1998 SEC filing.
41. Litterman (1996).
42. Black (1990d). The paper circulated before that as NBER Working Paper No. 2946 (April 1989), which was itself a revision of earlier drafts.
43. As before, he built his model on Robert Merton's 1973 intertemporal CAPM, as further developed by Brock (1982).
44. Fischer Black Papers, Box 12, Folder "Input-Output Model." In the eventual book (Black 1995b) the core model may be found on pages 19–84.
45. Fischer himself also thought of the book as a contribution to labor economics, but his interest in labor is mainly in the accumulation of human capital as a source of economic growth and fluctuation.
46. Robert Lucas to Fischer Black, November 30, 1993. Thanks to Robert Lucas for providing this document.
47. Prescott (1991) articulates this view as well.
48. Fischer Black Papers, Box 15, Folder "Neutral Technical Change."

EPILOGUE   Nothing Is Constant

1. Corzine, Cox, and Merton to FB, July 14, 1995.
2. FB to Corzine, Cox, and Merton, July 19, 1995.
3. In December 1995, the *Journal of Finance* published a review of Fischer's work by Robert Merton and Myron Scholes, and the *Journal of Derivatives* published a personal reminiscence by Stephen Figlewski, "Remembering Fischer Black." In September 1996, the London Business School organized a memorial conference in Sardinia on "The World of Fischer Black: Contingent

Claims, Corporate Finance, and the Macroeconomy," while the
Berkeley Program in Finance organized its own in Santa Barbara,
"On Finance: In Honor of Fischer Black." In December 1996 the
Journal of Portfolio Management published an entire special issue as
its tribute to Fischer Black. See also Lehmann (2004).

4. Breeden (1979) on the so-called consumption CAPM.
5. Treynor (1996) extends the memorial address.
6. Soros (1987, 44).
7. Black (1995b, xi).
8. The issue is nicely framed by the contributions of Burton Malkiel
   and Robert Shiller to a 2003 symposium on financial market efficiency (Malkiel 2003; Shiller 2003).
9. Black (1995b, 59)
10. The issue is nicely framed by the contributions of Andre Perold and
    Eugene Fama and Kenneth French to a 2004 symposium on the
    occasion of the 40th anniversary of CAPM (Perold 2004; Fama and
    French 2004).
11. Perold (1999) provides a detailed account of LTCM's trading strat-
    egy, as background for understanding why the firm decided to re-
    turn capital in 1997 and why it decided to solicit additional capital
    in 1998. The subsequent crisis is analyzed in numerous publications
    including Mehrling (2000), Lowenstein (2000), and MacKenzie
    (2003).
12. "Equilibrium and Politics" (April 1994). Thanks to Beverly Bell for
    providing this document.
13. "Doctoral Education, the Business School, and the University"
    (June 30, 1992). Fischer Black Papers, Box 26 (also Box 5).
14. "Doctoral Education, the Business School, and the University"
    (June 30, 1992). Fischer Black Papers, Box 26.

References

Adler, Michael, and Bernard Dumas. 1983. "International Portfolio Choice and Corporation Finance: A Synthesis." *Journal of Finance* 38 (No. 3, June): 925–984.

Adler, Michael, and Bhaskar Prasad. 1992. "On Universal Currency Hedges." *Journal of Financial and Quantitative Analysis* 20 (No. 1, March): 19–38.

Advisory Committee on Endowment Management. 1969. *Managing Educational Endowments.* New York: Ford Foundation.

Association for Investment Management and Research. 1997. *From Practice to Profession: A History of the Financial Analysts Federation and the Financial Profession.* Charlottesville, Virginia: Association for Investment Management and Research.

Bagehot, Walter [Jack Treynor]. 1971. "The Only Game in Town." *Financial Analysts Journal* 27 (No. 2, March/April): 12–14, 22.

Bagehot, Walter [Jack Treynor]. 1972. "Risk and Reward in Corporate Pension Funds." *Financial Analysts Journal* 28 (No. 1, January/February): 80–84.

Bank Administration Institute. 1968. *Measuring the Investment Performance of Pension Funds, for the Purpose of Inter-fund Comparison.* Park Ridge, Illinois: Bank Administration Institute.

Batt, W. F. J. 1970. "The Effect on the Forward-Exchange Market of More Flexible Rates." Pages 317–319 in Halm (1970).

Beaver, William H. 1989. *Financial Reporting: An Accounting Revolution.* 2nd edition. Englewood Cliffs, New Jersey: Prentice-Hall.

Beaver, William H., and R. E. Dukes. 1972. "Interperiod Tax Allocations, Earnings Expectations, and the Behavior of Security Prices." *Accounting Review* 47 (April): 320–332.

Bell, Beverly J. 1995. "Editing for Fischer." *Journal of Portfolio Management* Special Issue: 13–14.

Bell, Beverly J. 1997. "Fischer's Files." *Financial Analysts Journal* 53 (No. 5, September/October): 9–10.

Berkeley, Edmund C., and Daniel G. Bobrow. 1965. *The Programming Language LISP: Its Operation and Applications.* Cambridge, Mass.: MIT Press.

Bernstein, Peter L. 1992. *Capital Ideas: The Improbable Origins of Modern Wall Street.* New York: Free Press.

Black, Fischer. 1965. "Styles of Programming in LISP." Pages 96–107 in Berkeley and Bobrow (1965).

Black, Fischer. 1968. "A Deductive Question Answering System." Pages 354–402 in Minsky (1968).

Black, Fischer. 1970. "Banking and Interest Rates in a World without Money: The Effects of Uncontrolled Banking." *Journal of Bank Research* 1 (Autumn): 8–20. Reprinted as Ch. 1 in Black (1987).

Black, Fischer. 1971a. "Implications of the Random Walk Hypothesis for Portfolio Management." *Financial Analysts Journal* 27 (No. 2, March/April): 16–22.

Black, Fischer. 1971b. "Toward a Fully Automated Stock Exchange." *Financial Analysts Journal* 27, Part I (July/August): 28–35, 44; Part II (November/December): 24–28, 86–87.

Black, Fischer. 1972a. "Active and Passive Monetary Policy in a Neoclassical Model." *Journal of Finance* 27 (September): 801–814. Reprinted as Ch. 2 in Black (1987).

Black, Fischer. 1972b. "Capital Market Equilibrium with Restricted Borrowing." *Journal of Business* 45 (No. 3, July): 444–455.

Black, Fischer. 1972c. "Equilibrium in the Creation of Investment Goods under Uncertainty." Pages 249–265 in Jensen (1972).

Black, Fischer. 1973. "Yes, Virginia, There Is Hope: Tests of the Value Line Ranking System." *Financial Analysts Journal* 29 (No. 5, September/October): 10–14.

Black, Fischer. 1974a. "Can Portfolio Managers Outrun the Random Walkers?" *Journal of Portfolio Management* 1 (Fall): 32–36.

Black, Fischer. 1974b. "International Capital Market Equilibrium with Investment Barriers." *Journal of Financial Economics* 1 (No. 4, December): 337–352.

Black, Fischer. 1974c. "Uniqueness of the Price Level in Monetary Growth Models with Rational Expectations." *Journal of Economic Theory* 7 (January): 53–65. Reprinted as Ch. 4 in Black (1987).

Black, Fischer. 1975a. "Bank Funds Management in an Efficient Market." *Journal of Financial Economics* 2 (No. 4, December): 323–339.

Black, Fischer. 1975b. "Fact and Fantasy in the Use of Options." *Financial Analysts Journal* 31 (No. 4, July/August): 36–41, 61–72.

Black, Fischer. 1976a. "The Accountant's Job." *Financial Analysts Journal* 32 (No. 5, September/October): 18.

Black, Fischer. 1976b. "Comment [on Professor Stem]." Pages 336–337 in *Eurocurrencies and the International Monetary System*, edited by Carl H. Stem, John H. Makin, and Dennis E. Logue. Washington, DC: American Enterprise Institute for Public Policy Research.

Black, Fischer. 1976c. "The Dividend Puzzle." *Journal of Portfolio Management* 2 (No. 2, Winter): 5–8.

Black, Fischer. 1976d. "The Investment Policy Spectrum: Individuals, Endowment Funds, and Pension Funds." *Financial Analysts Journal* 32 (No. 1, January/February): 23–31.

Black, Fischer. 1976e. "The Pricing of Commodity Contracts." *Journal of Financial Economics* 3 (No. 1/2, January/March): 167–179.

Black, Fischer. 1976f. "Studies of Stock Price Volatility Changes." *Proceedings of the 1976 Meetings of the American Statistical Association, Business and Economics Statistics Section*, 177–181.

Black, Fischer. 1977. "What Should We Do about the Fools and the Gamblers?" *Journal of Portfolio Management* 3 (Winter): 71–73.

Black, Fischer. 1978a. "Global Monetarism in a World of National Currencies." *Columbia Journal of World Business* 51 (Spring): 27–32. Reprinted as Ch. 9 in Black (1987).

Black, Fischer. 1978b. "The Ins and Outs of Foreign Investment." *Financial Analysts Journal* 34 (No. 5, May/June): 25–32.

Black, Fischer. 1980a. "The Magic in Earnings: Economic Earnings versus Accounting Earnings." *Financial Analysts Journal* 36 (No. 6, November/December): 19–24.

Black, Fischer. 1980b. "The Tax Consequences of Long-Run Pension Policy." *Financial Analysts Journal* 36 (No. 4, July/August): 21–28.

Black, Fischer. 1981a. "The ABCs of Business Cycles." *Financial Analysts Journal* 37 (No. 6, November/December): 75–80. Reprinted as Ch. 10 in Black (1987).

Black, Fischer. 1981b. "An Open Letter to Jack Treynor." *Financial Analysts Journal* 37 (No. 4, July/August): 14.

Black, Fischer. 1982. "The Trouble with Econometric Models." *Financial Analysts Journal* 38 (No. 2, March/April): 29–37. Reprinted as Ch. 12 in Black (1987).

Black, Fischer. 1983. "Comment [on Investing for the Short and the Long Term]." Pages 223–230 in *Financial Aspects of the U.S. Pension System*, edited by Zvi Bodie and John B. Shoven. Chicago: University of Chicago Press.

Black, Fischer. 1985a. "Contingent Claims Valuation of Corporation Liabilities: Theory and Empirical Tests: Comment." Pages 262–263 in *Corporate Capital Structure in the United States*, edited by Benjamin M. Friedman. Chicago: University of Chicago Press.

Black, Fischer. 1985b. "The Future for Financial Services." Pages 223–230 in *Managing the Service Economy*, edited by Robert P. Inman. New York: Cambridge University Press.

Black, Fischer. 1985c. "Introduction." *Journal of Finance* 40 (No. 3, July): 619.

Black, Fischer. 1986. "Noise." *Journal of Finance* 41 (No. 3, July): 529–543.

Black, Fischer. 1987. *Business Cycles and Equilibrium*. Cambridge, Mass.: Basil Blackwell.

Black, Fischer. 1988a. "An Equilibrium Model of the Crash." Pages 269–275 in *NBER Macroeconomics Annual*, edited by Stanley Fischer. Cambridge, Mass.: MIT Press.

Black, Fischer. 1988b. "The Holes in Black-Scholes." *Risk* 1 (No. 4, March): 30–33.

Black, Fischer. 1988c. "Individual Investment and Consumption under Uncertainty." Pages 207–225 in *Portfolio Insurance, A Guide to Dynamic Hedging*, edited by Donald L. Luskin. New York: John Wiley & Sons.

Black, Fischer. 1988d. "On Robert C. Merton." *MIT Management* (Fall): 28.

Black, Fischer. 1988e. "A Simple Discounting Rule." *Financial Management* 17 (No. 2, Summer): 7–11.

Black, Fischer. 1989a. "Does Technology Matter?" Pages 151–152 in *The Challenge of Information Technology for the Securities Markets: Liquidity, Volatility, and Global Trading*, edited by Henry C. Lucas Jr. and Robert A. Schwartz. Homewood, Illinois: Dow Jones-Irwin.

Black, Fischer. 1989b. "How to Use the Holes in Black-Scholes." *Journal of Applied Corporate Finance* 1 (No. 4, Winter): 67–73.

Black, Fischer. 1989c. "How We Came Up with the Option Formula." *Journal of Portfolio Management* 15 (Winter): 4–8.

Black, Fischer. 1989d. "Should You Use Stocks to Hedge Your Pension Liability?" *Financial Analysts Journal* 45 (No. 1, January/February): 10–12.

Black, Fischer. 1989e. "Universal Hedging: Optimizing Currency Risk and Reward in International Equity Portfolios." *Financial Analysts Journal* 45 (No. 4, July/August): 16–22.

Black, Fischer. 1990a. "Equilibrium Exchange Rate Hedging." *Journal of Finance* 45 (No. 3, July): 899–907.

Black, Fischer. 1990b. "How I Discovered Universal Hedging." *Investing* [Japan] 4 (Winter): 60–64.

Black, Fischer. 1990c. "Living Up to the Model." *Risk* 3 (No. 3, March): 11–13.

Black, Fischer. 1990d. "Mean Reversion and Consumption Smoothing." *Review of Financial Studies* 3 (No. 1): 107–114.

Black, Fischer. 1990e. "Why Firms Pay Dividends." *Financial Analysts Journal* 46 (May/June): 5.

Black, Fischer. 1992a. "Doctoral Education, the Business School, and the University." Unpublished mimeo.

Black, Fischer. 1992b. "Global Reach." *Risk* 5 (No. 11, December): 27–32.

Black, Fischer. 1993a. "Beta and Return." *Journal of Portfolio Management* 20 (No. 1, Fall): 8–18.

Black, Fischer. 1993b. "Choosing Accounting Rules." *Accounting Horizons* 7 (No. 4, December): 1–17.

Black, Fischer. 1993c. "Estimating Expected Return." *Financial Analysts Journal* 49 (No. 5, September/October): 36–38.

Black, Fischer. 1993d. "U.S. Commercial Banking: Trends, Cycles, and Policy: Comment." Pages 368–371 in *NBER Macroeconomics Annual*, edited by Olivier Jean Blanchard and Stanley Fischer. Cambridge, Mass.: MIT Press.

Black, Fischer. 1995a. "Equilibrium Exchanges." *Financial Analysts Journal* 51 (No. 3, May/June): 23–29.

Black, Fischer. 1995b. *Exploring General Equilibrium*. Cambridge, Mass.: MIT Press.

Black, Fischer. 1995c. "Hedging, Speculation, and Systemic Risk." *Journal of Derivatives* (Summer): 6–8.

Black, Fischer. 1995d. "Interest Rates as Options." *Journal of Finance* 50 (No. 7, December): 1371–1376.

Black, Fischer. 1995e. "The Many Faces of Derivatives." Foreword to *Handbook of Equity Derivatives*, edited by Jack Francis, William Toy, and J. Gregg Whittaker. New York: John Wiley & Sons.

Black, Fischer. 1995f. "The Plan Sponsor's Goal." *Financial Analysts Journal* 51 (No. 4, July/August): 6–7.

Black, Fischer. 1997. "Fischer Black's Brave New World." *Risk* 10 (No. 11, December): 44–45.

Black, Fischer, and John C. Cox. 1976. "Valuing Corporate Securities: Some Effects of Bond Indenture Provisions." *Journal of Finance* 31 (No. 2, May): 351–368.

Black, Fischer, Emanuel Derman, and William Toy. 1990. "A One-Factor Model of Interest Rates and Its Application to Treasury Bond Options." *Financial Analysts Journal* 46 (No. 1, January/February): 33–39.

Black, Fischer, and Moray P. Dewhurst. 1981. "A New Investment Strategy for Pension Funds." *Journal of Portfolio Management* 7 (No. 4, Summer): 26–34.

Black, Fischer, and Peter Glasser. 1982. "Comment: A New Investment Strategy for Pension Funds." *Journal of Portfolio Management* 8 (No. 4, Summer): 74–76.

Black, Fischer, and Erol Hakanoglu. 1989. "Simplifying Portfolio Insurance for the Seller." Pages 709–726 in *Investment Management*, edited by Frank J. Fabozzi. Cambridge, Mass.: Ballinger.

Black, Fischer, Michael Jensen, and Myron Scholes. 1972. "The Capital Asset Pricing Model: Some Empirical Tests." Pages 79–121 in Jensen (1972).

Black, Fischer, and Robert Jones. 1987. "Simplifying Portfolio Insurance." *Journal of Portfolio Management* 14 (No. 1, Fall): 48–51.

Black, Fischer, and Robert Jones. 1988. "Simplifying Portfolio Insurance for Corporate Pension Plans." *Journal of Portfolio Management* 14 (No. 4, Summer): 33–37.

Black, Fischer, and Piotr Karasinski. 1991. "Bond and Option Pricing When Short Rates Are Lognormal." *Financial Analysts Journal* 47 (No. 4, July/August): 52–59.

Black, Fischer, and Robert Litterman. 1991. "Asset Allocation: Combining Investor Views with Market Equilibrium." *Journal of Fixed Income* 1 (September): 7–18.

Black, Fischer, and Robert Litterman. 1992. "Global Portfolio Optimization." *Financial Analysts Journal* 48 (No. 5, September/October): 28–43.

Black, Fischer, Merton Miller, and Richard Posner. 1978. "An Approach to the Regulation of Bank Holding Companies." *Journal of Business* 51 (No. 3, July): 379–412.

Black, Fischer, and Andre F. Perold. 1992. "Theory of Constant Proportion Portfolio Insurance." *Journal of Economic Dynamics and Control* 16: 403–426.

Black, Fischer, and Ramine Rouhani. 1989. "Constant Proportion Portfolio Insurance and the Synthetic Put Option: A Comparison." Pages 695–708 in *Investment Management*, edited by Frank J. Fabozzi. Cambridge, Mass.: Ballinger.

Black, Fischer, and Myron Scholes. 1972. "The Valuation of Option Contracts and a Test of Market Efficiency." *Journal of Finance* 27 (No. 2, May): 399–418.

Black, Fischer, and Myron Scholes. 1973. "The Pricing of Options and Corporate Liabilities." *Journal of Political Economy* 81 (May–June): 637–654.

Black, Fischer, and Myron Scholes. 1974a. "The Effects of Dividend Yield and Dividend Policy on Common Stock Prices and Returns." *Journal of Financial Economics* 1 (No. 1, May): 1–22.

Black, Fischer, and Myron Scholes. 1974b. "From Theory to a New Financial Product." *Journal of Finance* 19 (No. 2, May): 399–412.

Booth, David. 1973. "Selling Unconventional Financial Concepts: Can It Be Done?" Unpublished memo.

Bosworth, Barry, and James S. Duesenberry. 1974. "A Flow of Funds Model and Its Implications." Pages 39–149 in *Issues in Federal Debt Management*. Monetary Conference, Volume 10. Boston: Federal Reserve Bank of Boston.

Brady Commission. 1988. *Report of the Presidential Task Force on Market Mechanisms.* Washington, D.C.: Government Printing Office.

Brealey, Richard A., and Stewart C. Myers. 1981. *Principles of Corporate Finance.* New York: McGraw-Hill.

Breeden, Douglas T. 1979. "An Intertemporal Asset Pricing Model with Stochastic Consumption and Investment Opportunities." *Journal of Financial Economics* 7 (September): 265–296.

Brock, William A. 1982. "Asset Prices in a Production Economy." In *The Economics of Information and Uncertainty*, edited by John C. McCall. Chicago: University of Chicago Press.

Bronfenbrenner, M. 1962. "Observations on the 'Chicago School(s).'" *Journal of Political Economy* 70 (No. 1, February): 72–75.

Bruner, Jerome S. 1960. *The Process of Education*. Cambridge, Mass: Harvard University Press.

Bruner, Jerome S. 1962. *On Knowing: Essays for the Left Hand*. Cambridge, Mass.: Belknap Press of Harvard University Press.

Bruner, Jerome, and W. J. J. Gordon. 1957. *Conference on Creativity as a Process*. Boston: Institute of Contemporary Art.

Butters, J. Keith, and John Lintner. 1945. *Effects of Federal Taxes on Growing Enterprises*. Boston: Graduate School of Business, Harvard University.

Butters, J. Keith, John Lintner, and W. L. Cary. 1951. *Effects of Taxation on Corporate Mergers*. Boston: Graduate School of Business, Harvard University.

Carpenter, Ralph E. 1954. *The Arts and Crafts of Newport, Rhode Island, 1640–1820*. Newport, Rhode Island: Preservation Society of Newport.

Carpenter, Ralph E. 1955. *The Fifty Best Historic American Houses, Colonial and Federal, Now Furnished and Open to the Public*. New York: Dutton.

Cary, William L., and Craig B. Bright. 1969. *The Law and the Lore of Endowment Funds*. New York: Ford Foundation.

Chesnut, Mary Boykin. 1905. *A Diary from Dixie*. New York: D. Appleton & Co.

Chomsky, Noam. 1986. *Knowledge of Language: Its Nature, Origin, and Use*. Westport, Connecticut: Praeger.

Cohen, Avi, and Geoff Harcourt. 2003. "Whatever Happened to the Cambridge Capital Theory Controversies?" *Journal of Economic Perspectives* 17 (No. 1, Winter): 199–214.

Cootner, Paul H. 1964. *The Random Character of Stock Market Prices*. Cambridge, Mass.: MIT Press.

Copeland, Morris A. 1952. *A Study of Moneyflows in the United States*. New York: National Bureau of Economic Research.

Cox, John C., Jonathan E. Ingersoll Jr., and Stephen A. Ross. 1981. "The Relation between Forward Prices and Futures Prices." *Journal of Financial Economics* 9 (December): 321–346.

Cox, John C., Jonathan E. Ingersoll Jr., and Stephen A. Ross. 1985. "A Theory of the Term Structure of Interest Rates." *Econometrica* 53 (No. 2, March): 385–408.

Cox, John, Stephen Ross, and Mark Rubinstein. 1979. "Option Pricing: A Simplified Approach." *Journal of Financial Economics* 7 (October): 229–264.

Cox, John, and Mark Rubinstein. 1985. *Options Markets.* Englewood Cliffs, New Jersey: Prentice-Hall.

Crevier, Daniel. 1993. *AI: The Tumultuous History of the Search for Artificial Intelligence.* New York: Basic Books.

Cuneo, Larry J., and Wayne H. Wagner. 1975. "Reducing the Cost of Stock Trading." *Financial Analysts Journal* 31 (No. 6, November/December): 3–12.

DeBondt, Werner F. M., and Richard Thaler. 1985. "Does the Stock Market Overreact?" *Journal of Finance* 40 (No. 3, July): 793–805.

Derman, Emanuel. 2004. *My Life as a Quant, Reflections on Physics and Finance.* Hoboken, New Jersey: John Wiley & Sons.

Douglas, George. 1969. "Risk in the Equity Markets: An Empirical Appraisal of Market Efficiency." *Yale Economic Essays* 9 (No. 1): 3–41.

Dreyer, Jacob S. 1978. *Breadth and Depth in Economics: Fritz Machlup—the Man and His Ideas.* Lexington, Mass.: Lexington Books.

Duesenberry, James S., ed. 1965. *The Brookings Quarterly Econometric Model of the United States.* Chicago: Rand McNally.

Duesenberry, James S., Otto Eckstein, and Gary Fromm. 1960. "A Simulation of the United States Economy in Recession." *Econometrica* 28 (No. 4, October): 749–809.

Edwards, Paul N. 1996. *The Closed World: Computers and the Politics of Discourse in Cold War America.* Cambridge, Mass.: MIT Press.

Endlich, Lisa. 1999. *Goldman Sachs, the Culture of Success.* New York: Simon & Schuster.

Falloon, William D. 1998. *Market-Maker: A Sesquicentennial Look at the Chicago Board of Trade.* Chicago: Board of Trade of the City of Chicago.

Fama, Eugene. 1965. "The Behavior of Stock-Market Prices." *Journal of Business* 38 (No. 1, January): 34–105.

Fama, Eugene. 1968. "Risk, Return and Equilibrium: Some Clarifying Comments." *Journal of Finance* 23 (No. 1, March): 29–40.

Fama, Eugene. 1970a. "Efficient Capital Markets: A Review of Theory and Empirical Work." *Journal of Finance* 25 (No. 2, May): 383–417.

Fama, Eugene. 1970b. "Multi-period Consumption-Investment Decisions." *American Economic Review* 60: 163–174.

Fama, Eugene. 1971. "Risk, Return, and Equilibrium." *Journal of Political Economy* 79 (No. 1, January–February): 30–55.

Fama, Eugene. 1973. "A Note on the Market Model and the Two-Parameter Model." *Journal of Finance* 28 (No. 5, December): 1181–1185.

Fama, Eugene. 1977. "Risk-Adjusted Discount Rates and Capital Budgeting under Uncertainty." *Journal of Financial Economics* 5 (August): 3–24.

Fama, Eugene. 1980. "Banking in the Theory of Finance." *Journal of Monetary Economics* 6 (No. 1, January): 39–57.

Fama, Eugene. 1983. "Financial Intermediation and Price Level Control." *Journal of Monetary Economics* 12 (No. 1): 7–28.

Fama, Eugene. 1985. "What's Different About Banks?" *Journal of Monetary Economics* 15 (No. 1, January): 29–39.

Fama, Eugene. 1991. "Efficient Capital Markets: II." *Journal of Finance* 46 (No. 5, December): 1575–1617.

Fama, Eugene, Lawrence Fisher, Michael C. Jensen, and Richard Roll. 1969. "The Adjustment of Stock Prices to New Information." *International Economic Review* 10 (February): 1–21.

Fama, Eugene F., and Kenneth R. French. 2004. "The Capital Asset Pricing Model: Theory and Evidence." *Journal of Economic Perspectives* 18 (No. 3, Summer): 25–46.

Fama, Eugene, and Merton Miller. 1972. *The Theory of Finance*. Hinsdale, Illinois: Dryden Press.

Fama, Eugene, and Richard Roll. 1968. "Some Properties of Symmetric Stable Distributions." *Journal of the American Statistical Association* 63 (No. 323, September): 817–836.

Fama, Eugene, and Richard Roll. 1971. "Parameter Estimates for Symmetric Stable Distributions." *Journal of the American Statistical Association* 66 (No. 334, June): 331–338.

Farrar, Donald E. 1962. *The Investment Decision under Uncertainty*. Englewood Cliffs, New Jersey: Prentice-Hall, 1962.

Fisher, Irving. 1906. *The Nature of Capital and Income*. New York: Macmillan.

Fisher, Irving. 1907. *The Rate of Interest, Its Nature, Determination and Relation to Economic Phenomena.* New York: Macmillan.

Fisher, Irving. 1920. *Stabilizing the Dollar: A Plan to Stabilize the General Price Level without Fixing Individual Prices.* New York: Macmillan.

Fisher, Irving. 1930. *The Theory of Interest as Determined by Impatience to Spend Income and Opportunity to Invest It.* New York: Macmillan.

Fisher, Lawrence, and James Lorie. 1964. "Rates of Return on Investments in Common Stocks." *Journal of Business* 37 (No. 1, January): 1–24.

Fisher, Lawrence, and James H. Lorie. 1968. *Rates of Return on Investments in Common Stock: The Year-by-Year Record, 1926–65.* Chicago: University of Chicago Press.

Flesch, Rudolf. 1946. *The Art of Plain Talk.* New York: Harper.

Flesch, Rudolf. 1949. *The Art of Readable Writing.* New York: Harper.

Flesch, Rudolf. 1954. *How to Make Sense.* New York: Harper.

French, Craig. 2003. "The Treynor Capital Asset Pricing Model." *Journal of Investment Management* 1 (No. 2): 60–72.

Frenkel, Jacob A., and Harry G. Johnson, eds. 1976. *The Monetary Approach to the Balance of Payments.* London: Allen & Unwin.

Friedman, Milton. 1953. "The Case for Flexible Exchange Rates." Pages 157–203 in *Essays in Positive Economics.* Chicago: University of Chicago Press.

Friedman, Milton. 1956. *Studies in the Quantity Theory of Money.* Chicago: University of Chicago Press.

Friedman, Milton. 1968a. *Dollars and Deficits: Inflation, Monetary Policy and the Balance of Payments.* Englewood Cliffs, New Jersey: Prentice-Hall.

Friedman, Milton. 1968b. "The Role of Monetary Policy." *American Economic Review* 58 (March): 1–17.

Friedman, Milton. 1969. *The Optimum Quantity of Money and Other Essays.* Chicago: Aldine.

Friedman, Milton, and Anna J. Schwartz. 1963. *A Monetary History of the United States, 1867–1960.* Princeton, New Jersey: Princeton University Press.

Fullarton, John. 1845. *On the Regulation of Currencies: Being an Examination of the Principles, on Which It Is Proposed to Restrict, within Certain Fixed Limits, the Future Issues on Credit of the Bank of England, and of the Other Banking Establishments throughout the Country.* London: J. Murray.

Galai, Dan. 1975. *Pricing of Options and the Efficiency of the Chicago Board Options Exchange*. PhD dissertation. Graduate School of Business, University of Chicago, Chicago, Illinois.

Gersh, Harry. 1959. "Gentlemen's Agreement in Bronxville." *Commentary* 27 (No. 2, February): 109–116.

Glosten, Lawrence R., and Paul R. Milgrom. 1985. "Bid, Ask and Transactions Prices in a Specialist Market with Heterogenously Informed Traders." *Journal of Financial Economics* 14 (No. 1, March): 71–100.

Good, Walter R., Robert Ferguson, and Jack Treynor. 1976. "An Investor's Guide to the Index Fund Controversy." *Financial Analysts Journal* 32 (No. 6, November/December): 27–36.

Graham, Benjamin, and David L. Dodd. 1934. *Security Analysis*. New York: Whittlesey House, McGraw-Hill.

Grauer, Frederick L. A., Richard H. Litzenberger, and Richard E. Stehle. 1976. "Sharing Rules and Equilibrium in an International Capital Market Under Uncertainty." *Journal of Financial Economics* 3 (No. 3, June): 233–256.

Grossman, Sanford J., and Joseph E. Stiglitz. 1980. "On the Impossibility of Informationally Efficient Markets." *American Economic Review* 70 (No. 3, June): 393–408.

Gurley, John, and Edward Stone Shaw. 1960. *Money in a Theory of Finance*. Washington, D.C.: Brookings Institution.

Hafner, Katie, and Matthew Lyon. 1996. *Where Wizards Stay Up Late: The Origins of the Internet*. New York: Touchstone/Simon Schuster.

Halm, George N., ed. 1970. *Approaches to Greater Flexibility of Exchange Rates*. The Burgenstock Papers. Princeton, New Jersey: Princeton University Press.

Hayek, Friedrich A. von. 1933. *Monetary Theory and the Trade Cycle*. London: Jonathan Cape.

Herling, John. 1962. *The Great Price Conspiracy: The Story of the Antitrust Violations in the Electrical Industry*. Washington, D.C.: Robert B. Luce, Inc.

Hilbert, David (trans. Maby Winton Newson). 1902. "Mathematical Problems." *Bulletin of the American Mathematical Society* 8: 437–479.

Hoover, Kevin D. 1988. *The New Classical Macroeconomics, a Sceptical Inquiry*. New York: Basil Blackwell.

Hull, John, and Alan White. 1990. "Pricing Interest Rate Derivative Securities." *Review of Financial Studies* 3 (No. 4): 573–592.

Humphrey, Thomas. 1970. "The Monetarist-Nonmonetarist Debate, Some 19th Century Controversies Revisited." Federal Reserve Bank of Richmond *Monthly Review* (December): 2–6.

Jahnke, William W. 1990. "The Development of Structured Portfolio Management: A Contextual View." Pages 153–181 in *Quantitative International Investing: A Handbook of Analytical and Modeling Techniques and Strategies*, edited by Brian R. Bruce. Chicago: Probus.

Jensen, Michael C. 1968. "The Performance of Mutual Funds in the Period 1945–1964." *Journal of Finance* 23 (No. 2, May): 389–416.

Jensen, Michael C., ed. 1972. *Studies in the Theory of Capital Markets*. New York: Praeger.

Johnson, Harry. 1969. "The Case for Flexible Exchange Rates." In *UK and Floating Exchanges*, by Harry G. Johnson and John E. Nash. London: Institute of Economic Affairs.

Kahn, E. J. 1986. *The Problem Solvers: A History of Arthur D. Little, Inc.* Boston: Little, Brown.

Kahneman, Daniel, Paul Slovic, and Amos Tversky. 1982. *Judgment Under Uncertainty: Heuristics and Biases*. New York: Cambridge University Press.

Kassouf, Sheen T. 1968. "Stock Price Random Walks: Some Supporting Evidence." *Review of Economics and Statistics* 50 (No. 2, May): 275-278.

Kendall, Maurice G. 1953. "The Analysis of Time Series, Part I: Prices." *Journal of the Royal Statistical Society* Series A (General), 116 (No. 1): 11–25.

Kephart, Horace. 1913. *Our Southern Highlanders*. New York: Outing Publishing Company.

Keynes, John Maynard. 1936. *The General Theory of Employment, Interest, and Money*. New York: Harcourt Brace.

Kindleberger, Charles. 1978. *Manias, Panics, and Crashes: A History of Financial Crises*. New York: Basic Books.

King, Benjamin. 1966. "Market and Industry Factors in Stock Price Behavior." *Journal of Business* 30 (No. 1, Part 2, January): 139–190.

Kirkland, Thomas J., and Robert M. Kennedy. 1905. *Historic Camden*. Part One: *Colonial and Revolutionary*. Part Two: *Nineteenth Century*. Columbia, South Carolina: State Company.

Korajczyk, Robert A. 1999. *Asset Pricing and Portfolio Performance*. London: Risk Books.

Kotlikoff, Laurence J. 1996. Review of *Exploring General Equilibrium. Journal of Economic Literature* 35 (No. 1): 127–129.

Kouri, Pentti. 1976. "The Exchange Rate and the Balance of Payments in the Short Run and in the Long Run: A Monetary Approach." *Scandinavian Journal of Economics* 78: 280–301.

Kydland, Finn E., and Edward C. Prescott. 1982. "Time to Build and Aggregate Fluctuations." *Econometrica* 50 (No. 6, November): 1345–1370.

Kyle, Albert. 1985. "Continuous Auctions and Insider Trading." *Econometrica* 53 (No. 6, November): 1315–1335.

Laffer, Arthur. 1970. "Trade Credit and the Money Market." *Journal of Political Economy* 78 (No. 2, March–April): 239–267.

Laffer, Arthur B. 1974. "Balance of Payments and Exchange Rate Systems." *Financial Analysts Journal* 30 (No. 4, July/August): 26–32, 76–82.

Laffer, Arthur B. 1976. "Economic Consequences of Devaluation of a Reserve Currency Country." Pages 79–89 in *World Monetary Disorder*, edited by Patrick M. Boarman and David G. Tuerck. New York: Praeger.

Laidler, David. 1991. *The Golden Age of the Quantity Theory*. Princeton, New Jersey: Princeton University Press.

Lawrence, Gordon. 1993. *People Types and Tiger Stripes*. 3rd edition. Gainesville, Florida: Center for Applications of Psychological Type.

Leary, Timothy. 1983. *Flashbacks: A Personal and Cultural History of an Era; An Autobiography*. New York: G. P. Putnam's Sons.

Lehmann, Bruce N., ed. 2004. *The Legacy of Fischer Black*. New York: Oxford University Press.

Leland, Hayne E. 1980. "Who Should Buy Portfolio Insurance?" *Journal of Finance* 35 (No. 2, May): 581–594.

Leland, Hayne E. 1985. "Option Pricing and Replication with Transactions Costs." *Journal of Finance* 40 (No. 5, December): 1283–1301.

Licklider, J. C. R. 1960. "Man-Computer Symbiosis." *IRE Transactions on Human Factors in Electronics*, Vol. HFE-1 (March): 4–11.

Licklider, J. C. R. 1965. *Libraries of the Future*. Cambridge, Mass.: MIT Press.

Lintner, John. 1947. "The Theory of Money and Prices." Pages 503–537 in *The New Economics: Keynes' Influence on Theory and Public Policy*, edited by Seymour E. Harris. New York: Knopf.

Lintner, John. 1948. *Mutual Savings Banks in the Savings and Mortgage Markets.* Boston: Graduate School of Business Administration, Harvard University.

Lintner, John. 1956. "Distribution of Incomes of Corporations among Dividends, Retained Earnings, and Taxes." *American Economic Review* 46 (No. 2, May): 97–113.

Lintner, John. 1959. "The Financing of Corporations." Pages 166–201 in *The Corporation in Modern Society*, edited by Edward S. Mason. Cambridge, Mass.: Harvard University Press.

Lintner, John. 1962. "Dividends, Earnings, Leverage, Stock Prices and the Supply of Capital to Corporations." *Review of Economics and Statistics* 44 (No. 3, August): 243–269.

Lintner, John. 1963. "The Cost of Capital and Optimal Financing of Corporate Growth." *Journal of Finance* 18 (No. 2, May): 292–310.

Lintner, John. 1964. "Optimal Dividends and Corporate Growth under Uncertainty." *Quarterly Journal of Economics* 78 (No. 1, February): 49–95.

Lintner, John. 1965a. "Security Prices, Risk and Maximal Gains from Diversification." *Journal of Finance* 20 (No. 4, December): 587–615.

Lintner, John. 1965b. "The Valuation of Risk Assets and the Selection of Risky Investments in Stock Portfolios and Capital Budgets." *Review of Economics and Statistics* 47 (No. 1, February): 13–37.

Lintner, John. 1965c. "What Is Left of the Business Cycles in the United States?" Pages 388–394 in *Proceedings of the Business and Economic Statistics Section*, American Statistical Association.

Lintner, John. 1969. "The Aggregation of Investors' Diverse Judgments and Preferences in Purely Competitive Securities Markets." *Journal of Financial and Quantitative Analysis* 4 (No. 4, December): 347–400.

Lintner, John. 1971. "Optimum or Maximum Corporate Growth under Uncertainty." Pages 172–241 in *The Corporate Economy: Growth, Competition and Innovative Potential*, edited by Robin Marris and Adrian Wood. Cambridge, Mass.: Harvard University Press.

Lintner, John. 1972. *Finance and Capital Markets.* Fiftieth Anniversary Colloquium, Vol. II. NBER General Series No. 96. National Bureau of Economic Research.

Lintner, John. 1981. "Some New Perspectives on Tests of CAPM and Other Capital Asset Pricing Models and Issues of Market Efficiency."

Pages 129–162 in *Economic Activity and Finance*, edited by Marshall E. Blume, Jean Crockett, and Paul Taubman. Cambridge, Mass.: Ballinger.

Lintner, John, and Robert Glauber. 1972. "Higgledy Piggledy Growth in America." Pages 645–662 in *Modern Developments in Investment Management: A Book of Readings*, edited by James Lorie and Richard Brealey. New York: Praeger.

Litterman, Robert. 1996. "Hot Spots and Hedges." *Journal of Portfolio Management* Special Issue (December): 52–75.

Litterman, Robert. 2003. *Modern Investment Management: an Equilibrium Approach.* New York: John Wiley & Sons.

Long, John B., Jr., and Charles I. Plosser. 1983. "Real Business Cycles." *Journal of Political Economy* 91 (No. 1, February): 39–69.

Lowenstein, Roger. 2000. *When Genius Failed: The Rise and Fall of Long-Term Capital Management.* New York: Random House.

Lucas, Robert E. 1972. "Expectations and the Neutrality of Money." *Journal of Economic Theory* 4 (April): 103–124.

Lucas, Robert E. 1975. "An Equilibrium Model of the Business Cycle." *Journal of Political Economy* 83 (No. 6, December): 1113–1144.

Lucas, Robert E. 1976. "Econometric Policy Evaluation: A Critique." Pages 19–46 in *The Phillips Curve and Labor Markets*, edited by Karl Brunner and Allan H. Meltzer. Carnegie-Rochester Conference Series on Public Policy, Vol. 1. Amsterdam: North-Holland.

Lucas, Robert E. 1977. "Understanding Business Cycles." Pages 7–29 in *Stabilization of the Domestic and International Economy*, edited by Karl Brunner and Allan H. Meltzer. Carnegie-Rochester Conference Series on Public Policy, Vol. 5. Amsterdam: North-Holland.

Machlup, Fritz. 1963. *Essays on Economic Semantics*, edited by Merton H. Miller. Englewood Cliffs, New Jersey: Prentice-Hall.

Machlup, Fritz. 1970. "The Forward-Exchange Market: Misunderstandings between Practitioners and Economists." Pages 297–306 in Halm (1970).

MacKenzie, Donald. 2003. "Long-Term Capital Management and the Sociology of Arbitrage." *Economy and Society* 32 (No. 3, August): 349–380.

Malkiel, Burton G. 2003. "The Efficient Market Hypothesis and Its Critics." *Journal of Economic Perspectives* 17 (No. 1, Winter): 59-82.

Mandelbrot, Benoit. 1963. "The Variation of Certain Speculative Prices." *Journal of Business* 36 (No. 4, October): 394–419.

Mandelbrot, Benoit. 1966. "Forecasts of Future Prices, Unbiased Markets, and 'Martingale' Models." *Journal of Business* 39 (No. 1, Supplement): 242–255.

Mandelbrot, Benoit. 1967. "The Variation of Some Other Speculative Prices." *Journal of Business* 40 (No. 4, October): 393–413.

Mandelbrot, Benoit. 1971. "When Can Price Be Arbitraged Efficiently? A Limit to the Validity of the Random Walk and Martingale Model." *Review of Economics and Statistics* 53 (No. 3, August): 225–236.

Mandelbrot, Benoit. 1997. *Fractals and Scaling in Finance: Discontinuity, Concentration, Risk*. New York: Springer.

Mandelbrot, Benoit, and Richard L. Hudson. 2004. *The (Mis)behavior of Markets: A Fractal View of Risk, Ruin, and Reward*. New York: Basic Books.

Markowitz, Harry. 1952. "Portfolio Selection." *Journal of Finance* 7 (No. 1, March): 77–91.

Markowitz, Harry. 1959. *Portfolio Selection: Efficient Diversification of Investments*. New York: John Wiley & Sons.

Mayers, David. 1972. "Nonmarketable Assets and Capital Market Equilibrium under Uncertainty." Pages 223–248 in Jensen (1972).

McCloskey, Donald N., and J. Richard Zecher. 1976. "How the Gold Standard Worked, 1880–1913." Pages 357–385 in Frenkel and Johnson (1976).

McCloskey, Donald N., and J. Richard Zecher. 1984. "The Success of Purchasing Power Parity: Historical Evidence and Its Implications for Macroeconomics." Pages 121–170 in *A Retrospective on the Classical Gold Standard, 1821–1931*, edited by Michael D. Bordo and Anna J. Schwartz. Chicago: University of Chicago Press.

McCulloch, Rachel. 1988. "Unexpected Real Consequences of Floating Exchange Rates." Pages 223–244 in Melamed (1988).

Mehrling, Perry. 1997. *The Money Interest and the Public Interest*. Cambridge, Mass.: Harvard University Press.

Mehrling, Perry. 2000. "Minsky and Modern Finance: The Case of Long Term Capital Management." *Journal of Portfolio Management* 26 (No. 2, Winter): 81–88.

Mehrling, Perry. 2001. "Love and Death: The Wealth of Irving Fisher." Pages 47–61 in *Research in the History of Economic Thought and Methodology*, edited by Warren J. Samuels and Jeff E. Biddle. Amsterdam: Elsevier Science.

Mehrling, Perry. 2002. "Economists and the Fed: Beginnings." *Journal of Economic Perspectives* 16 (No. 4, Fall): 207–218.

Melamed, Leo, ed. 1988. *The Merits of Flexible Exchange Rates: An Anthology*. Fairfax, Virginia: George Mason University Press.

Melamed, Leo (with Bob Tamarkin). 1996. *Leo Melamed, Escape to the Futures*. New York: John Wiley & Sons.

Merton, Robert C. 1969. "Lifetime Portfolio Selection under Uncertainty: The Continuous-Time Case." *Review of Economics and Statistics* 51 (No. 3, August): 247–257.

Merton, Robert C. 1970. "A Dynamic General Equilibrium Model of the Asset Market and Its Application to the Pricing of the Capital Structure of the Firm." Massachusetts Institute of Technology Working Paper No. 497-70. Reprinted as Chapter 11 in Merton (1990).

Merton, Robert C. 1973a. "An Intertemporal Capital Asset Pricing Model." *Econometrica* 41 (September): 867–887. Reprinted as Chapter 15 in Merton (1990).

Merton, Robert C. 1973b. "Theory of Rational Option Pricing." *Bell Journal of Economics and Management Science* 4 (Spring): 141–183. Reprinted as Chapter 8 in Merton (1990).

Merton, Robert C. 1974. "On the Pricing of Corporate Debt: The Risk Structure of Interest Rates." Reprinted as Chapter 12 in Merton (1990).

Merton, Robert C. 1990. *Continuous-Time Finance*. Cambridge, Mass.: Basil Blackwell.

Merton, Robert C. 1997. *Robert C. Merton*. Stockholm: Nobel Foundation.

Merton, Robert C., and Myron S. Scholes. 1995. "Fischer Black." *Journal of Finance* 50 (No. 5, December): 1359–1370.

Miller, George A., Eugene Galanter, and Karl H. Pribram. 1960. *Plans and the Structure of Behavior*. New York: Henry Holt.

Miller, H. Laurence, Jr. 1962. "On the 'Chicago School of Economics.'" *Journal of Political Economy* 70 (No. 1, February): 64–69.

Miller, Merton H. 1963. "Preface" in Machlup (1963), v–vi.

Miller, Merton H. 1977. "Debt and Taxes." *Journal of Finance* 32 (No. 2, May): 261–275.

Miller, Merton H. 1991. *Financial Innovations and Market Volatility*. Cambridge, Mass.: Basil Blackwell.

Miller, Merton H. 1993. "Introduction" to Tamarkin (1993).

Miller, Merton H. 1997. *Merton Miller on Derivatives*. New York: John Wiley & Sons.

Miller, Merton, and Myron Scholes. 1972. "Rates of Return in Relation to Risk: A Re-examination of Some Recent Findings." Pages 47–78 in Jensen (1972).

Miller, Merton, and Myron Scholes. 1978. "Dividends and Taxes." *Journal of Financial Economics* 6 (No. 4, December): 333–364.

Miller, Merton, and Myron Scholes. 1981. "Executive Compensation, Taxes, and Incentives." Pages 179–201 in *Financial Economics: Essays in Honor of Paul Cootner*, edited by Cathryn Cootner and William Sharpe. Englewood Cliffs, New Jersey: Prentice-Hall.

Miller, Merton, and Myron Scholes. 1982. "Dividends and Taxes: Some Empirical Results." *Journal of Political Economy* 90 (No. 6, December): 1118–1141.

Miller, Merton, and Charles Upton. 1974. *Macroeconomics: A Neoclassical Introduction*. Homewood, Illinois: Richard Irwin.

Mills, Frederick C. 1927. *The Behavior of Prices*. New York: National Bureau of Economic Research.

Minsky, Marvin. 1968. *Semantic Information Processing*. Cambridge, Mass.: MIT Press.

Mints, Lloyd N. 1945. *A History of Banking Theory in Great Britain and the United States*. Chicago: University of Chicago Press.

Mitchell, Wesley C. 1915. "The Making and Using of Index Numbers." Introduction to *Index Numbers and Wholesale Prices in the United States and Foreign Countries*. U.S. Bureau of Labor Statistics Bulletin 173. Reprinted in 1921 as Bulletin 284.

Modigliani, Franco. 1944. "Liquidity Preference and the Theory of Interest and Money." *Econometrica* 12 (No. 1, January): 45–88.

Modigliani, Franco. 1963. "The Monetary Mechanism and Its Interaction with Real Phenomena." *Review of Economics and Statistics* 45 (No. 1, Supplement, February): 79–107.

Modigliani, Franco. 1968. "Liquidity Preference." Pages 394–409 in *International Encyclopedia of the Social Sciences*, Vol. 9, edited by David L. Sills. New York: Macmillan.

Modigliani, Franco. 1971. "Monetary Policy and Consumption: Linkages via Interest Rate and Wealth Effects in the FMP Model." Pages 9–84 in *Consumer Spending and Monetary Policy: The Linkages*. Conference Series No. 5. Boston: Federal Reserve Bank of Boston.

Modigliani, Franco. 1972. "The Dynamics of Portfolio Adjustment and the Flow of Savings through Financial Intermediaries." Pages 63–102 in *Savings Deposits, Mortgages, and Housing: Studies for the Federal Reserve–MIT–Penn Econometric Model*, edited by Edward M. Gramlich and Dwight M. Jaffee. Lexington, Mass.: Lexington Books.

Modigliani, Franco. 1988. "MM—Past, Present, Future." *Journal of Economic Perspectives* 2 (No. 4, Autumn): 149–158.

Modigliani, Franco. 2003. "The Keynesian Gospel According to Modigliani." *American Economist* 47 (No. 1, Spring): 3–24.

Modigliani, Franco, and Hossein Askari. 1971. *The Reform of the International Payments System*. Essays in International Finance, No. 89. International Finance Section, Department of Economics, Princeton University.

Modigliani, Franco, and Peter Kenen. 1966. "A Suggestion for Solving the International Liquidity Problem." Banca Nazionale del Lavoro *Quarterly Review* (No. 76, March): 3–17.

Modigliani, Franco, and Merton Miller. 1958. "The Cost of Capital, Corporation Finance, and the Theory of Investment." *American Economic Review* 48 (No. 3, June): 261–297.

Modigliani, Franco, Robert Rasche, and J. Phillip Cooper. 1970. "Central Bank Policy, the Money Supply, and the Short-Term Rate of Interest." *Journal of Money, Credit, and Banking* 2 (No. 2, May): 166–218.

Modigliani, Franco, and Richard Sutch. 1966. "Innovations in Interest Rate Policy." *American Economic Review* 56 (No. 2, May): 178–197.

Molodovsky, Nicholas. 1974. *Investment Values in a Dynamic World: The Collected Papers of Nicholas Molodovsky*, edited by Robert D. Milne. Homewood, Illinois: Richard Irwin, for the Financial Analysts Research Foundation.

Mossin, Jan. 1966. "Equilibrium in a Capital Asset Market." *Econometrica* 34 (No. 4, October): 768–783.

Mundell, Robert A. 1968a. *International Economics*. New York: Macmillan.

Mundell, Robert A. 1968b. *Man and Economics*. New York: McGraw-Hill.

Mundell, Robert A. 1971. *Monetary Theory*. Pacific Palisades, California: Goodyear Publishing Co.

Mundell, Robert A. 1973. "Uncommon Arguments for a Common Currency." Pages 114–132 in *The Economics of Common Currencies*, edited by Harry G. Johnson and A. Swoboda. Cambridge, Mass.: Harvard University Press.

Myers, Stewart C. 1996. "Fischer Black's Contributions to Corporate Finance." *Financial Management* 25 (No. 4, Winter): 95–103.

Myers, Stewart C., and S. M. Turnbull. 1977. "Capital Budgeting and the Capital Asset Pricing Model: Good News and Bad News." *Journal of Finance* 32 (No. 2, May): 321–332.

O'Hara, Maureen. 1995. *Market Microstructure Theory*. Cambridge, Mass.: Basil Blackwell.

Perold, Andre F. 1999. *Long-Term Capital Management, L.P.* Boston: Harvard Business School Publishing.

Perold, Andre F. 2004. "The Capital Asset Pricing Model." *Journal of Economic Perspectives* 18 (No. 3, Summer): 3–24.

Perold, Andre F., and Evan C. Schulman. 1988. "The Free Lunch in Currency Hedging: Implications for Investment Policy and Performance Standards." *Financial Analysts Journal* 44 (No. 3, May/June): 45–50.

Phelps, Edmund S. 1968. "Money Wage Dynamics and Labor Market Equilibrium." *Journal of Political Economy* 76 (No. 4, Part 2, July/August): 687–711.

Plosser, Charles I. 1989. "Understanding Real Business Cycles." *Journal of Economic Perspectives* 3 (No. 3, Summer): 51–77.

Pratt, John W., Howard Raiffa, and Robert Schlaifer. 1965. *Introduction to Statistical Decision Theory*. New York: McGraw-Hill.

Prescott, Edward C. 1991. "Real Business Cycle Theory: What Have We Learned?" *Revista de Analisis Economico* 6: 3–19.

Quine, W. V. O. 1950. *Methods of Logic*. New York: Henry Holt.

Quine, W. V. O. 1953. "Two Dogmas of Empiricism." Pages 20–46 in *From a Logical Point of View*. Cambridge, Mass.: Harvard University Press.

Quine, W. V. O. 1987. *Quiddities: An Intermittently Philosophical Dictionary.* Cambridge, Mass.: Belknap Press of Harvard University Press.

Reder, Melvin W. 1980. "Chicago Economics: Permanence and Change." *Journal of Economic Literature* 20 (No. 1, March): 1–38.

Regan, Nancy. 1987. *The Institute of Chartered Financial Analysts: A Twenty-Five Year History.* Charlottesville, Virginia: Association for Investment Management and Research.

Reichers, Edwin A., and Harold Van B. Cleveland. 1970. "Flexible Exchange Rates and Forward Markets." Pages 323–331 in Halm (1970).

Ritter, Jay R. 1996. "How I Helped to Make Fischer Black Wealthier." *Financial Management* 25 (No. 4, Winter): 104–107.

Roberts, Harry V. 1959. "Stock Market 'Patterns' and Financial Analysis: Methodological Suggestions." *Journal of Finance* 14 (No. 1, March): 1–10.

Roll, Richard. 1969. "Bias in Fitting the Sharpe Model to Time Series Data." *Journal of Financial and Quantitative Analysis* 4 (September): 271–289.

Roll, Richard. 1970. *The Behavior of Interest Rates.* New York: Basic Books.

Roll, Richard. 1971. "Investment Diversification and Bond Maturity." *Journal of Finance* 26 (No. 1, March): 51–66.

Roll, Richard. 1977. "A Critique of the Asset Pricing Theory's Tests, Part I: On Past and Potential Testability of the Theory." *Journal of Financial Economics* 4 (No. 2, March): 129–176.

Roll, Richard, and Stephen A. Ross. 1980. "An Empirical Investigation of the Arbitrage Pricing Theory." *Journal of Finance* 35 (No. 5, December): 1073–1103.

Ross, Stephen A. 1976. "The Arbitrage Theory of Capital Asset Pricing." *Journal of Economic Theory* 13 (December): 341–360.

Rubin, Robert. 2003. *In an Uncertain World, Tough Choices from Wall Street to Washington.* New York: Random House.

Samuelson, Paul A. 1947. *Foundations of Economic Analysis.* Harvard Economic Studies No. 80. Cambridge, Mass.: Harvard University Press.

Samuelson, Paul A. 1952. "Economic Theory and Mathematics—An Appraisal." *American Economic Review* 42 (No. 2, May): 56–66.

Samuelson, Paul A. 1962. "Economists and the History of Ideas." *American Economic Review* 52 (No. 1, March): 1–18.

Samuelson, Paul A. 1965a. "Proof That Properly Anticipated Prices Fluctuate Randomly." *Industrial Management Review* 6 (No. 2, Spring): 41–49.

Samuelson, Paul A. 1965b. "Rational Theory of Warrant Pricing." *Industrial Management Review* 6 (Spring): 13–31.

Samuelson, Paul A. 1966. "A Summing Up." *Quarterly Journal of Economics* 80 (No. 4, November): 568–583.

Samuelson, Paul A. 1967. "Irving Fisher and the Theory of Capital." Pages 17–37 in *Ten Economic Studies in the Tradition of Irving Fisher*, edited by William Fellner. New York: John Wiley & Sons.

Samuelson, Paul A. 1968. Review of *Beat the Market. Journal of the American Statistical Association* 63 (No. 323, September): 1049–1051.

Samuelson, Paul A. 1972. "Maximum Principles in Analytical Economics." *American Economic Review* 62 (No. 3, June): 249–262.

Samuelson, Paul A., and Robert C. Merton. 1969. "A Complete Model of Warrant Pricing That Maximizes Utility." *Industrial Management Review* 10 (Winter): 17–46. Reprinted as Ch. 7 in Merton (1990).

Scholes, Myron. 1972. "The Market for Securities: Substitution versus Price Pressure and the Effects of Information on Share Prices." *Journal of Business* 45 (No. 2, April): 179–211.

Scholes, Myron S. 1998. "Derivatives in a Dynamic Environment." *American Economic Review* 88 (No. 3, June): 350–370.

Schumpeter, Joseph A. 1934. *The Theory of Economic Development: An Inquiry into Profits, Capital, Credit, Interest, and the Business Cycle.* Cambridge, Mass.: Harvard University Press.

Sercu, Piet. 1980. "A Generalization of the International Asset Pricing Model." *Revue de l'Association Française de Finance* 1: 91–135.

Sharpe, William. 1961. "Portfolio Analysis Based on a Simplified Model of the Relationships among Securities." Unpublished PhD dissertation. University of California, Los Angeles.

Sharpe, William. 1963. "A Simplified Model for Portfolio Analysis." *Management Science* 9 (No. 2, January): 277–293.

Sharpe, William. 1964. "Capital Asset Prices: A Theory of Market Equilibrium under Conditions of Risk." *Journal of Finance* 19 (No. 3, September): 425–442.

Sharpe, William. 1966a. "Mutual Fund Performance." *Journal of Business* 39 (Part 2, January): 119–138.

Sharpe, William. 1966b. "Security Prices, Risk, and Maximal Gains from Diversification: Reply." *Journal of Finance* 21 (No. 4, December): 743–444.

Shefrin, Hersh. 2000. *Beyond Greed and Fear, Understanding Behavioral Finance and the Psychology of Investing.* Boston: Harvard Business School Press.

Shefrin, Hersh, and Meir Statman. 1984. "Explaining Investor Preference for Cash Dividends." *Journal of Financial Economics* 13 (No. 2, June): 253–282.

Shefrin, Hersh, and Meir Statman. 1985. "The Disposition to Sell Winners Too Early and Ride Losers Too Long: Theory and Evidence." *Journal of Finance* 40 (No. 3, July): 777–790.

Shiller, Robert J. 1989. *Market Volatility.* Cambridge, Mass.: MIT Press.

Shiller, Robert J. 2000. *Irrational Exuberance.* Princeton, New Jersey: Princeton University Press.

Shiller, Robert J. 2003. "From Efficient Markets Theory to Behavioral Finance." *Journal of Economic Perspectives* 17 (No. 1, Winter): 83–104.

Shleifer, Andre. 2000. *Inefficient Markets: An Introduction to Behavioral Finance.* Oxford: Oxford University Press.

Siegel, Jeremy J. 1972. "Risk, Interest Rates, and the Forward Exchange." *Quarterly Journal of Economics* 86 (No. 2, May): 303–309.

Siegel, Jeremy J. 1994. *Stocks for the Long Run: A Guide to Selecting Markets for Long-Term Growth.* Burr Ridge, Illinois: Richard Irwin.

Silver, Edward A., Alan L. Loss, and Fischer Black. 1971. "A Quantitative Rule for the Use of Resources in a Multiprogrammed Computer System." *INFOR* 9 (No. 2, July): 96–110.

Simonton, Dean Keith. 1988. "Age and Outstanding Achievement: What Do We Know after a Century of Research?" *Psychological Bulletin* 104 (No. 2): 251–267.

Sohmen, Egon. 1961. *Flexible Exchange Rates, Theory and Controversy.* Chicago: University of Chicago Press.

Sohmen, Egon. 1970. "Exchange Risks and Forward Coverage in Different Monetary Systems." Pages 311–315 in Halm (1970).

Solnik, Bruno H. 1974. "An Equilibrium Model of the International Capital Market." *Journal of Economic Theory* 8 (August): 500–524.

Solnik, Bruno, and Michael Adler. 1990. "The Individuality of 'Universal' Hedging." *Financial Analysts Journal* 46 (No. 3, May/June): 7–8.

Solow, Robert. 1956. "A Contribution to the Theory of Economic Growth." *Quarterly Journal of Economics* 70 (No. 1, February): 65–94.

Solow, Robert. 1957. "Technical Change and the Aggregate Production Function." *Review of Economics and Statistics* 39 (No. 3, August): 312–320.

Soros, George. 1987. *The Alchemy of Finance: Reading the Mind of the Market*. New York: Simon & Schuster.

Sprenkle, Case. 1964. "Warrant Prices as Indicators of Expectations and Preferences." Pages 412–474 in Cootner (1964).

Stigler, George J. 1962. "On the 'Chicago School of Economics': Comment." *Journal of Political Economy* 70 (No. 1, February): 70–71.

Stone, Bernell Kenneth. 1970. *Risk, Return and Equilibrium; A General Single-Period Theory of Asset Selection and Capital Market Equilibrium*. Cambridge, Mass.: MIT Press.

Stulz, Rene. 1981. "A Model of International Asset Pricing." *Journal of Financial Economics* 9 (December): 383–406.

Swoboda, Alexander K. 1973. "Monetary Policy under Fixed Exchange Rates: Effectiveness, the Speed of Adjustment and Proper Use." *Economica*, New Series, 40 (No. 158, May): 136–154.

Tamarkin, Bob. 1993. *The Merc: The Emergence of a Global Financial Powerhouse*. New York: HarperCollins.

Thomasson, Lillian Franklin. 1965. *Swain County, Early History and Educational Development*. Bryson City, North Carolina.

Thorp, Edward O., and Sheen T. Kassouf. 1967. *Beat the Market*. New York: Random House.

Tobin, James. 1958. "Liquidity Preference as Behavior toward Risk." *Review of Economic Studies* 67 (February): 65–86.

Tobin, James. 1965. "The Theory of Portfolio Selection." Pages 3–51 in F. H. Hahn and F. B. R. Brechling, *The Theory of Interest Rates*. London: Macmillan.

Tobin, James. 1980. *Asset Accumulation and Economic Activity, Reflections on Contemporary Macroeconomic Theory*. Chicago: University of Chicago Press.

Treynor, Jack L. 1961. "Market Value, Time, and Risk." Unpublished manuscript (August 8).

Treynor, Jack L. 1962. "Toward a Theory of Market Value of Risky Assets." Pages 15–22 in Korajczyk (1999).

Treynor, Jack L. 1963. "Implications for a Theory of Finance." Unpublished manuscript.

Treynor, Jack L. 1965. "How to Rate Management of Investment Funds." *Harvard Business Review* 43 (January/February): 63–75.

Treynor, Jack L. 1972. "The Trouble with Earnings." *Financial Analysts Journal* 28 (No. 5, September/October): 41–43.

Treynor, Jack L. 1977. "The Principles of Corporate Pension Finance." *Journal of Finance* 32 (No. 2, May): 627–638.

Treynor, Jack. 1981. "What Does It Take to Win the Trading Game?" *Financial Analysts Journal* 37 (No. 1, January/February): 55–60.

Treynor, Jack. 1983. "Implementation of Strategy: Execution." Chapter 12 in *Managing Investment Portfolios: A Dynamic Process*, edited by John L. Maginn and Donald Tuttle. Boston: Warren, Gorham, and Lamont.

Treynor, Jack. 1987. "Market Efficiency and the Bean Jar Experiment." *Financial Analysts Journal* 43 (No. 3, May/June): 50–53.

Treynor, Jack. 1989. "Information Based Investing." *Financial Analysts Journal* 45 (No. 3, May/June): 6–7.

Treynor, Jack L. 1990. "The 10 Most Important Questions to Ask in Selecting a Money Manager." *Financial Analysts Journal* 46 (No. 3, May/June): 4–5.

Treynor, Jack L. 1993. "In Defense of CAPM." *Financial Analysts Journal* 49 (No. 3, May/June): 11–13.

Treynor, Jack L. 1994. "The Invisible Costs of Trading." *Journal of Portfolio Management* (Fall): 71–78.

Treynor, Jack L. 1996. "Remembering Fischer Black." *Journal of Portfolio Management* Special Issue (December): 92–95.

Treynor, Jack L., and Fischer Black. 1972. "Portfolio Selection Using Special Information, under the Assumptions of the Diagonal Model, with Mean-Variance Portfolio Objectives, and without Constraints." Pages 367–384 in *Mathematical Methods in Investment and Finance* 4, edited by George P. Szego and Karl Shell. Amsterdam: North-Holland.

Treynor, Jack L., and Fischer Black. 1973. "How to Use Security Analysis to Improve Portfolio Selection." *Journal of Business* 46 (No. 1, January): 66–86.

Treynor, Jack L., and Fischer Black. 1976. "Corporate Investment Decisions." Pages 310–327 in *Modern Developments in Financial Management*, edited by Stewart C. Myers. New York: Praeger.

Treynor, Jack L., and Kay Mazuy. 1966. "Can Mutual Funds Outguess the Market?" *Harvard Business Review* 44 (January/February): 131–136.

Treynor, Jack L., William L. Priest Jr., Lawrence Fisher, and Catherine A. Higgins. 1968. "Using Portfolio Composition to Estimate Risk." *Financial Analysts Journal* 24 (No. 5, September/October): 93–100.

Treynor, Jack L., Patrick J. Regan, and William M. Priest Jr. 1976. *The Financial Reality of Pension Funding under ERISA*. Homewood, Illinois: Dow Jones-Irwin.

Treynor, Jack L., and Richard F. Vancil. 1956. *Machine Tool Leasing*. Boston: Management Analysis Center.

Waldrop, M. Mitchell. 2001. *The Dream Machine: J. C. R. Licklider and the Revolution That Made Computing Personal*. New York: Viking.

Walras, Leon. 1874. *Elements of Pure Economics*. Lausanne: L. Borbax.

Williams, John Burr. 1938. *The Theory of Investment Value*. Cambridge, Mass.: Harvard University Press.

Wilson, Edward O. 1998. *Consilience: The Unity of Knowledge*. New York: Knopf.

Woodford, Michael. 2003. *Interest and Prices: Foundations of a Theory of Monetary Policy*. Princeton, New Jersey: Princeton University Press.

Woofter, T. J., Jr., and Ellen Winston. 1939. *Seven Lean Years*. Chapel Hill: University of North Carolina Press.

Index